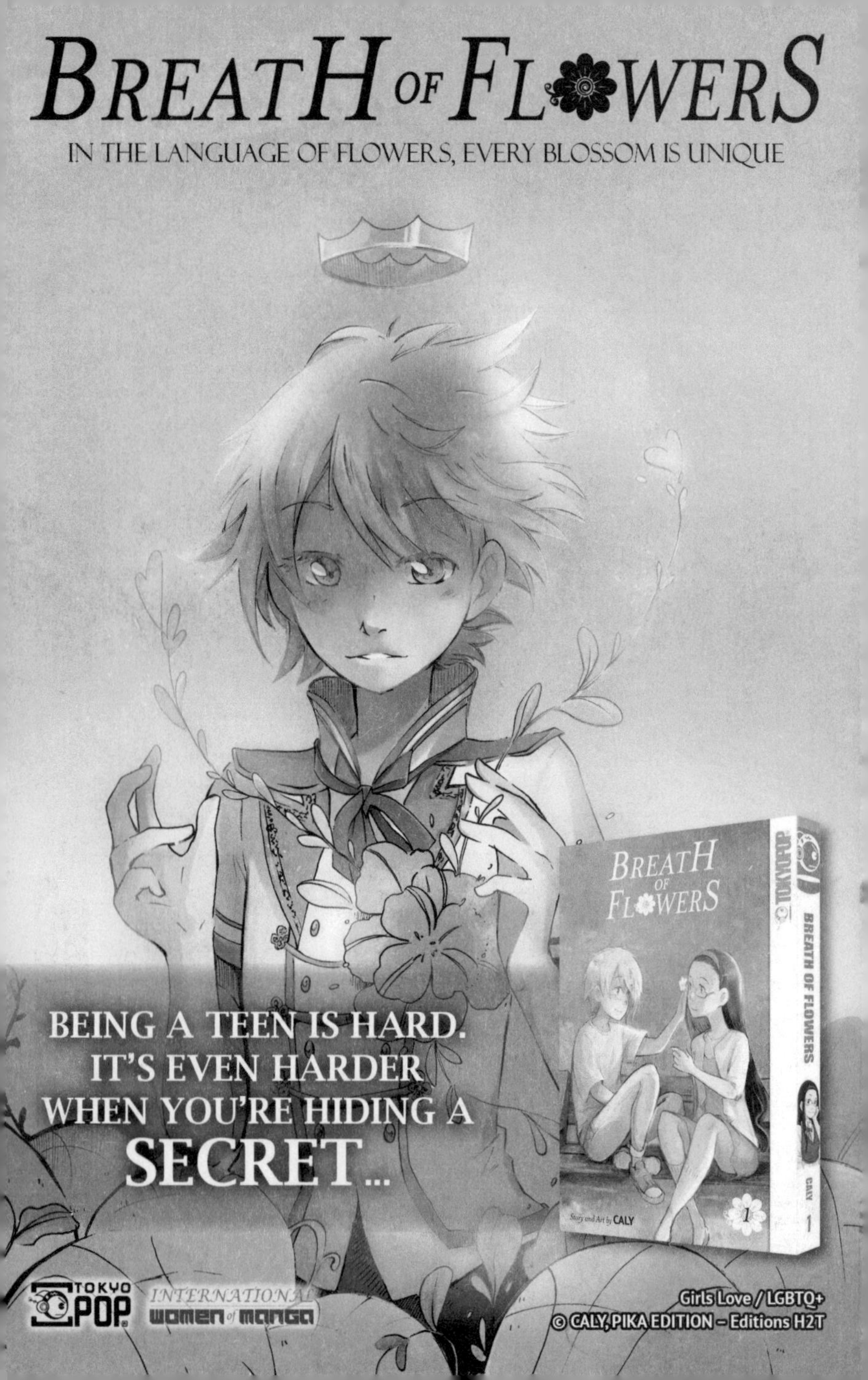
BREATH OF FLOWERS
IN THE LANGUAGE OF FLOWERS, EVERY BLOSSOM IS UNIQUE
BREATH OF FLOWERS
BREATH OF FLOWERS
Story and Art by CALY
CALY
1
BEING A TEEN IS HARD. IT'S EVEN HARDER WHEN YOU'RE HIDING A SECRET...
TOKYOPOP
INTERNATIONAL women of manga
Girls Love / LGBTQ+
© CALY, PIKA EDITION – Editions H2T

OSSAN IDOL! 01

CONTENTS

OSSAN IDOL! 01

MANGA   ICHIKA KINO

ORIGINAL   MOCHIKO MOCHIDA
STORY

CHARACTER   MIZUKI
DESIGN   SAKAKIBARA

Chapter 1

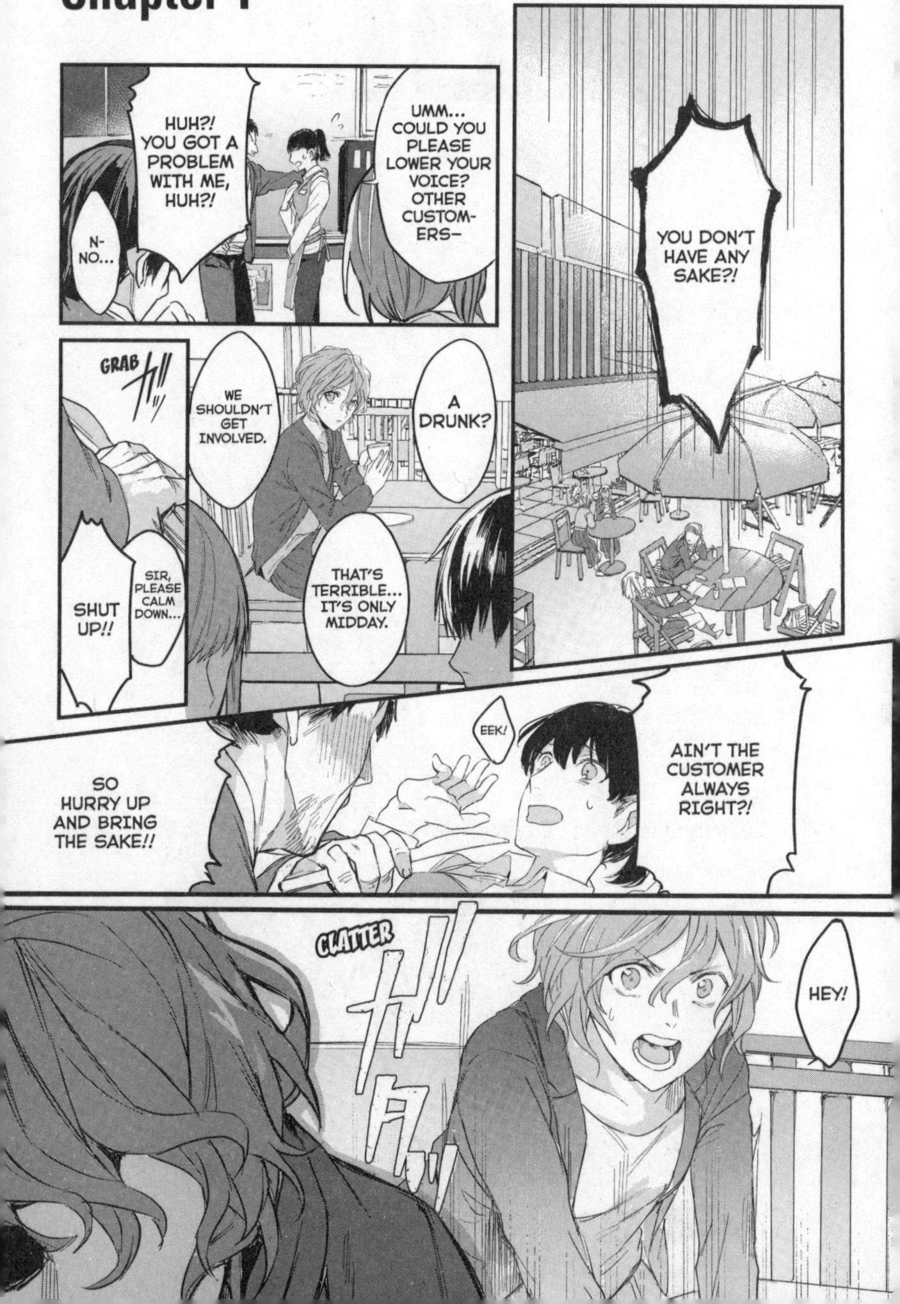
YOU DON'T HAVE ANY SAKE?!
UMM... COULD YOU PLEASE LOWER YOUR VOICE? OTHER CUSTOMERS–
HUH?! YOU GOT A PROBLEM WITH ME, HUH?!
N-NO...
A DRUNK?
WE SHOULDN'T GET INVOLVED.
GRAB
THAT'S TERRIBLE... IT'S ONLY MIDDAY.
SIR, PLEASE CALM DOWN...
SHUT UP!!
AIN'T THE CUSTOMER ALWAYS RIGHT?!
EEK!
SO HURRY UP AND BRING THE SAKE!!
HEY!
CLATTER

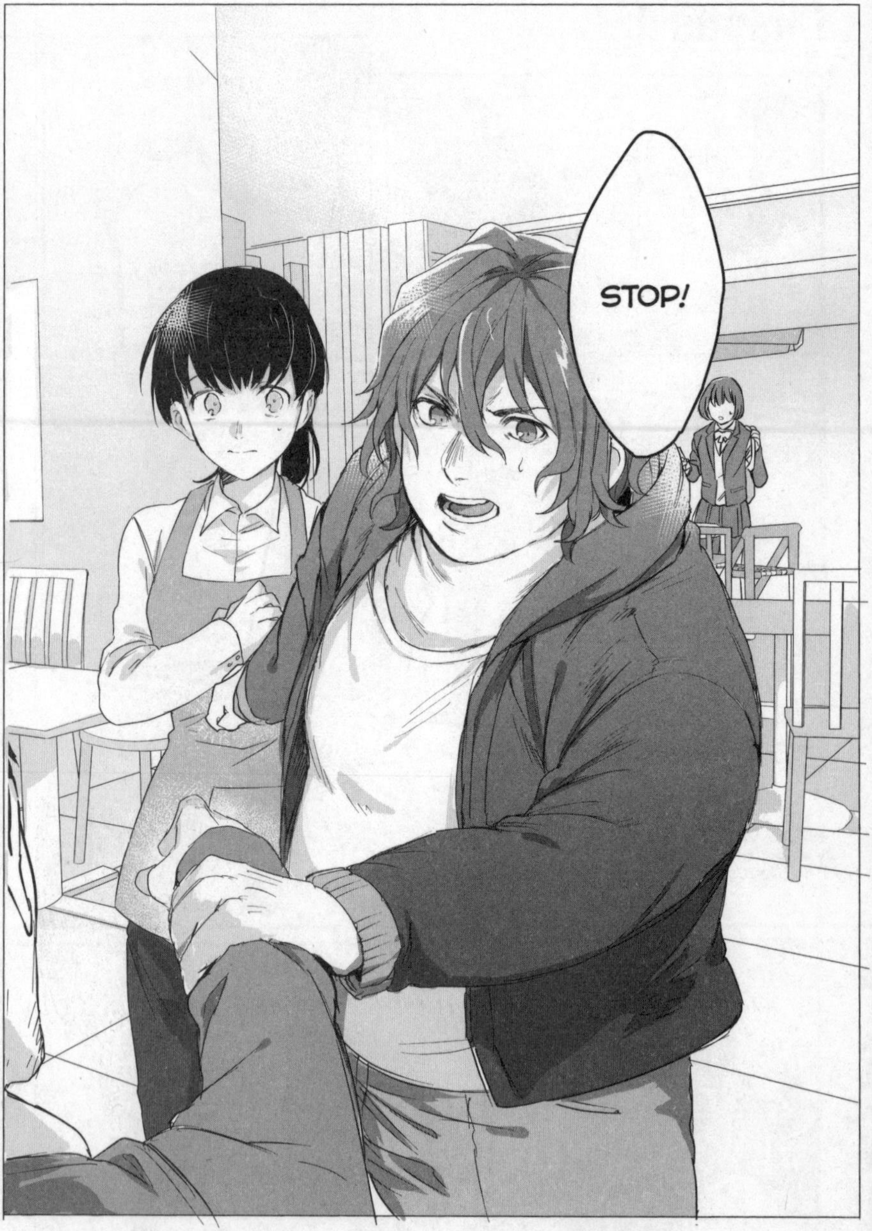
STOP!

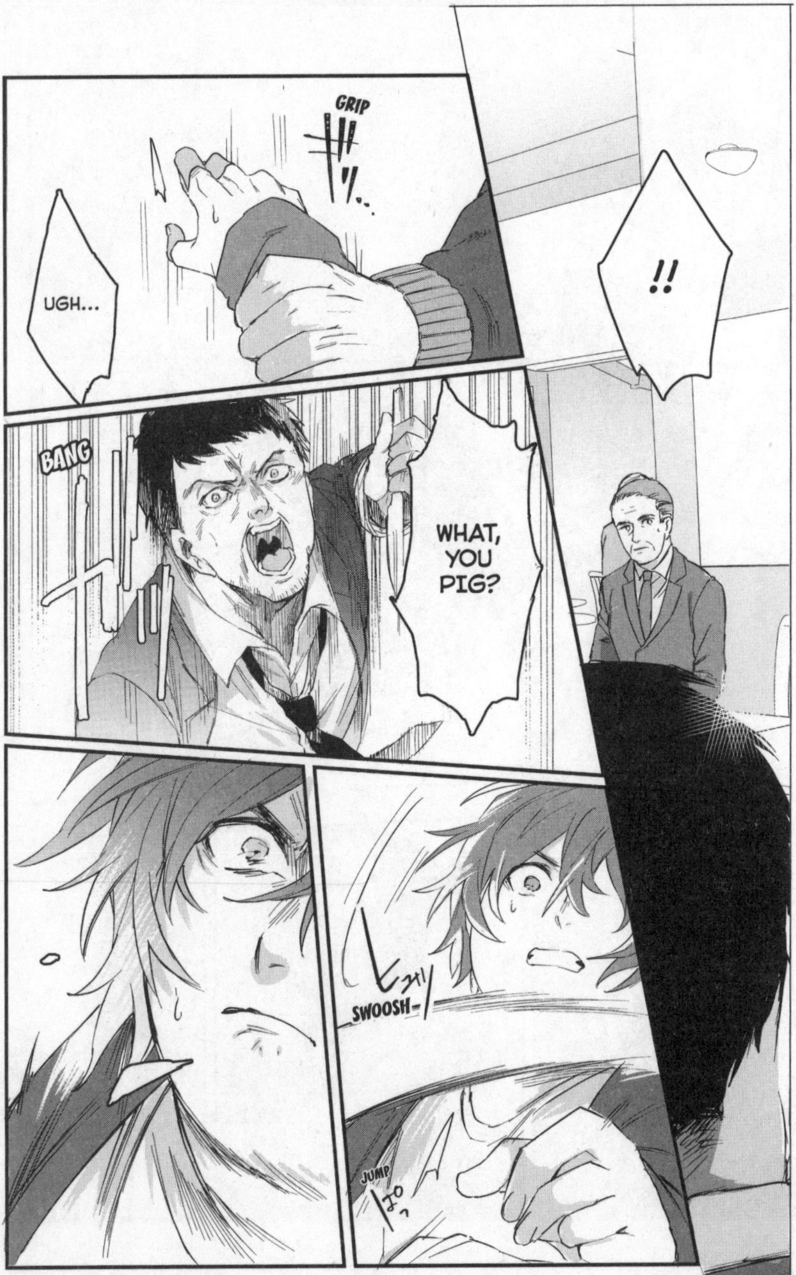
!!
GRIP
UGH...
WHAT, YOU PIG?
BANG
SWOOSH
JUMP

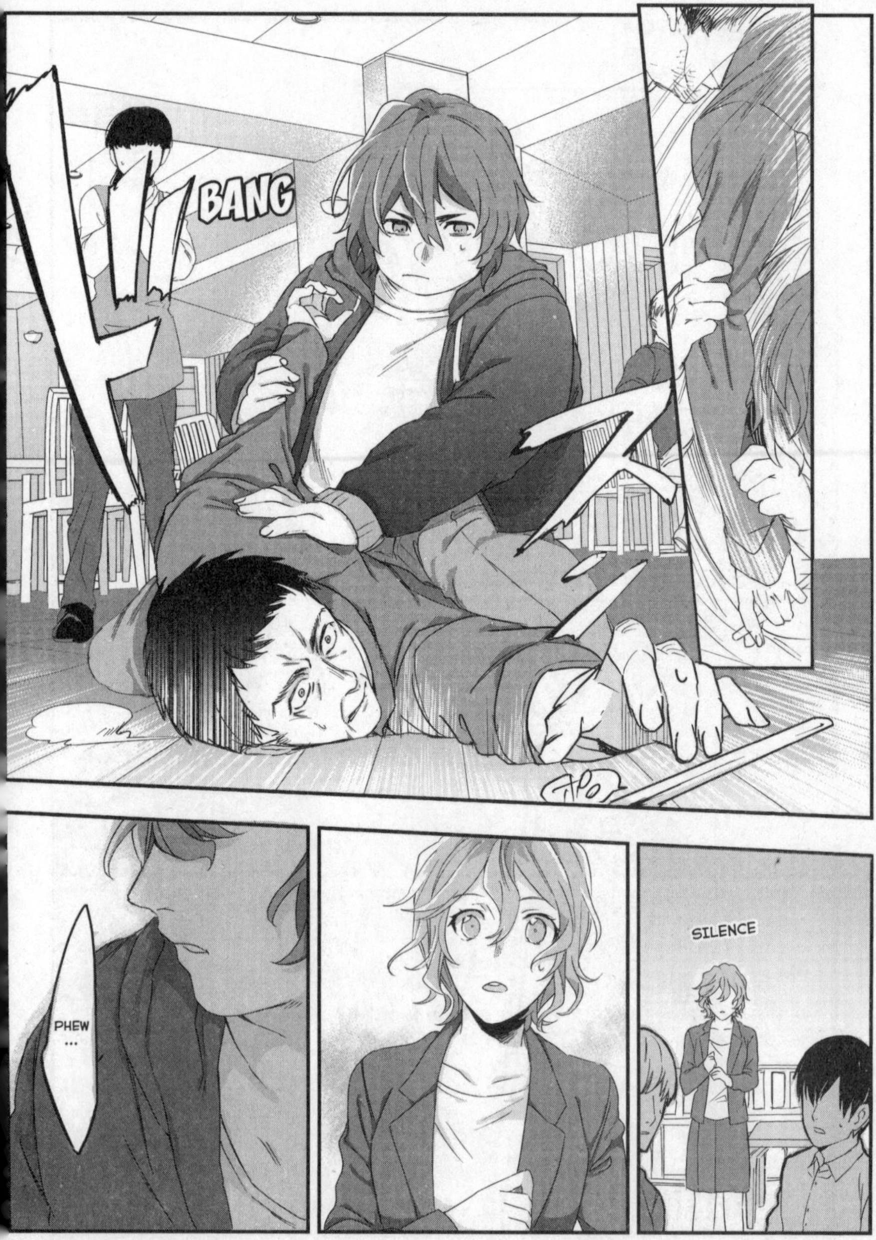
BANG
SILENCE
PHEW
...

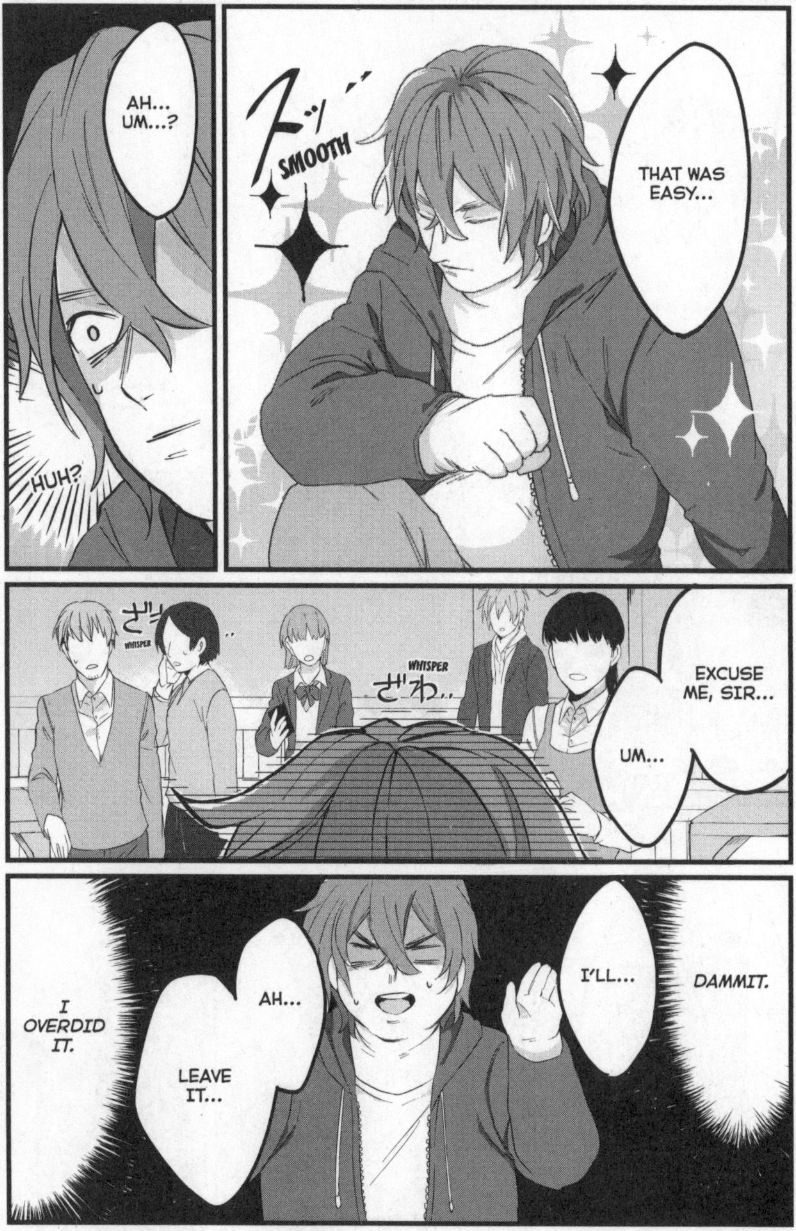
THAT WAS EASY...
SMOOTH
AH... UM...?
HUH?
EXCUSE ME, SIR...
UM...
WHISPER
ざわ..
WHISPER
DAMMIT.
I'LL...
AH...
LEAVE IT...
I OVERDID IT.

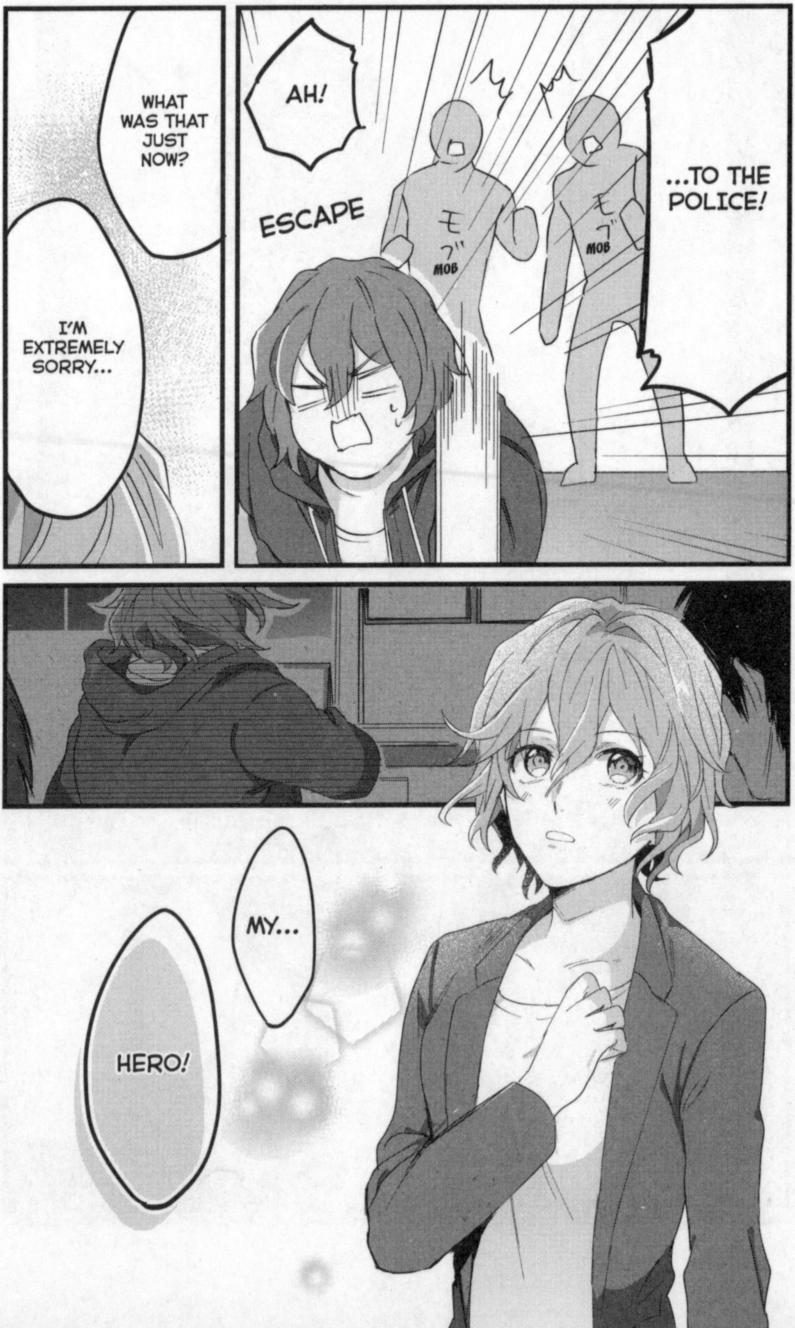
...TO THE POLICE!
AH!
ESCAPE
モブ
MOB
モブ
MOB
WHAT WAS THAT JUST NOW?
I'M EXTREMELY SORRY...
MY...
HERO!

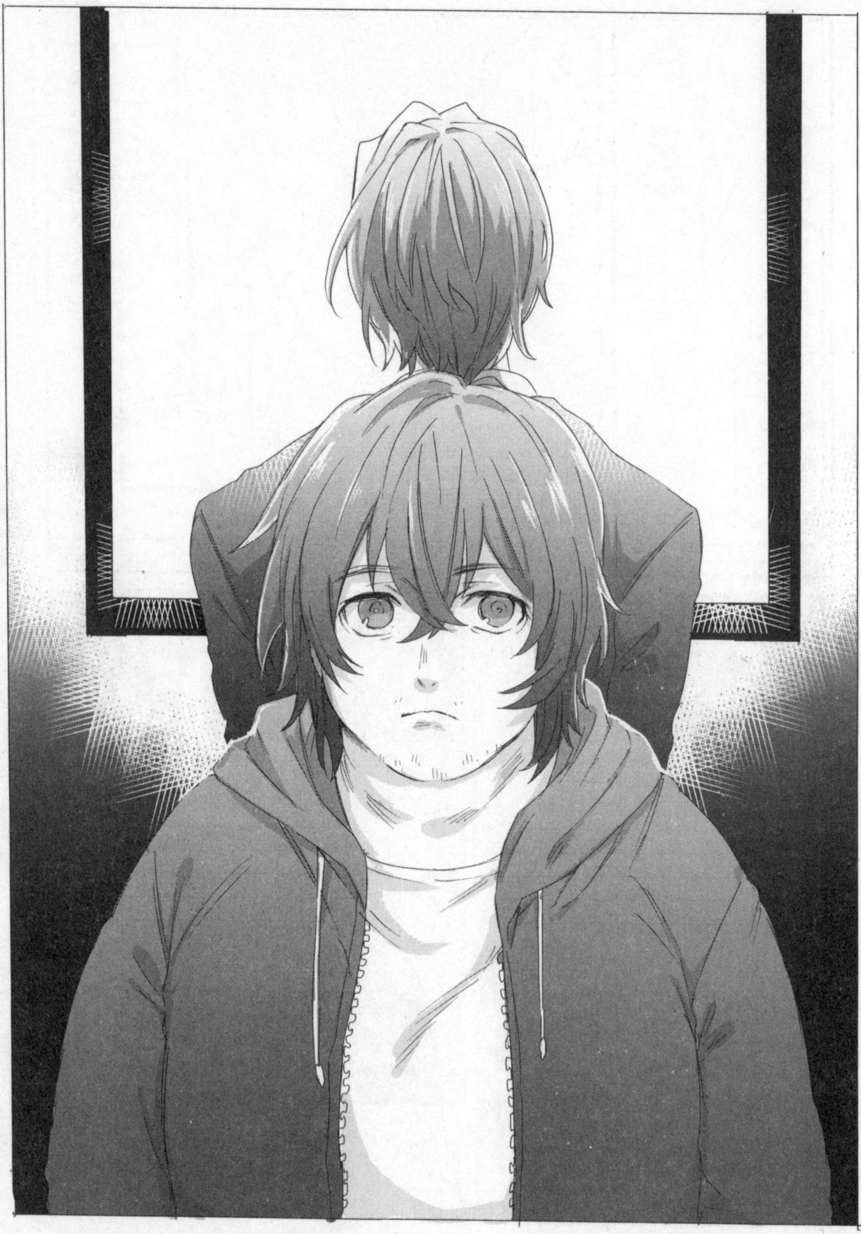

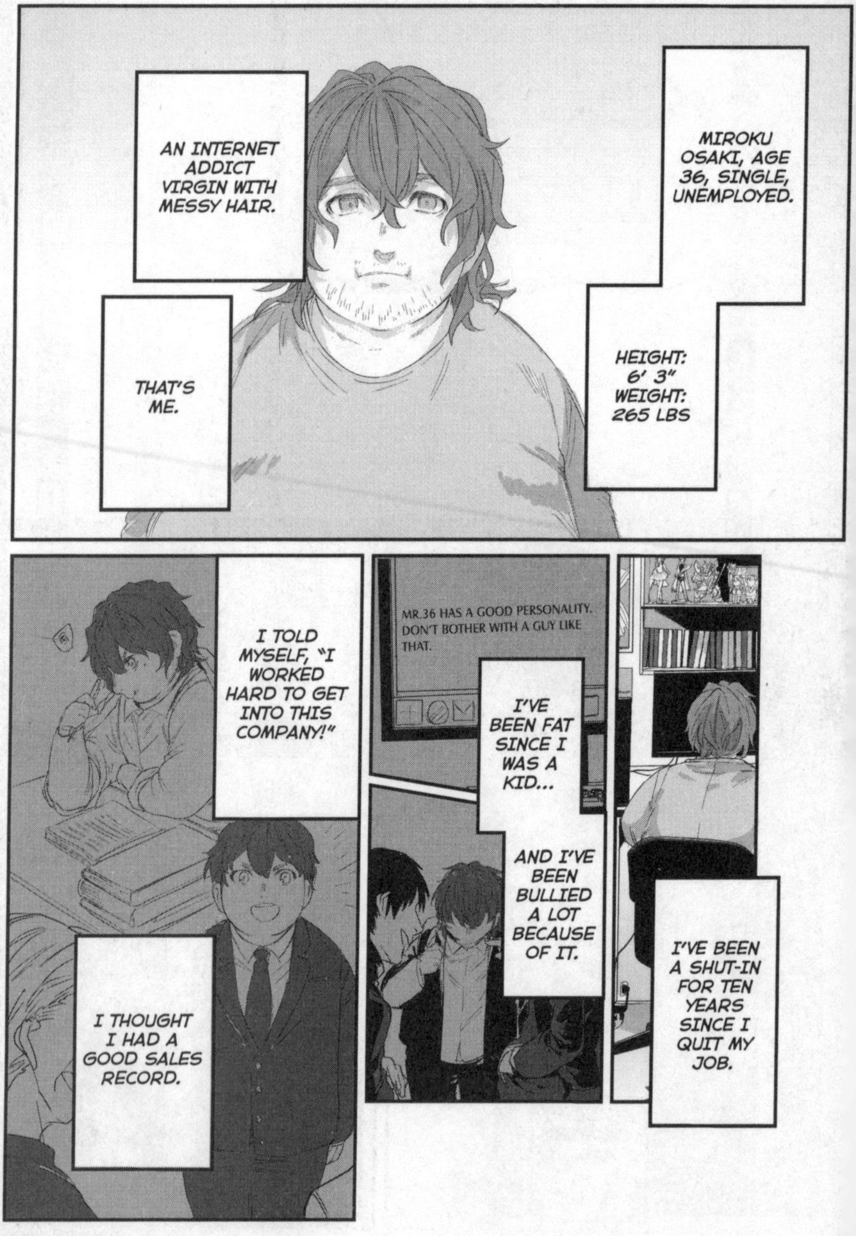
MIROKU OSAKI, AGE 36, SINGLE, UNEMPLOYED.
HEIGHT: 6' 3" WEIGHT: 265 LBS
AN INTERNET ADDICT VIRGIN WITH MESSY HAIR.
THAT'S ME.
I'VE BEEN A SHUT-IN FOR TEN YEARS SINCE I QUIT MY JOB.
MR.36 HAS A GOOD PERSONALITY. DON'T BOTHER WITH A GUY LIKE THAT.
I'VE BEEN FAT SINCE I WAS A KID...
AND I'VE BEEN BULLIED A LOT BECAUSE OF IT.
I TOLD MYSELF, "I WORKED HARD TO GET INTO THIS COMPANY!"
I THOUGHT I HAD A GOOD SALES RECORD.

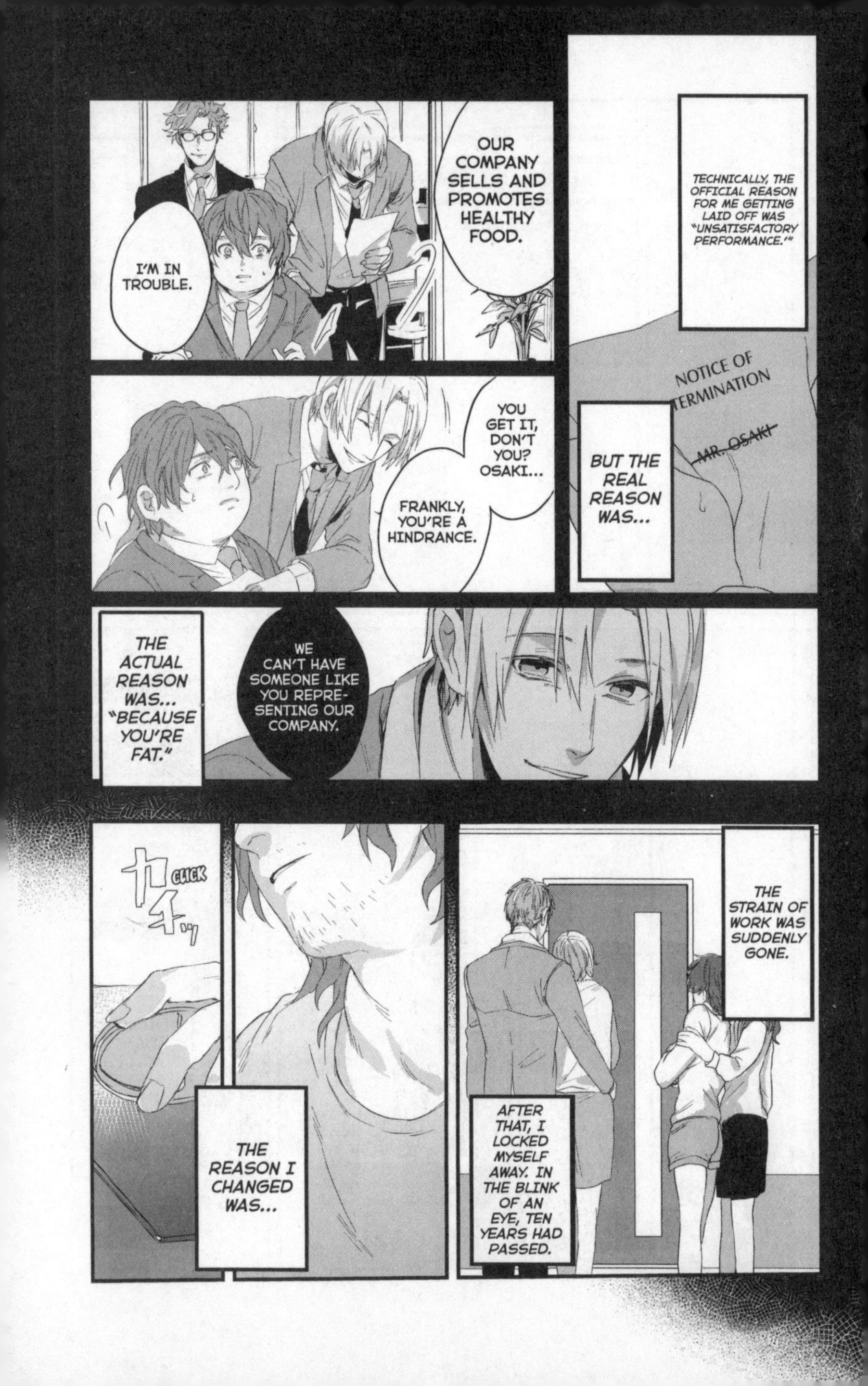

TECHNICALLY, THE OFFICIAL REASON FOR ME GETTING LAID OFF WAS "UNSATISFACTORY PERFORMANCE."
NOTICE OF TERMINATION
MR. OSAKI
BUT THE REAL REASON WAS...
OUR COMPANY SELLS AND PROMOTES HEALTHY FOOD.
I'M IN TROUBLE.
YOU GET IT, DON'T YOU? OSAKI...
FRANKLY, YOU'RE A HINDRANCE.
WE CAN'T HAVE SOMEONE LIKE YOU REPRESENTING OUR COMPANY.
THE ACTUAL REASON WAS... "BECAUSE YOU'RE FAT."
THE STRAIN OF WORK WAS SUDDENLY GONE.
AFTER THAT, I LOCKED MYSELF AWAY. IN THE BLINK OF AN EYE, TEN YEARS HAD PASSED.
THE REASON I CHANGED WAS...
カチッ
CLICK

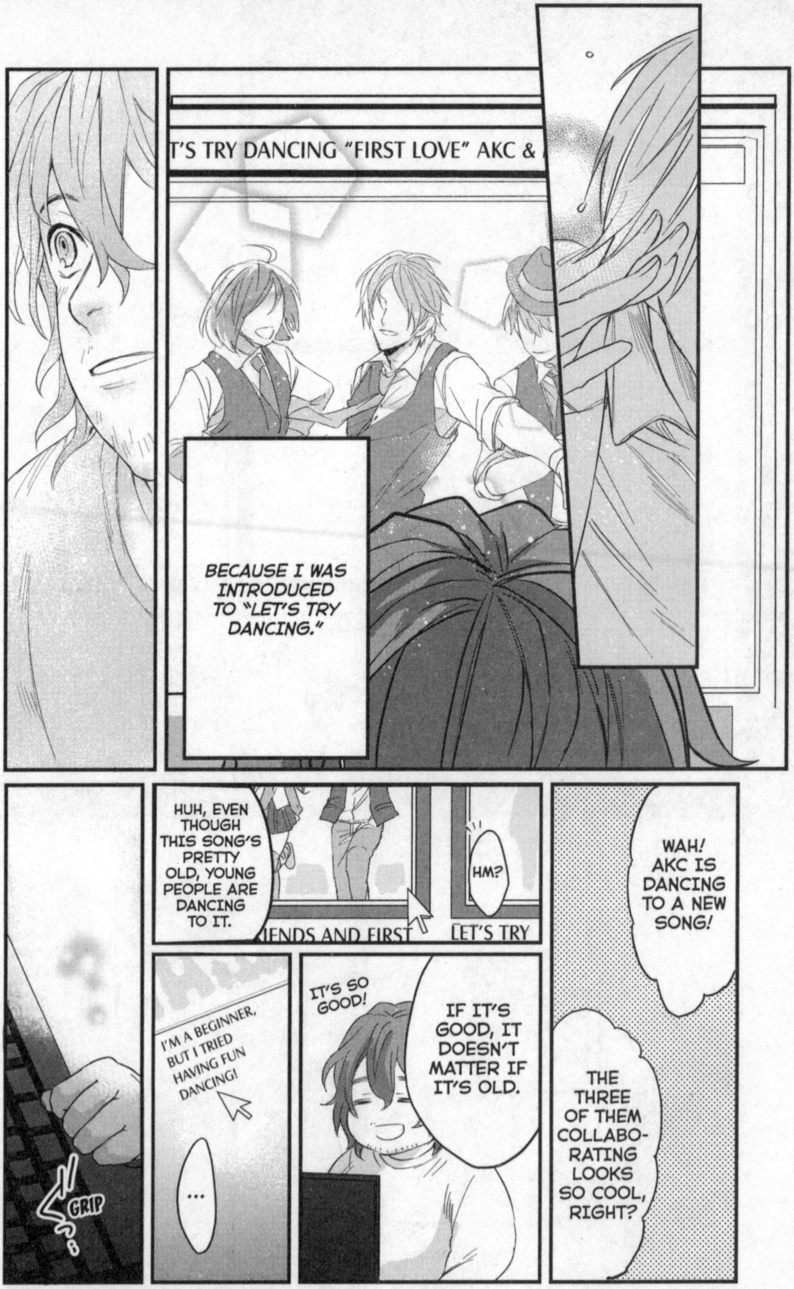
T'S TRY DANCING "FIRST LOVE" AKC &
BECAUSE I WAS INTRODUCED TO "LET'S TRY DANCING."
WAH! AKC IS DANCING TO A NEW SONG!
THE THREE OF THEM COLLABORATING LOOKS SO COOL, RIGHT?
HM?
LET'S TRY
HUH, EVEN THOUGH THIS SONG'S PRETTY OLD, YOUNG PEOPLE ARE DANCING TO IT.
RIENDS AND FIRST
IF IT'S GOOD, IT DOESN'T MATTER IF IT'S OLD.
IT'S SO GOOD!
I'M A BEGINNER, BUT I TRIED HAVING FUN DANCING!
...
GRIP

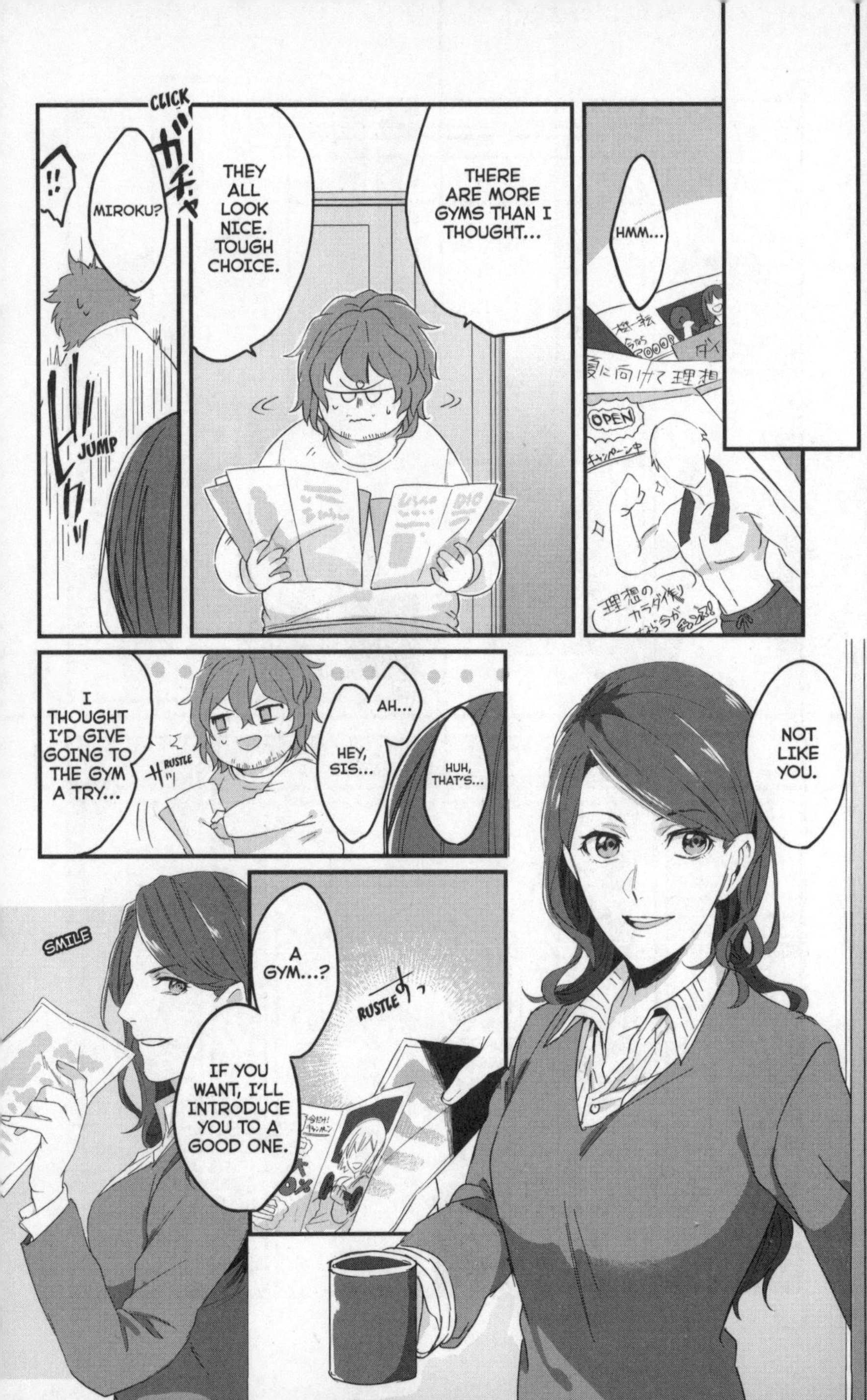

HMM...
OPEN
THERE ARE MORE GYMS THAN I THOUGHT...
THEY ALL LOOK NICE. TOUGH CHOICE.
CLICK ガチャ
MIROKU?
!!
JUMP ビクッ
NOT LIKE YOU.
AH...
HEY, SIS...
HUH, THAT'S...
I THOUGHT I'D GIVE GOING TO THE GYM A TRY...
RUSTLE
A GYM...?
RUSTLE
IF YOU WANT, I'LL INTRODUCE YOU TO A GOOD ONE.
SMILE

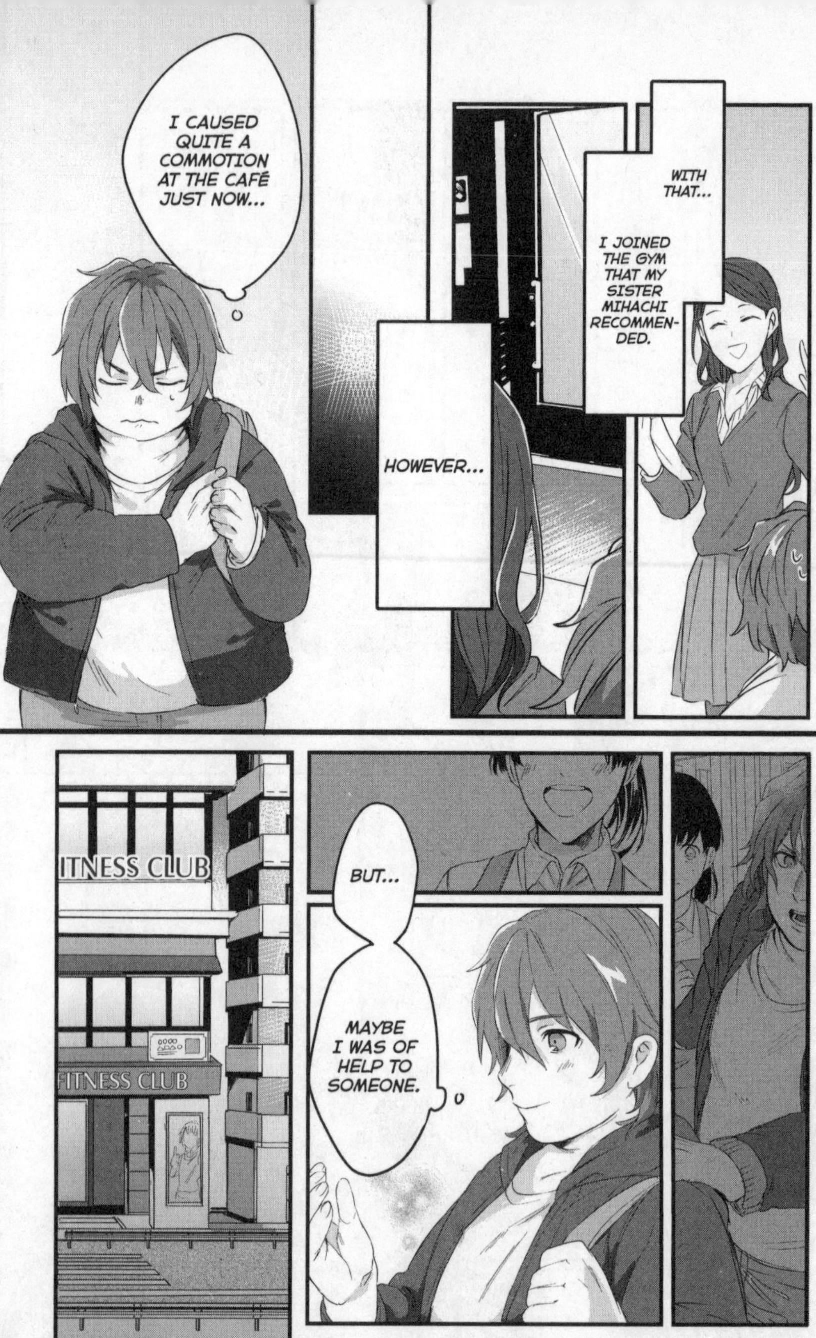
WITH THAT...
I JOINED THE GYM THAT MY SISTER MIHACHI RECOMMEN-DED.
HOWEVER...
I CAUSED QUITE A COMMOTION AT THE CAFÉ JUST NOW...
BUT...
MAYBE I WAS OF HELP TO SOMEONE.
ITNESS CLUB
FITNESS CLUB

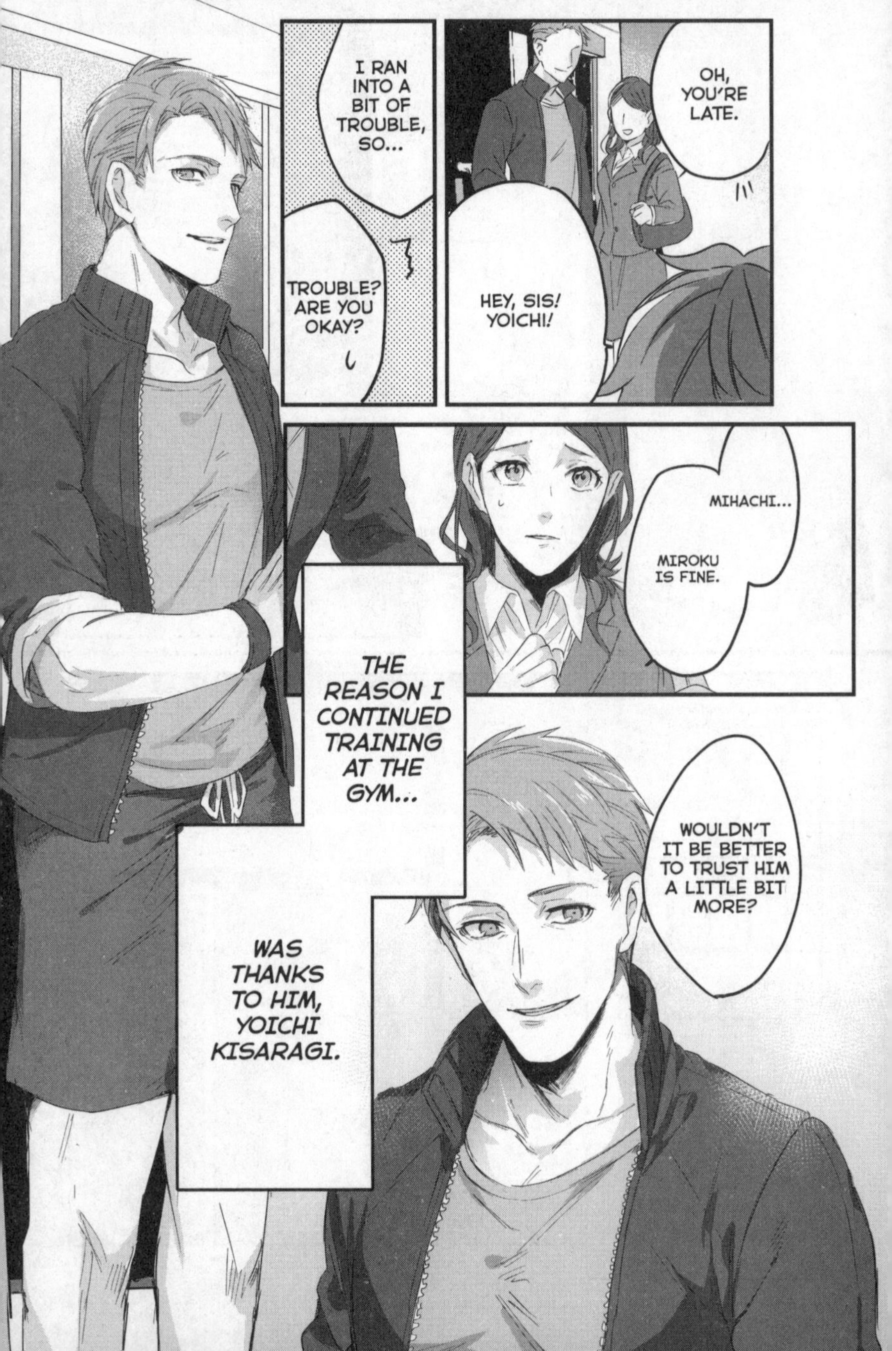
OH, YOU'RE LATE.
HEY, SIS! YOICHI!
I RAN INTO A BIT OF TROUBLE, SO...
TROUBLE? ARE YOU OKAY?
MIHACHI...
MIROKU IS FINE.
WOULDN'T IT BE BETTER TO TRUST HIM A LITTLE BIT MORE?
THE REASON I CONTINUED TRAINING AT THE GYM...
WAS THANKS TO HIM, YOICHI KISARAGI.

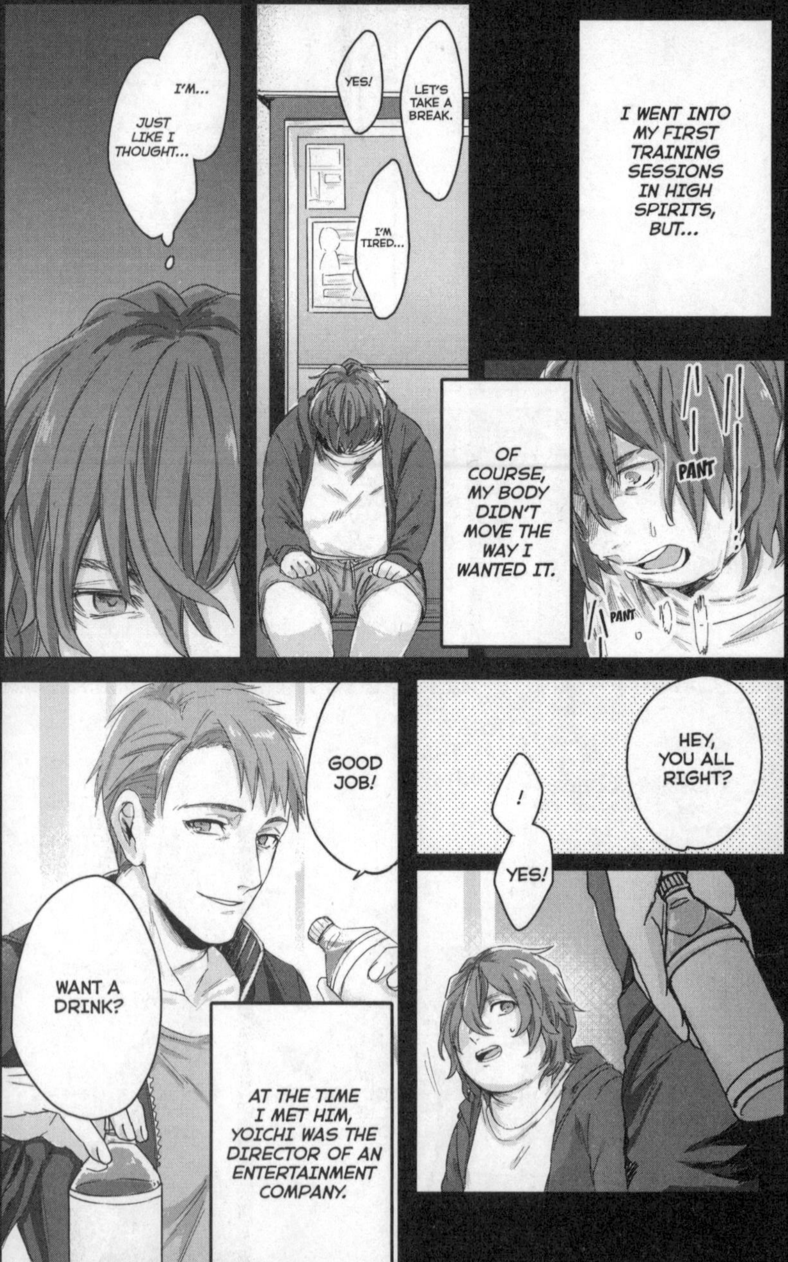
I WENT INTO MY FIRST TRAINING SESSIONS IN HIGH SPIRITS, BUT...
OF COURSE, MY BODY DIDN'T MOVE THE WAY I WANTED IT.
PANT
PANT
LET'S TAKE A BREAK.
YES!
I'M TIRED...
I'M...
JUST LIKE I THOUGHT...
HEY, YOU ALL RIGHT?
!
YES!
GOOD JOB!
WANT A DRINK?
AT THE TIME I MET HIM, YOICHI WAS THE DIRECTOR OF AN ENTERTAINMENT COMPANY.

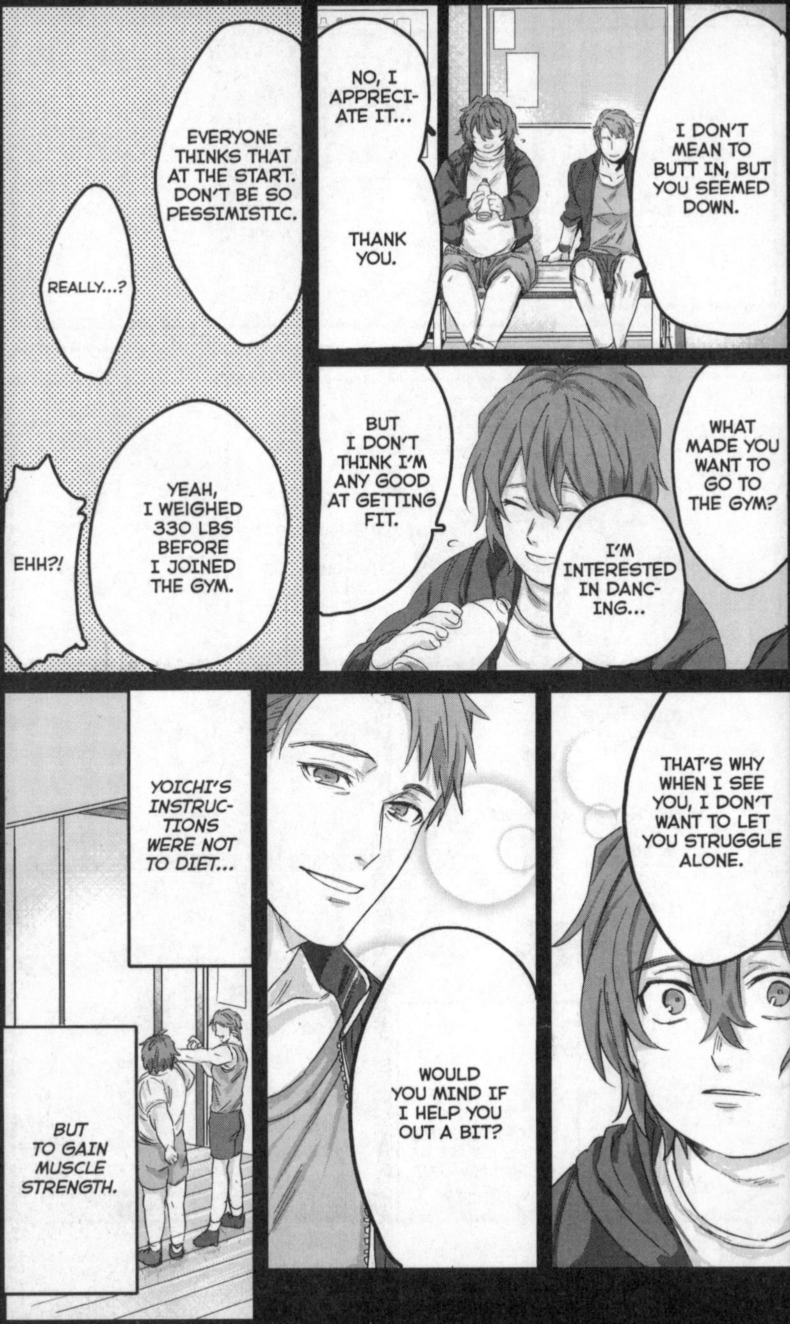

I DON'T MEAN TO BUTT IN, BUT YOU SEEMED DOWN.
NO, I APPRECIATE IT...
THANK YOU.
WHAT MADE YOU WANT TO GO TO THE GYM?
I'M INTERESTED IN DANCING...
BUT I DON'T THINK I'M ANY GOOD AT GETTING FIT.
EVERYONE THINKS THAT AT THE START. DON'T BE SO PESSIMISTIC.
REALLY...?
YEAH, I WEIGHED 330 LBS BEFORE I JOINED THE GYM.
EHH?!
THAT'S WHY WHEN I SEE YOU, I DON'T WANT TO LET YOU STRUGGLE ALONE.
WOULD YOU MIND IF I HELP YOU OUT A BIT?
YOICHI'S INSTRUCTIONS WERE NOT TO DIET...
BUT TO GAIN MUSCLE STRENGTH.

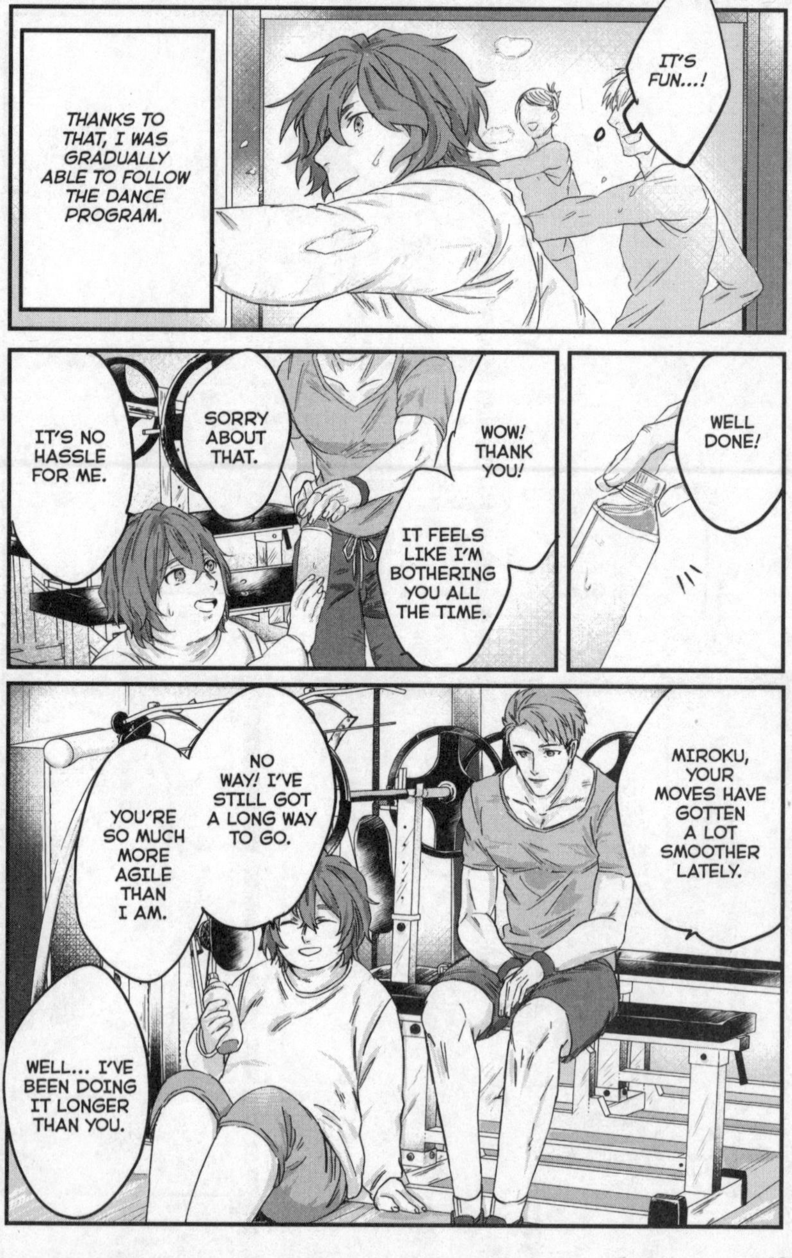
IT'S FUN...!
THANKS TO THAT, I WAS GRADUALLY ABLE TO FOLLOW THE DANCE PROGRAM.
WELL DONE!
WOW! THANK YOU!
IT FEELS LIKE I'M BOTHERING YOU ALL THE TIME.
SORRY ABOUT THAT.
IT'S NO HASSLE FOR ME.
MIROKU, YOUR MOVES HAVE GOTTEN A LOT SMOOTHER LATELY.
NO WAY! I'VE STILL GOT A LONG WAY TO GO.
YOU'RE SO MUCH MORE AGILE THAN I AM.
WELL... I'VE BEEN DOING IT LONGER THAN YOU.

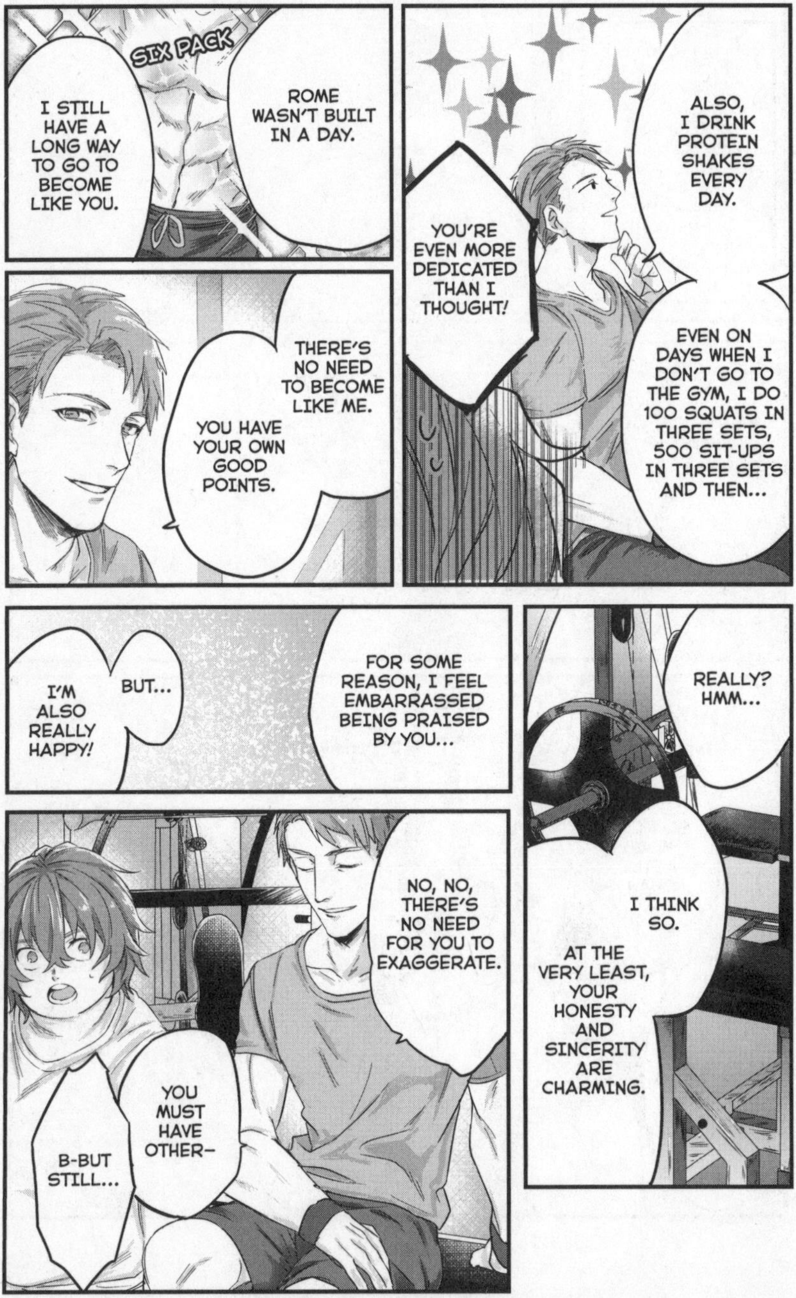
ALSO, I DRINK PROTEIN SHAKES EVERY DAY.
EVEN ON DAYS WHEN I DON'T GO TO THE GYM, I DO 100 SQUATS IN THREE SETS, 500 SIT-UPS IN THREE SETS AND THEN...
YOU'RE EVEN MORE DEDICATED THAN I THOUGHT!
SIX PACK
ROME WASN'T BUILT IN A DAY.
I STILL HAVE A LONG WAY TO GO TO BECOME LIKE YOU.
THERE'S NO NEED TO BECOME LIKE ME.
YOU HAVE YOUR OWN GOOD POINTS.
REALLY? HMM...
I THINK SO.
AT THE VERY LEAST, YOUR HONESTY AND SINCERITY ARE CHARMING.
FOR SOME REASON, I FEEL EMBARRASSED BEING PRAISED BY YOU...
BUT...
I'M ALSO REALLY HAPPY!
NO, NO, THERE'S NO NEED FOR YOU TO EXAGGERATE.
YOU MUST HAVE OTHER—
B-BUT STILL...

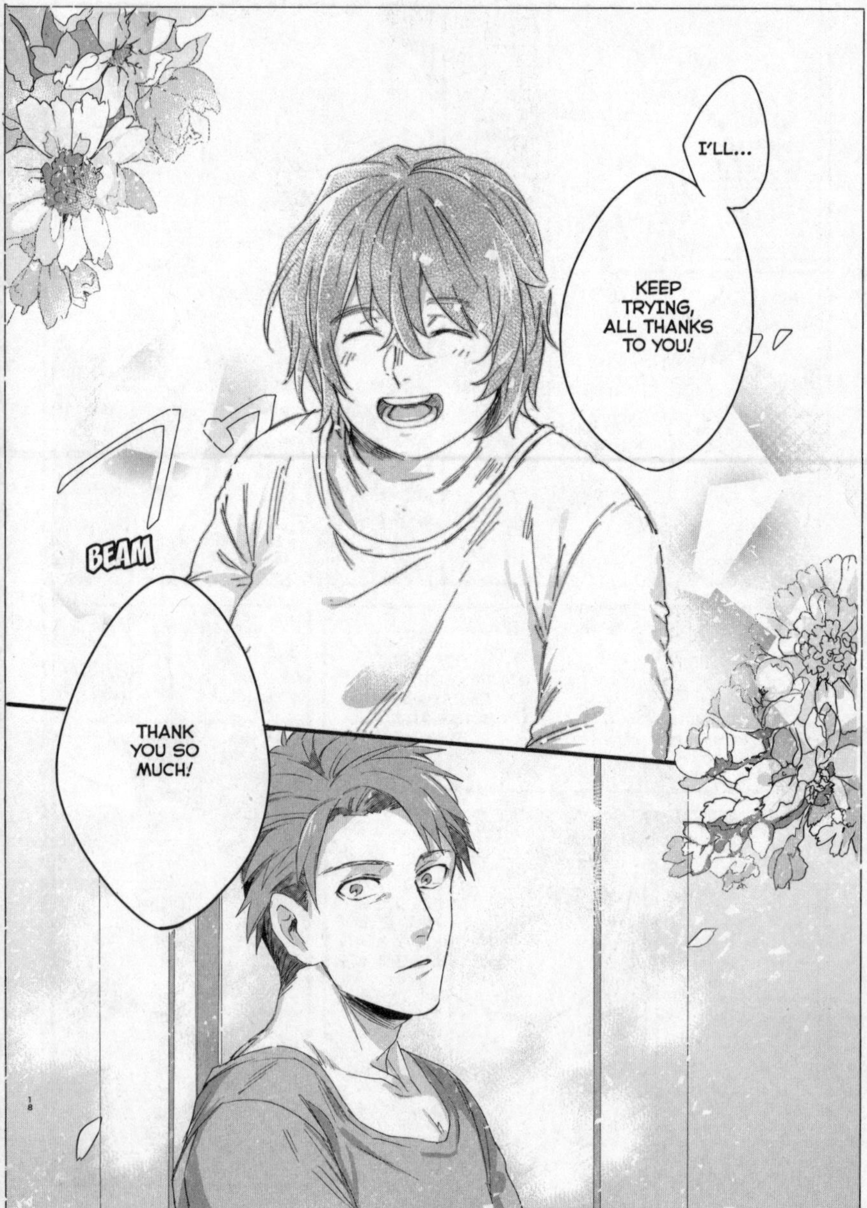
I'LL...
KEEP TRYING, ALL THANKS TO YOU!
BEAM
THANK YOU SO MUCH!

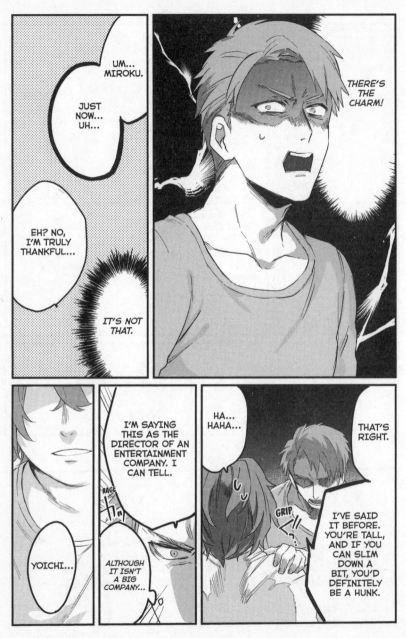

THERE'S THE CHARM!
UM... MIROKU.
JUST NOW... UH...
EH? NO, I'M TRULY THANKFUL...
IT'S NOT THAT.
THAT'S RIGHT.
HA... HAHA...
GRIP
I'VE SAID IT BEFORE. YOU'RE TALL, AND IF YOU CAN SLIM DOWN A BIT, YOU'D DEFINITELY BE A HUNK.
I'M SAYING THIS AS THE DIRECTOR OF AN ENTERTAINMENT COMPANY. I CAN TELL.
RAGE
ALTHOUGH IT ISN'T A BIG COMPANY...
YOICHI...

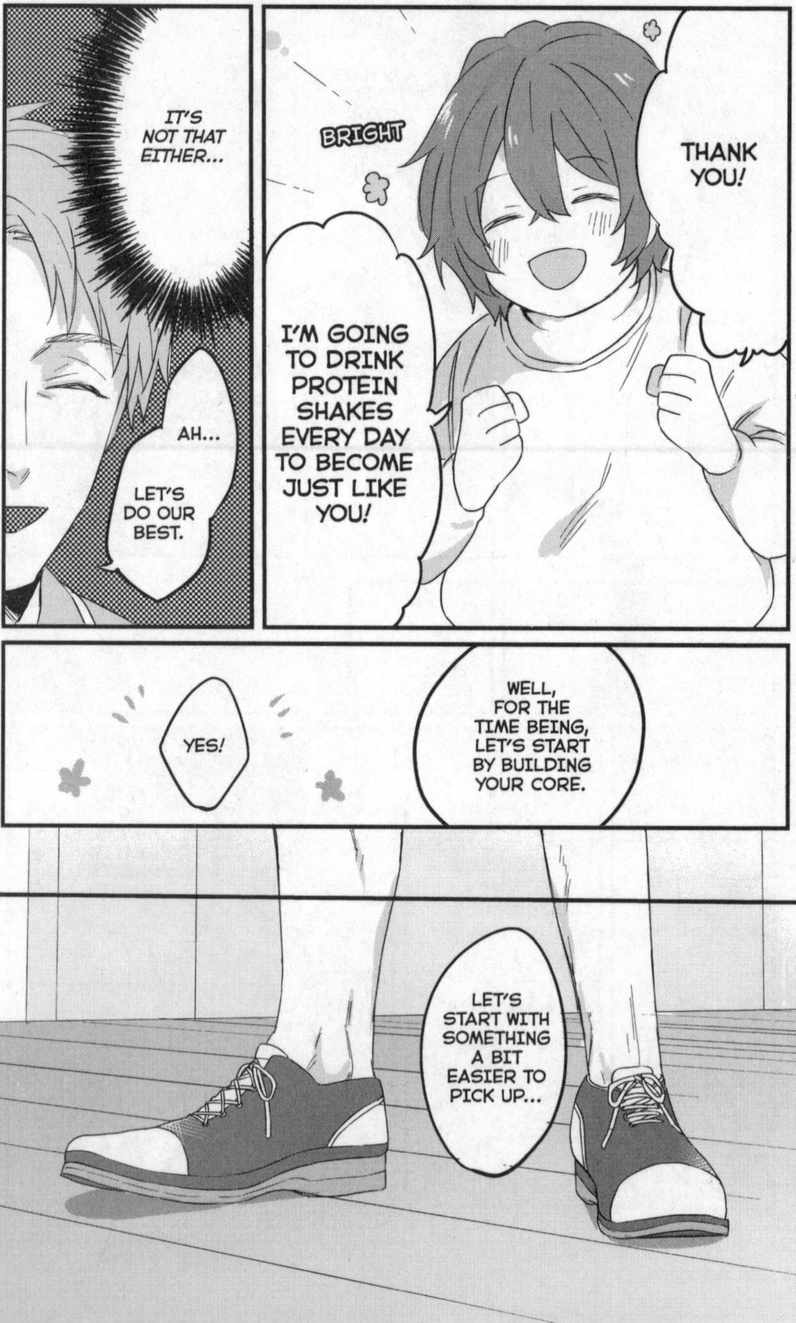
THANK YOU!
BRIGHT
I'M GOING TO DRINK PROTEIN SHAKES EVERY DAY TO BECOME JUST LIKE YOU!
IT'S NOT THAT EITHER...
AH...
LET'S DO OUR BEST.
WELL, FOR THE TIME BEING, LET'S START BY BUILDING YOUR CORE.
YES!
LET'S START WITH SOMETHING A BIT EASIER TO PICK UP...

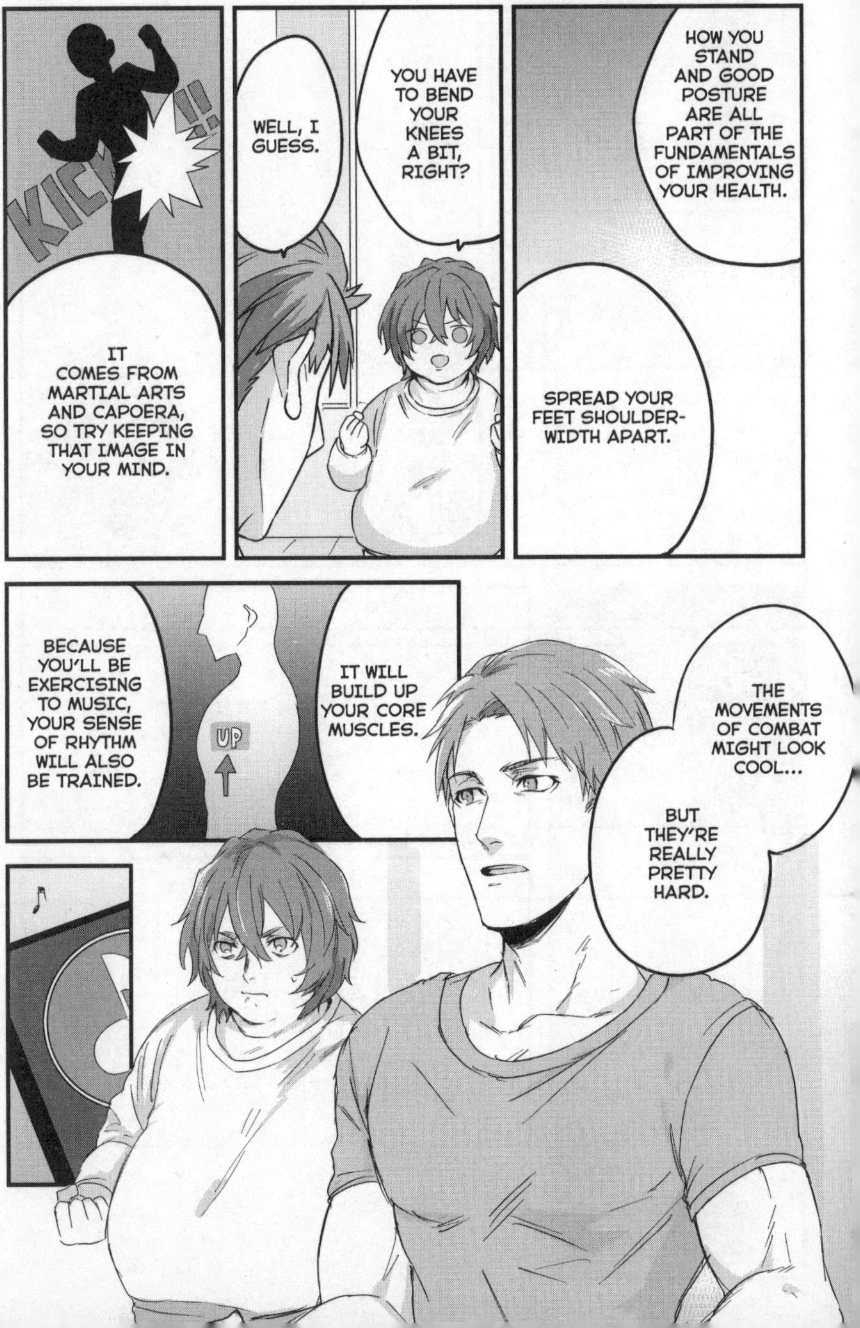
HOW YOU STAND AND GOOD POSTURE ARE ALL PART OF THE FUNDAMENTALS OF IMPROVING YOUR HEALTH.
SPREAD YOUR FEET SHOULDER-WIDTH APART.
YOU HAVE TO BEND YOUR KNEES A BIT, RIGHT?
WELL, I GUESS.
IT COMES FROM MARTIAL ARTS AND CAPOERA, SO TRY KEEPING THAT IMAGE IN YOUR MIND.
THE MOVEMENTS OF COMBAT MIGHT LOOK COOL...
BUT THEY'RE REALLY PRETTY HARD.
IT WILL BUILD UP YOUR CORE MUSCLES.
UP
BECAUSE YOU'LL BE EXERCISING TO MUSIC, YOUR SENSE OF RHYTHM WILL ALSO BE TRAINED.

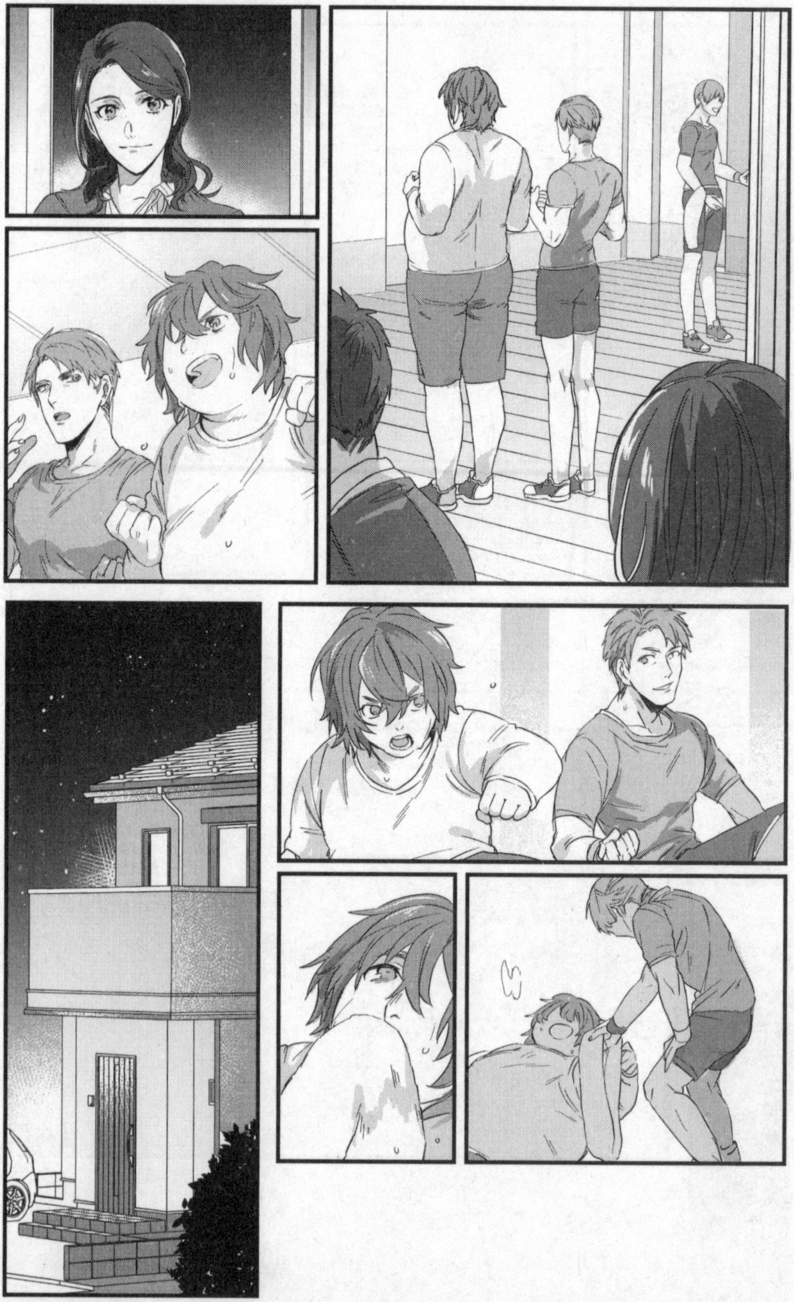

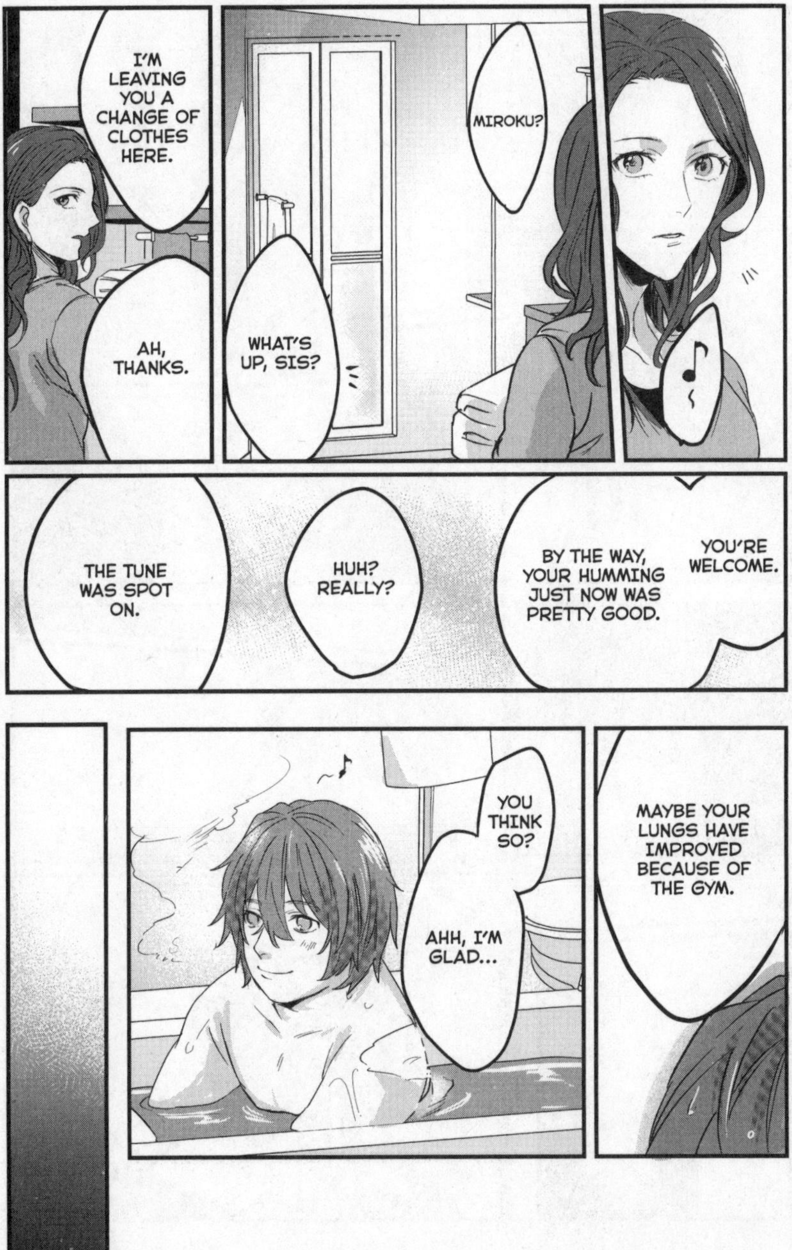
MIROKU?
WHAT'S UP, SIS?
I'M LEAVING YOU A CHANGE OF CLOTHES HERE.
AH, THANKS.
YOU'RE WELCOME.
BY THE WAY, YOUR HUMMING JUST NOW WAS PRETTY GOOD.
HUH? REALLY?
THE TUNE WAS SPOT ON.
MAYBE YOUR LUNGS HAVE IMPROVED BECAUSE OF THE GYM.
YOU THINK SO?
AHH, I'M GLAD...

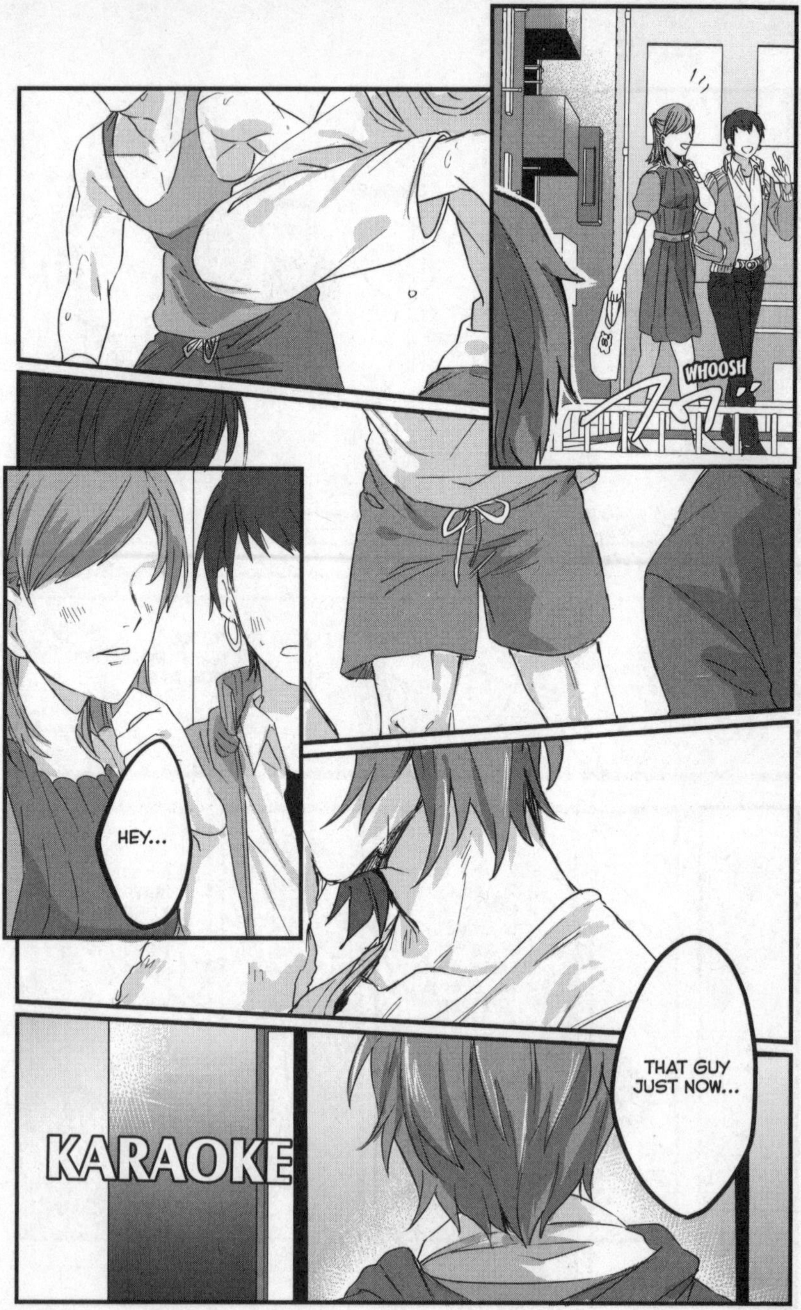
WHOOSH
HEY...
THAT GUY JUST NOW...
KARAOKE

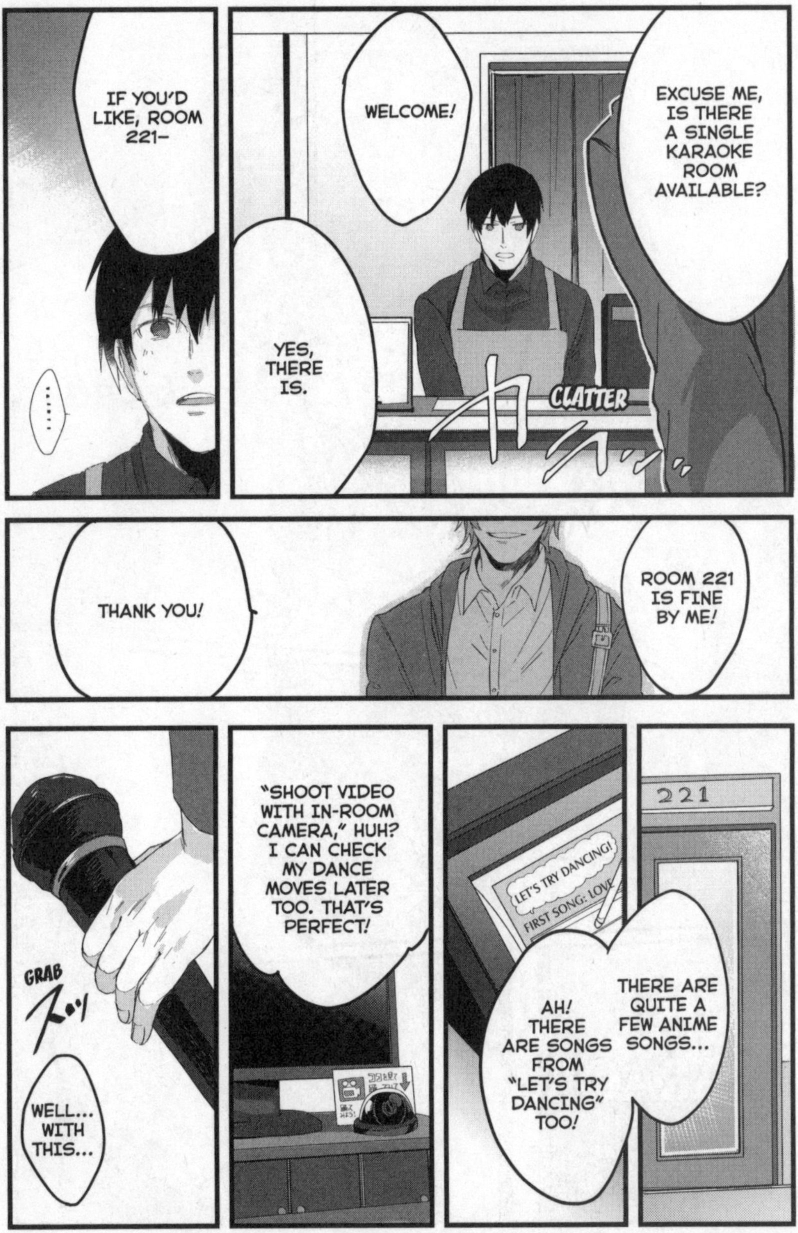
EXCUSE ME, IS THERE A SINGLE KARAOKE ROOM AVAILABLE?
WELCOME!
CLATTER
YES, THERE IS.
IF YOU'D LIKE, ROOM 221–
......
ROOM 221 IS FINE BY ME!
THANK YOU!
221
THERE ARE QUITE A FEW ANIME SONGS...
AH! THERE ARE SONGS FROM "LET'S TRY DANCING" TOO!
LET'S TRY DANCING!
FIRST SONG: LOVE
"SHOOT VIDEO WITH IN-ROOM CAMERA," HUH? I CAN CHECK MY DANCE MOVES LATER TOO. THAT'S PERFECT!
GRAB
WELL... WITH THIS...

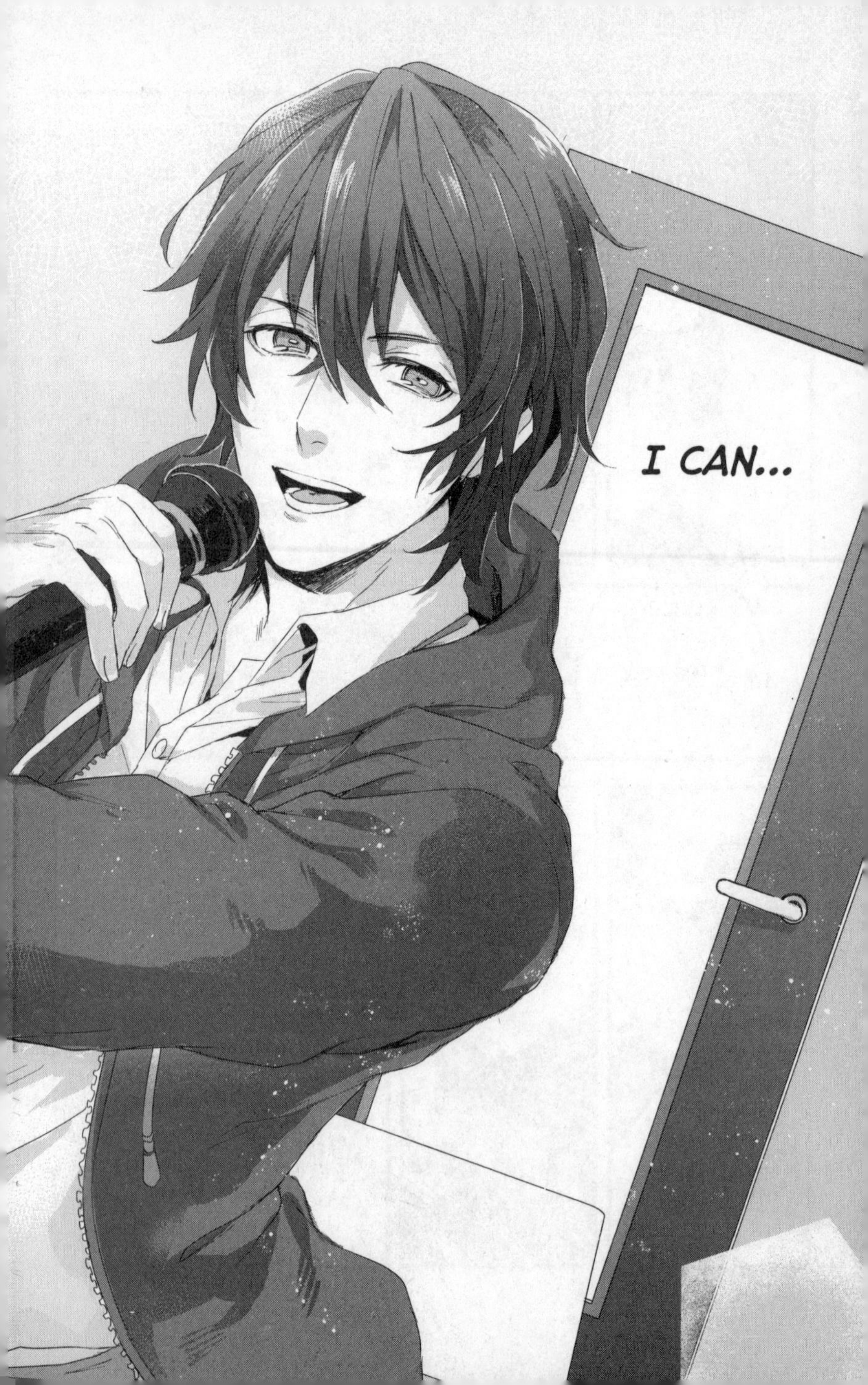
I CAN...

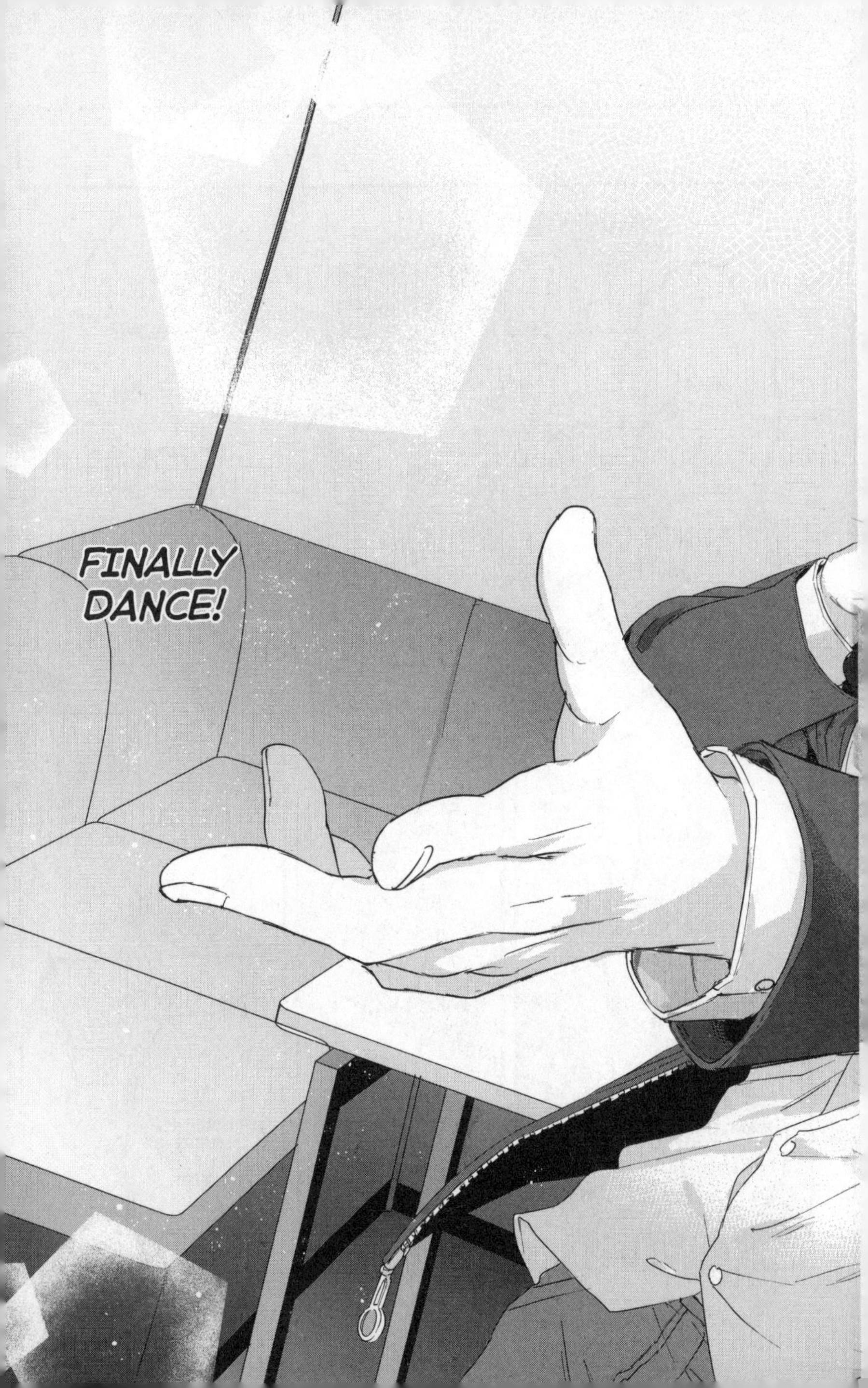
FINALLY DANCE!

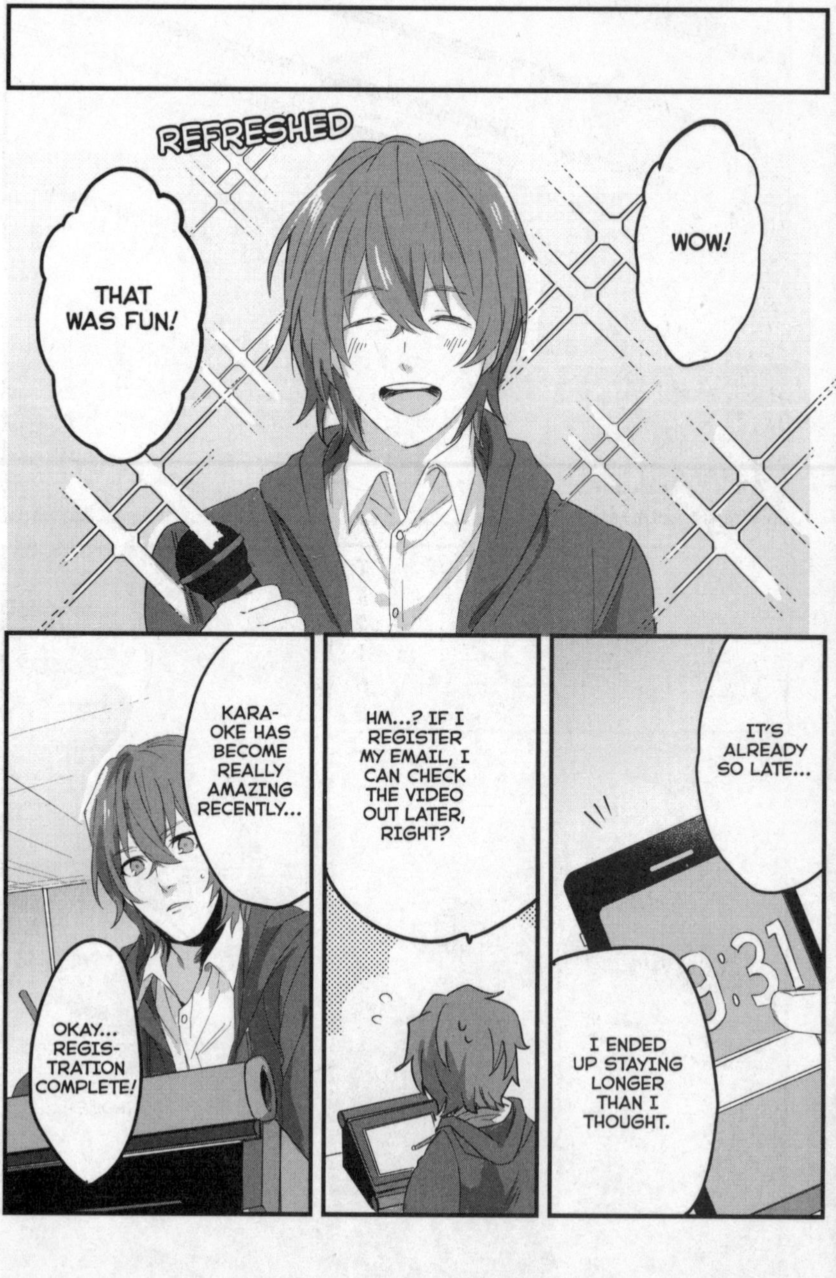
WOW!
REFRESHED
THAT WAS FUN!
IT'S ALREADY SO LATE...
I ENDED UP STAYING LONGER THAN I THOUGHT.
HM...? IF I REGISTER MY EMAIL, I CAN CHECK THE VIDEO OUT LATER, RIGHT?
KARA-OKE HAS BECOME REALLY AMAZING RECENTLY...
OKAY... REGIS-TRATION COMPLETE!

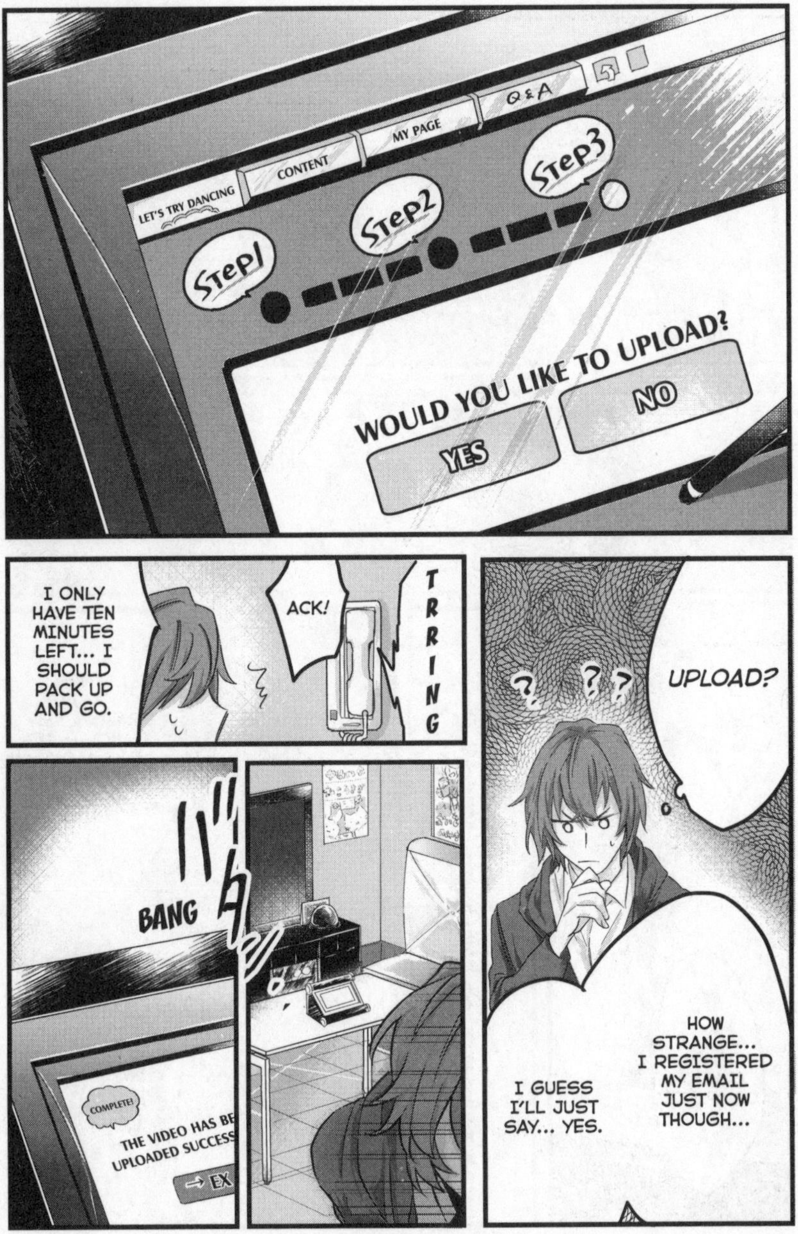
Q&A
MY PAGE
CONTENT
LET'S TRY DANCING
Step3
Step2
Step1
WOULD YOU LIKE TO UPLOAD?
NO
YES
UPLOAD?
? ? ?
HOW STRANGE... I REGISTERED MY EMAIL JUST NOW THOUGH...
I GUESS I'LL JUST SAY... YES.
TRRRING
ACK!
I ONLY HAVE TEN MINUTES LEFT... I SHOULD PACK UP AND GO.
バン
BANG
COMPLETE!
THE VIDEO HAS BE
UPLOADED SUCCESS
→ EX

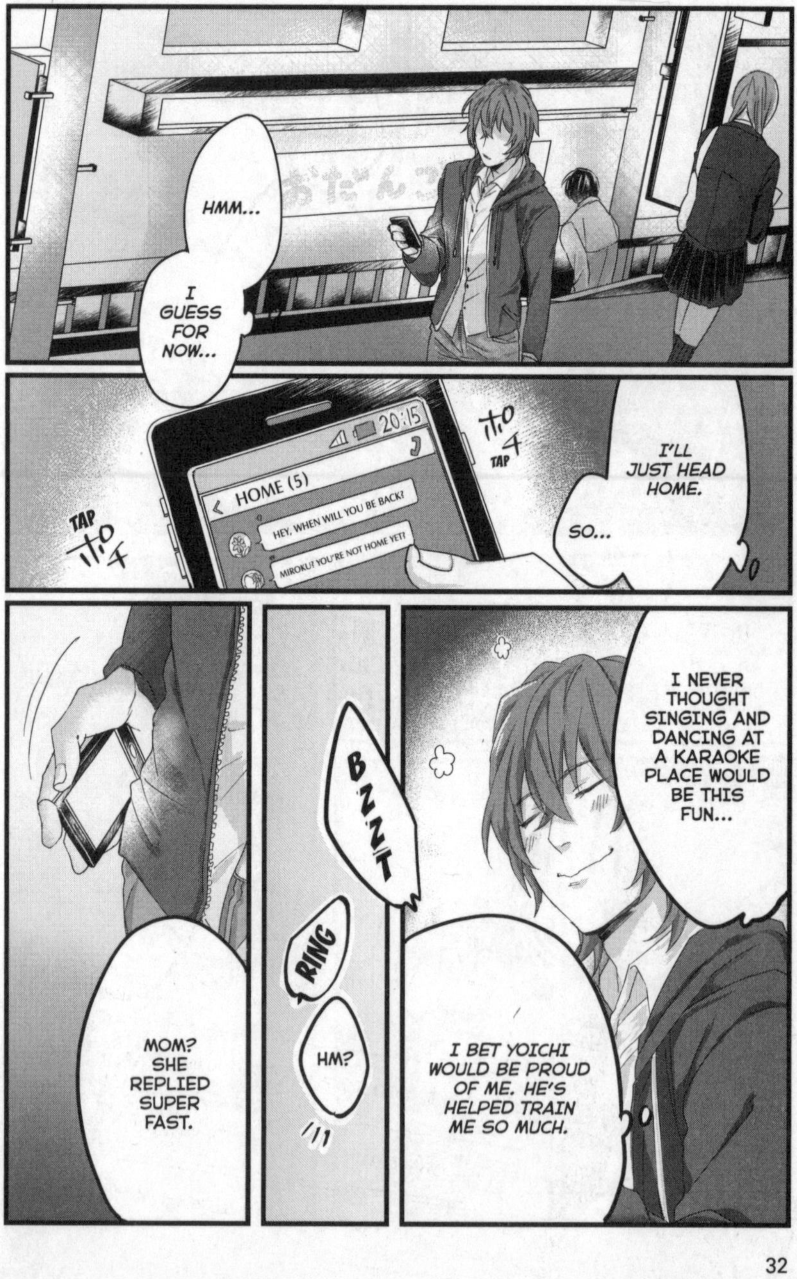
HMM...
I GUESS FOR NOW...
I'LL JUST HEAD HOME.
SO...
TAP
20:15
HOME (5)
HEY, WHEN WILL YOU BE BACK?
MIROKU? YOU'RE NOT HOME YET?
TAP
I NEVER THOUGHT SINGING AND DANCING AT A KARAOKE PLACE WOULD BE THIS FUN...
I BET YOICHI WOULD BE PROUD OF ME. HE'S HELPED TRAIN ME SO MUCH.
BZZZT
RING
HM?
MOM? SHE REPLIED SUPER FAST.

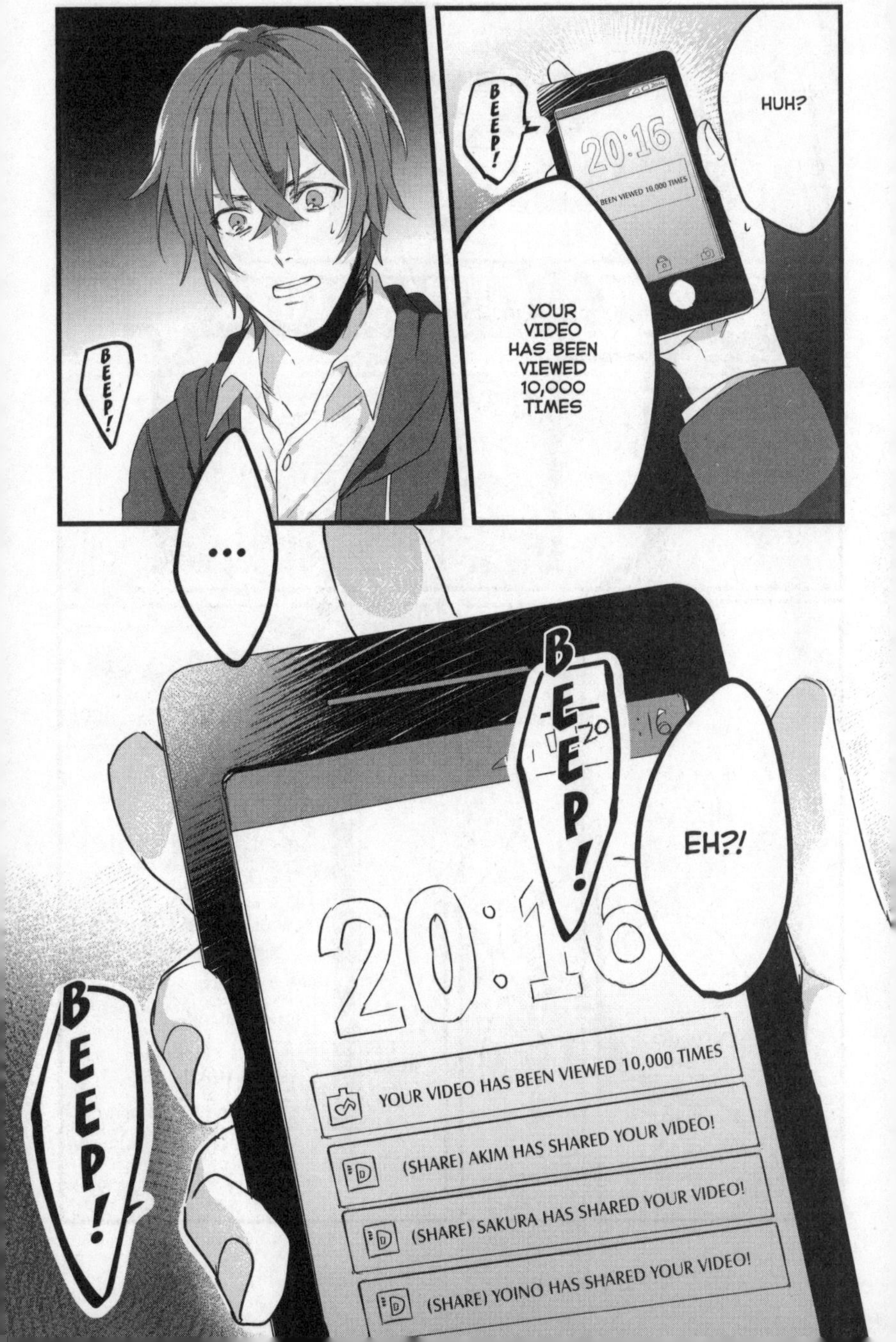

HUH?
BEEP!
20:16
BEEN VIEWED 10,000 TIMES
YOUR VIDEO HAS BEEN VIEWED 10,000 TIMES
BEEP!
...
EH?!
BEEP!
20:16
YOUR VIDEO HAS BEEN VIEWED 10,000 TIMES
(SHARE) AKIM HAS SHARED YOUR VIDEO!
(SHARE) SAKURA HAS SHARED YOUR VIDEO!
(SHARE) YOINO HAS SHARED YOUR VIDEO!
BEEP!

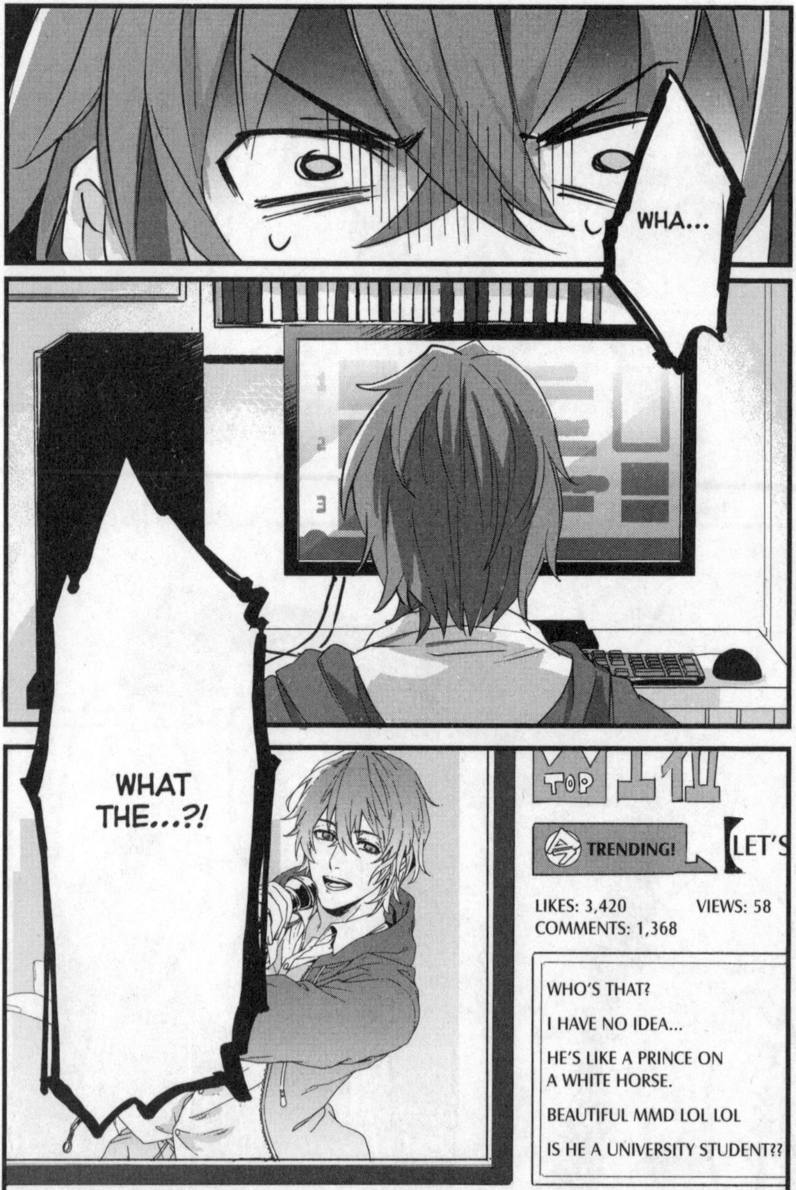
WHA...
TOP
TRENDING!
LET'S
LIKES: 3,420
VIEWS: 58
COMMENTS: 1,368
WHO'S THAT?
I HAVE NO IDEA...
HE'S LIKE A PRINCE ON A WHITE HORSE.
BEAUTIFUL MMD LOL LOL
IS HE A UNIVERSITY STUDENT??
WHAT THE...?!

Chapter 2

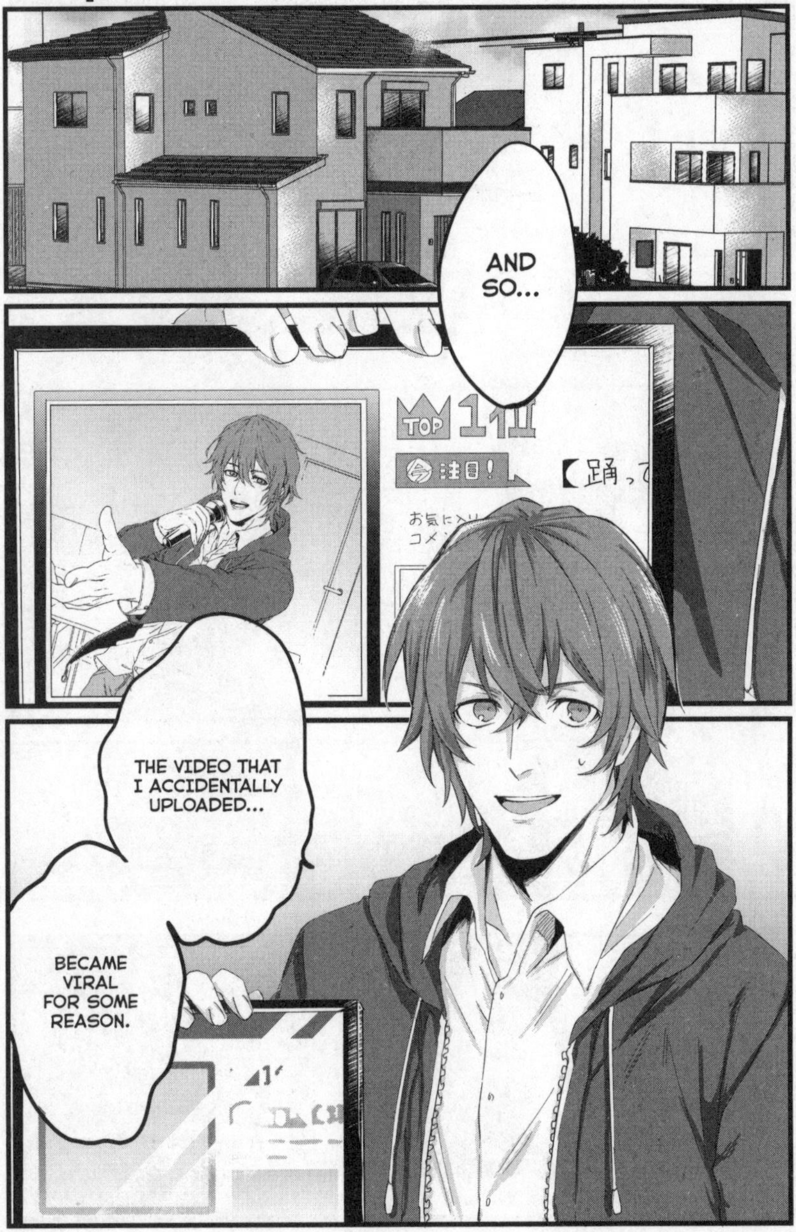
AND SO...
THE VIDEO THAT I ACCIDENTALLY UPLOADED...
BECAME VIRAL FOR SOME REASON.

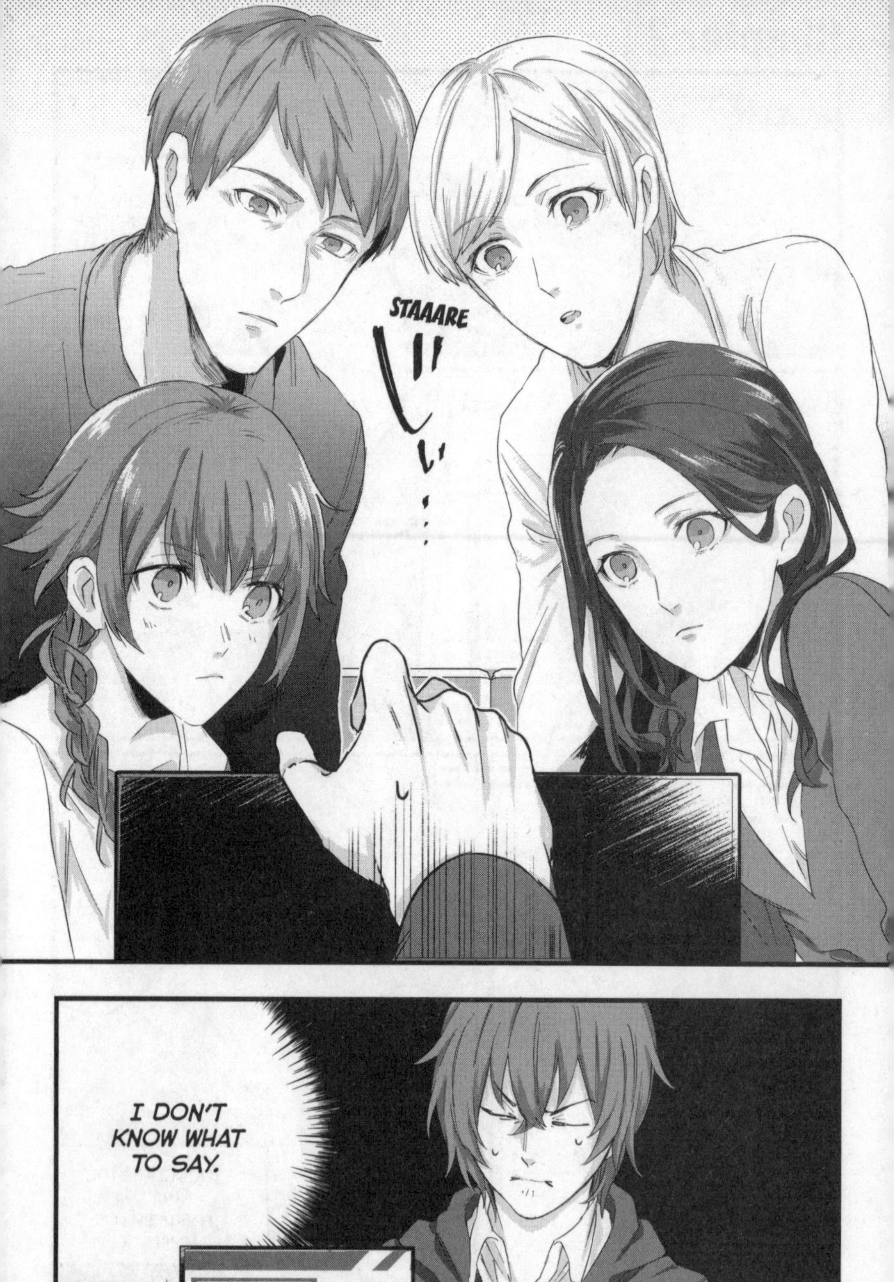
STAARE
じぃ…
I DON'T KNOW WHAT TO SAY.

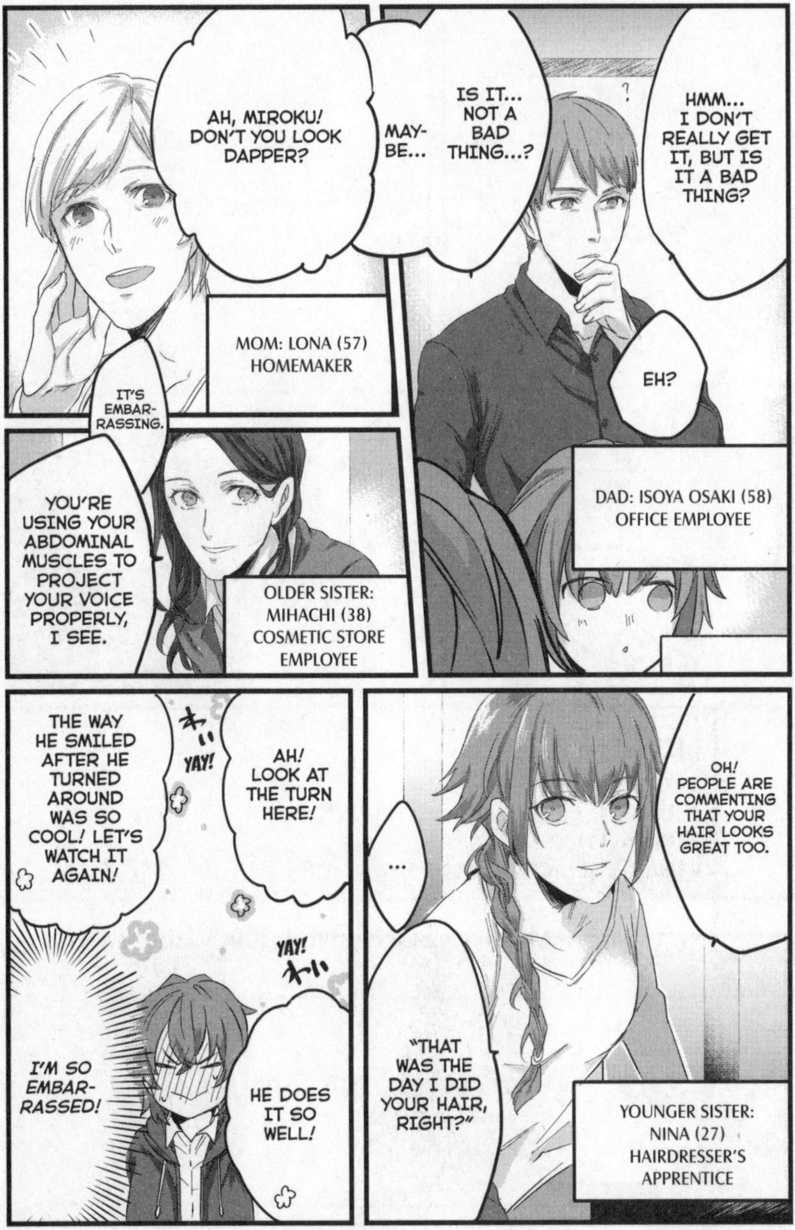
HMM... I DON'T REALLY GET IT, BUT IS IT A BAD THING?
IS IT... NOT A BAD THING...?
MAY-BE...
EH?
DAD: ISOYA OSAKI (58) OFFICE EMPLOYEE
AH, MIROKU! DON'T YOU LOOK DAPPER?
MOM: LONA (57) HOMEMAKER
IT'S EMBAR-RASSING.
YOU'RE USING YOUR ABDOMINAL MUSCLES TO PROJECT YOUR VOICE PROPERLY, I SEE.
OLDER SISTER: MIHACHI (38) COSMETIC STORE EMPLOYEE
OH! PEOPLE ARE COMMENTING THAT YOUR HAIR LOOKS GREAT TOO.
...
"THAT WAS THE DAY I DID YOUR HAIR, RIGHT?"
YOUNGER SISTER: NINA (27) HAIRDRESSER'S APPRENTICE
AH! LOOK AT THE TURN HERE!
YAY!
THE WAY HE SMILED AFTER HE TURNED AROUND WAS SO COOL! LET'S WATCH IT AGAIN!
YAY!
HE DOES IT SO WELL!
I'M SO EMBAR-RASSED!

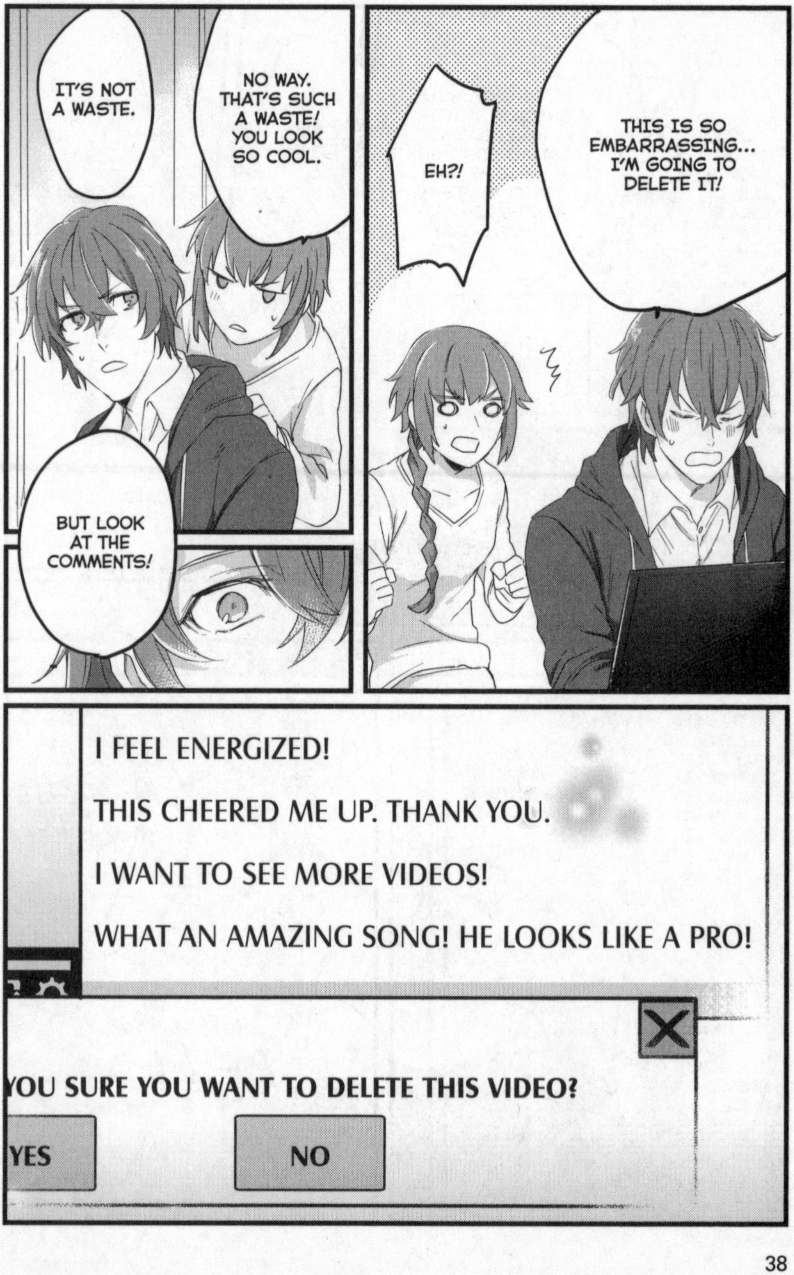
THIS IS SO EMBARRASSING... I'M GOING TO DELETE IT!
EH?!
NO WAY. THAT'S SUCH A WASTE! YOU LOOK SO COOL.
IT'S NOT A WASTE.
BUT LOOK AT THE COMMENTS!
I FEEL ENERGIZED!
THIS CHEERED ME UP. THANK YOU.
I WANT TO SEE MORE VIDEOS!
WHAT AN AMAZING SONG! HE LOOKS LIKE A PRO!
YOU SURE YOU WANT TO DELETE THIS VIDEO?
YES
NO

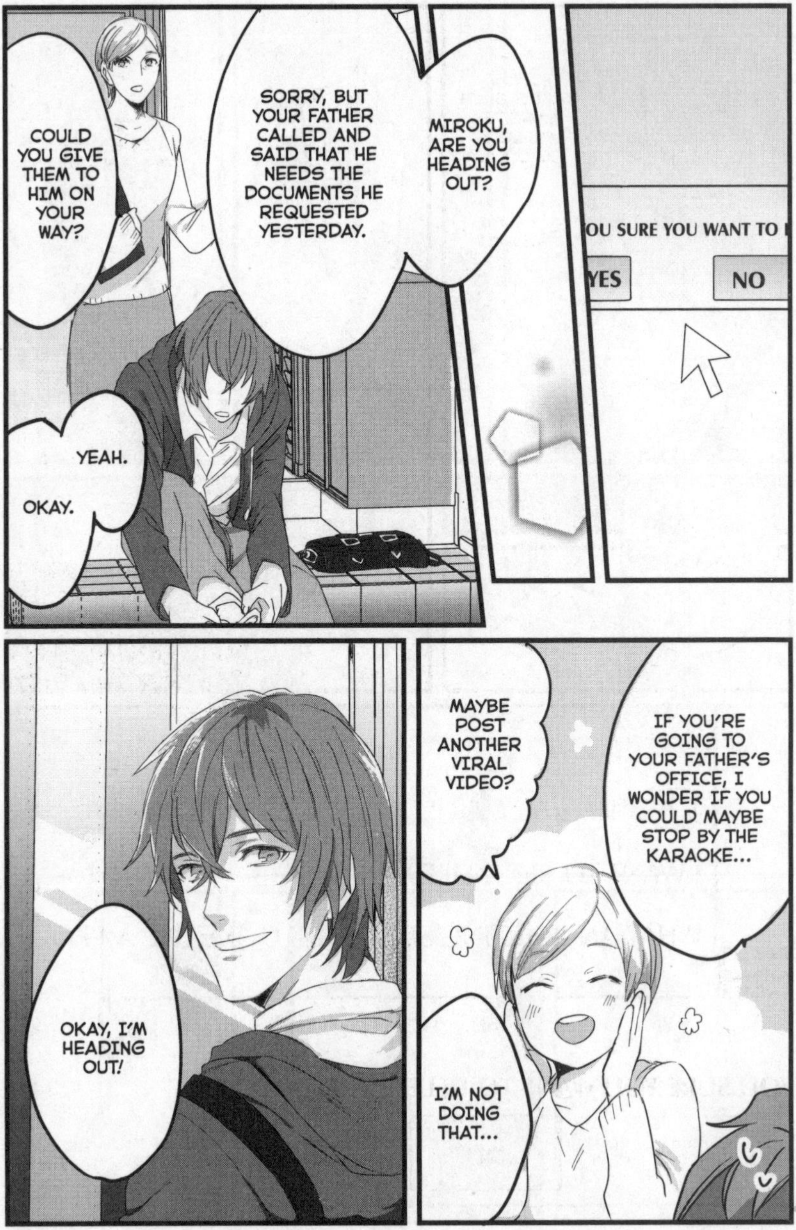
OU SURE YOU WANT TO
YES
NO
MIROKU, ARE YOU HEADING OUT?
SORRY, BUT YOUR FATHER CALLED AND SAID THAT HE NEEDS THE DOCUMENTS HE REQUESTED YESTERDAY.
COULD YOU GIVE THEM TO HIM ON YOUR WAY?
YEAH.
OKAY.
IF YOU'RE GOING TO YOUR FATHER'S OFFICE, I WONDER IF YOU COULD MAYBE STOP BY THE KARAOKE...
MAYBE POST ANOTHER VIRAL VIDEO?
I'M NOT DOING THAT...
OKAY, I'M HEADING OUT!

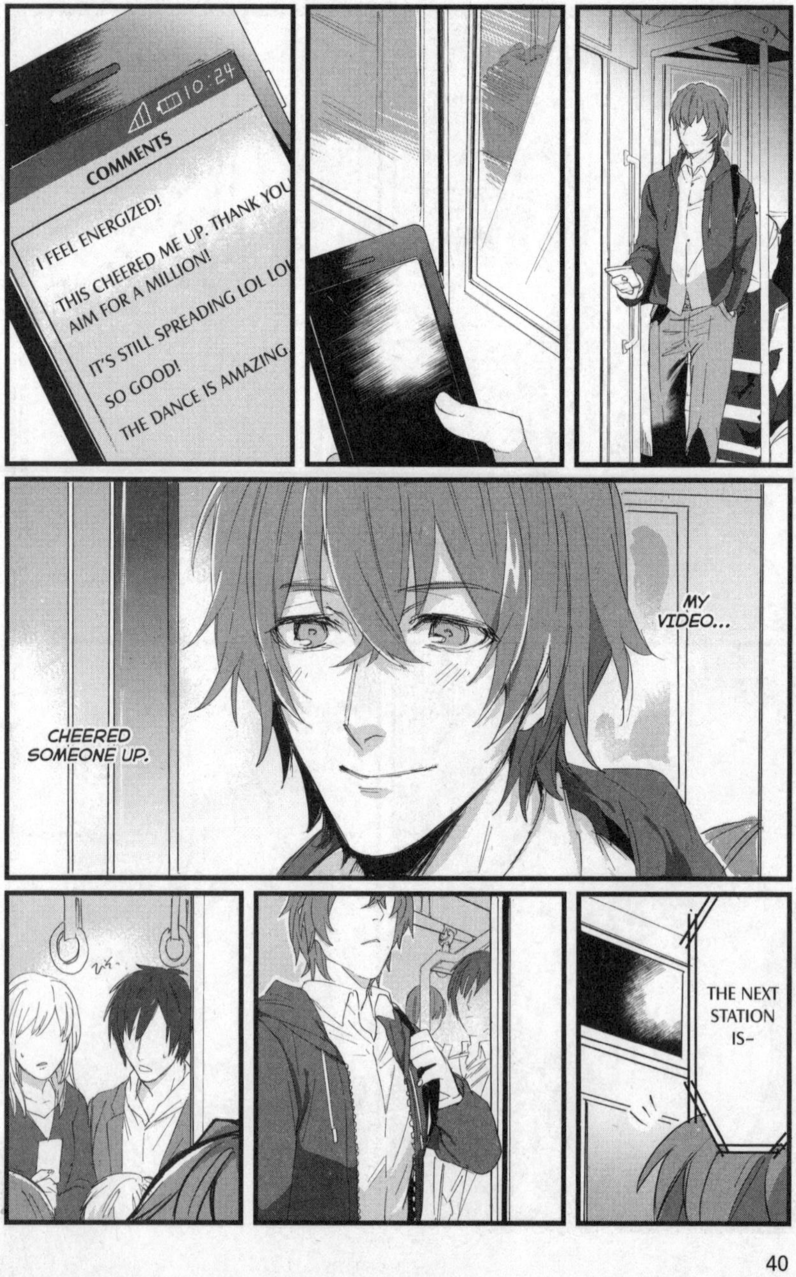
10:24
COMMENTS
I FEEL ENERGIZED!
THIS CHEERED ME UP. THANK YOU
AIM FOR A MILLION!
IT'S STILL SPREADING LOL LO
SO GOOD!
THE DANCE IS AMAZING.
MY VIDEO...
CHEERED SOMEONE UP.
THE NEXT STATION IS–

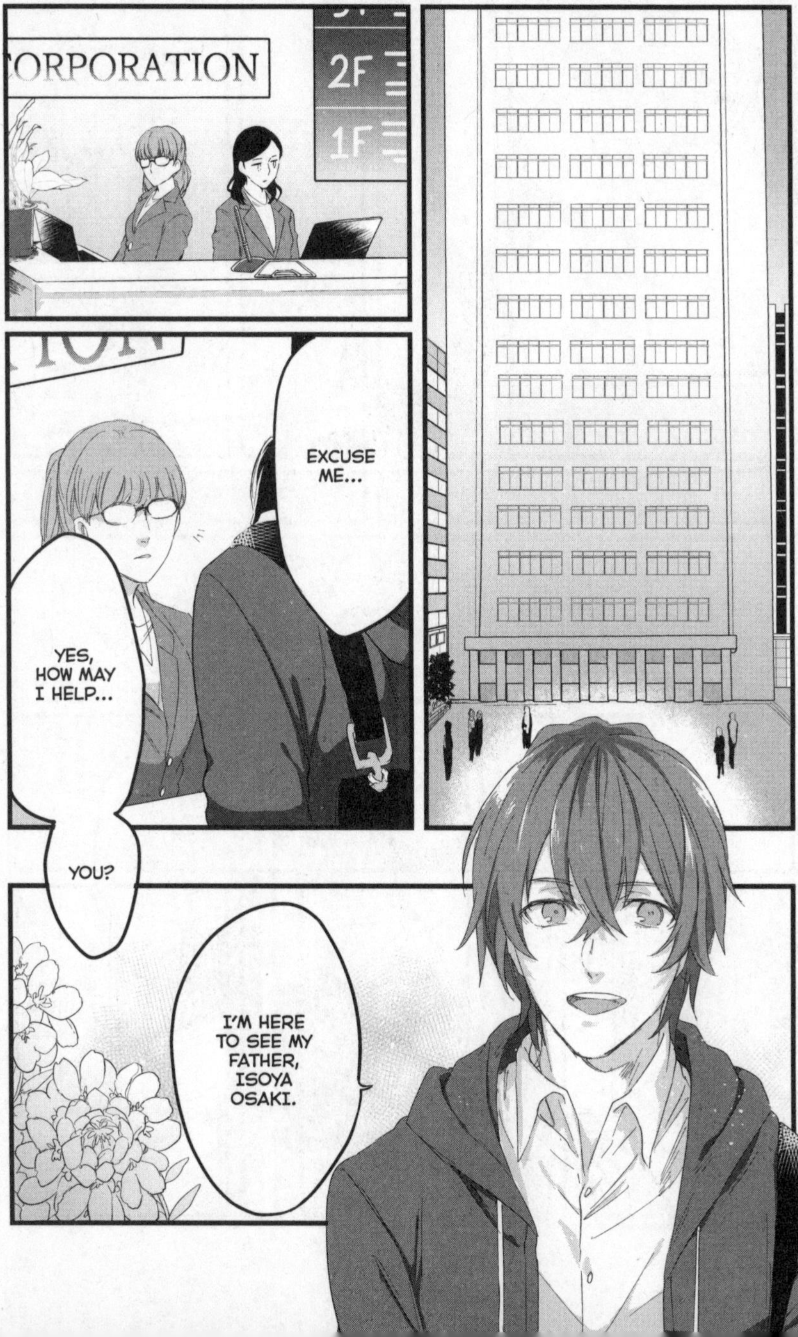
CORPORATION
2F
1F
EXCUSE ME...
YES, HOW MAY I HELP...
YOU?
I'M HERE TO SEE MY FATHER, ISOYA OSAKI.

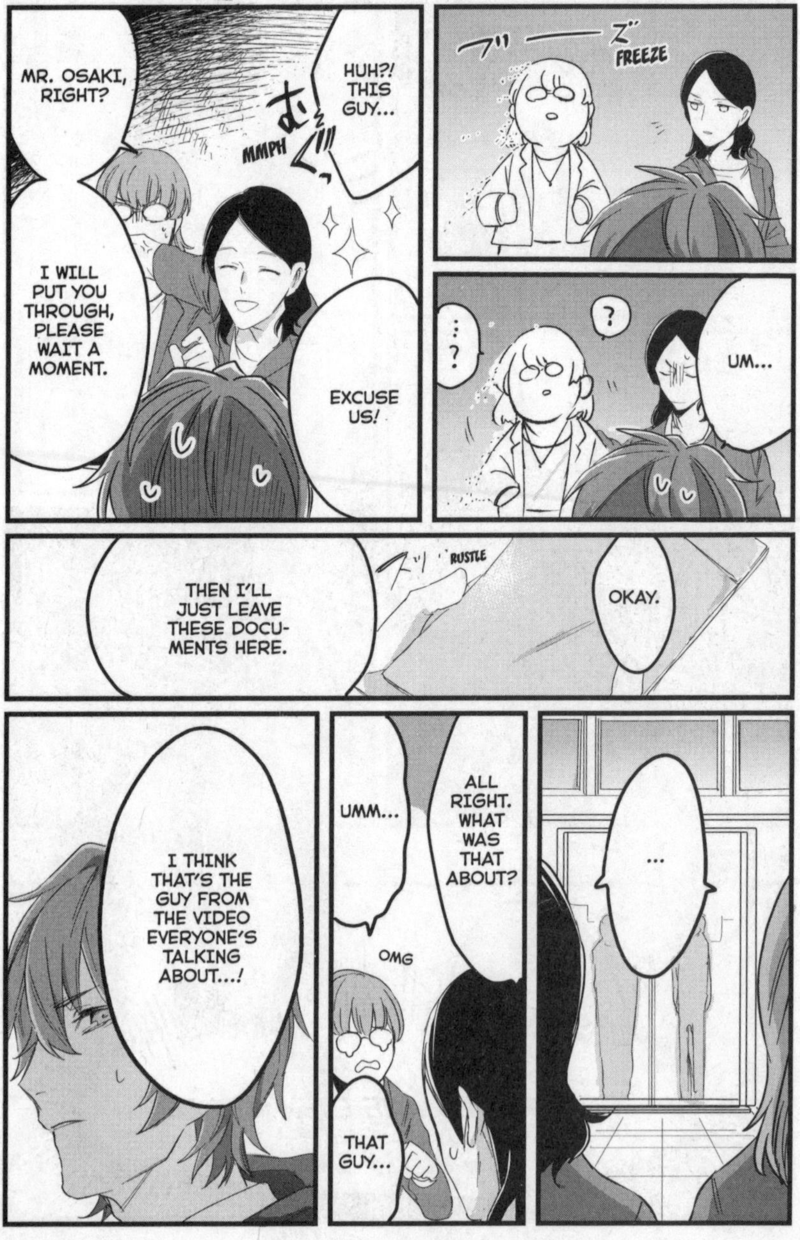
FREEZE
?
...?
UM...
HUH?! THIS GUY...
MMPH
MR. OSAKI, RIGHT?
EXCUSE US!
I WILL PUT YOU THROUGH, PLEASE WAIT A MOMENT.
OKAY.
RUSTLE
THEN I'LL JUST LEAVE THESE DOCU-MENTS HERE.
...
ALL RIGHT. WHAT WAS THAT ABOUT?
UMM...
OMG
THAT GUY...
I THINK THAT'S THE GUY FROM THE VIDEO EVERYONE'S TALKING ABOUT...!

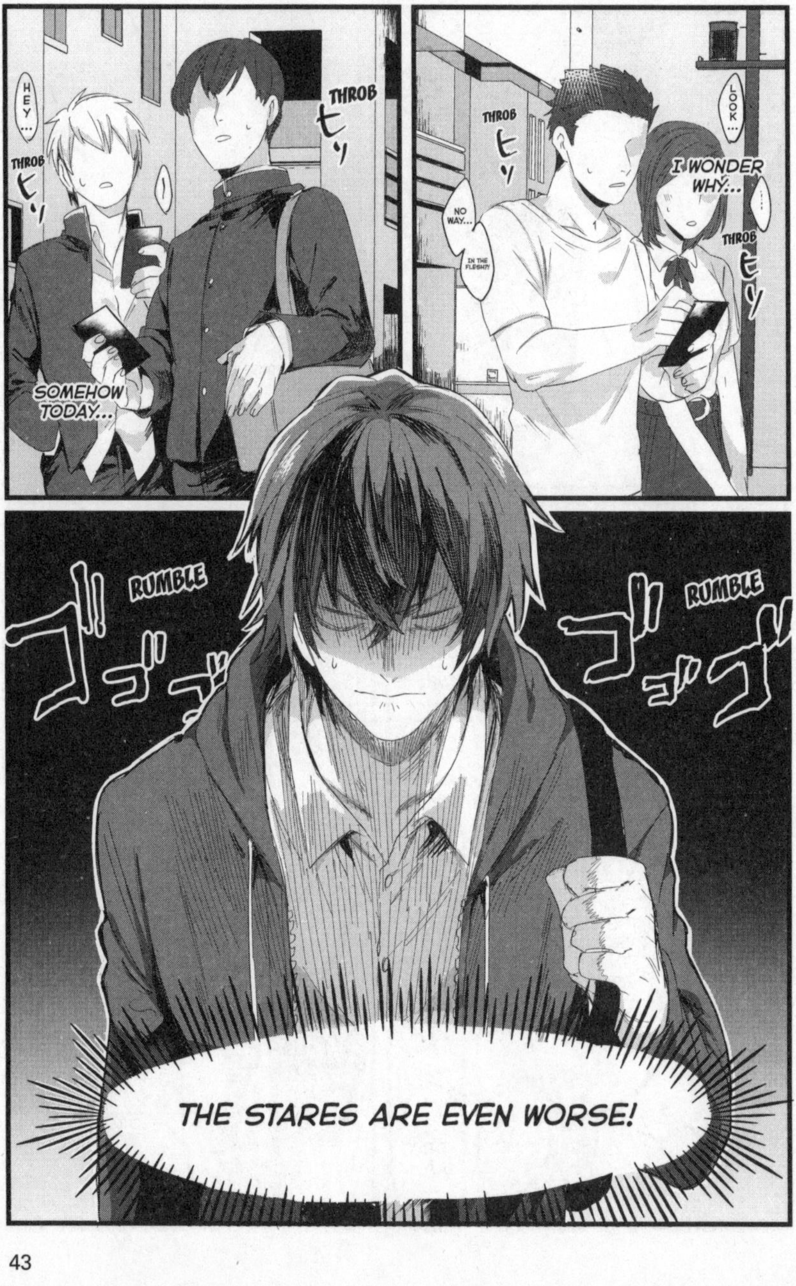
LOOK...
I WONDER WHY...
....
THROB
THROB
NO WAY...
IN THE FLESH?!
THROB
HEY...
!
THROB
SOMEHOW TODAY...
RUMBLE
RUMBLE
THE STARES ARE EVEN WORSE!

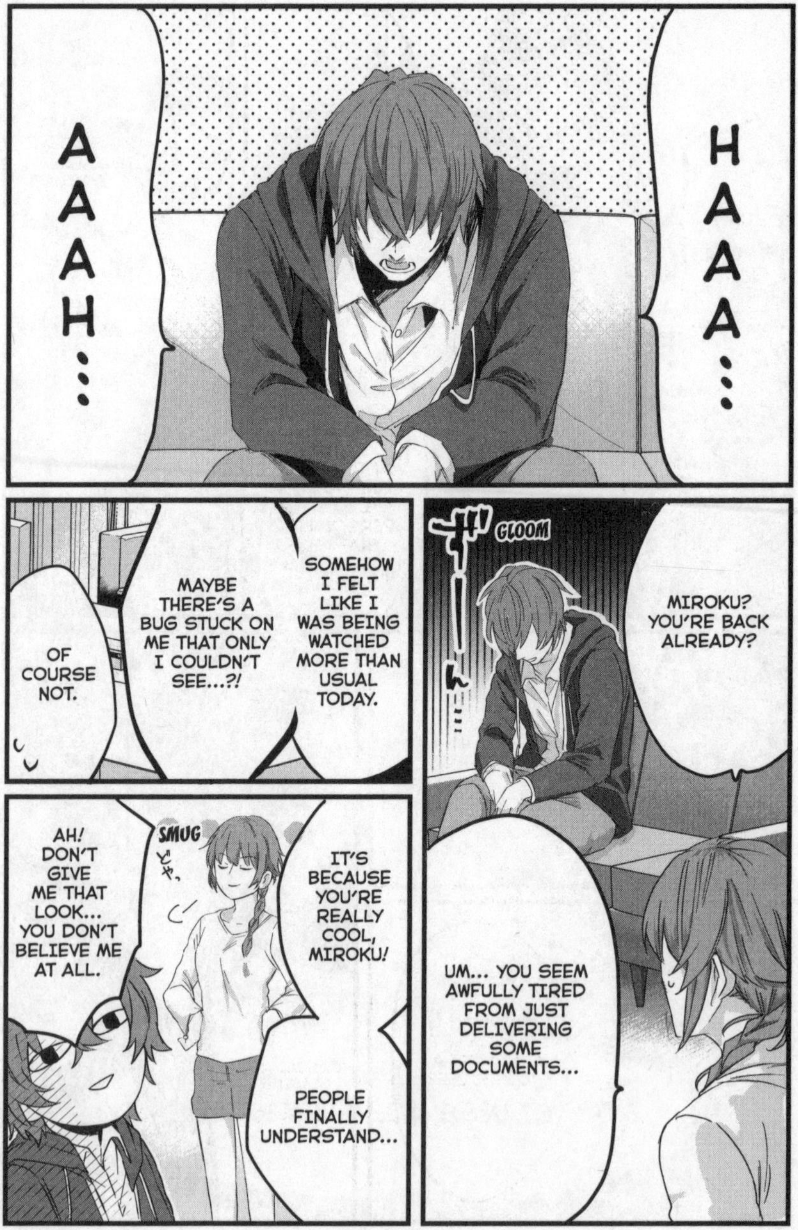
HAAA...
AAAH...
GLOOM
MIROKU? YOU'RE BACK ALREADY?
UM... YOU SEEM AWFULLY TIRED FROM JUST DELIVERING SOME DOCUMENTS...
SOMEHOW I FELT LIKE I WAS BEING WATCHED MORE THAN USUAL TODAY.
MAYBE THERE'S A BUG STUCK ON ME THAT ONLY I COULDN'T SEE...?!
OF COURSE NOT.
IT'S BECAUSE YOU'RE REALLY COOL, MIROKU!
SMUG
どや、
PEOPLE FINALLY UNDERSTAND...
AH! DON'T GIVE ME THAT LOOK... YOU DON'T BELIEVE ME AT ALL.

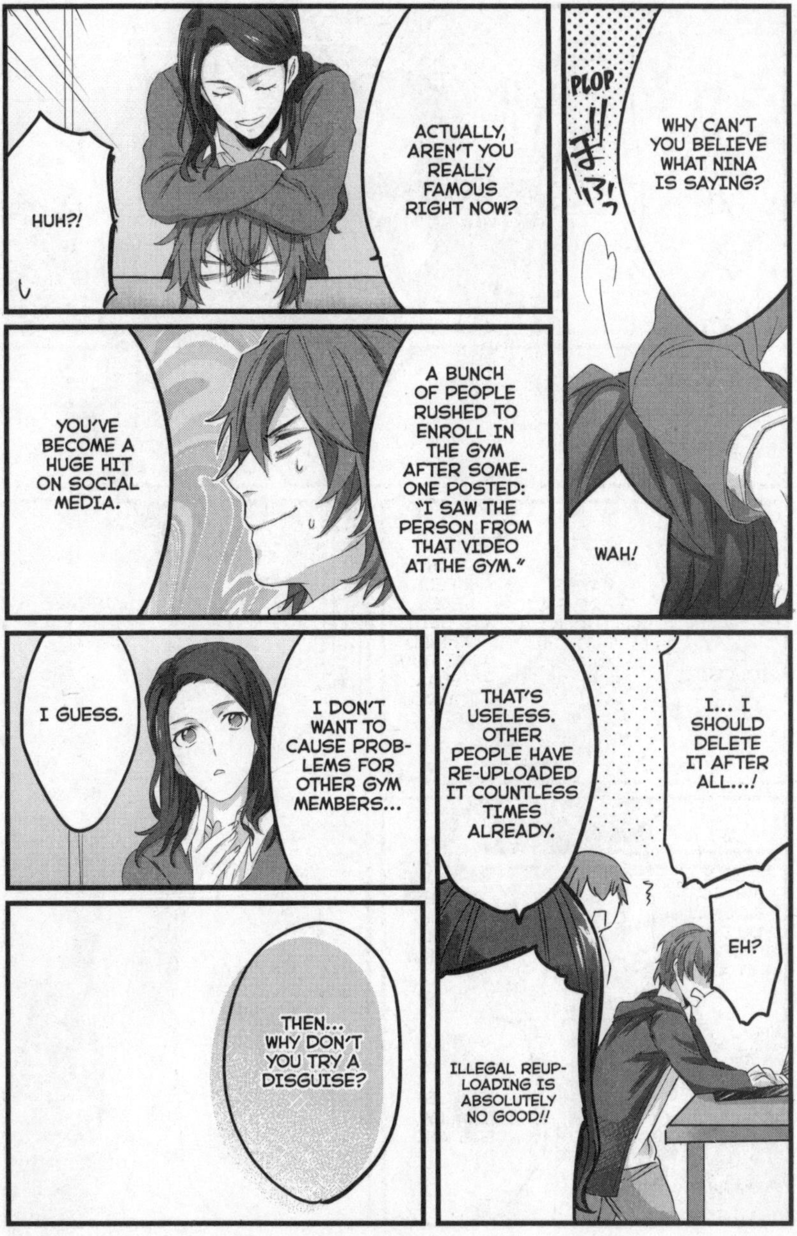
WHY CAN'T YOU BELIEVE WHAT NINA IS SAYING?
PLOP
WAH!
ACTUALLY, AREN'T YOU REALLY FAMOUS RIGHT NOW?
HUH?!
A BUNCH OF PEOPLE RUSHED TO ENROLL IN THE GYM AFTER SOME-ONE POSTED: "I SAW THE PERSON FROM THAT VIDEO AT THE GYM."
YOU'VE BECOME A HUGE HIT ON SOCIAL MEDIA.
I... I SHOULD DELETE IT AFTER ALL...!
THAT'S USELESS. OTHER PEOPLE HAVE RE-UPLOADED IT COUNTLESS TIMES ALREADY.
EH?
ILLEGAL REUP-LOADING IS ABSOLUTELY NO GOOD!!
I DON'T WANT TO CAUSE PROB-LEMS FOR OTHER GYM MEMBERS...
I GUESS.
THEN... WHY DON'T YOU TRY A DISGUISE?

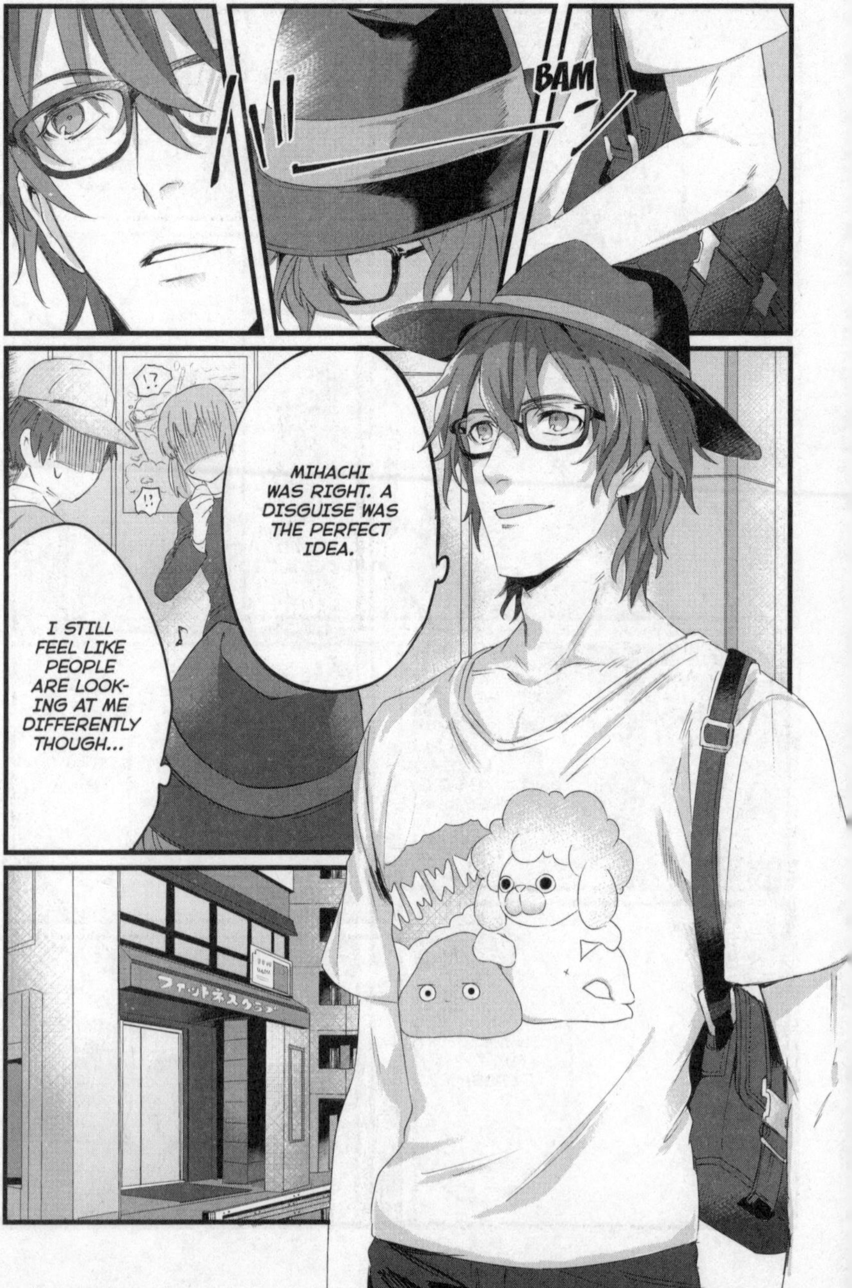
BAM
MIHACHI WAS RIGHT. A DISGUISE WAS THE PERFECT IDEA.
I STILL FEEL LIKE PEOPLE ARE LOOKING AT ME DIFFERENTLY THOUGH...

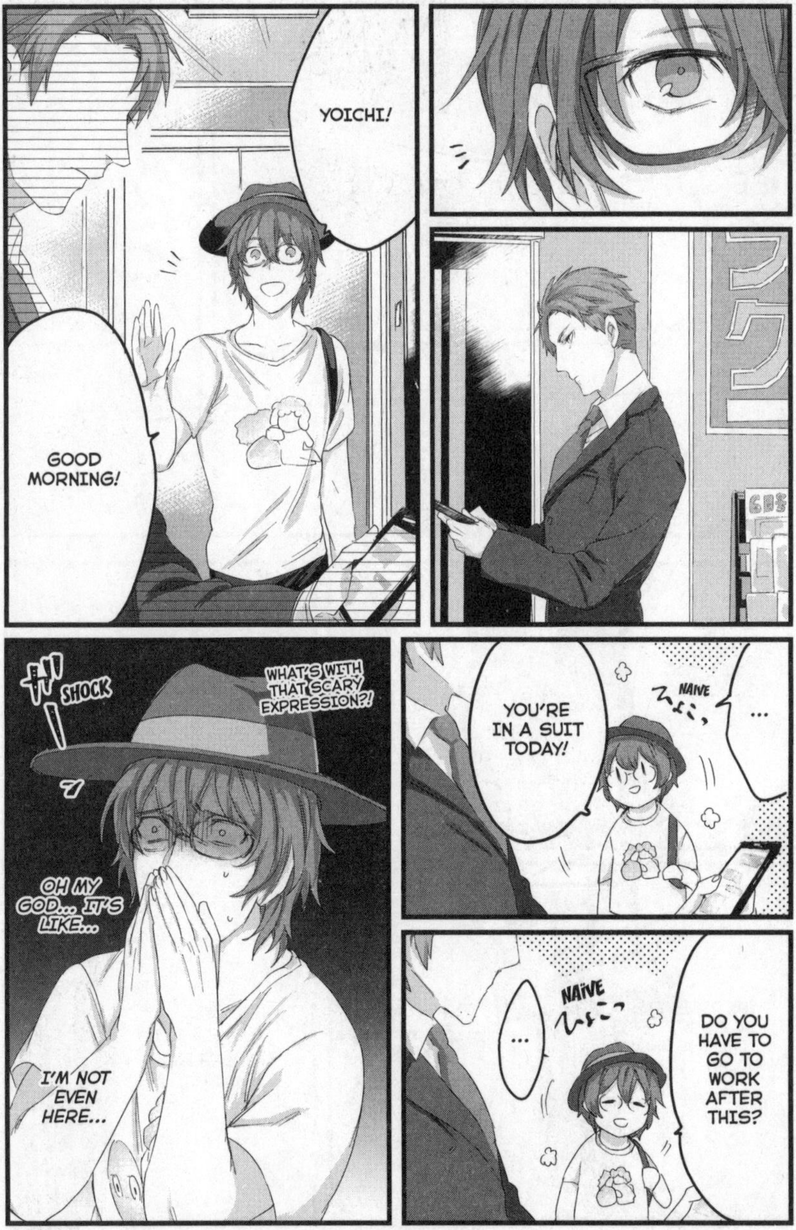
YOICHI!
GOOD MORNING!
...
NAÏVE
YOU'RE IN A SUIT TODAY!
DO YOU HAVE TO GO TO WORK AFTER THIS?
NAÏVE
...
WHAT'S WITH THAT SCARY EXPRESSION?!
SHOCK
OH MY GOD... IT'S LIKE...
I'M NOT EVEN HERE...

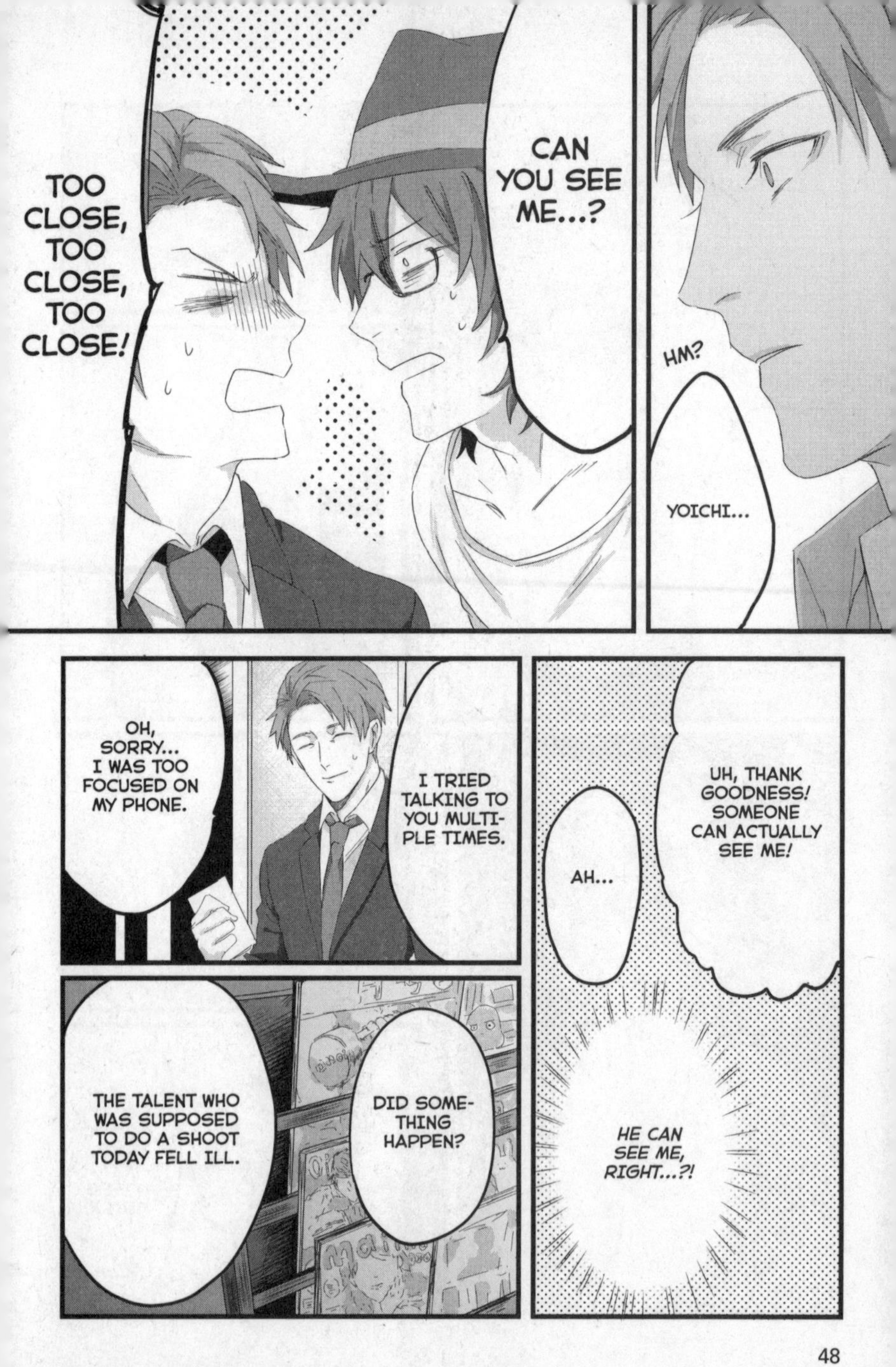
HM?
YOICHI...
CAN YOU SEE ME...?
TOO CLOSE, TOO CLOSE, TOO CLOSE!
UH, THANK GOODNESS! SOMEONE CAN ACTUALLY SEE ME!
AH...
HE CAN SEE ME, RIGHT...?!
I TRIED TALKING TO YOU MULTIPLE TIMES.
OH, SORRY... I WAS TOO FOCUSED ON MY PHONE.
DID SOMETHING HAPPEN?
THE TALENT WHO WAS SUPPOSED TO DO A SHOOT TODAY FELL ILL.

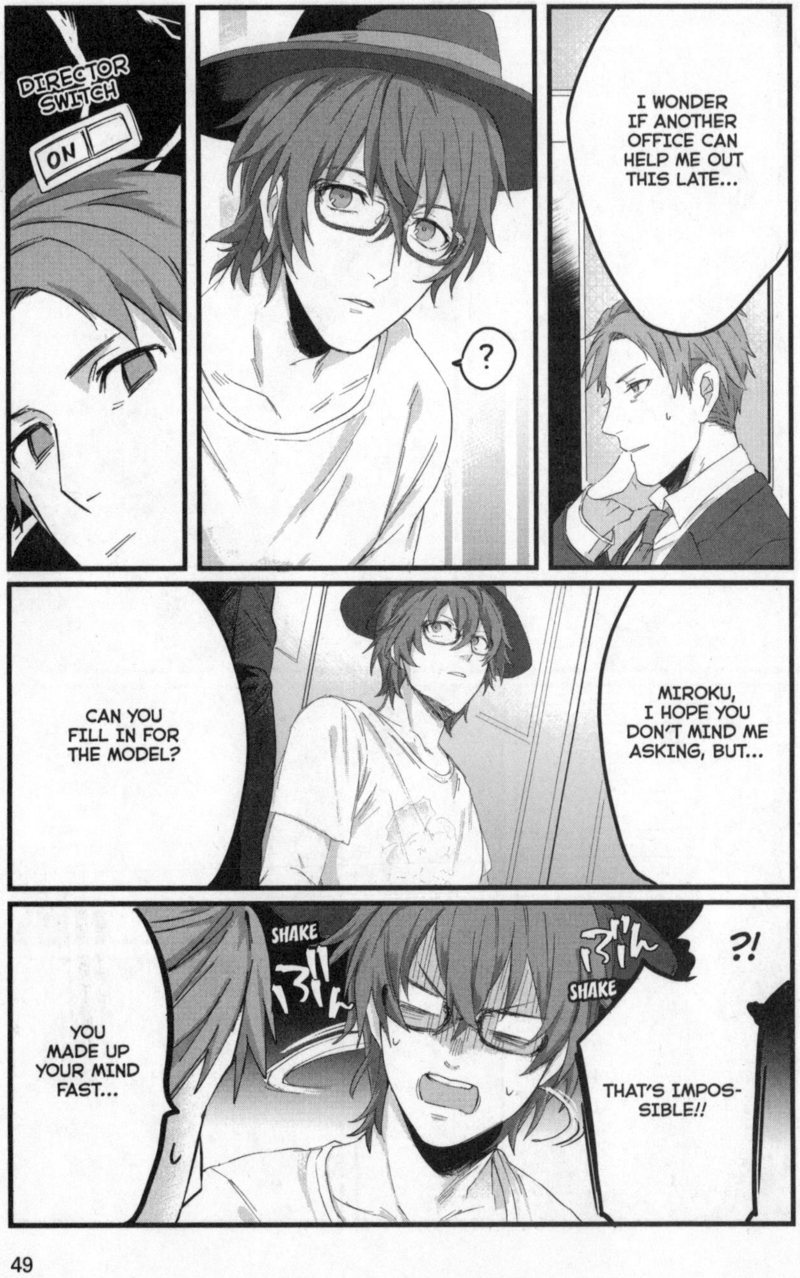
I WONDER IF ANOTHER OFFICE CAN HELP ME OUT THIS LATE...
?
DIRECTOR SWITCH
ON
MIROKU, I HOPE YOU DON'T MIND ME ASKING, BUT...
CAN YOU FILL IN FOR THE MODEL?
?!
ぶん
SHAKE
THAT'S IMPOS-SIBLE!!
SHAKE
ぶん
YOU MADE UP YOUR MIND FAST...

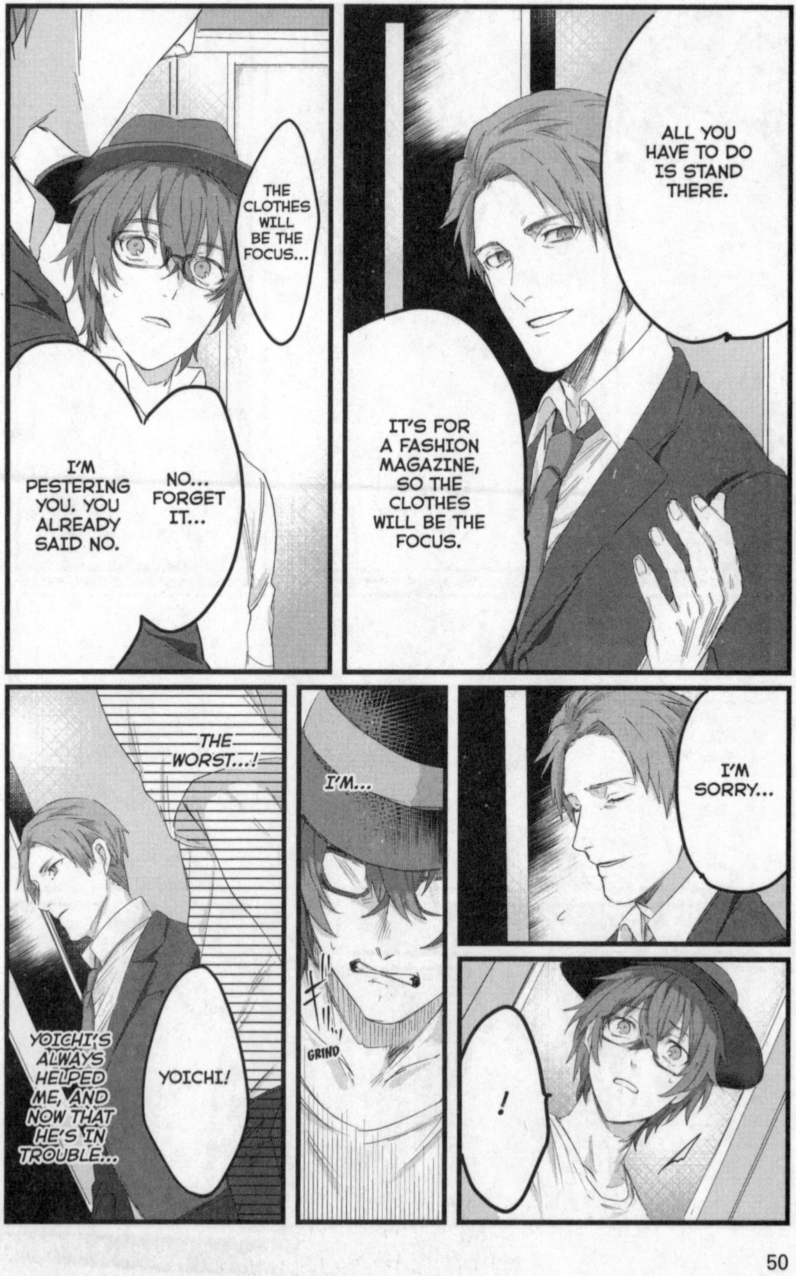
ALL YOU HAVE TO DO IS STAND THERE.
IT'S FOR A FASHION MAGAZINE, SO THE CLOTHES WILL BE THE FOCUS.
THE CLOTHES WILL BE THE FOCUS...
NO... FORGET IT...
I'M PESTERING YOU. YOU ALREADY SAID NO.
I'M SORRY...
!
I'M...
GRIND
THE WORST...!
YOICHI!
YOICHI'S ALWAYS HELPED ME, AND NOW THAT HE'S IN TROUBLE...

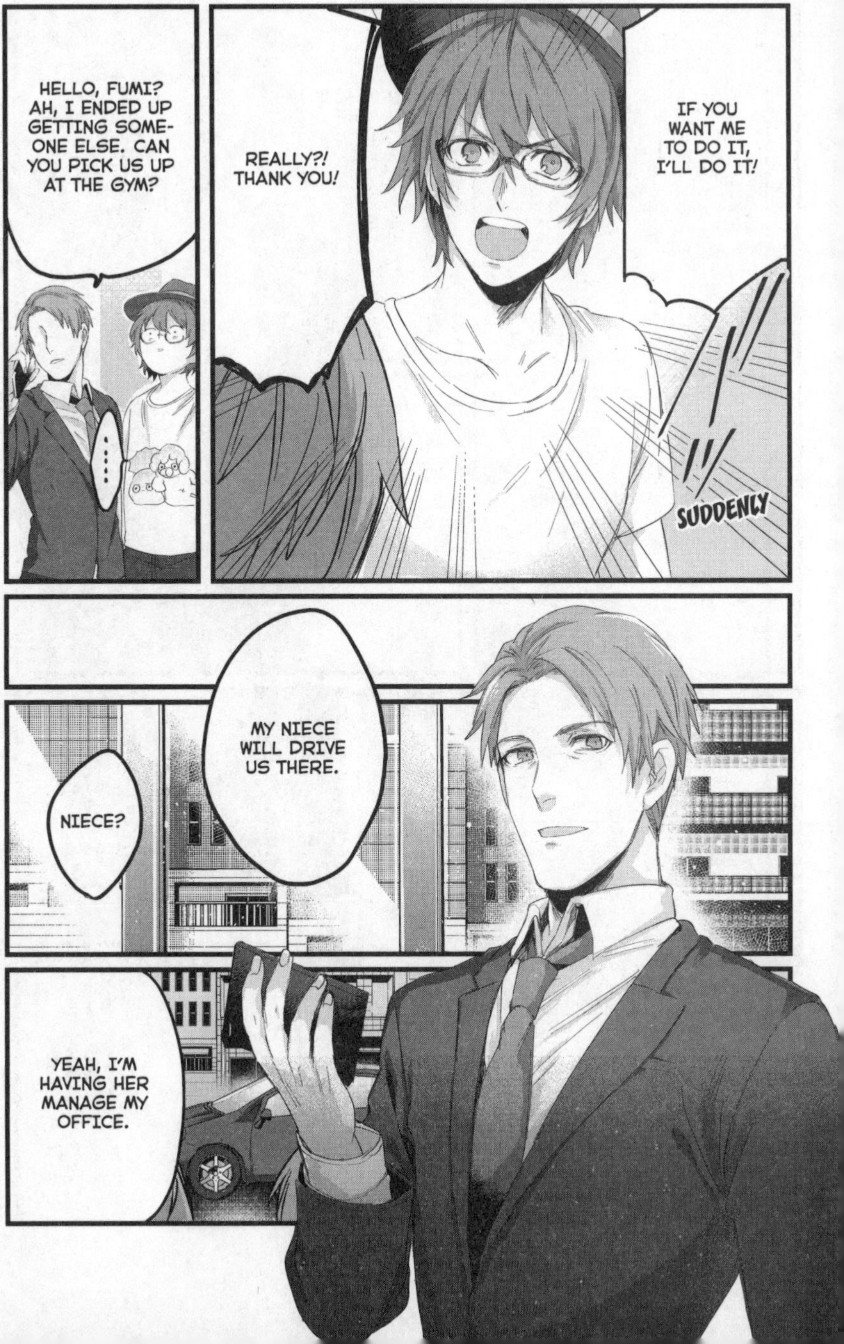
IF YOU WANT ME TO DO IT, I'LL DO IT!
REALLY?! THANK YOU!
SUDDENLY
HELLO, FUMI? AH, I ENDED UP GETTING SOME-ONE ELSE. CAN YOU PICK US UP AT THE GYM?
......
MY NIECE WILL DRIVE US THERE.
NIECE?
YEAH, I'M HAVING HER MANAGE MY OFFICE.

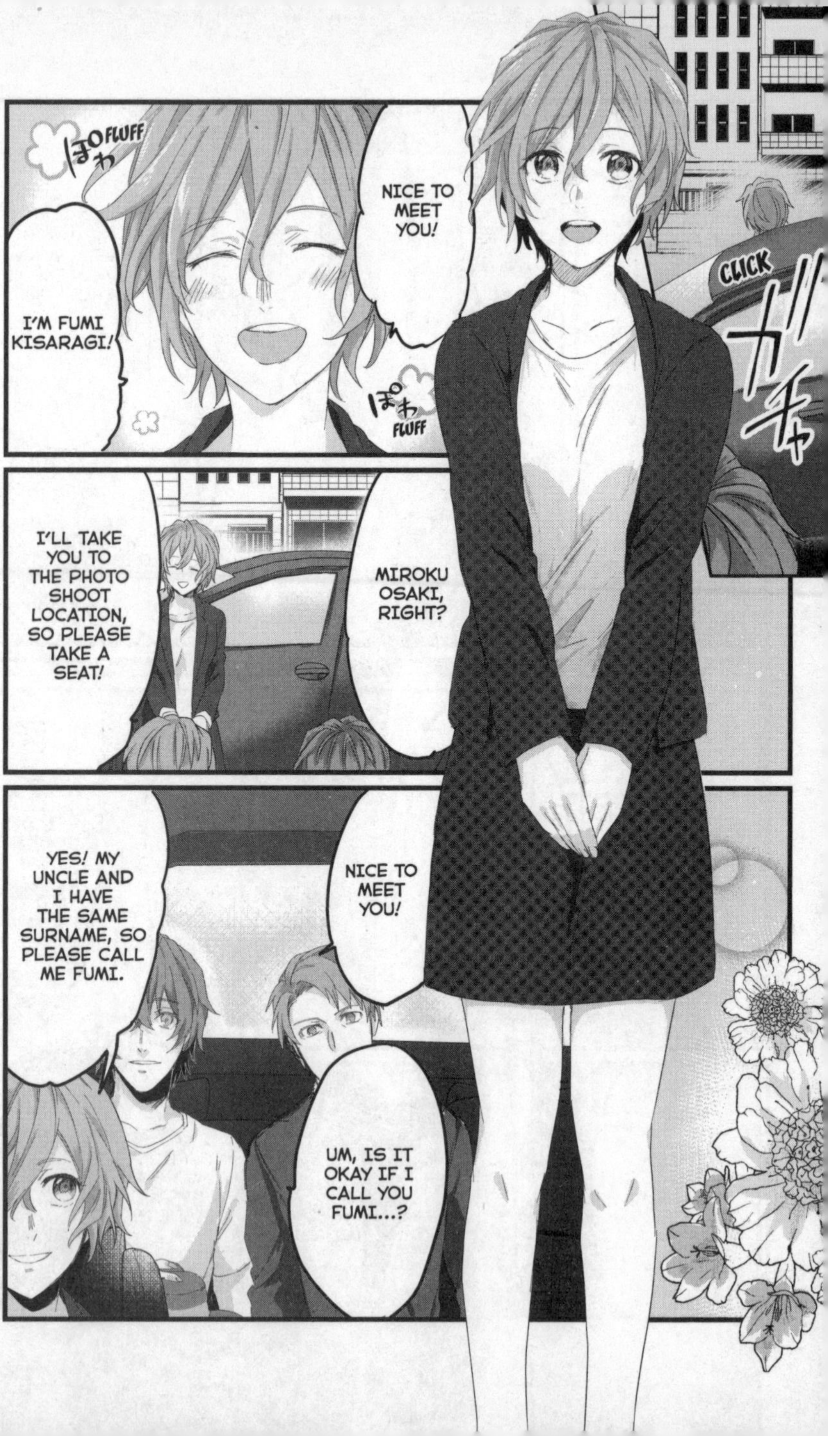

ガチャ
CLICK
ほわ
FLUFF
NICE TO MEET YOU!
I'M FUMI KISARAGI!
ぽわ
FLUFF
MIROKU OSAKI, RIGHT?
I'LL TAKE YOU TO THE PHOTO SHOOT LOCATION, SO PLEASE TAKE A SEAT!
NICE TO MEET YOU!
YES! MY UNCLE AND I HAVE THE SAME SURNAME, SO PLEASE CALL ME FUMI.
UM, IS IT OKAY IF I CALL YOU FUMI...?

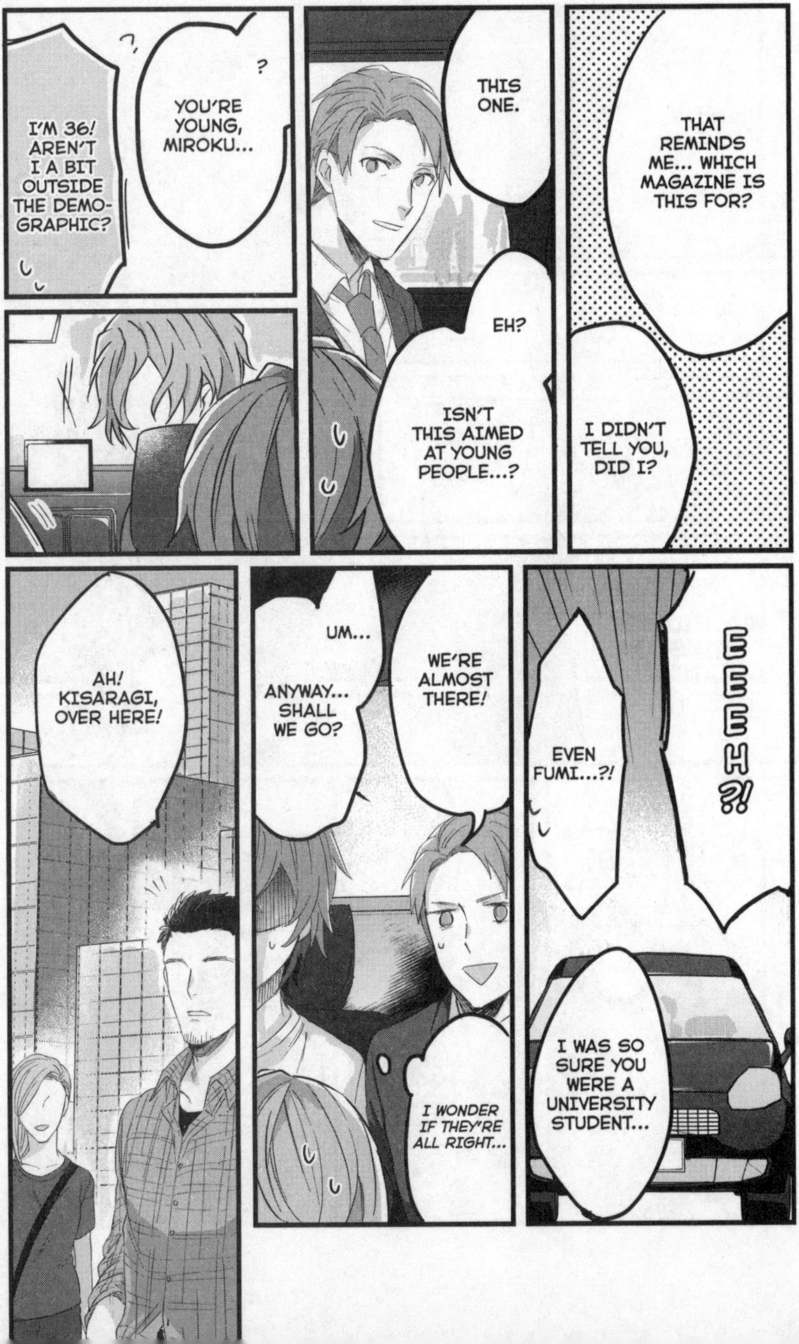
THAT REMINDS ME... WHICH MAGAZINE IS THIS FOR?
I DIDN'T TELL YOU, DID I?
THIS ONE.
EH?
ISN'T THIS AIMED AT YOUNG PEOPLE...?
YOU'RE YOUNG, MIROKU...
I'M 36! AREN'T I A BIT OUTSIDE THE DEMO-GRAPHIC?
EEEH?!
EVEN FUMI...?!
I WAS SO SURE YOU WERE A UNIVERSITY STUDENT...
WE'RE ALMOST THERE!
UM...
ANYWAY... SHALL WE GO?
I WONDER IF THEY'RE ALL RIGHT...
AH! KISARAGI, OVER HERE!

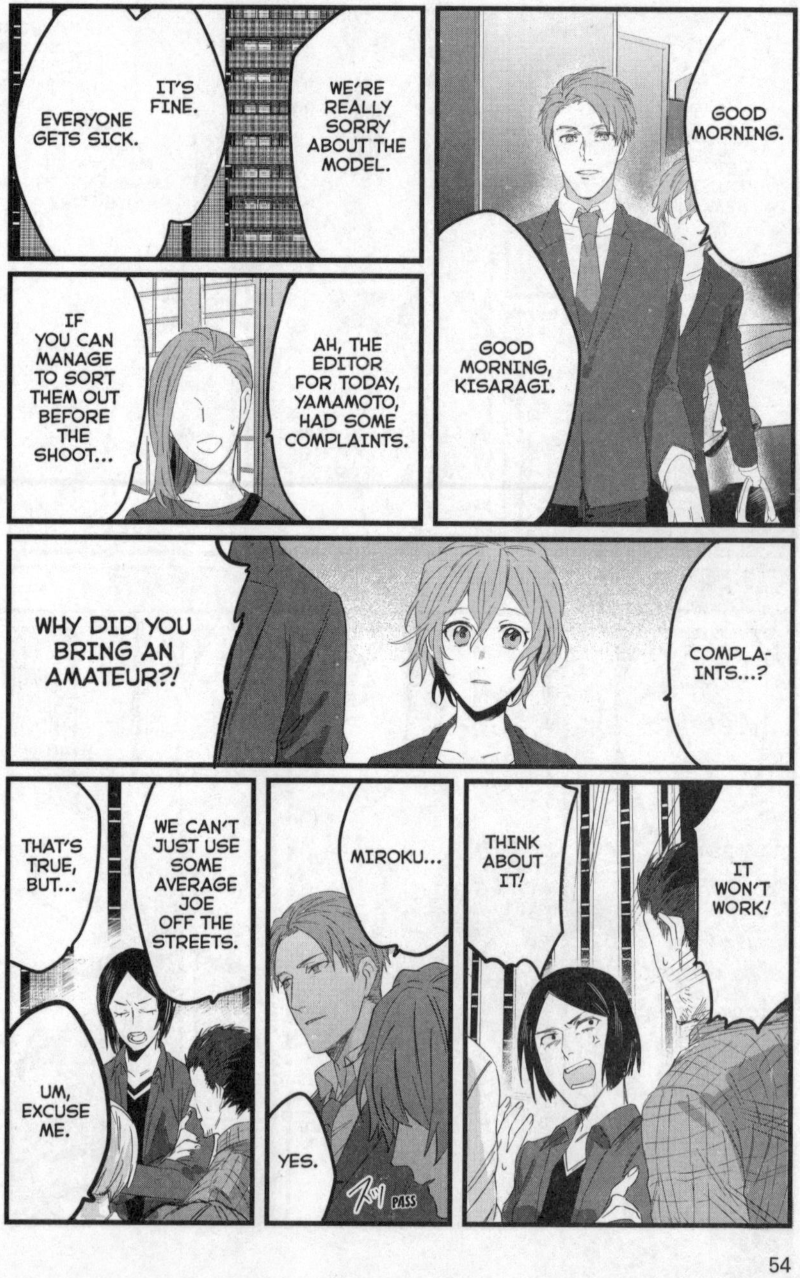
GOOD MORNING.
GOOD MORNING, KISARAGI.
WE'RE REALLY SORRY ABOUT THE MODEL.
IT'S FINE.
EVERYONE GETS SICK.
AH, THE EDITOR FOR TODAY, YAMAMOTO, HAD SOME COMPLAINTS.
IF YOU CAN MANAGE TO SORT THEM OUT BEFORE THE SHOOT...
COMPLAINTS...?
WHY DID YOU BRING AN AMATEUR?!
IT WON'T WORK!
THINK ABOUT IT!
MIROKU...
YES.
PASS
WE CAN'T JUST USE SOME AVERAGE JOE OFF THE STREETS.
THAT'S TRUE, BUT...
UM, EXCUSE ME.

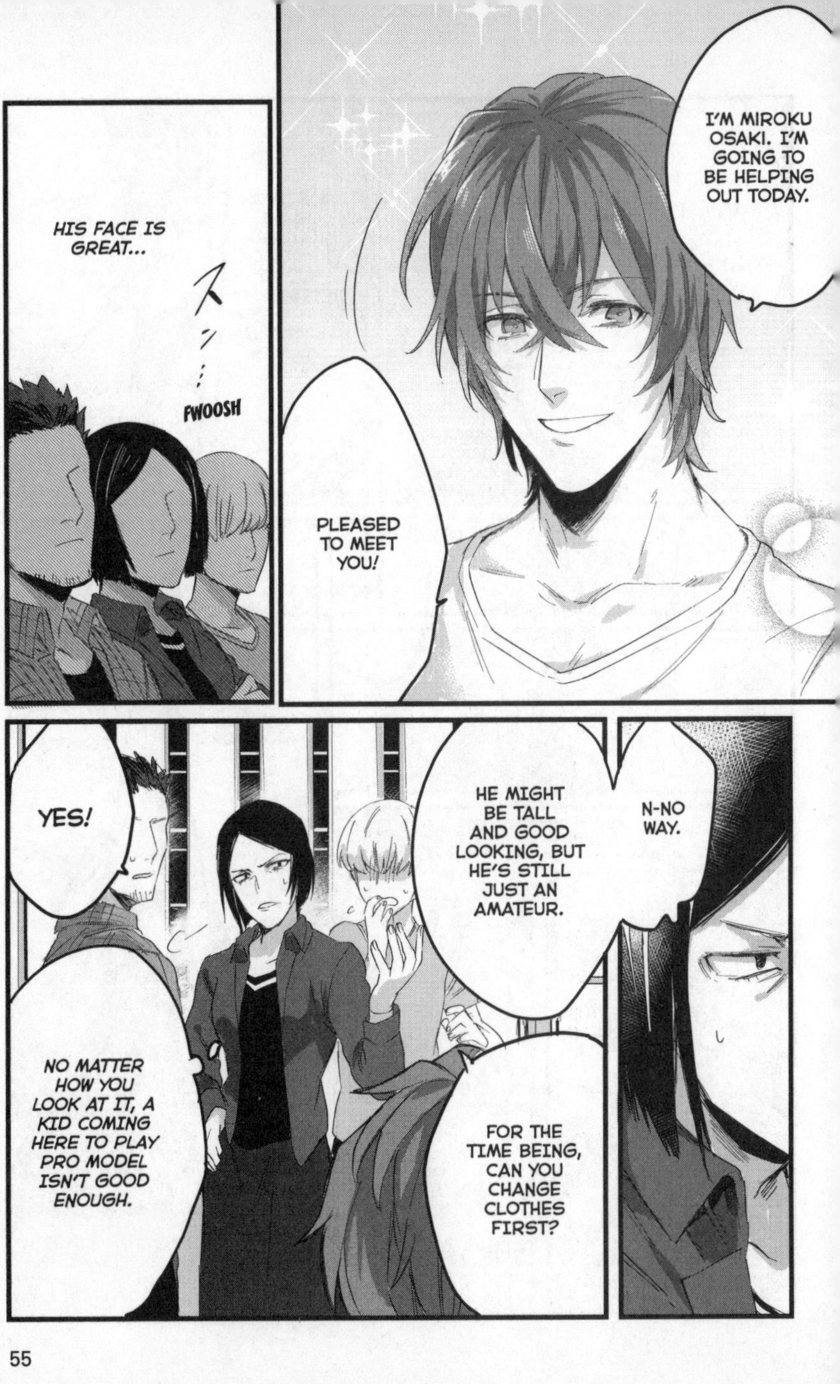
I'M MIROKU OSAKI. I'M GOING TO BE HELPING OUT TODAY.
PLEASED TO MEET YOU!
HIS FACE IS GREAT...
スッ…
FWOOSH
N-NO WAY.
HE MIGHT BE TALL AND GOOD LOOKING, BUT HE'S STILL JUST AN AMATEUR.
YES!
FOR THE TIME BEING, CAN YOU CHANGE CLOTHES FIRST?
NO MATTER HOW YOU LOOK AT IT, A KID COMING HERE TO PLAY PRO MODEL ISN'T GOOD ENOUGH.

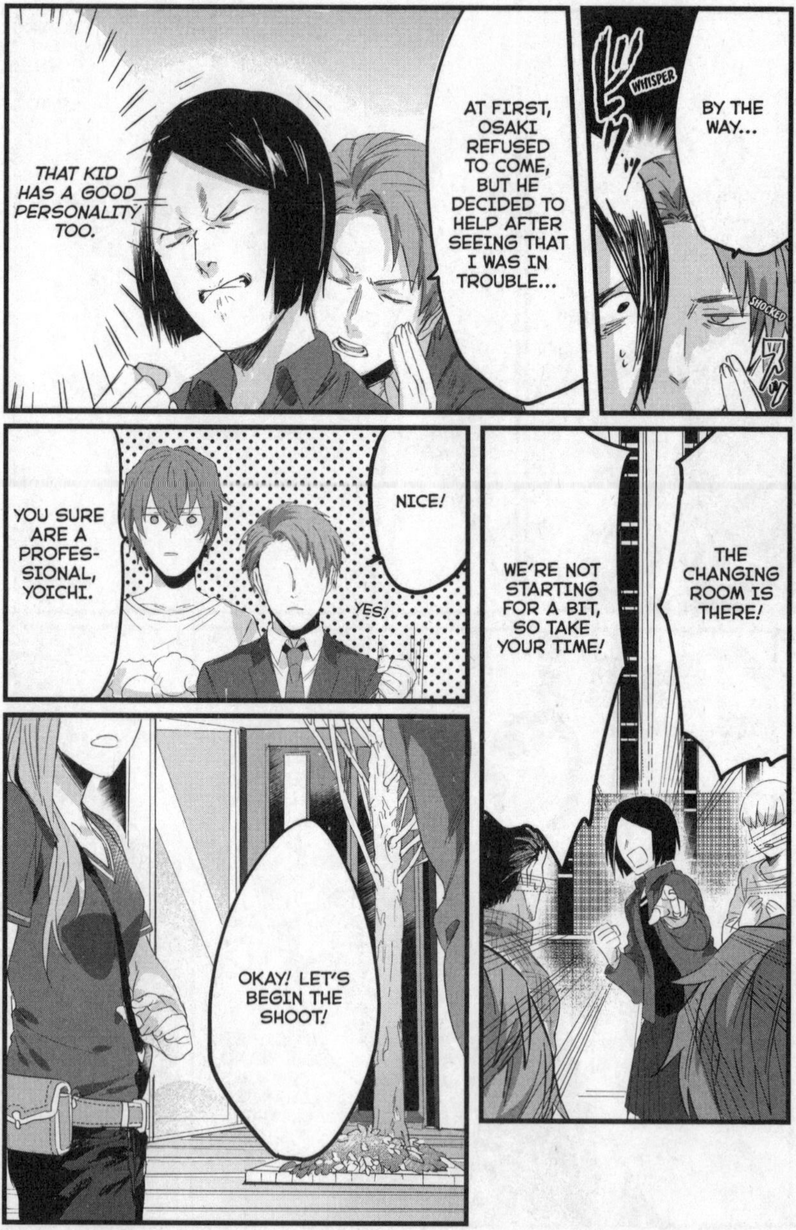
BY THE WAY...
WHISPER
SHOCKED
AT FIRST, OSAKI REFUSED TO COME, BUT HE DECIDED TO HELP AFTER SEEING THAT I WAS IN TROUBLE...
THAT KID HAS A GOOD PERSONALITY TOO.
THE CHANGING ROOM IS THERE!
WE'RE NOT STARTING FOR A BIT, SO TAKE YOUR TIME!
NICE!
YES!
YOU SURE ARE A PROFES-SIONAL, YOICHI.
OKAY! LET'S BEGIN THE SHOOT!

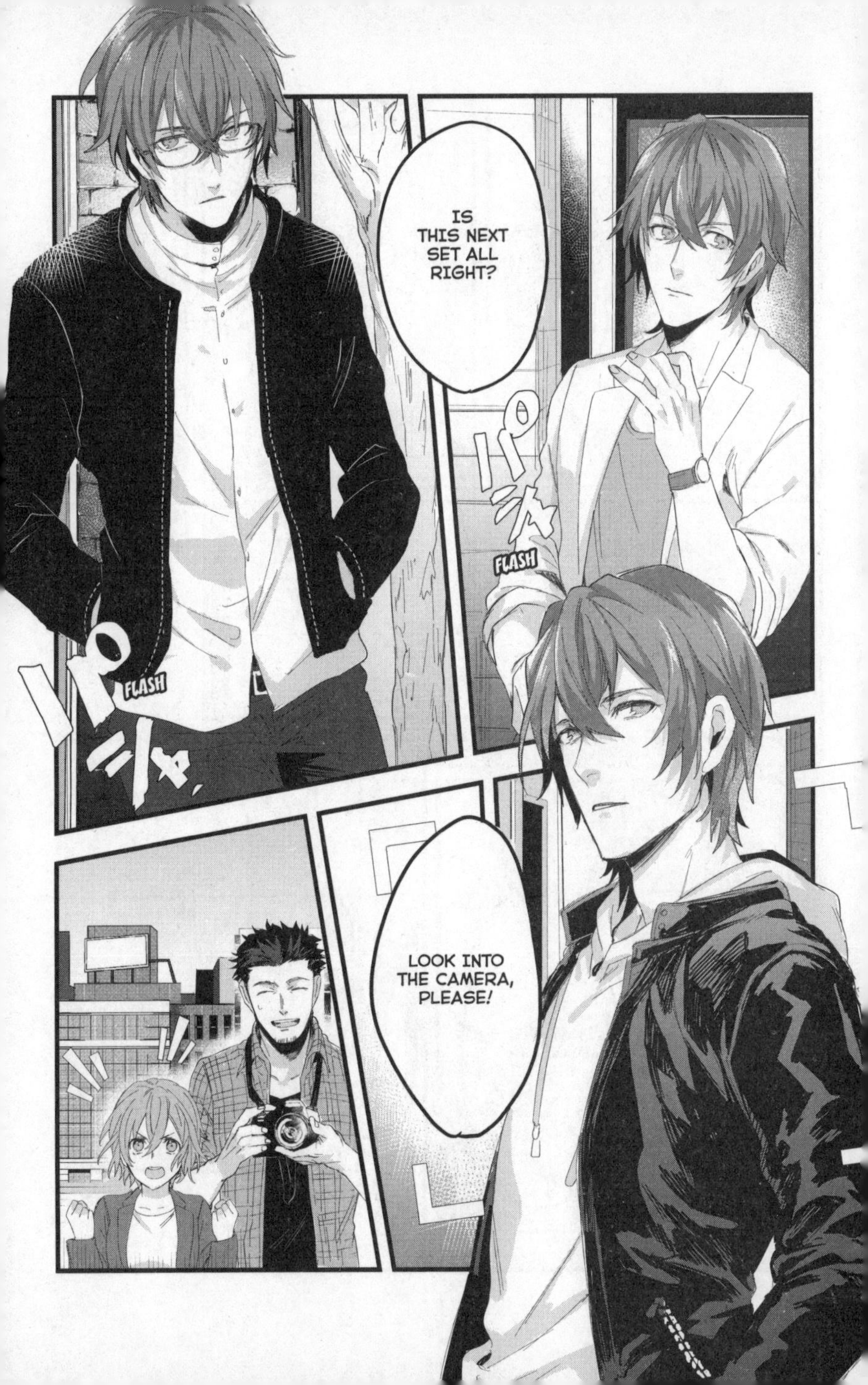
IS THIS NEXT SET ALL RIGHT?
FLASH
FLASH
LOOK INTO THE CAMERA, PLEASE!

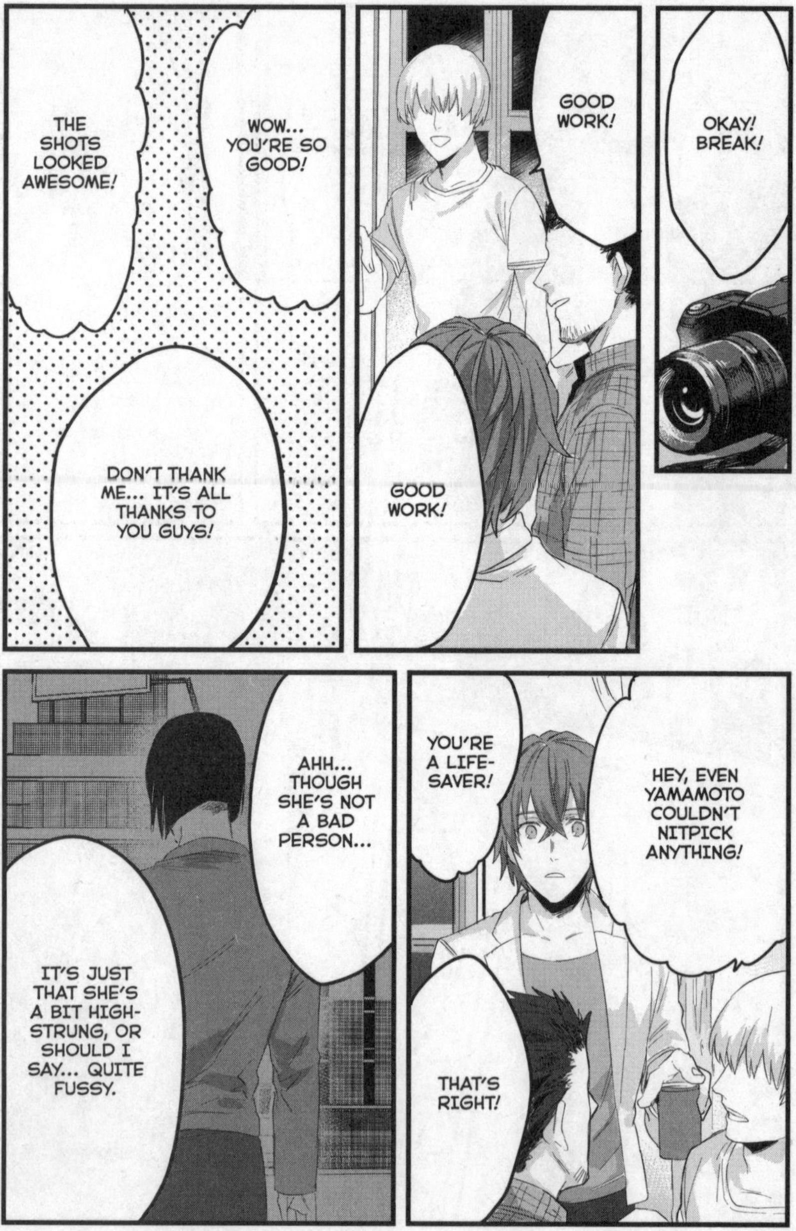
OKAY! BREAK!
GOOD WORK!
GOOD WORK!
WOW... YOU'RE SO GOOD!
THE SHOTS LOOKED AWESOME!
DON'T THANK ME... IT'S ALL THANKS TO YOU GUYS!
HEY, EVEN YAMAMOTO COULDN'T NITPICK ANYTHING!
YOU'RE A LIFE-SAVER!
THAT'S RIGHT!
AHH... THOUGH SHE'S NOT A BAD PERSON...
IT'S JUST THAT SHE'S A BIT HIGH-STRUNG, OR SHOULD I SAY... QUITE FUSSY.

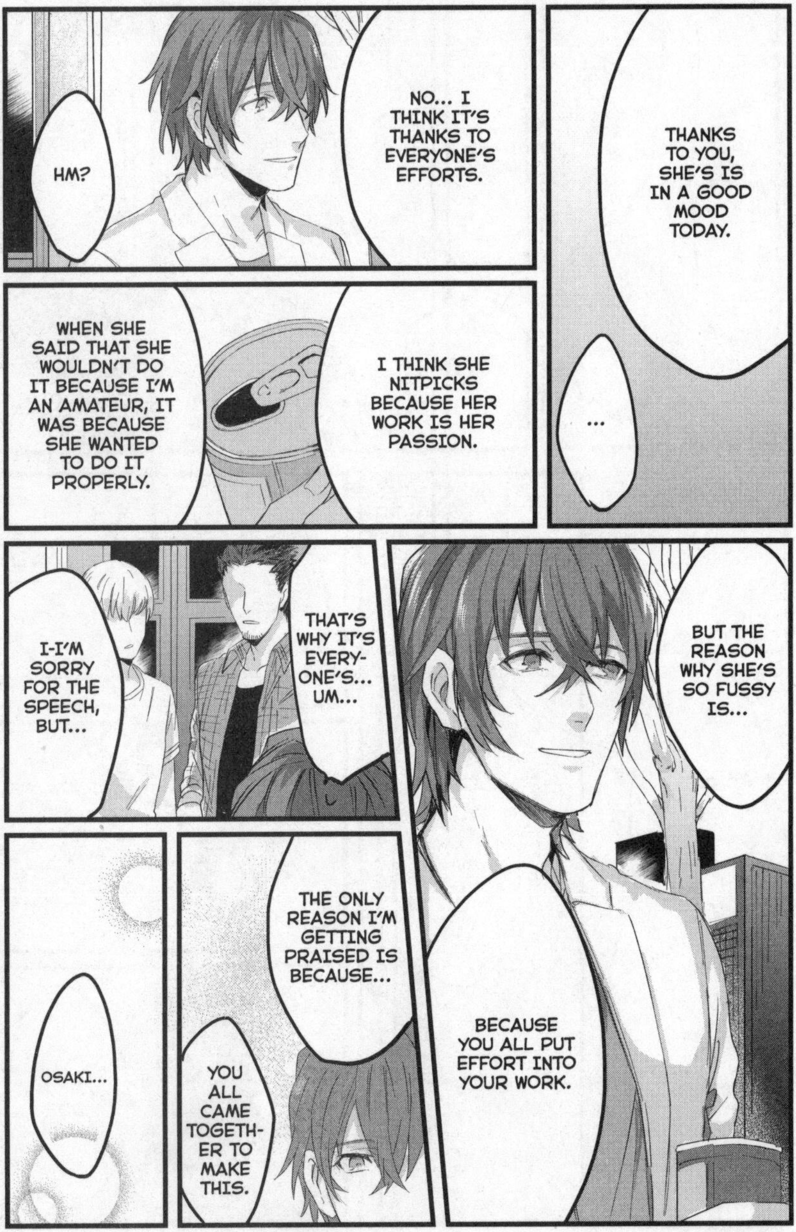
THANKS TO YOU, SHE'S IS IN A GOOD MOOD TODAY.
...
NO... I THINK IT'S THANKS TO EVERYONE'S EFFORTS.
HM?
I THINK SHE NITPICKS BECAUSE HER WORK IS HER PASSION.
WHEN SHE SAID THAT SHE WOULDN'T DO IT BECAUSE I'M AN AMATEUR, IT WAS BECAUSE SHE WANTED TO DO IT PROPERLY.
BUT THE REASON WHY SHE'S SO FUSSY IS...
BECAUSE YOU ALL PUT EFFORT INTO YOUR WORK.
THAT'S WHY IT'S EVERY-ONE'S... UM...
I-I'M SORRY FOR THE SPEECH, BUT...
THE ONLY REASON I'M GETTING PRAISED IS BECAUSE...
YOU ALL CAME TOGETH-ER TO MAKE THIS.
OSAKI...

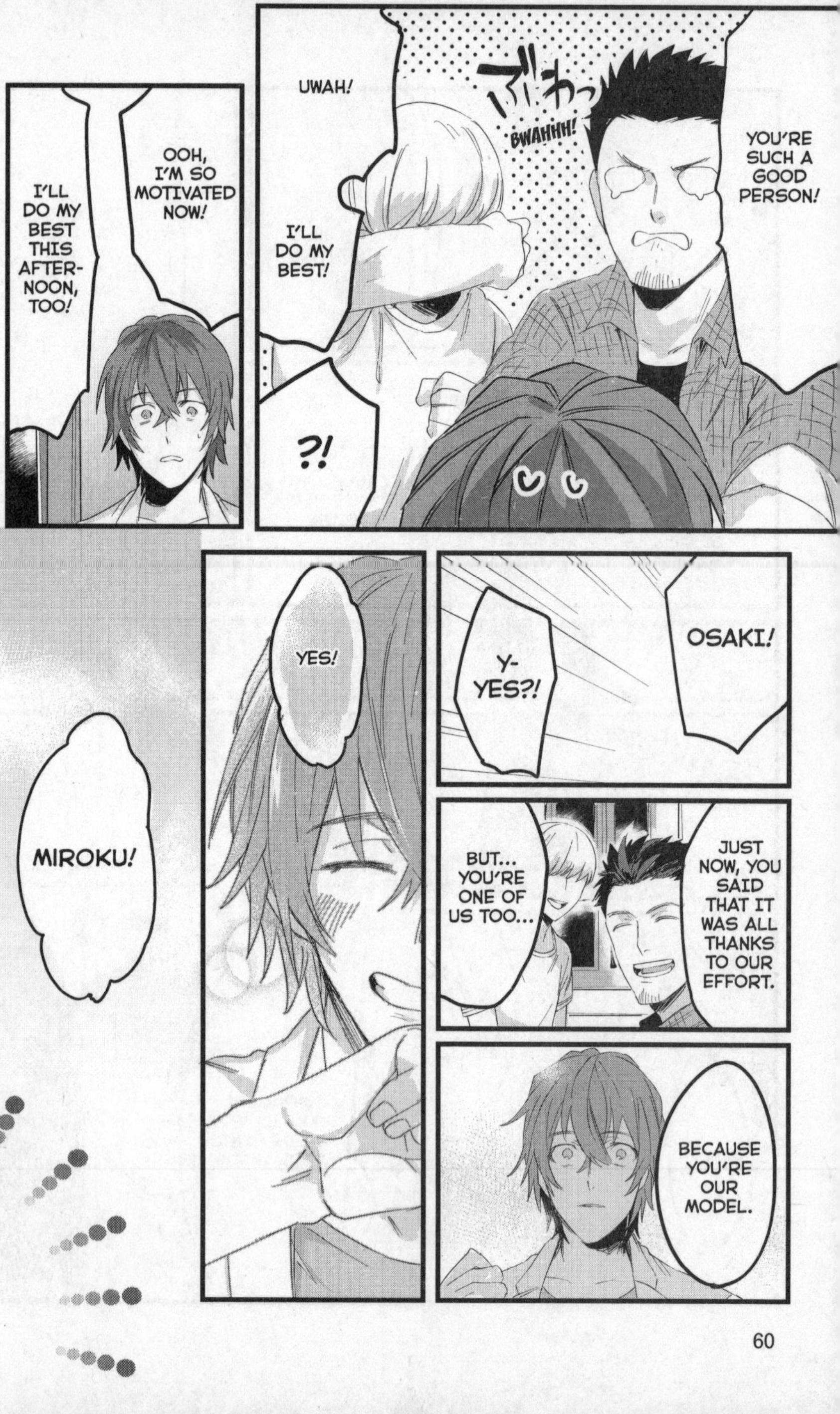
YOU'RE SUCH A GOOD PERSON!
BWAHHH!
UWAH!
I'LL DO MY BEST!
?!
OOH, I'M SO MOTIVATED NOW!
I'LL DO MY BEST THIS AFTERNOON, TOO!
OSAKI!
Y-YES?!
JUST NOW, YOU SAID THAT IT WAS ALL THANKS TO OUR EFFORT.
BUT... YOU'RE ONE OF US TOO...
BECAUSE YOU'RE OUR MODEL.
YES!
MIROKU!

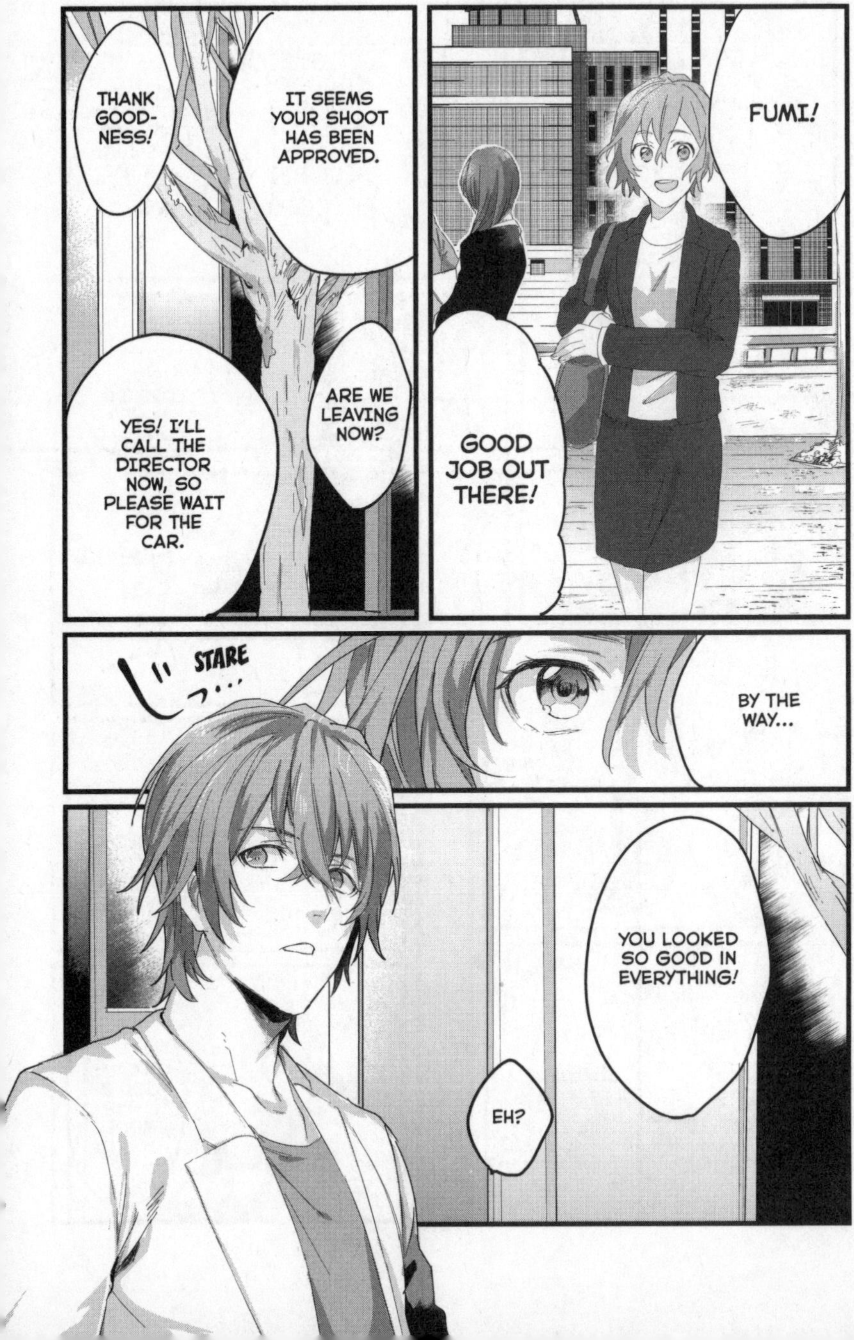
FUMI!
GOOD JOB OUT THERE!
IT SEEMS YOUR SHOOT HAS BEEN APPROVED.
THANK GOODNESS!
ARE WE LEAVING NOW?
YES! I'LL CALL THE DIRECTOR NOW, SO PLEASE WAIT FOR THE CAR.
BY THE WAY...
STARE
じっ…
YOU LOOKED SO GOOD IN EVERYTHING!
EH?

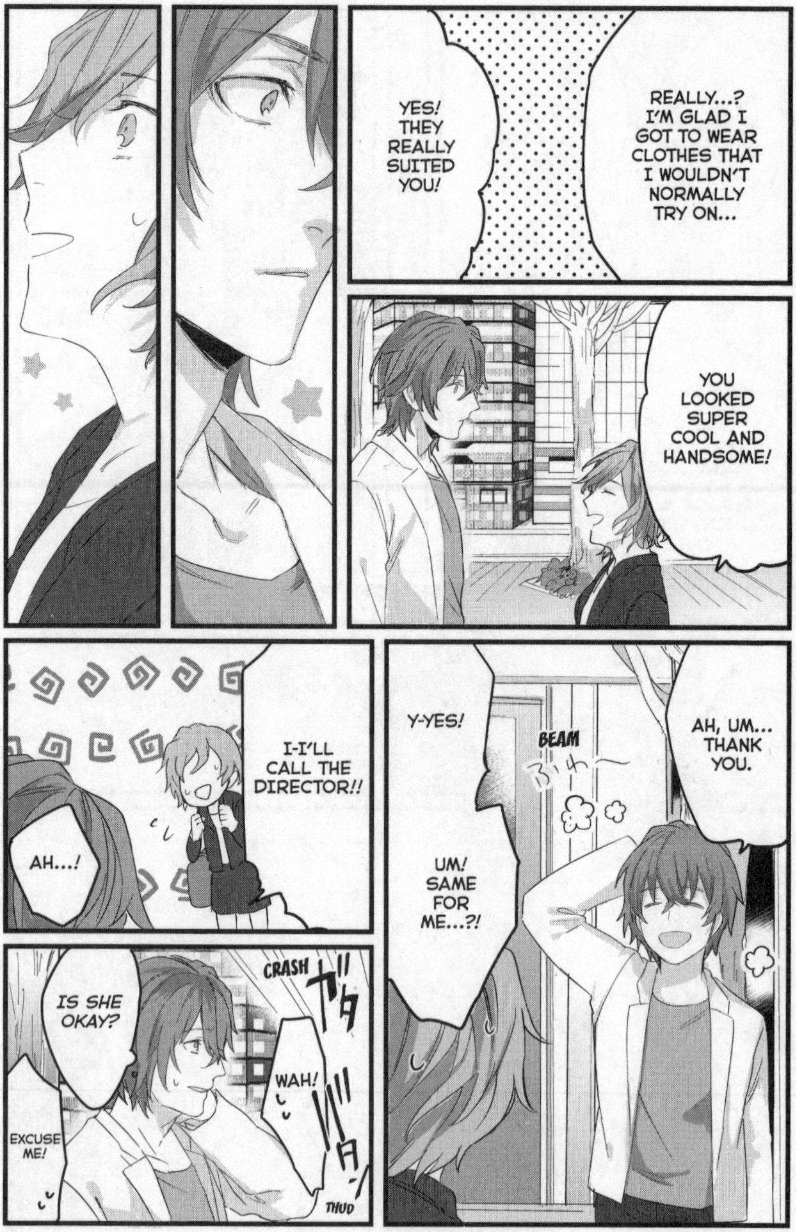
REALLY...? I'M GLAD I GOT TO WEAR CLOTHES THAT I WOULDN'T NORMALLY TRY ON...
YES! THEY REALLY SUITED YOU!
YOU LOOKED SUPER COOL AND HANDSOME!
AH, UM... THANK YOU.
BEAM
ぶわ〜
Y-YES!
UM! SAME FOR ME...?!
I-I'LL CALL THE DIRECTOR!!
AH...!
CRASH
WAH!
IS SHE OKAY?
EXCUSE ME!
THUD

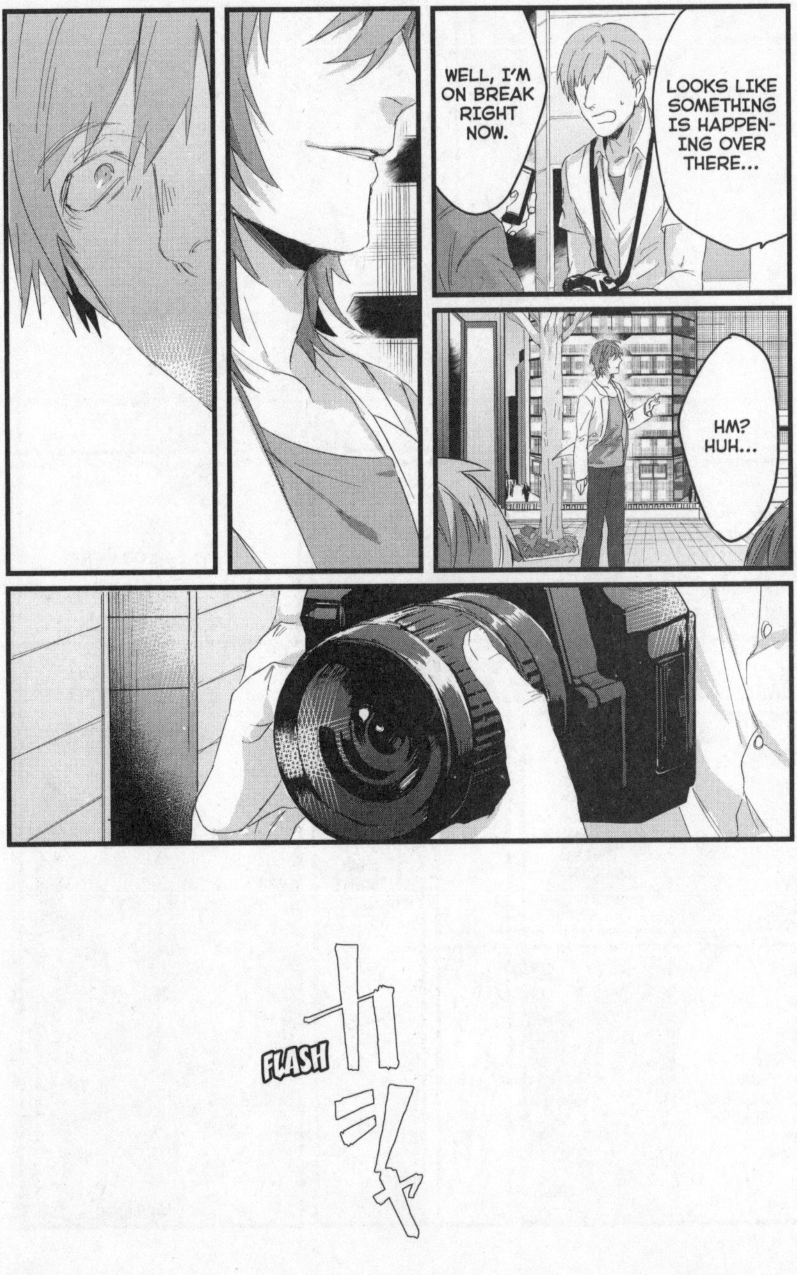
LOOKS LIKE SOMETHING IS HAPPEN-ING OVER THERE...
WELL, I'M ON BREAK RIGHT NOW.
HM? HUH...
カシャ
FLASH

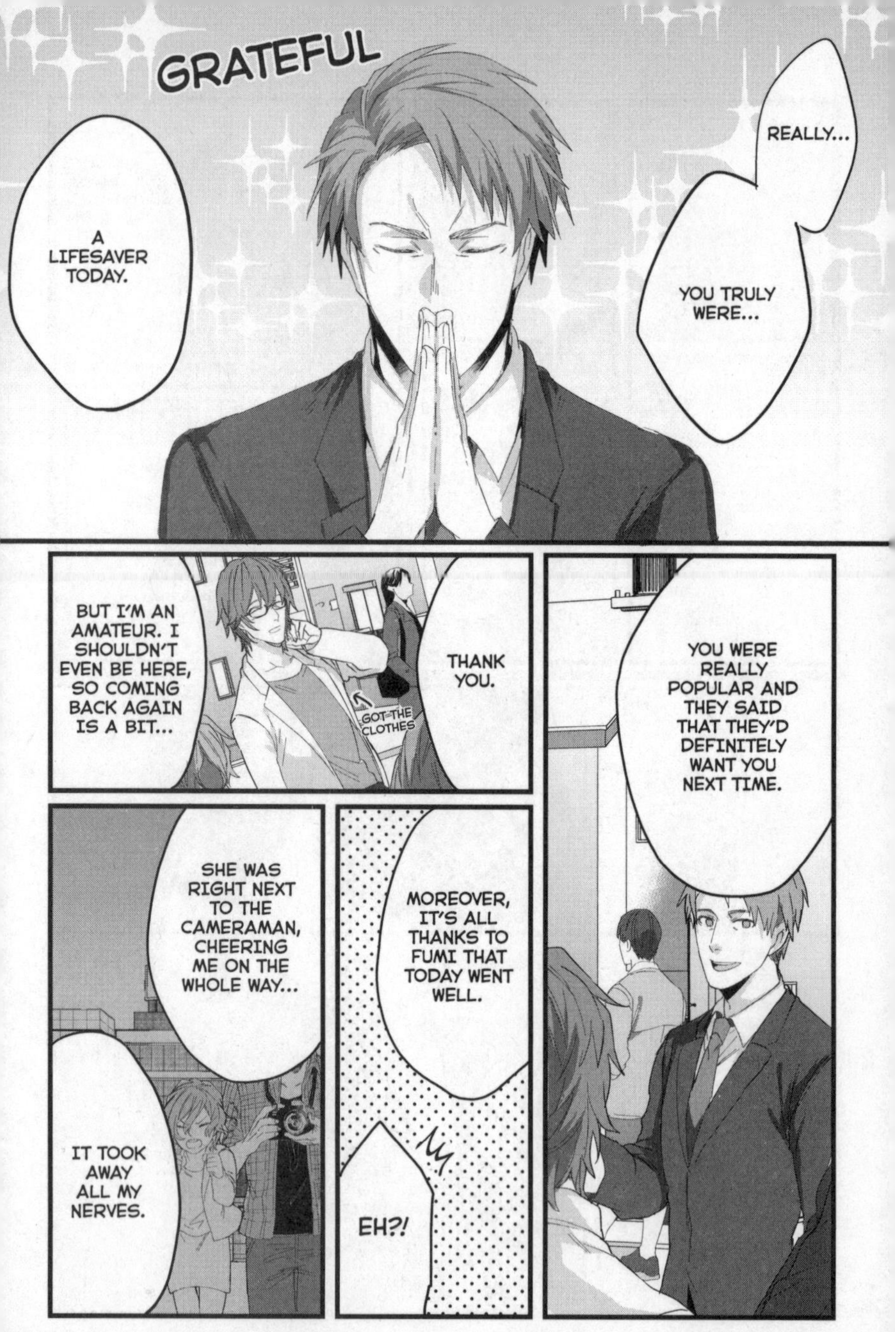
GRATEFUL
REALLY...
YOU TRULY WERE...
A LIFESAVER TODAY.
YOU WERE REALLY POPULAR AND THEY SAID THAT THEY'D DEFINITELY WANT YOU NEXT TIME.
THANK YOU.
BUT I'M AN AMATEUR. I SHOULDN'T EVEN BE HERE, SO COMING BACK AGAIN IS A BIT...
GOT THE CLOTHES
MOREOVER, IT'S ALL THANKS TO FUMI THAT TODAY WENT WELL.
EH?!
SHE WAS RIGHT NEXT TO THE CAMERAMAN, CHEERING ME ON THE WHOLE WAY...
IT TOOK AWAY ALL MY NERVES.

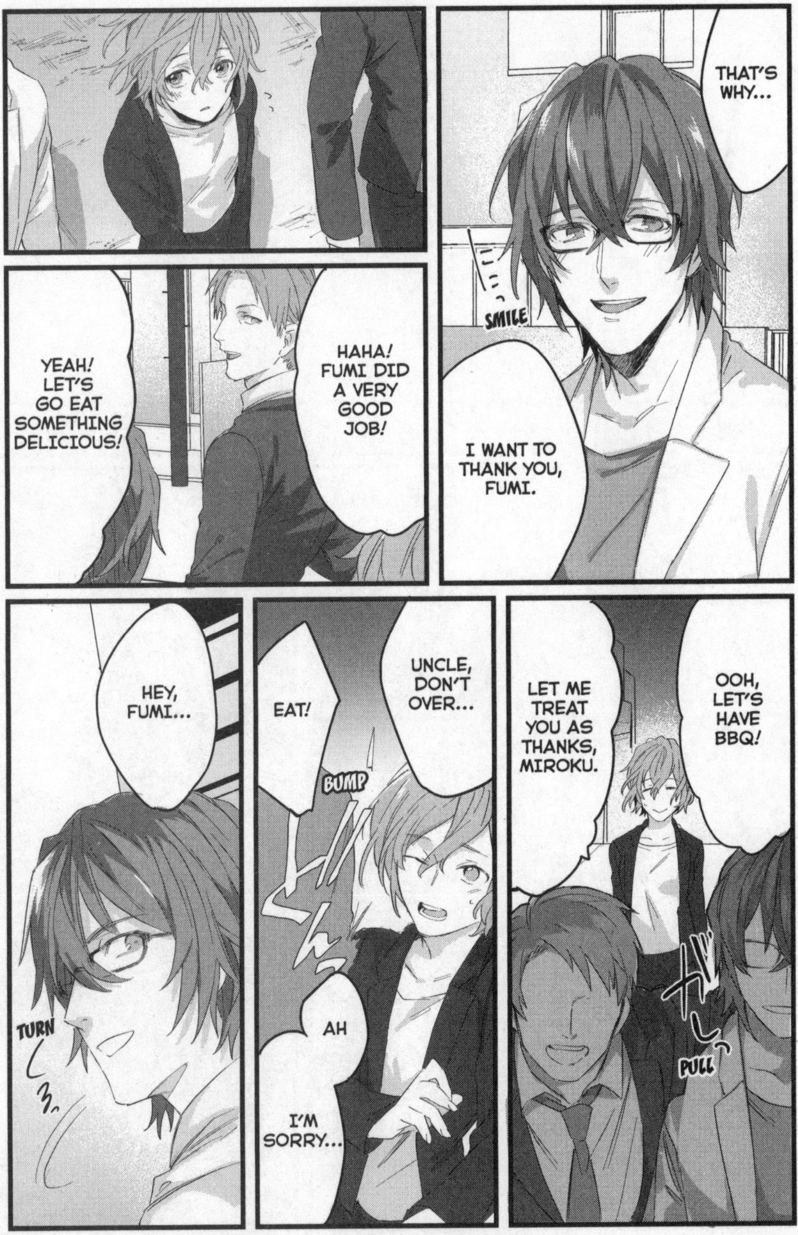
THAT'S WHY...
SMILE
I WANT TO THANK YOU, FUMI.
HAHA! FUMI DID A VERY GOOD JOB!
YEAH! LET'S GO EAT SOMETHING DELICIOUS!
OOH, LET'S HAVE BBQ!
LET ME TREAT YOU AS THANKS, MIROKU.
PULL
UNCLE, DON'T OVER...
EAT!
BUMP
AH
I'M SORRY...
HEY, FUMI...
TURN

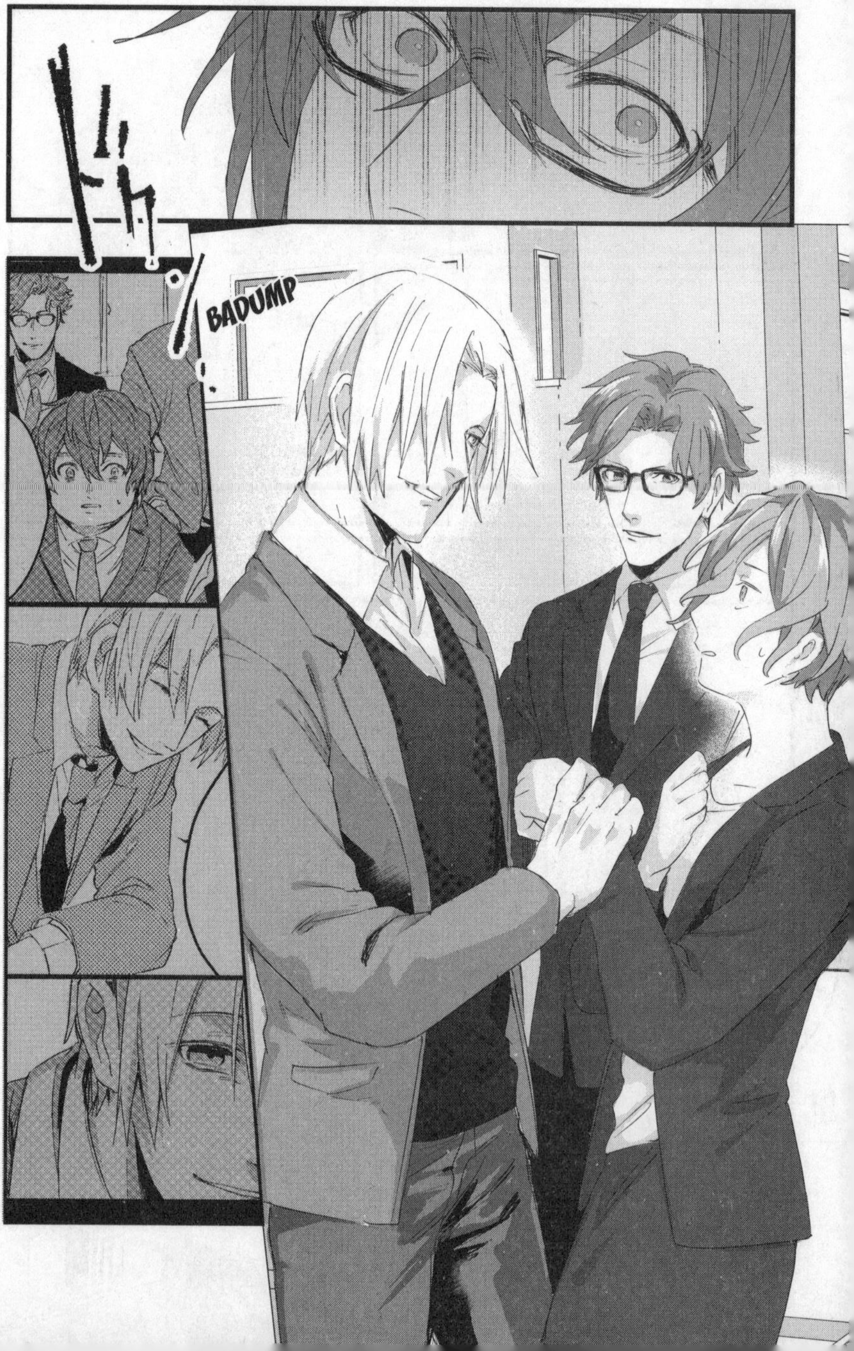
ドクッ
BADUMP

Chapter 3

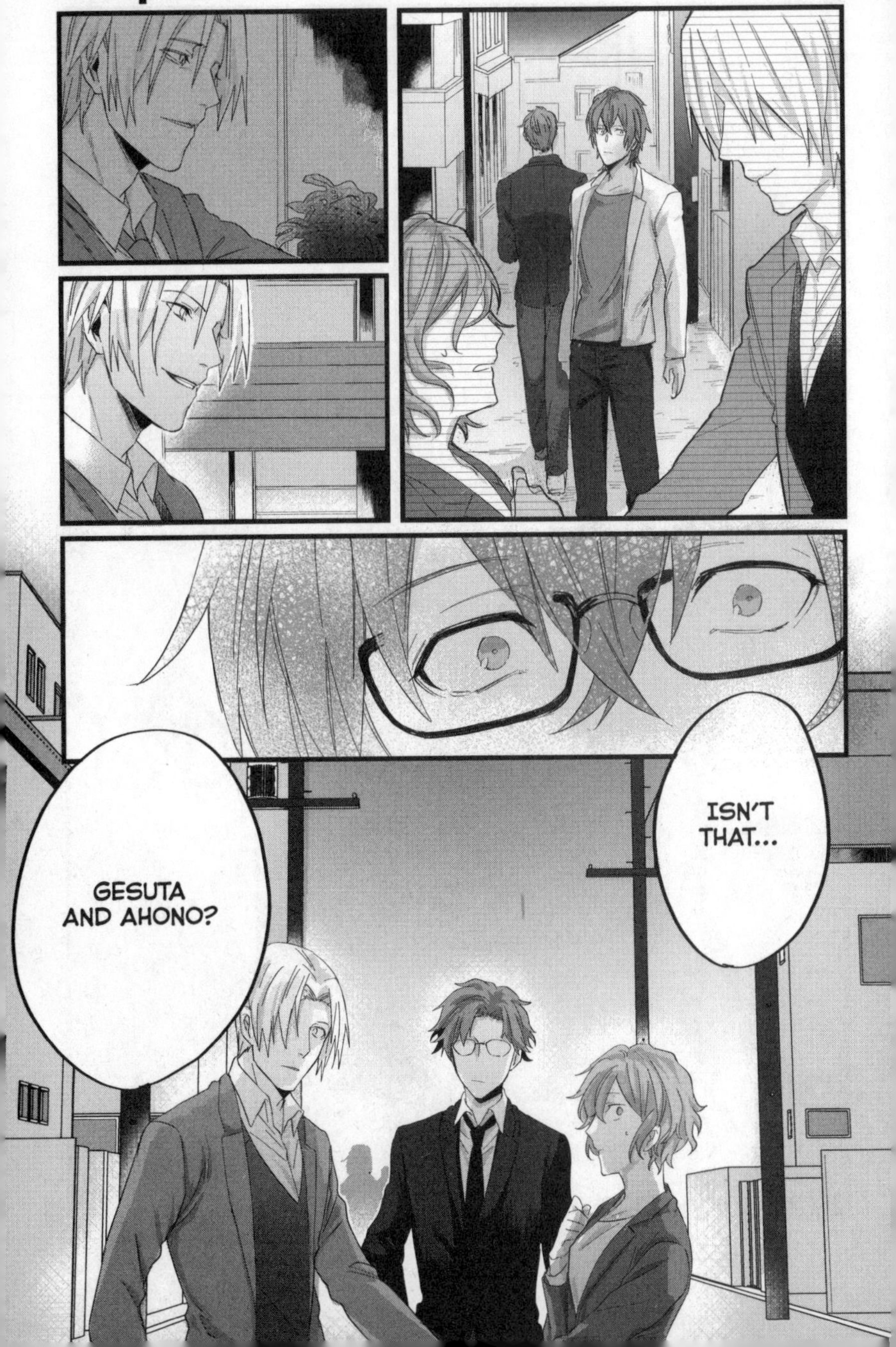
ISN'T THAT...
GESUTA AND AHONO?

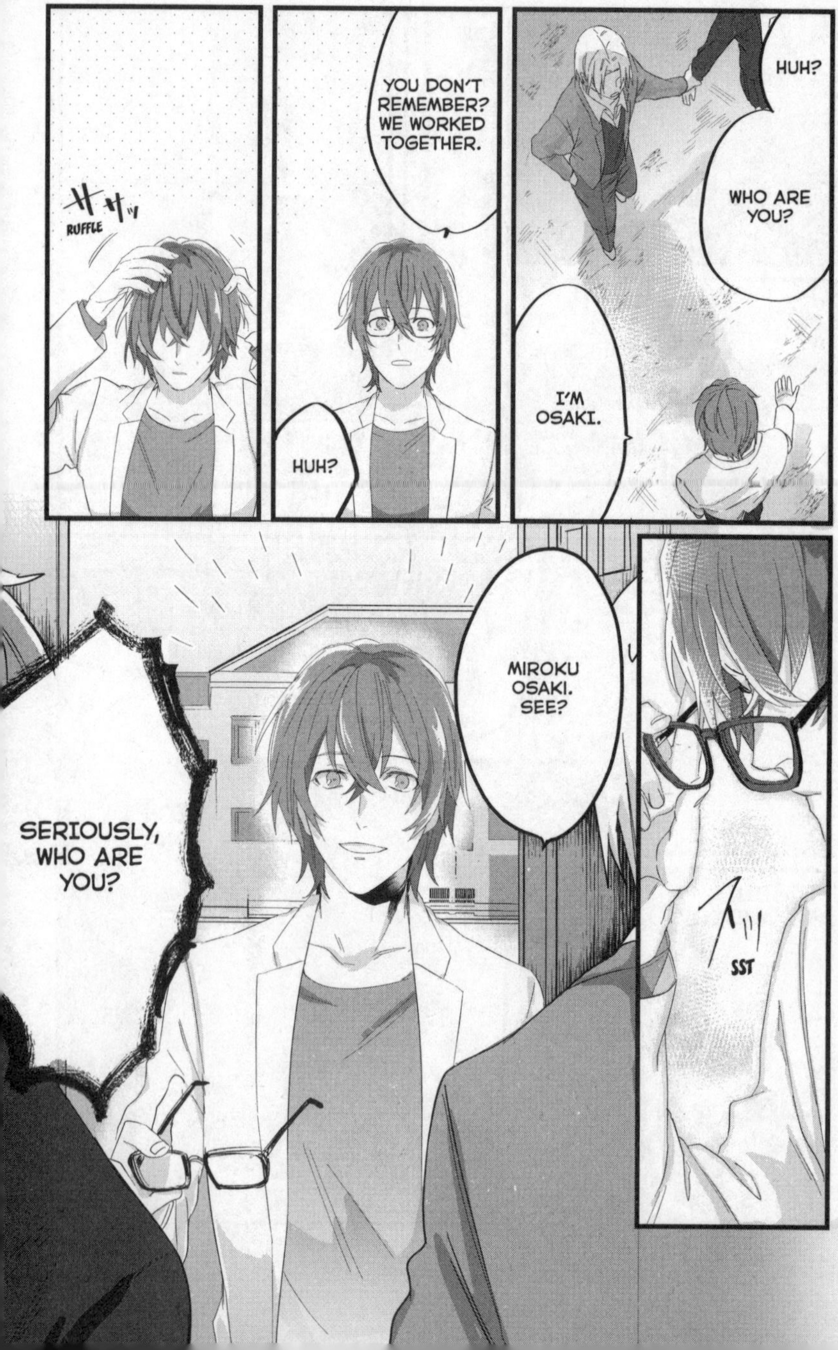
HUH?
WHO ARE YOU?
I'M OSAKI.
YOU DON'T REMEMBER? WE WORKED TOGETHER.
HUH?
RUFFLE
SST
MIROKU OSAKI. SEE?
SERIOUSLY, WHO ARE YOU?

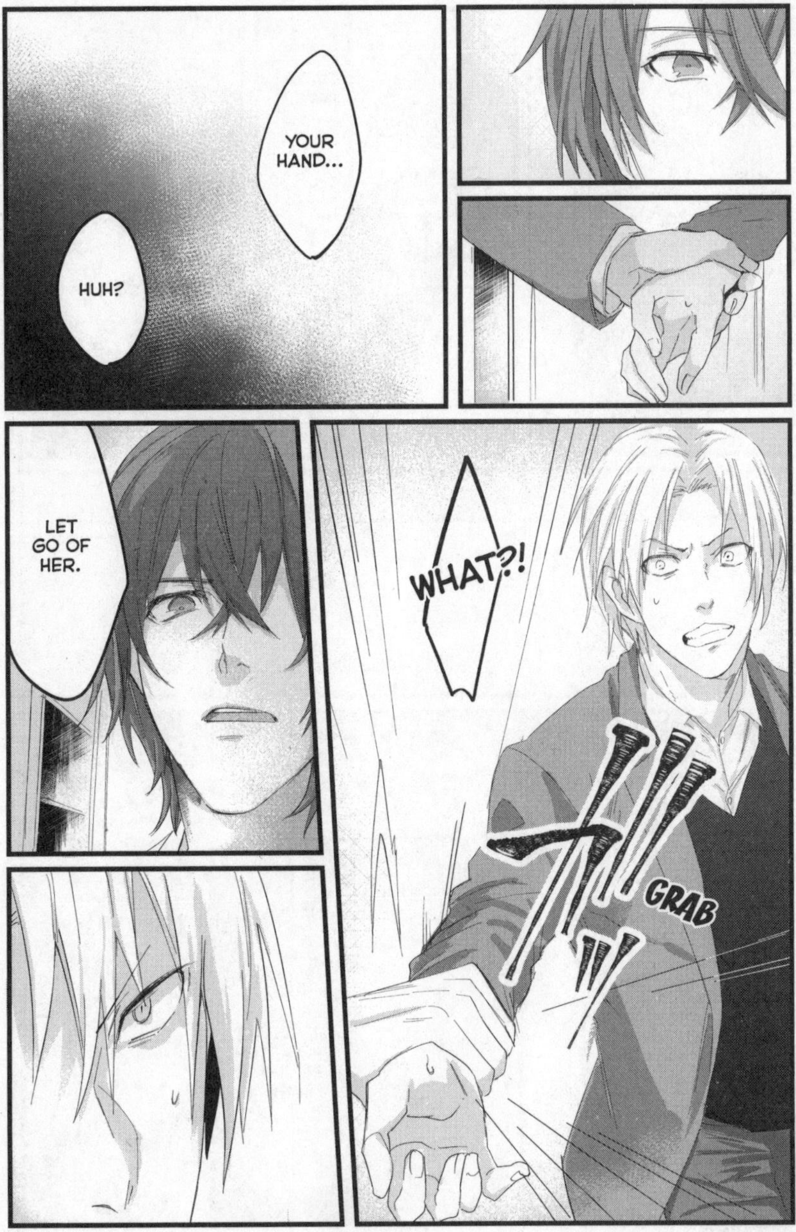
YOUR HAND...
HUH?
WHAT?!
GRAB
LET GO OF HER.

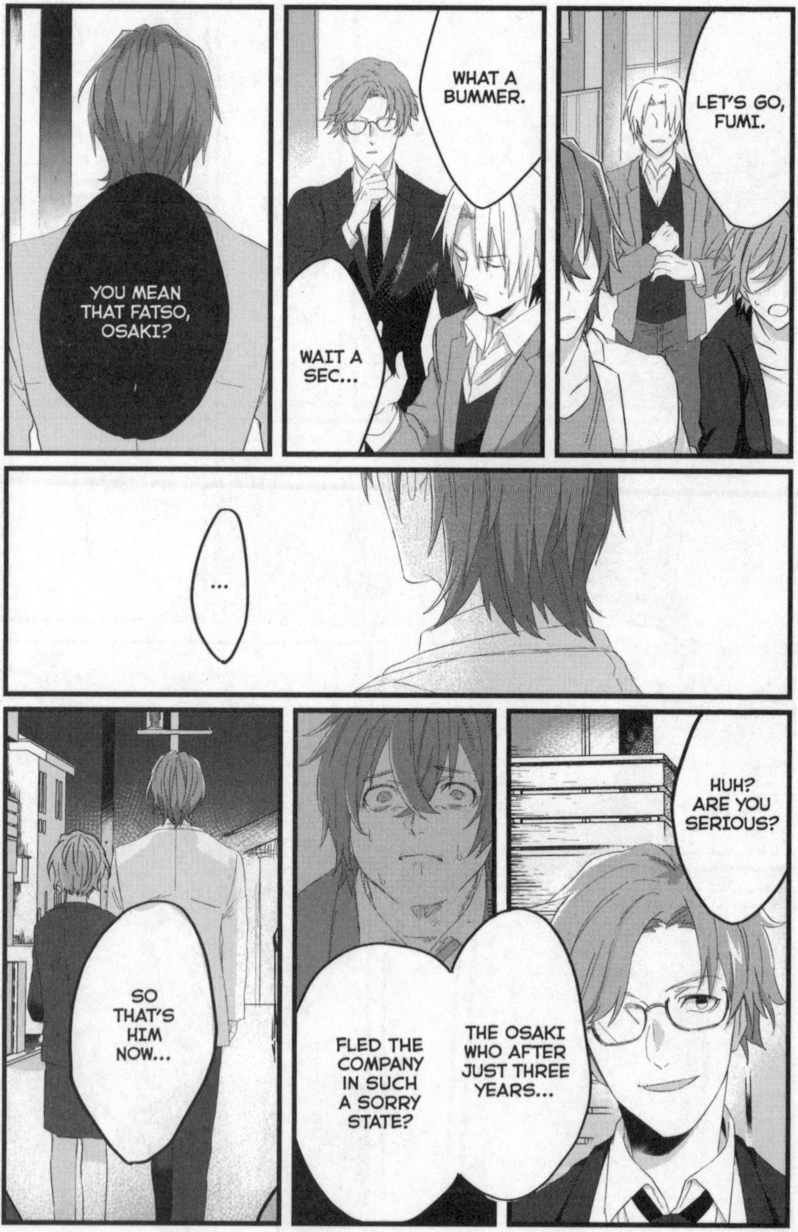
LET'S GO, FUMI.
WHAT A BUMMER.
WAIT A SEC...
YOU MEAN THAT FATSO, OSAKI?
...
HUH? ARE YOU SERIOUS?
THE OSAKI WHO AFTER JUST THREE YEARS...
FLED THE COMPANY IN SUCH A SORRY STATE?
SO THAT'S HIM NOW...

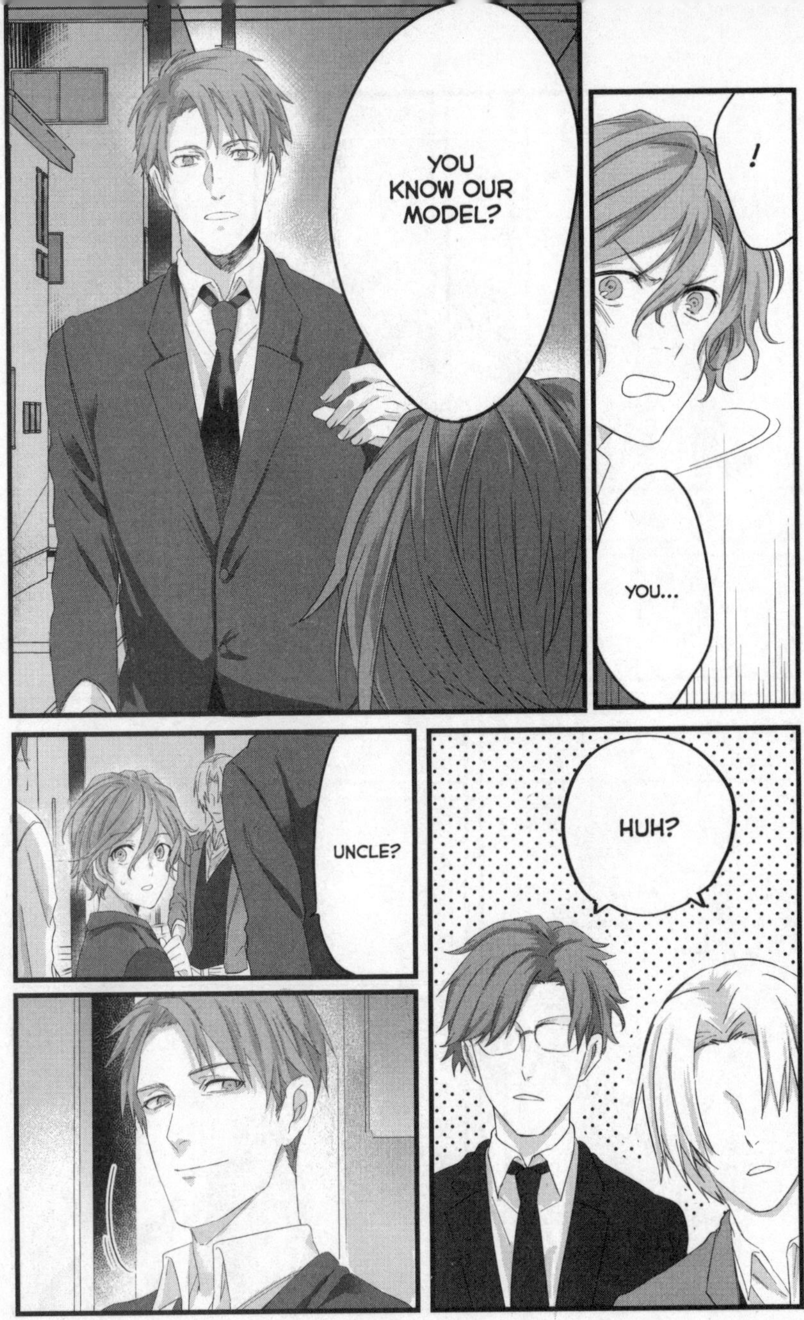
!
YOU...
YOU KNOW OUR MODEL?
HUH?
UNCLE?

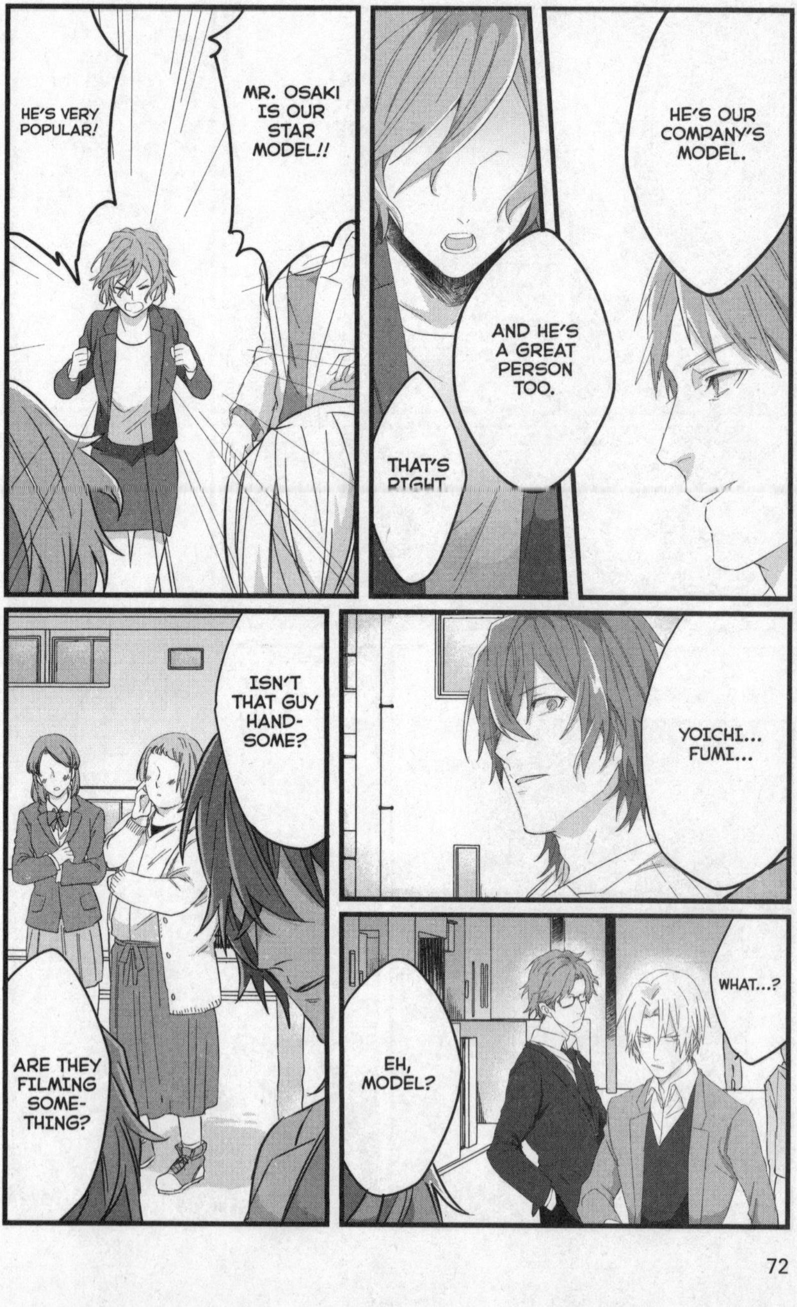
HE'S OUR COMPANY'S MODEL.
AND HE'S A GREAT PERSON TOO.
THAT'S RIGHT
MR. OSAKI IS OUR STAR MODEL!!
HE'S VERY POPULAR!
YOICHI... FUMI...
WHAT...?
EH, MODEL?
ISN'T THAT GUY HAND-SOME?
ARE THEY FILMING SOME-THING?

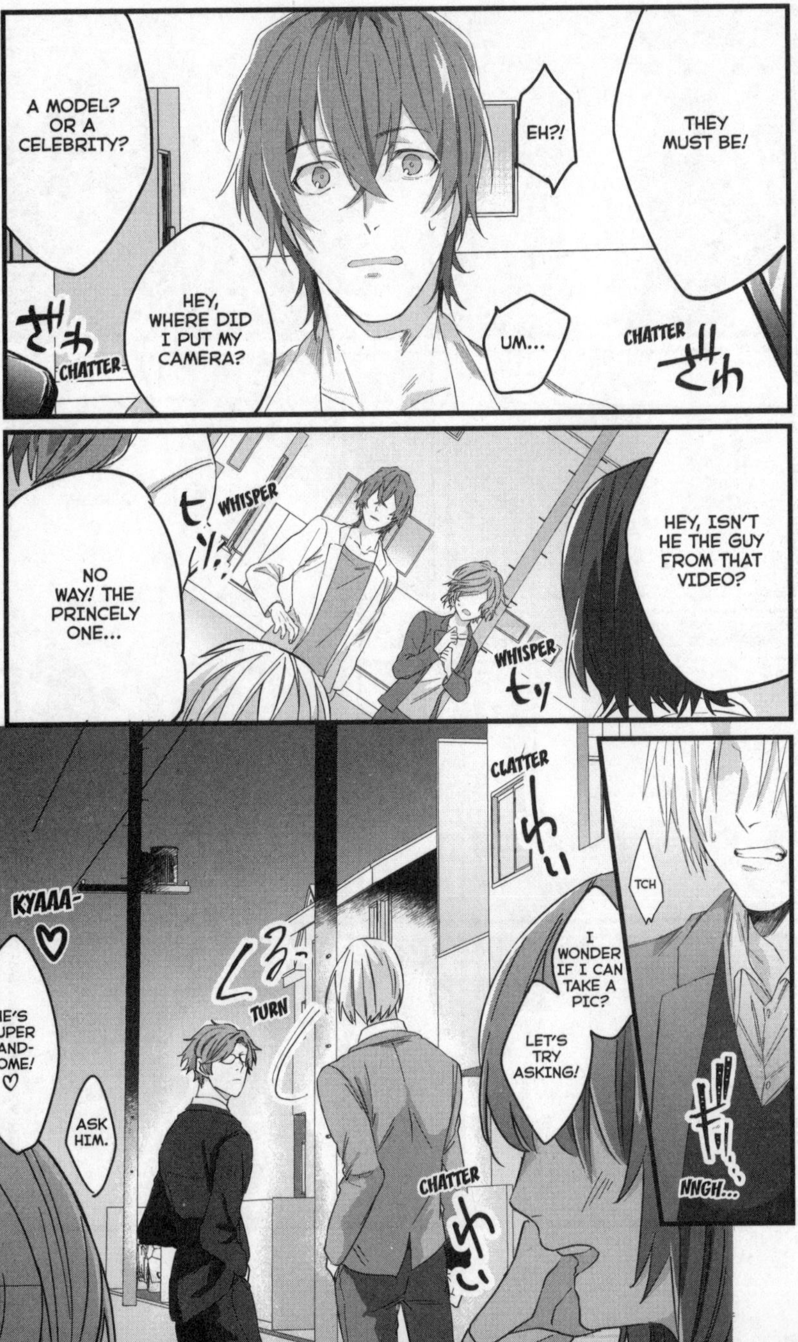
THEY MUST BE!
EH?!
A MODEL? OR A CELEBRITY?
CHATTER
ざわ
UM...
HEY, WHERE DID I PUT MY CAMERA?
ざわ
CHATTER
HEY, ISN'T HE THE GUY FROM THAT VIDEO?
WHISPER
WHISPER
NO WAY! THE PRINCELY ONE...
TCH
NNGH...
CLATTER
I WONDER IF I CAN TAKE A PIC?
LET'S TRY ASKING!
TURN
CHATTER
KYAAA- ♡
HE'S SUPER HAND-SOME! ♡
ASK HIM.

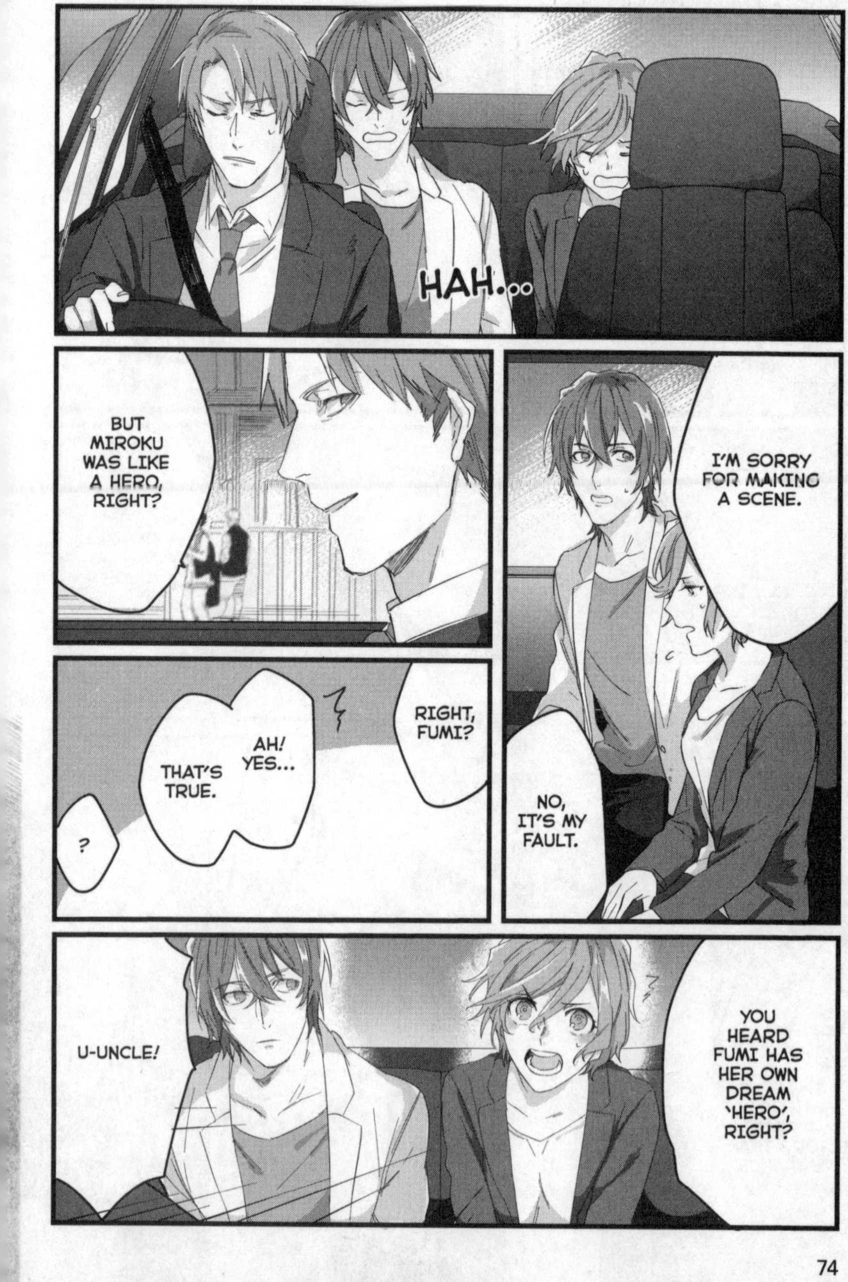
HAH...
I'M SORRY FOR MAKING A SCENE.
NO, IT'S MY FAULT.
BUT MIROKU WAS LIKE A HERO, RIGHT?
RIGHT, FUMI?
AH! YES... THAT'S TRUE.
?
YOU HEARD FUMI HAS HER OWN DREAM 'HERO', RIGHT?
U-UNCLE!

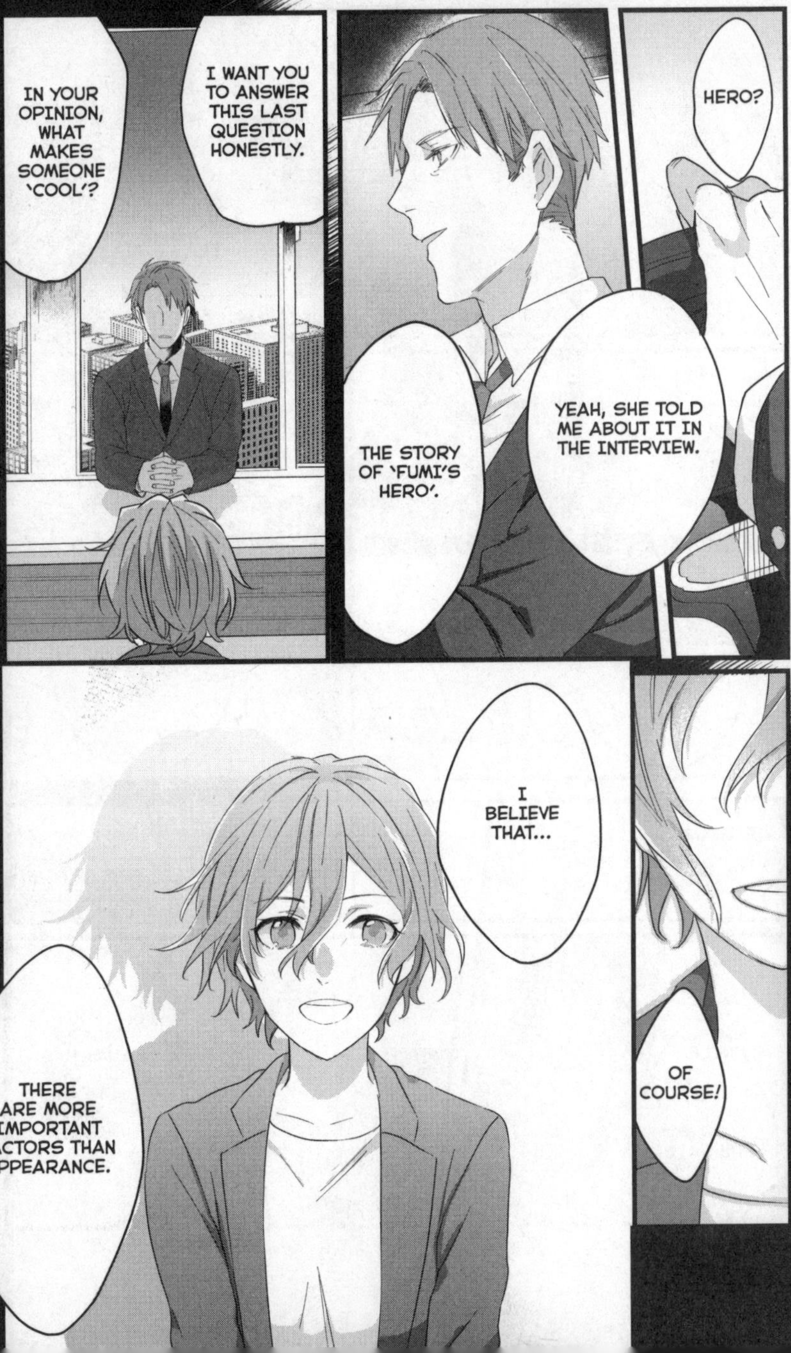
HERO?
YEAH, SHE TOLD ME ABOUT IT IN THE INTERVIEW.
THE STORY OF 'FUMI'S HERO'.
I WANT YOU TO ANSWER THIS LAST QUESTION HONESTLY.
IN YOUR OPINION, WHAT MAKES SOMEONE 'COOL'?
OF COURSE!
I BELIEVE THAT...
THERE ARE MORE IMPORTANT FACTORS THAN APPEARANCE.

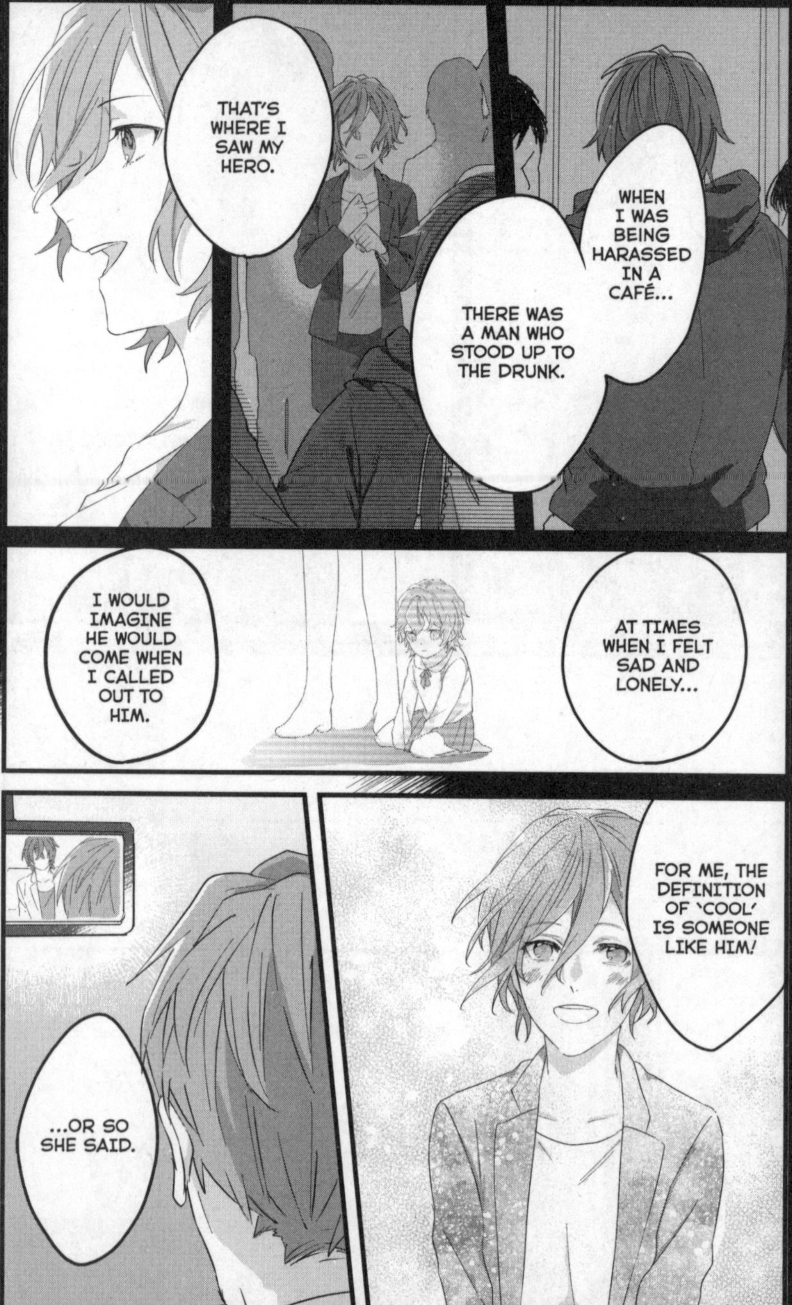
WHEN I WAS BEING HARASSED IN A CAFÉ...
THERE WAS A MAN WHO STOOD UP TO THE DRUNK.
THAT'S WHERE I SAW MY HERO.
AT TIMES WHEN I FELT SAD AND LONELY...
I WOULD IMAGINE HE WOULD COME WHEN I CALLED OUT TO HIM.
FOR ME, THE DEFINITION OF 'COOL' IS SOMEONE LIKE HIM!
...OR SO SHE SAID.

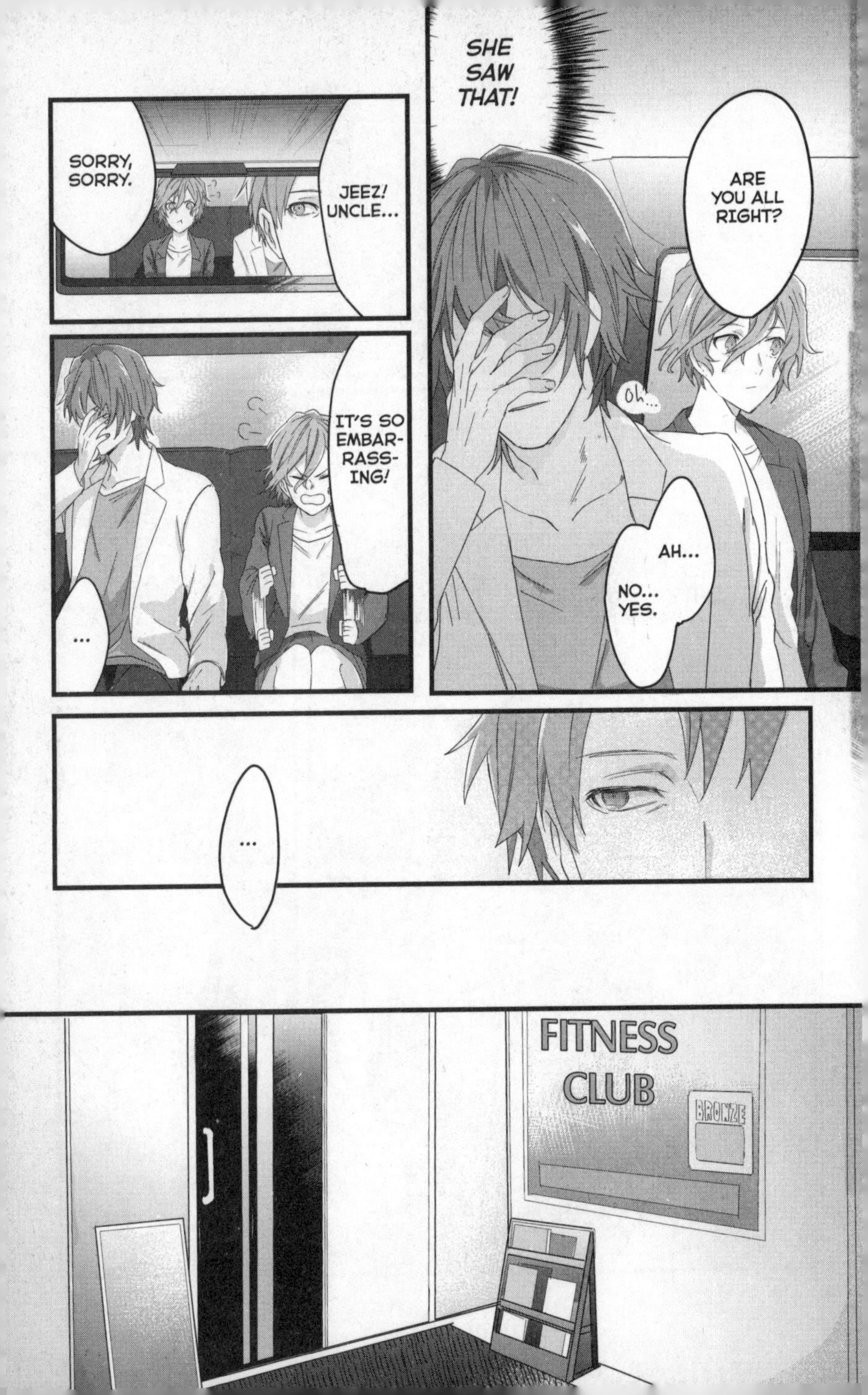
SHE SAW THAT!
ARE YOU ALL RIGHT?
Oh...
AH... NO... YES.
JEEZ! UNCLE...
SORRY, SORRY.
IT'S SO EMBARRASSING!
...
...
FITNESS CLUB
BRONZE

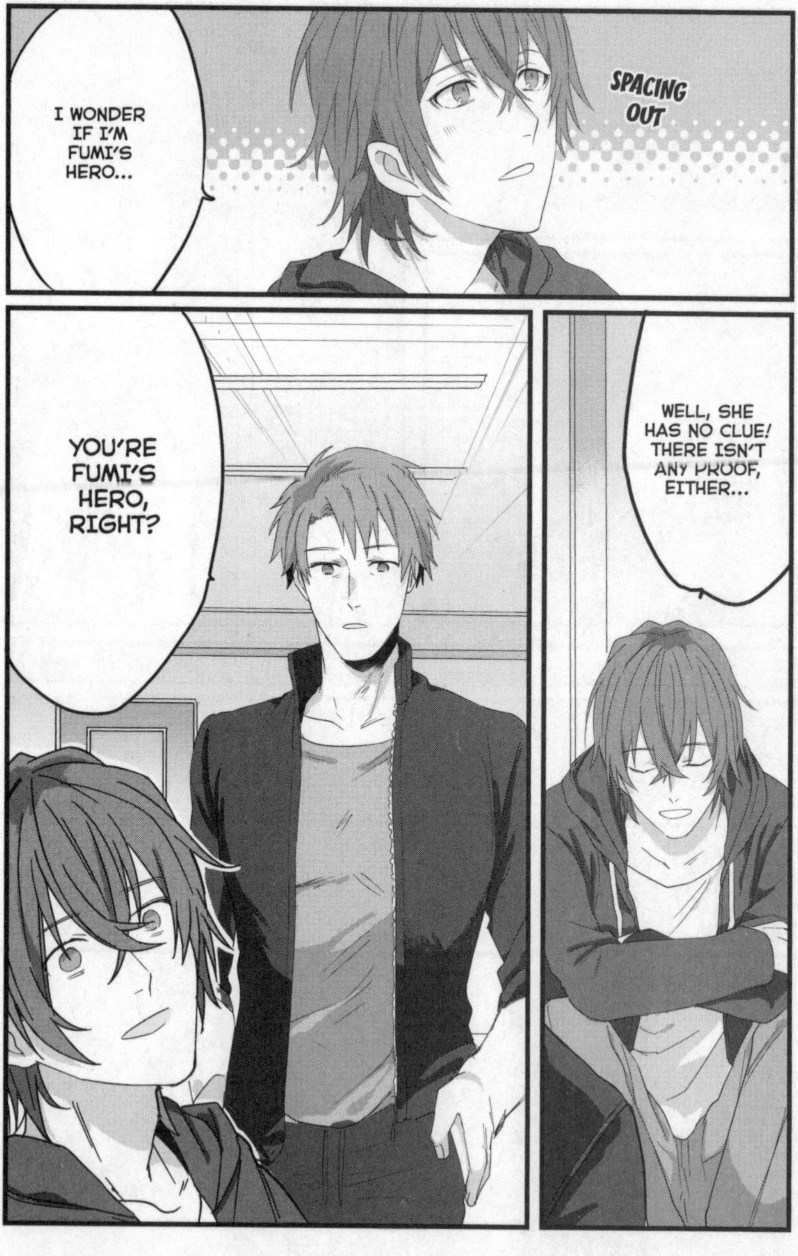
SPACING OUT
I WONDER IF I'M FUMI'S HERO...
WELL, SHE HAS NO CLUE! THERE ISN'T ANY PROOF, EITHER...
YOU'RE FUMI'S HERO, RIGHT?

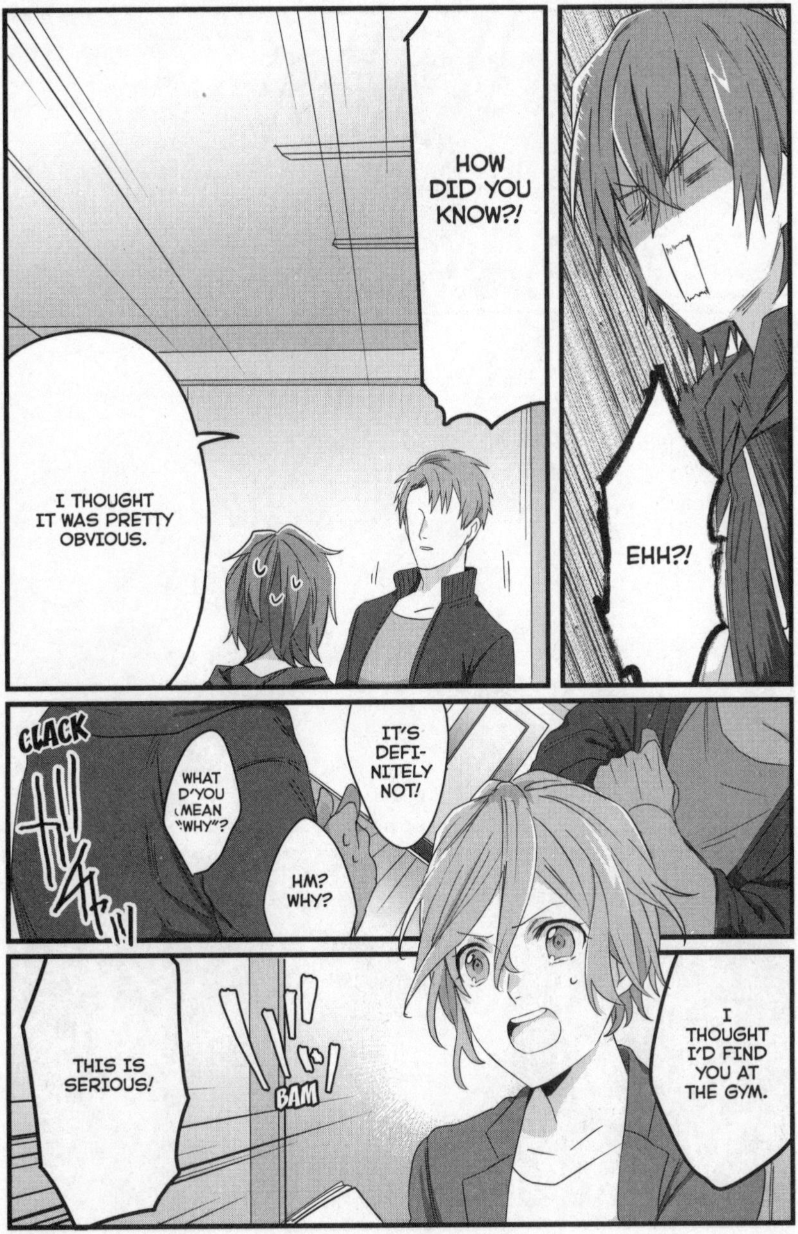
EHH?!
HOW DID YOU KNOW?!
I THOUGHT IT WAS PRETTY OBVIOUS.
IT'S DEFINITELY NOT!
HM? WHY?
WHAT D'YOU MEAN "WHY"?
CLACK
I THOUGHT I'D FIND YOU AT THE GYM.
BAM
THIS IS SERIOUS!

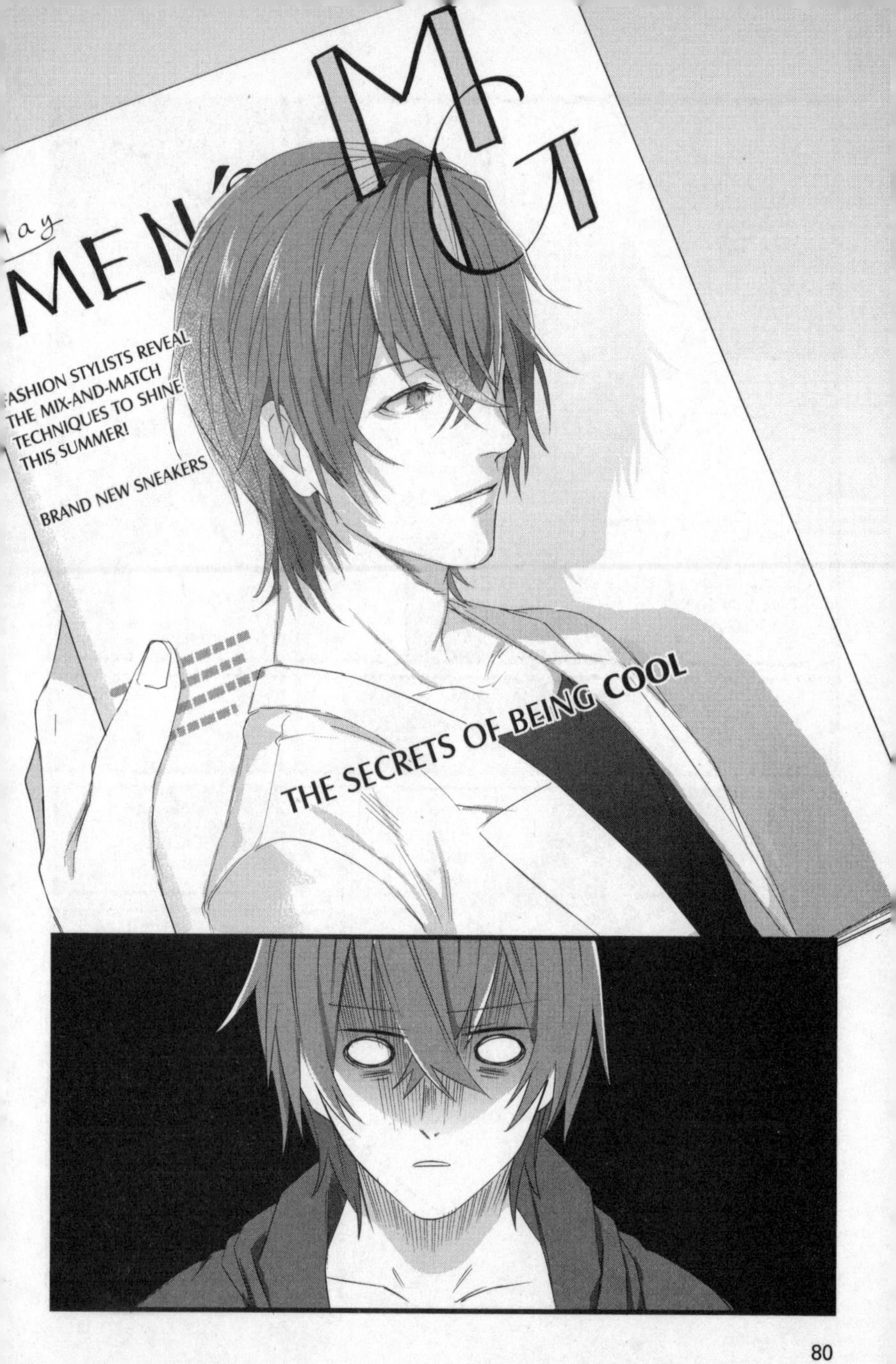

MEN'S
FASHION STYLISTS REVEAL THE MIX-AND-MATCH TECHNIQUES TO SHINE THIS SUMMER!
BRAND NEW SNEAKERS
THE SECRETS OF BEING COOL

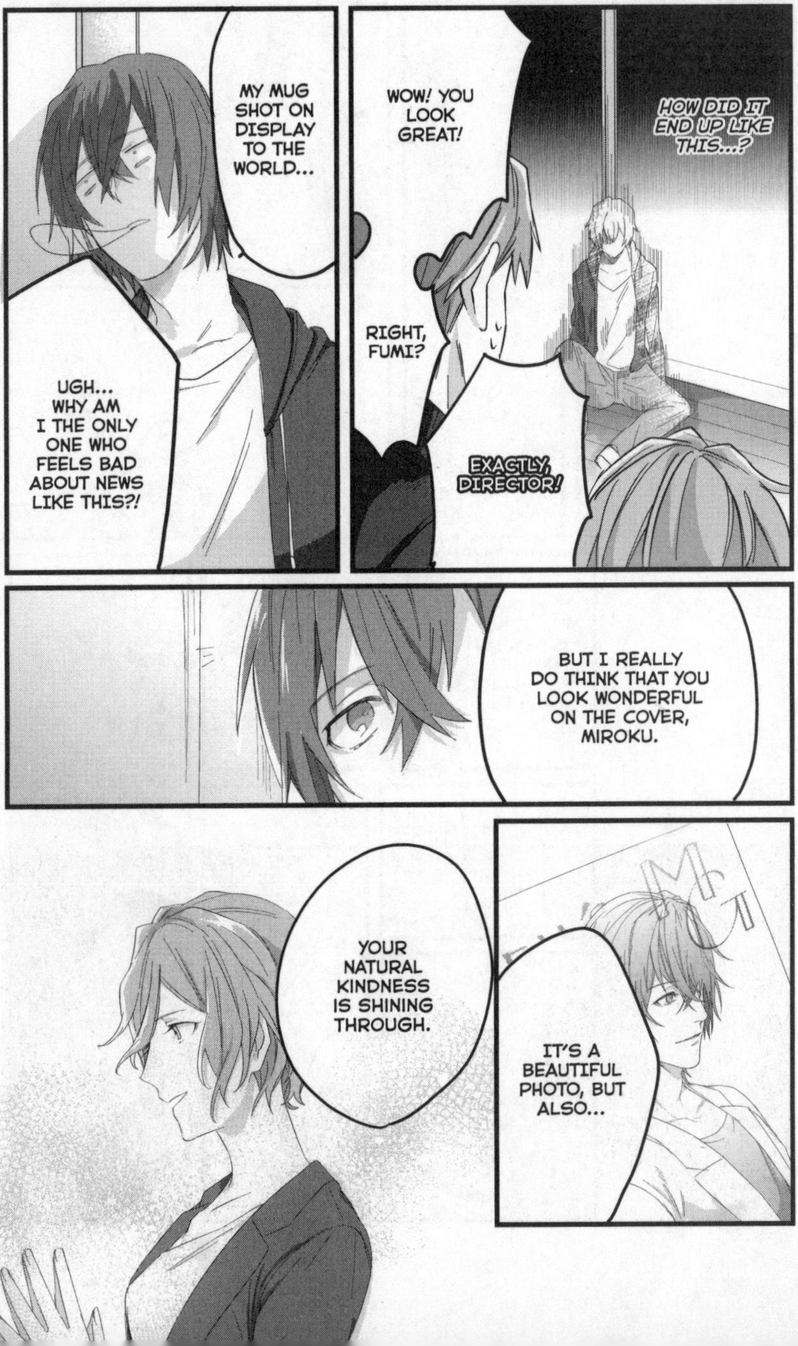
HOW DID IT END UP LIKE THIS...?
WOW! YOU LOOK GREAT!
RIGHT, FUMI?
EXACTLY, DIRECTOR!
MY MUG SHOT ON DISPLAY TO THE WORLD...
UGH... WHY AM I THE ONLY ONE WHO FEELS BAD ABOUT NEWS LIKE THIS?!
BUT I REALLY DO THINK THAT YOU LOOK WONDERFUL ON THE COVER, MIROKU.
IT'S A BEAUTIFUL PHOTO, BUT ALSO...
YOUR NATURAL KINDNESS IS SHINING THROUGH.

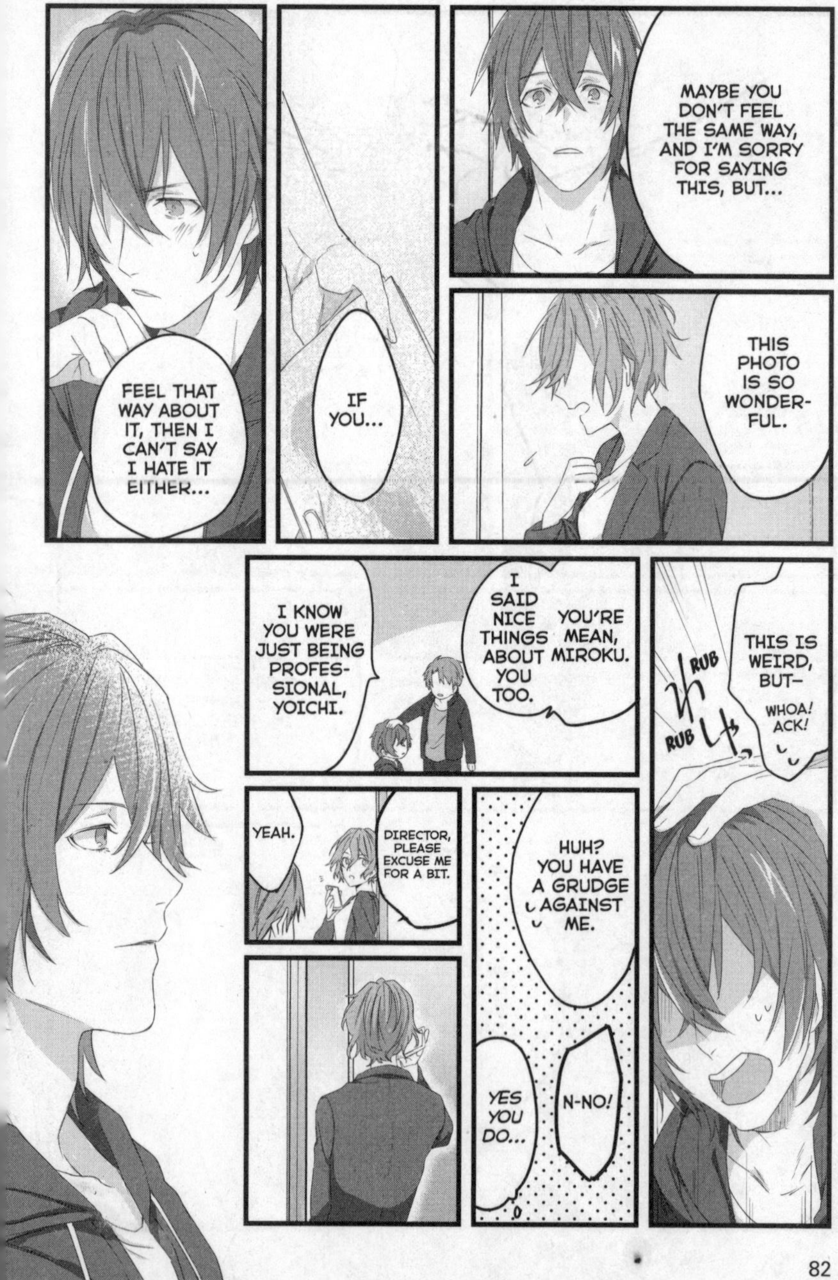
MAYBE YOU DON'T FEEL THE SAME WAY, AND I'M SORRY FOR SAYING THIS, BUT...
THIS PHOTO IS SO WONDER-FUL.
IF YOU...
FEEL THAT WAY ABOUT IT, THEN I CAN'T SAY I HATE IT EITHER...
THIS IS WEIRD, BUT–
RUB
RUB
WHOA! ACK!
YOU'RE MEAN, MIROKU.
I SAID NICE THINGS ABOUT YOU TOO.
I KNOW YOU WERE JUST BEING PROFES-SIONAL, YOICHI.
HUH? YOU HAVE A GRUDGE AGAINST ME.
N-NO!
YES YOU DO...
DIRECTOR, PLEASE EXCUSE ME FOR A BIT.
YEAH.

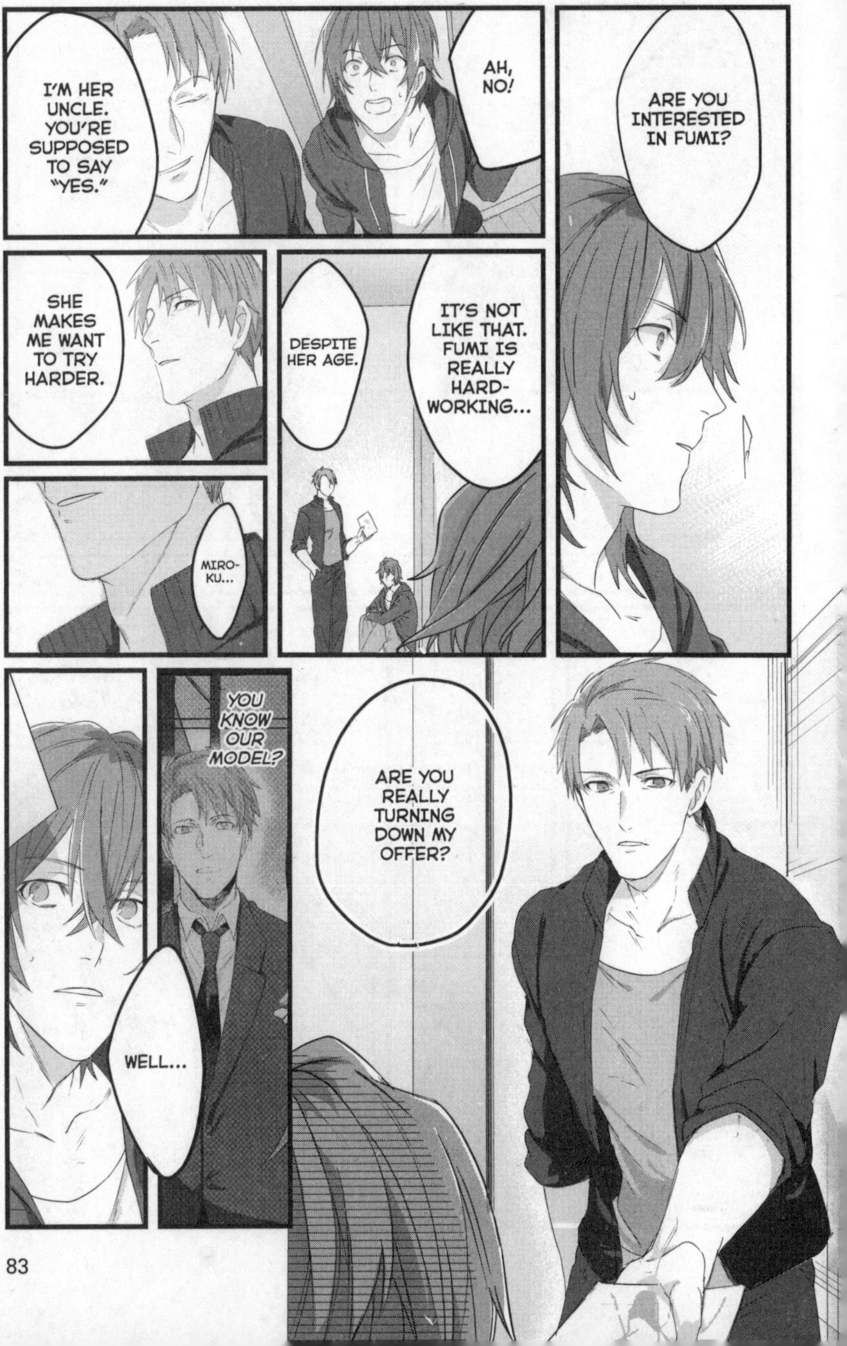

ARE YOU INTERESTED IN FUMI?
AH, NO!
I'M HER UNCLE. YOU'RE SUPPOSED TO SAY "YES."
IT'S NOT LIKE THAT. FUMI IS REALLY HARD-WORKING...
DESPITE HER AGE.
SHE MAKES ME WANT TO TRY HARDER.
MIRO-KU...
ARE YOU REALLY TURNING DOWN MY OFFER?
YOU KNOW OUR MODEL?
WELL...

*OSSAN: A CASUAL TERM IN JAPANESE FOR A MIDDLE-AGED MAN

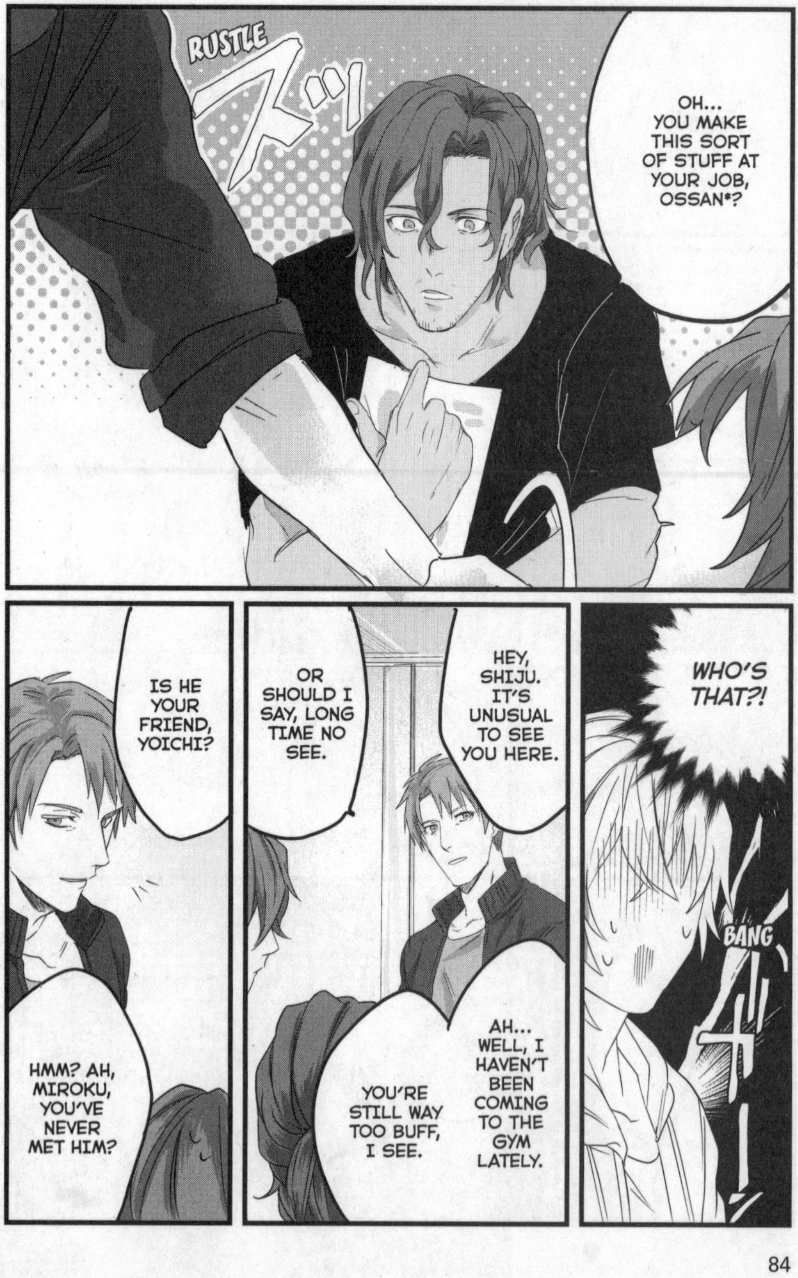
OH... YOU MAKE THIS SORT OF STUFF AT YOUR JOB, OSSAN*?
RUSTLE
WHO'S THAT?!
BANG
HEY, SHIJU. IT'S UNUSUAL TO SEE YOU HERE.
OR SHOULD I SAY, LONG TIME NO SEE.
AH... WELL, I HAVEN'T BEEN COMING TO THE GYM LATELY.
YOU'RE STILL WAY TOO BUFF, I SEE.
IS HE YOUR FRIEND, YOICHI?
HMM? AH, MIROKU, YOU'VE NEVER MET HIM?

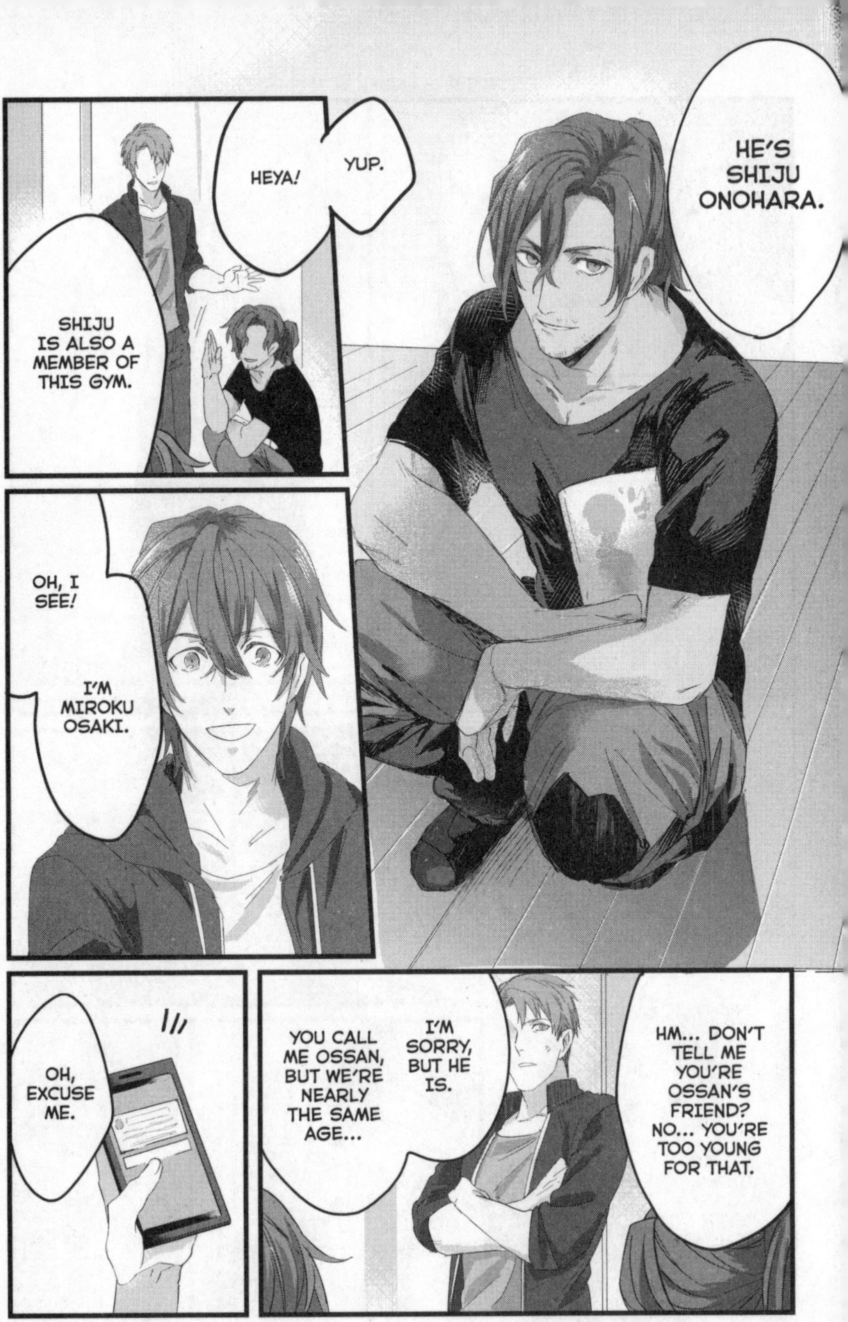
HE'S SHIJU ONOHARA.
YUP.
HEYA!
SHIJU IS ALSO A MEMBER OF THIS GYM.
OH, I SEE!
I'M MIROKU OSAKI.
HM... DON'T TELL ME YOU'RE OSSAN'S FRIEND? NO... YOU'RE TOO YOUNG FOR THAT.
I'M SORRY, BUT HE IS.
YOU CALL ME OSSAN, BUT WE'RE NEARLY THE SAME AGE...
OH, EXCUSE ME.

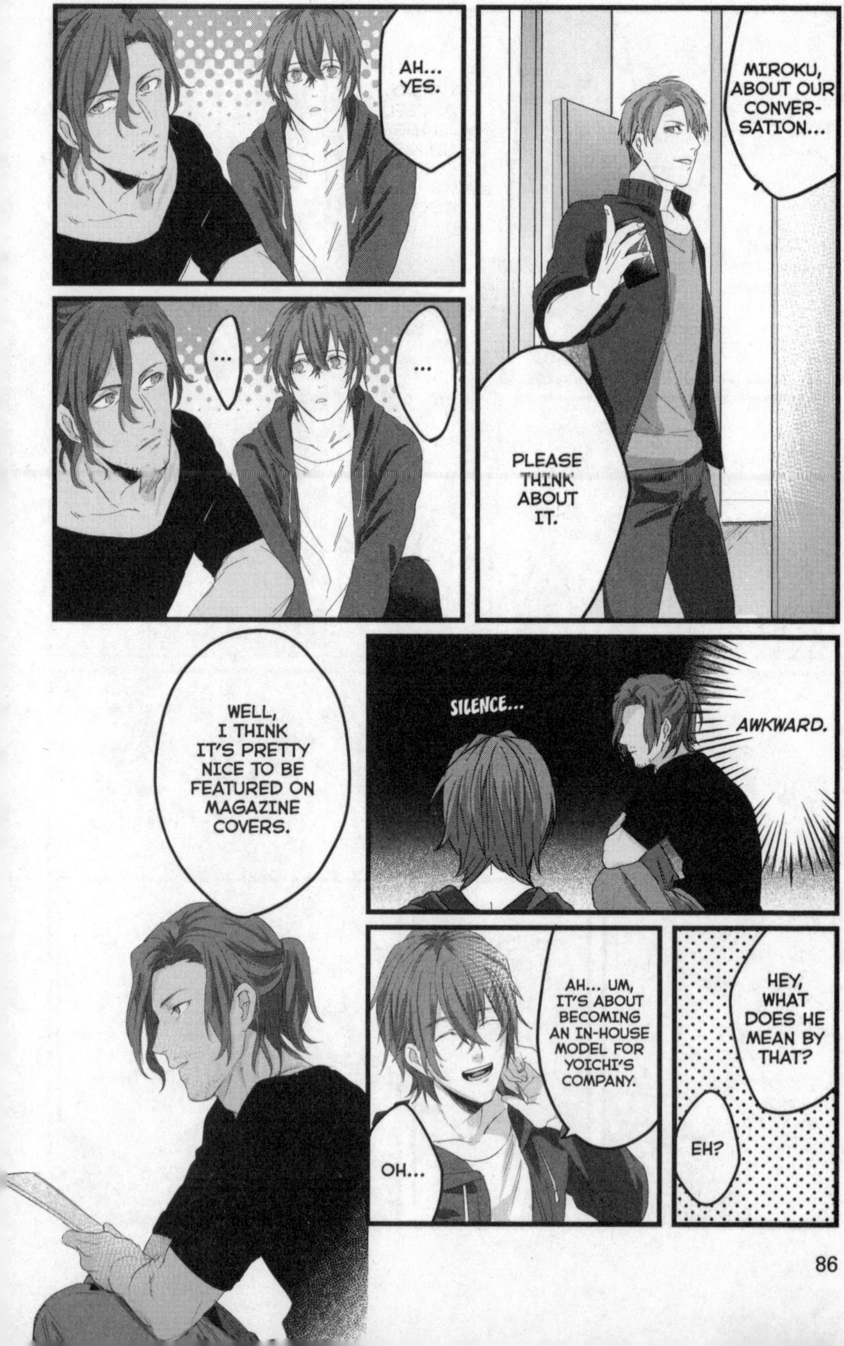
MIROKU, ABOUT OUR CONVER-SATION...
PLEASE THINK ABOUT IT.
AH... YES.
...
...
AWKWARD.
SILENCE...
WELL, I THINK IT'S PRETTY NICE TO BE FEATURED ON MAGAZINE COVERS.
HEY, WHAT DOES HE MEAN BY THAT?
EH?
AH... UM, IT'S ABOUT BECOMING AN IN-HOUSE MODEL FOR YOICHI'S COMPANY.
OH...

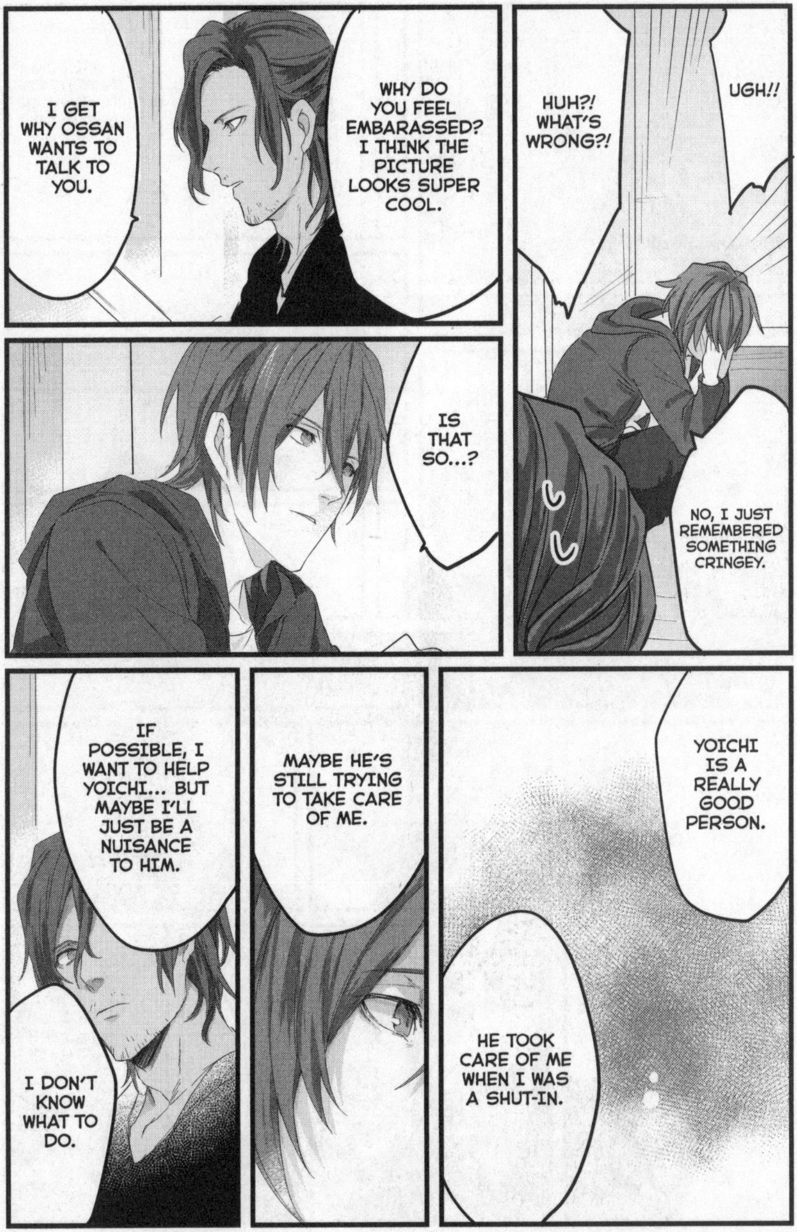
UGH!!
HUH?! WHAT'S WRONG?!
NO, I JUST REMEMBERED SOMETHING CRINGEY.
WHY DO YOU FEEL EMBARASSED? I THINK THE PICTURE LOOKS SUPER COOL.
I GET WHY OSSAN WANTS TO TALK TO YOU.
IS THAT SO...?
YOICHI IS A REALLY GOOD PERSON.
HE TOOK CARE OF ME WHEN I WAS A SHUT-IN.
MAYBE HE'S STILL TRYING TO TAKE CARE OF ME.
IF POSSIBLE, I WANT TO HELP YOICHI... BUT MAYBE I'LL JUST BE A NUISANCE TO HIM.
I DON'T KNOW WHAT TO DO.

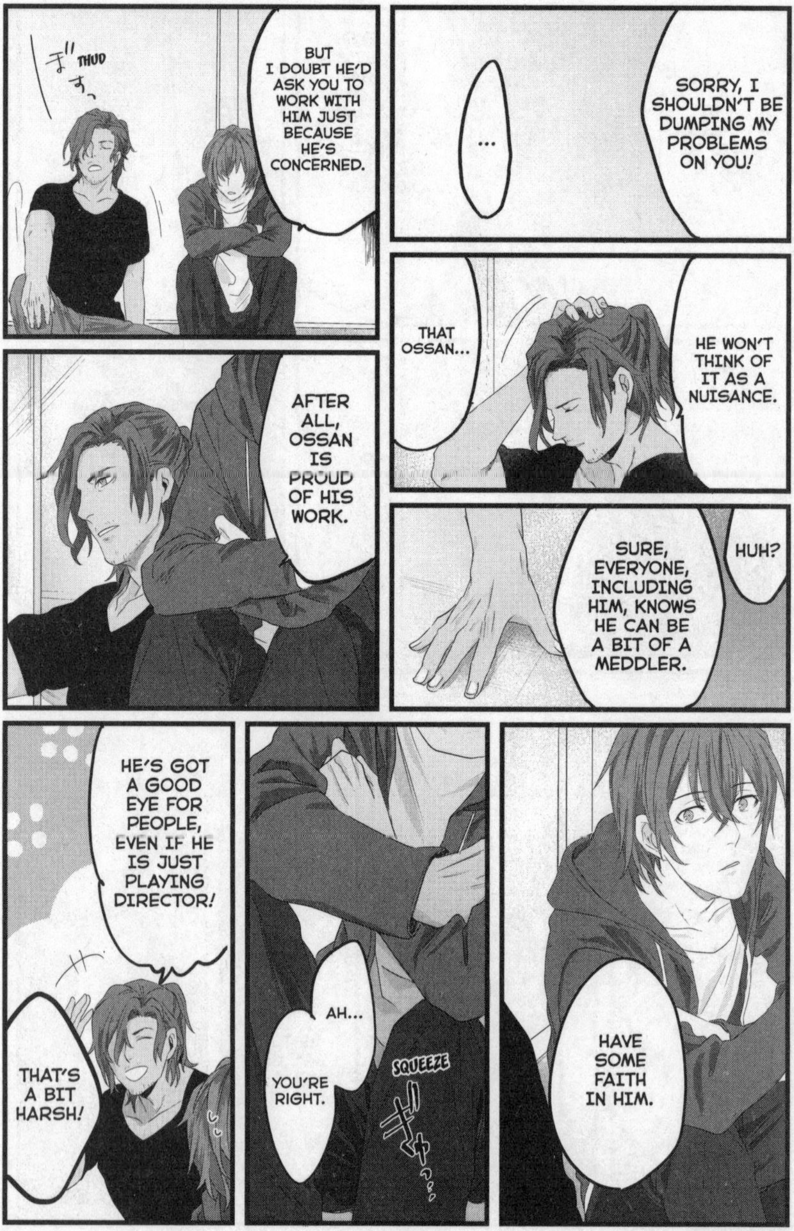
SORRY, I SHOULDN'T BE DUMPING MY PROBLEMS ON YOU!
...
HE WON'T THINK OF IT AS A NUISANCE.
THAT OSSAN...
HUH?
SURE, EVERYONE, INCLUDING HIM, KNOWS HE CAN BE A BIT OF A MEDDLER.
BUT I DOUBT HE'D ASK YOU TO WORK WITH HIM JUST BECAUSE HE'S CONCERNED.
THUD
AFTER ALL, OSSAN IS PROUD OF HIS WORK.
HAVE SOME FAITH IN HIM.
AH...
YOU'RE RIGHT.
SQUEEZE
HE'S GOT A GOOD EYE FOR PEOPLE, EVEN IF HE IS JUST PLAYING DIRECTOR!
THAT'S A BIT HARSH!

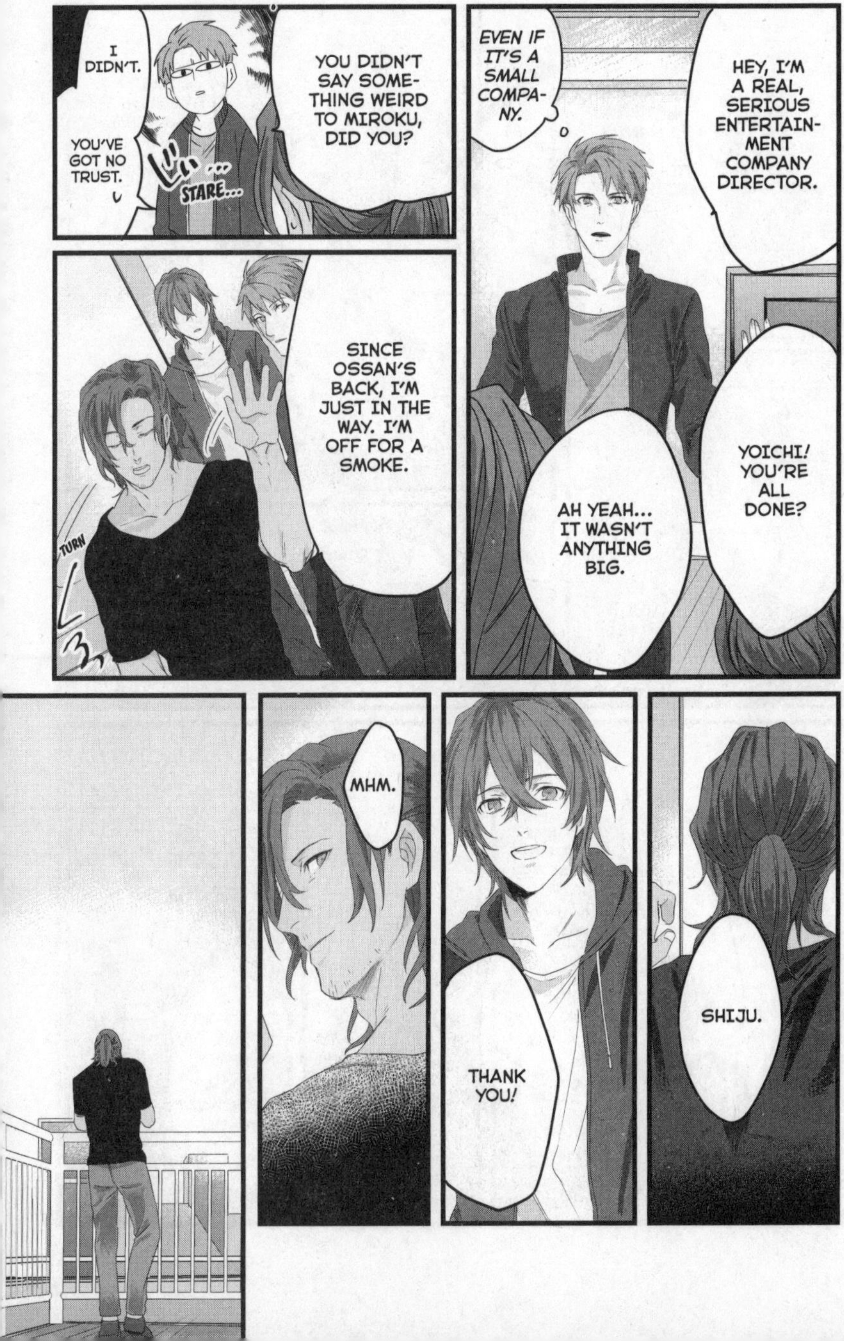
HEY, I'M A REAL, SERIOUS ENTERTAINMENT COMPANY DIRECTOR.
EVEN IF IT'S A SMALL COMPANY.
YOICHI! YOU'RE ALL DONE?
AH YEAH... IT WASN'T ANYTHING BIG.
YOU DIDN'T SAY SOMETHING WEIRD TO MIROKU, DID YOU?
I DIDN'T.
YOU'VE GOT NO TRUST.
STARE...
SINCE OSSAN'S BACK, I'M JUST IN THE WAY. I'M OFF FOR A SMOKE.
TURN
SHIJU.
THANK YOU!
MHM.

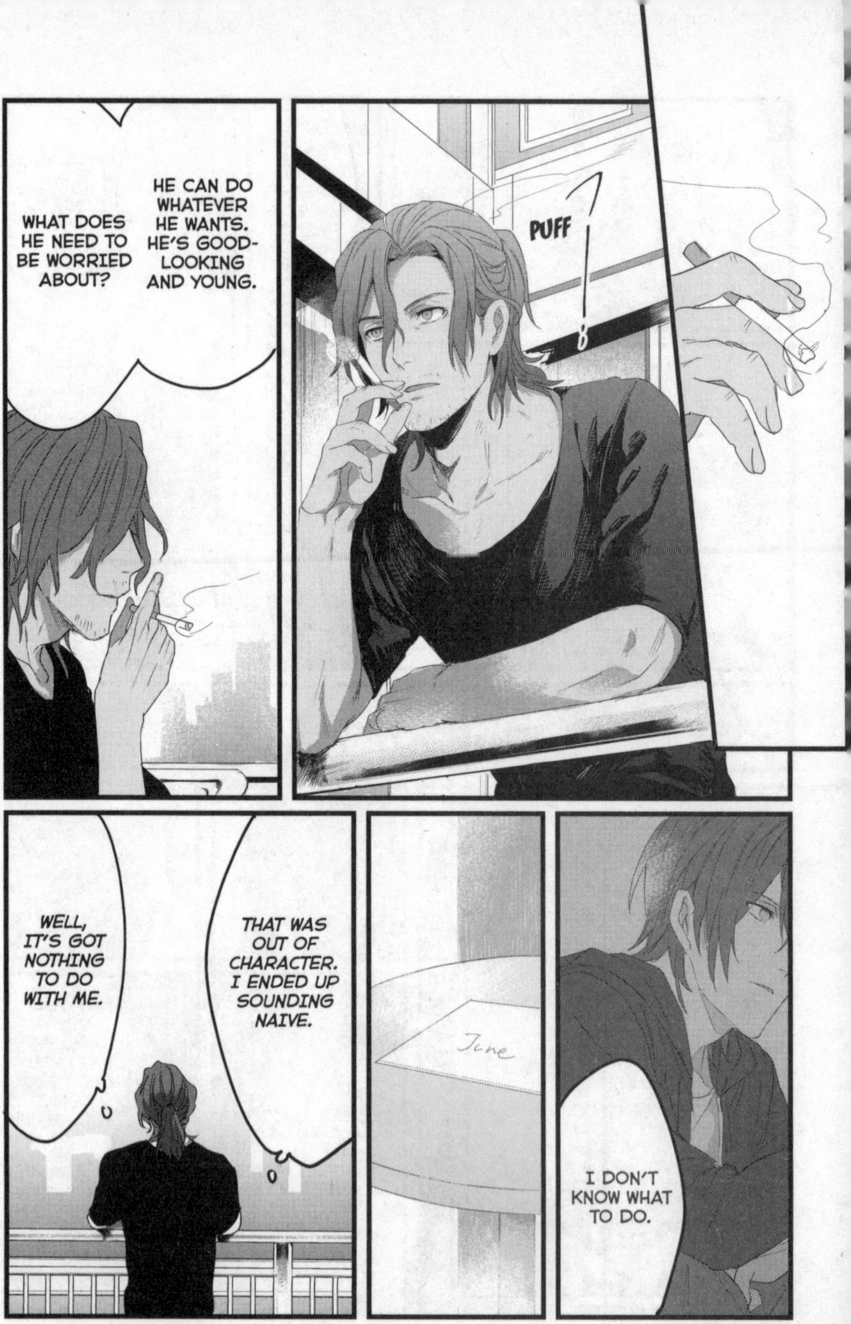
PUFF
HE CAN DO WHATEVER HE WANTS. HE'S GOOD-LOOKING AND YOUNG.
WHAT DOES HE NEED TO BE WORRIED ABOUT?
I DON'T KNOW WHAT TO DO.
June
THAT WAS OUT OF CHARACTER. I ENDED UP SOUNDING NAIVE.
WELL, IT'S GOT NOTHING TO DO WITH ME.

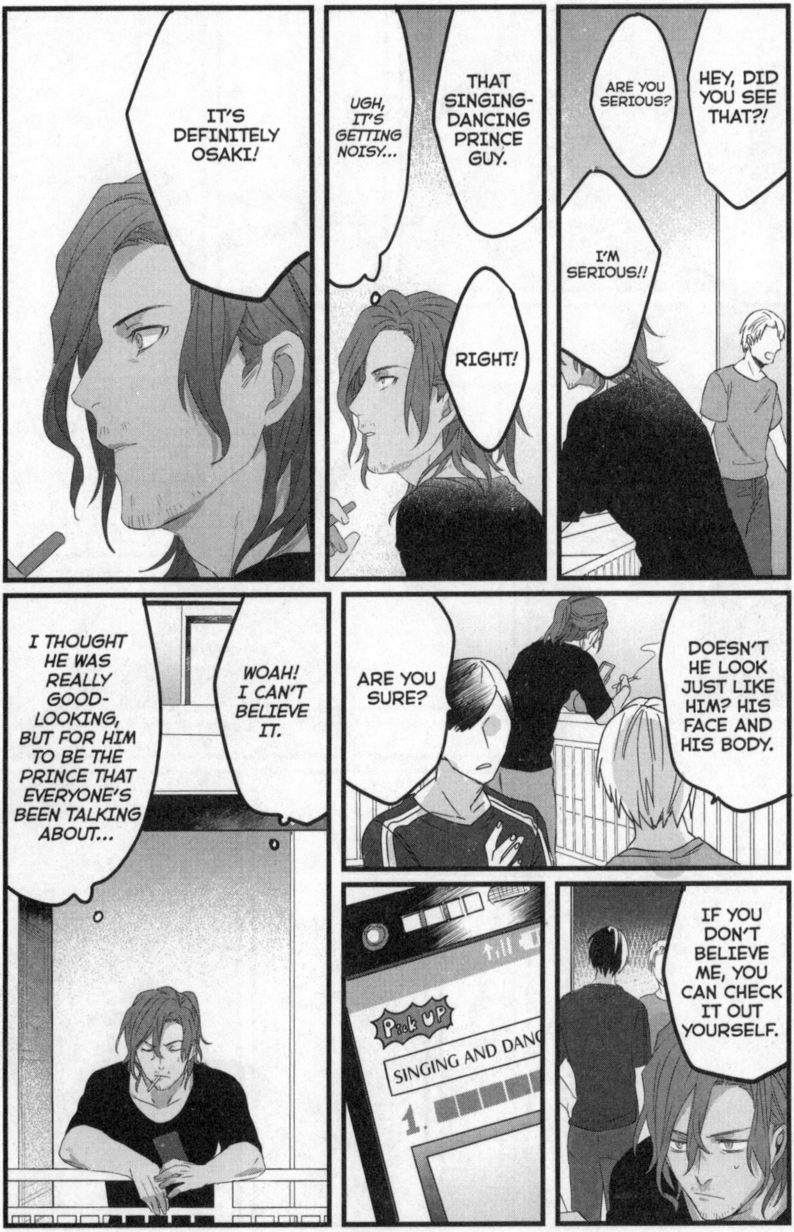
HEY, DID YOU SEE THAT?!
ARE YOU SERIOUS?
I'M SERIOUS!!
THAT SINGING-DANCING PRINCE GUY.
UGH, IT'S GETTING NOISY...
RIGHT!
IT'S DEFINITELY OSAKI!
DOESN'T HE LOOK JUST LIKE HIM? HIS FACE AND HIS BODY.
ARE YOU SURE?
IF YOU DON'T BELIEVE ME, YOU CAN CHECK IT OUT YOURSELF.
Pick up
SINGING AND DANC
1.
WOAH! I CAN'T BELIEVE IT.
I THOUGHT HE WAS REALLY GOOD-LOOKING, BUT FOR HIM TO BE THE PRINCE THAT EVERYONE'S BEEN TALKING ABOUT...

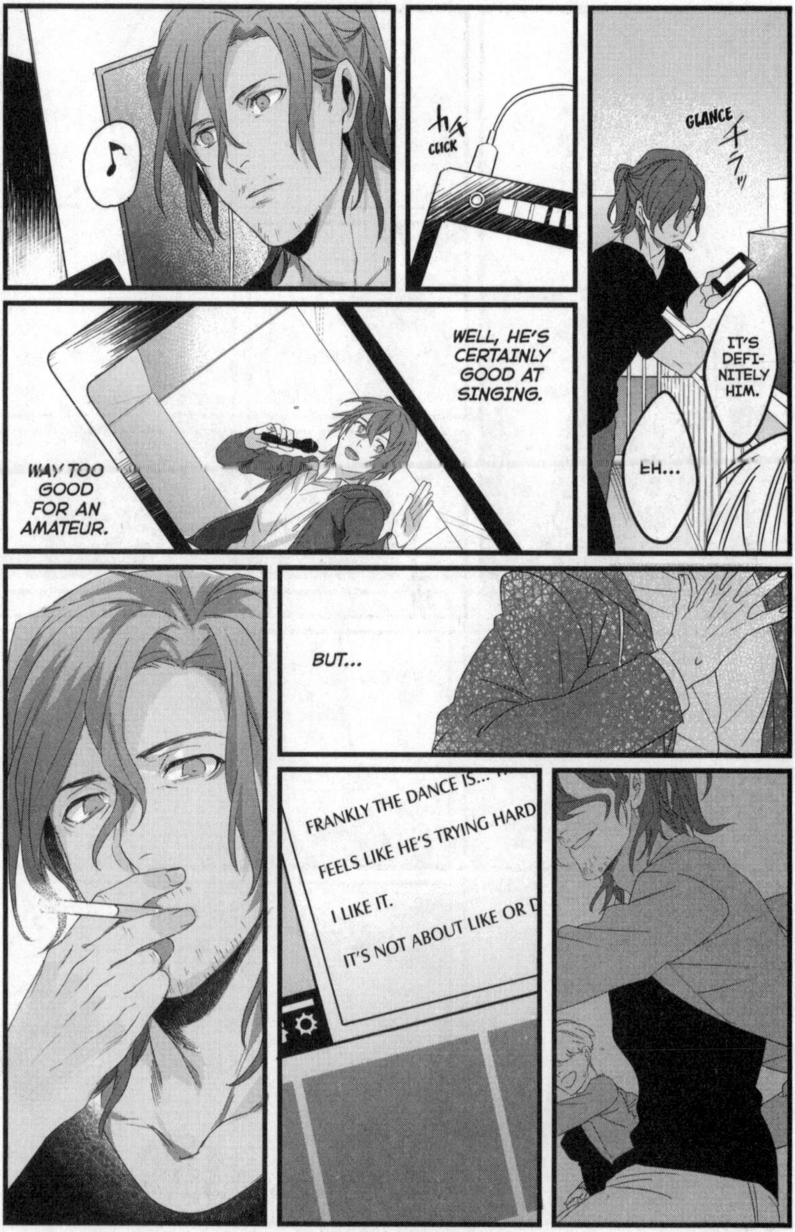
GLANCE
チラッ
IT'S DEFINITELY HIM.
EH...
カチ
CLICK
♪
WELL, HE'S CERTAINLY GOOD AT SINGING.
WAY TOO GOOD FOR AN AMATEUR.
BUT...
FRANKLY THE DANCE IS...
FEELS LIKE HE'S TRYING HARD
I LIKE IT.
IT'S NOT ABOUT LIKE OR D

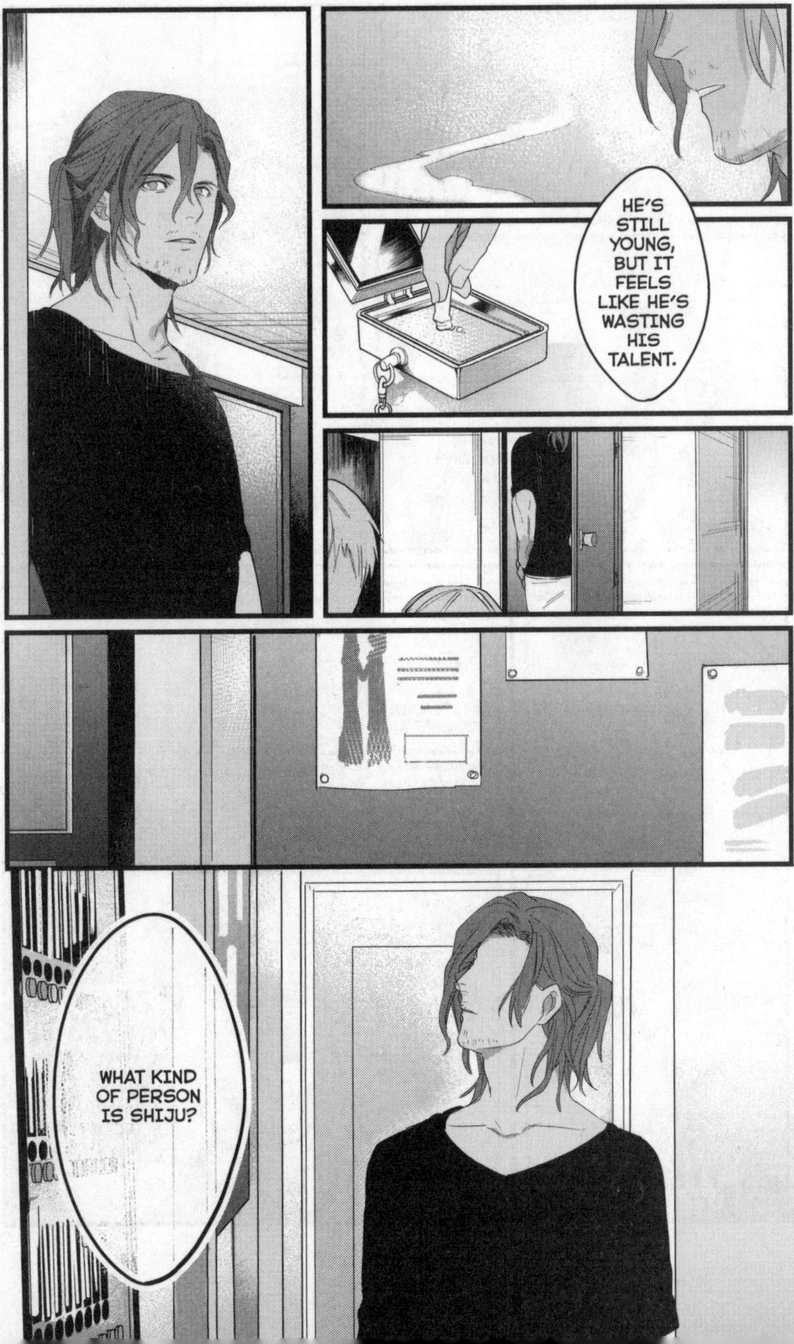
HE'S STILL YOUNG, BUT IT FEELS LIKE HE'S WASTING HIS TALENT.
WHAT KIND OF PERSON IS SHIJU?

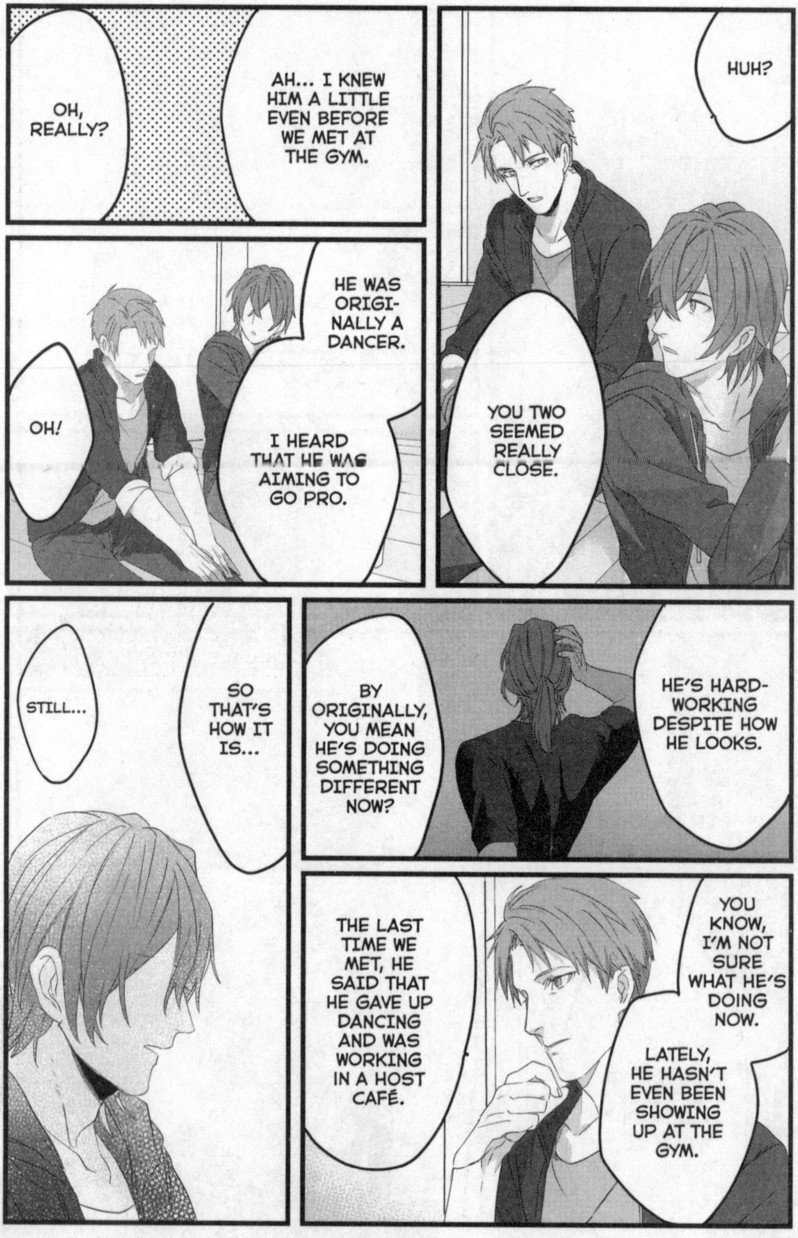
HUH?
YOU TWO SEEMED REALLY CLOSE.
AH... I KNEW HIM A LITTLE EVEN BEFORE WE MET AT THE GYM.
OH, REALLY?
HE WAS ORIGINALLY A DANCER.
I HEARD THAT HE WAS AIMING TO GO PRO.
OH!
HE'S HARD-WORKING DESPITE HOW HE LOOKS.
BY ORIGINALLY, YOU MEAN HE'S DOING SOMETHING DIFFERENT NOW?
YOU KNOW, I'M NOT SURE WHAT HE'S DOING NOW.
LATELY, HE HASN'T EVEN BEEN SHOWING UP AT THE GYM.
THE LAST TIME WE MET, HE SAID THAT HE GAVE UP DANCING AND WAS WORKING IN A HOST CAFÉ.
SO THAT'S HOW IT IS...
STILL...

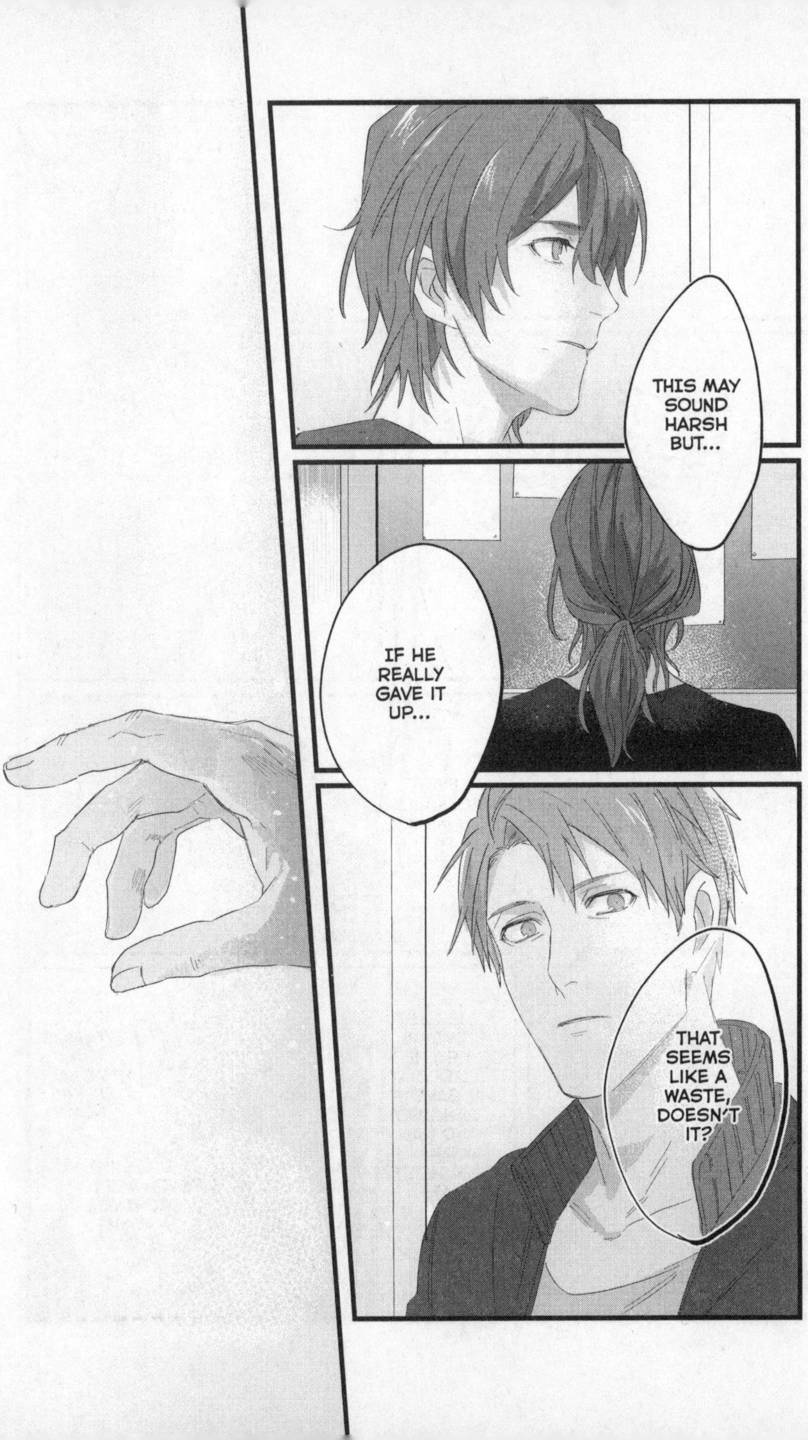
THIS MAY SOUND HARSH BUT...
IF HE REALLY GAVE IT UP...
THAT SEEMS LIKE A WASTE, DOESN'T IT?

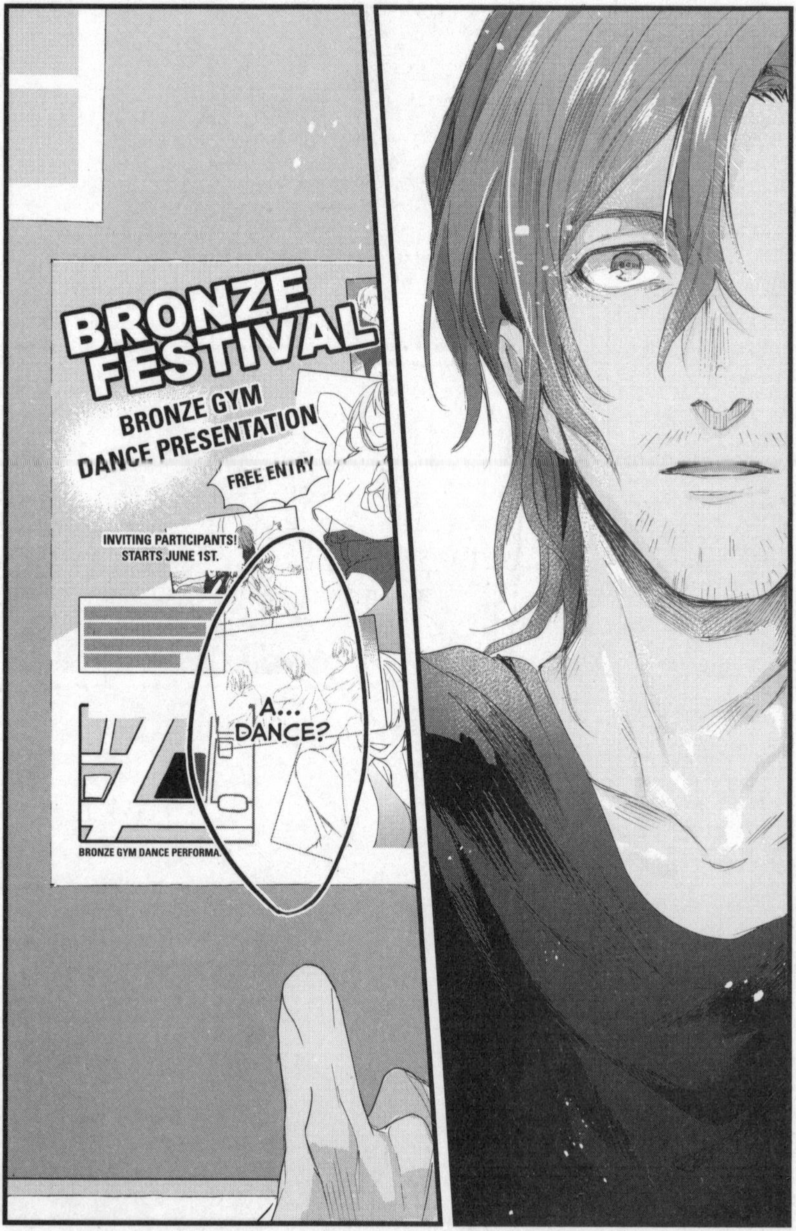
BRONZE FESTIVAL
BRONZE GYM
DANCE PRESENTATION
FREE ENTRY
INVITING PARTICIPANTS!
STARTS JUNE 1ST.
BRONZE GYM DANCE PERFORMA
A... DANCE?

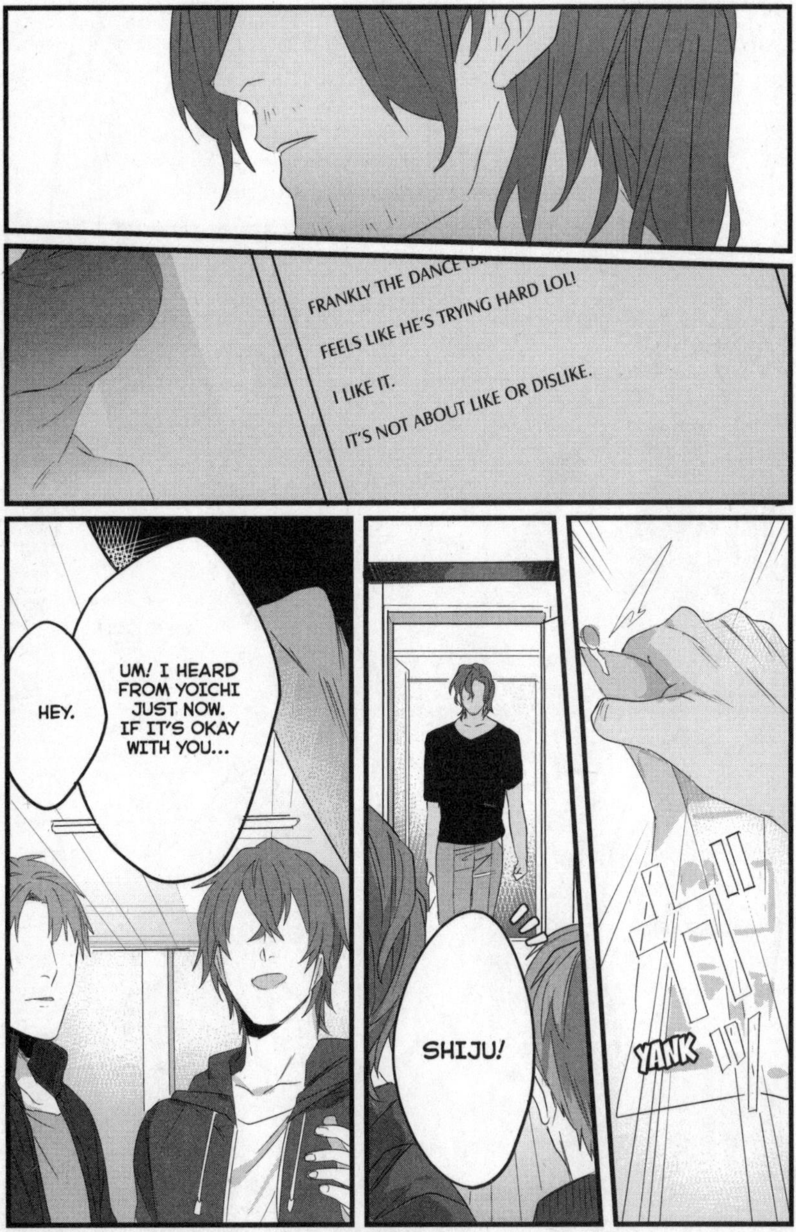
FRANKLY THE DANCE IS...
FEELS LIKE HE'S TRYING HARD LOL!
I LIKE IT.
IT'S NOT ABOUT LIKE OR DISLIKE.
YANK
SHIJU!
UM! I HEARD FROM YOICHI JUST NOW. IF IT'S OKAY WITH YOU...
HEY.

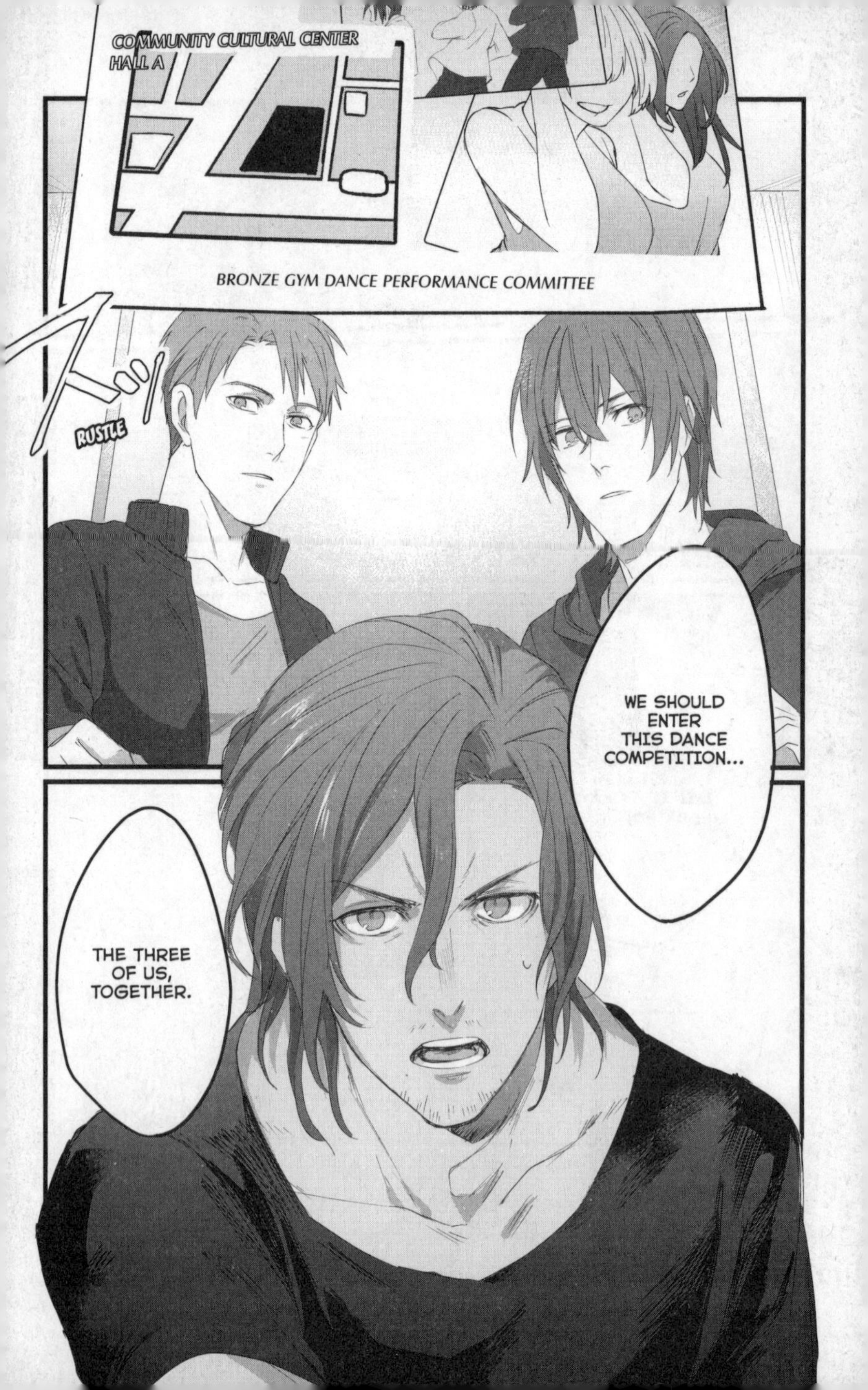
COMMUNITY CULTURAL CENTER HALL A
BRONZE GYM DANCE PERFORMANCE COMMITTEE
RUSTLE
WE SHOULD ENTER THIS DANCE COMPETITION...
THE THREE OF US, TOGETHER.

Chapter 4

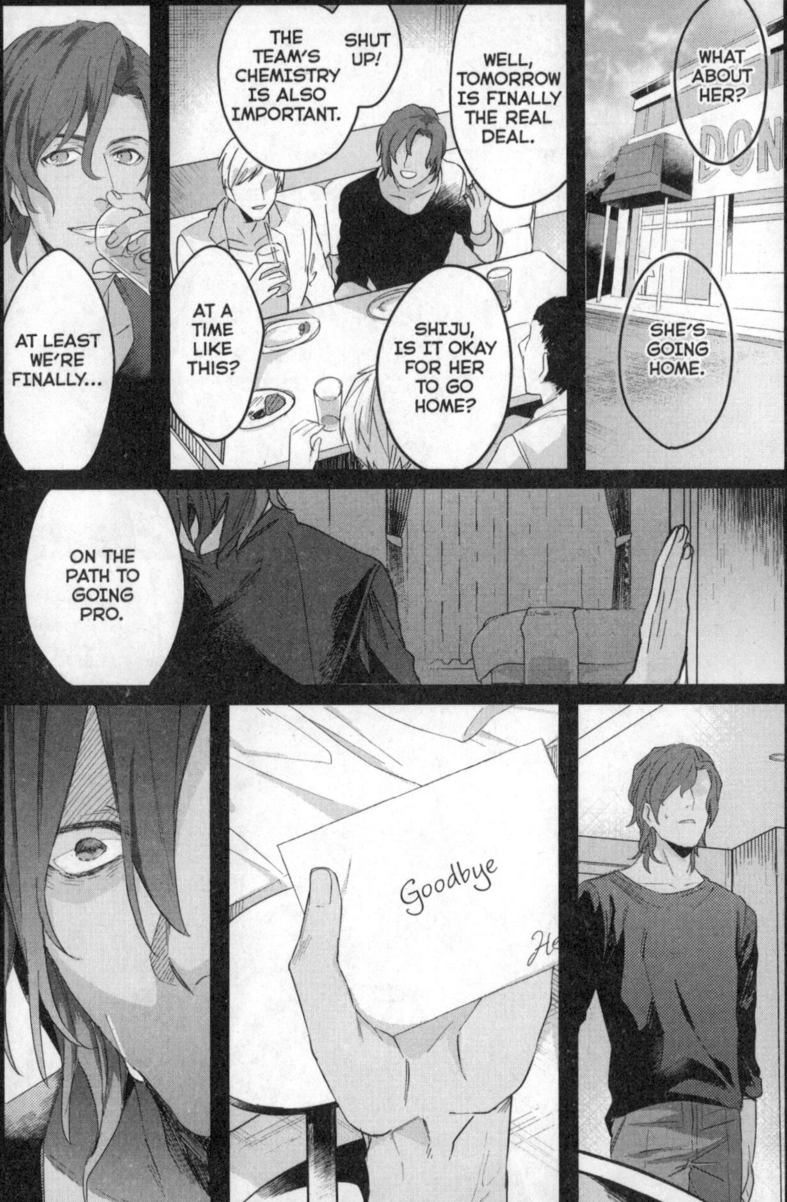
WHAT ABOUT HER?
SHE'S GOING HOME.
WELL, TOMORROW IS FINALLY THE REAL DEAL.
SHUT UP!
THE TEAM'S CHEMISTRY IS ALSO IMPORTANT.
SHIJU, IS IT OKAY FOR HER TO GO HOME?
AT A TIME LIKE THIS?
AT LEAST WE'RE FINALLY...
ON THE PATH TO GOING PRO.
Goodbye

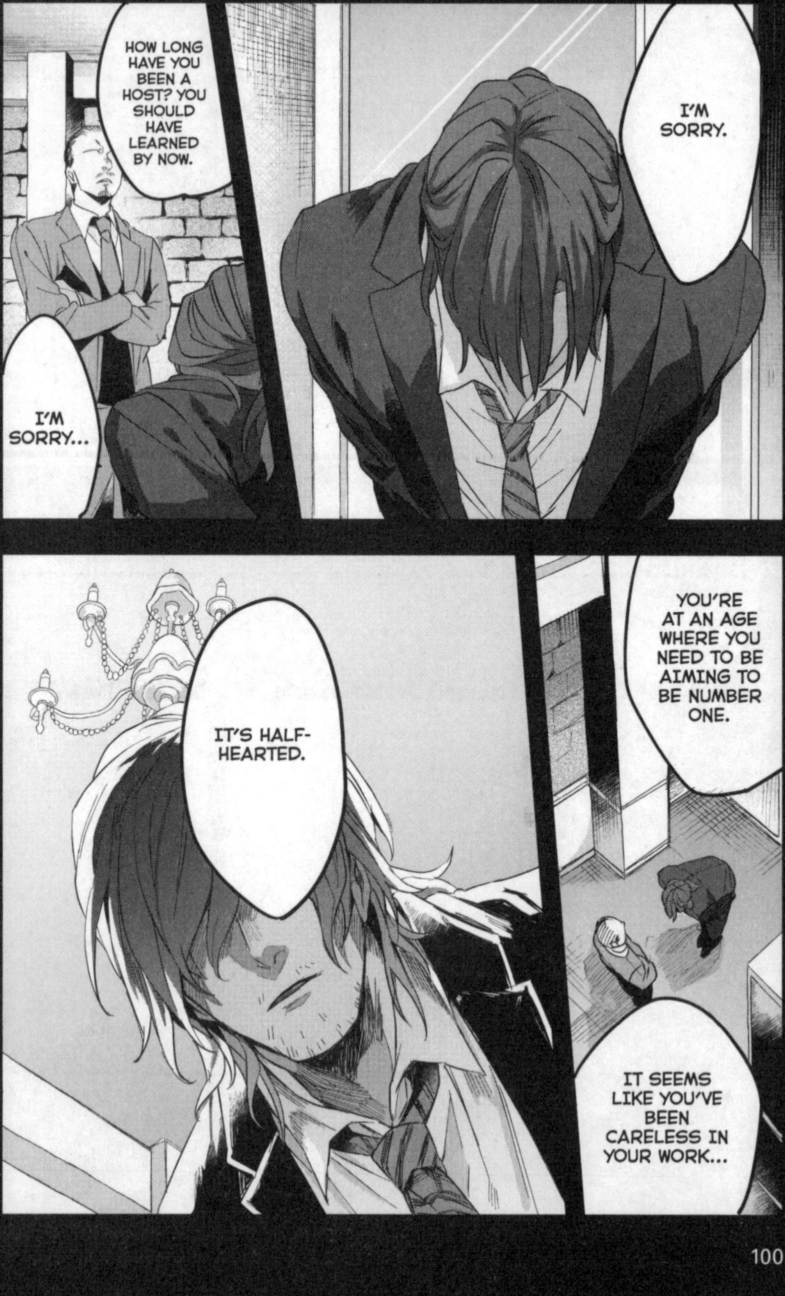
I'M SORRY.
HOW LONG HAVE YOU BEEN A HOST? YOU SHOULD HAVE LEARNED BY NOW.
I'M SORRY...
YOU'RE AT AN AGE WHERE YOU NEED TO BE AIMING TO BE NUMBER ONE.
IT SEEMS LIKE YOU'VE BEEN CARELESS IN YOUR WORK...
IT'S HALF-HEARTED.

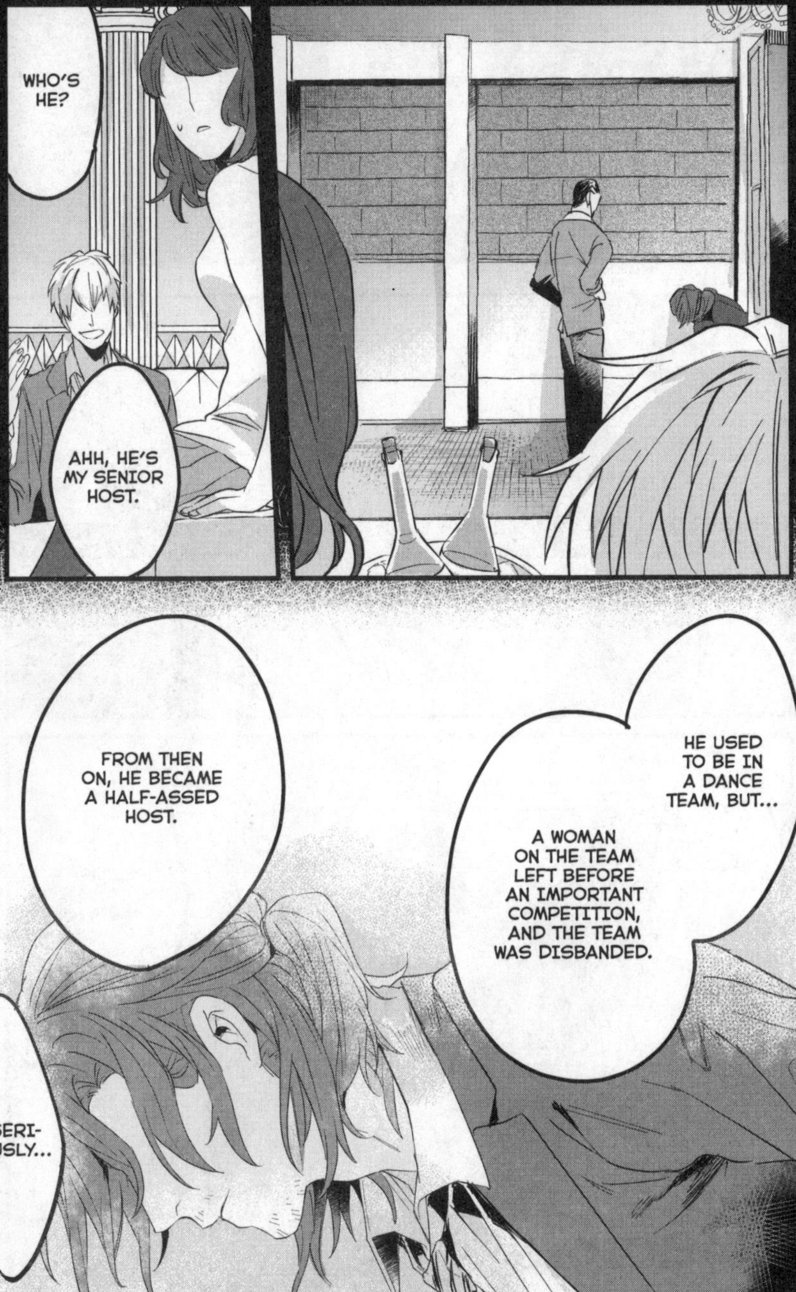
WHO'S HE?
AHH, HE'S MY SENIOR HOST.
HE USED TO BE IN A DANCE TEAM, BUT...
A WOMAN ON THE TEAM LEFT BEFORE AN IMPORTANT COMPETITION, AND THE TEAM WAS DISBANDED.
FROM THEN ON, HE BECAME A HALF-ASSED HOST.
SERIOUSLY...

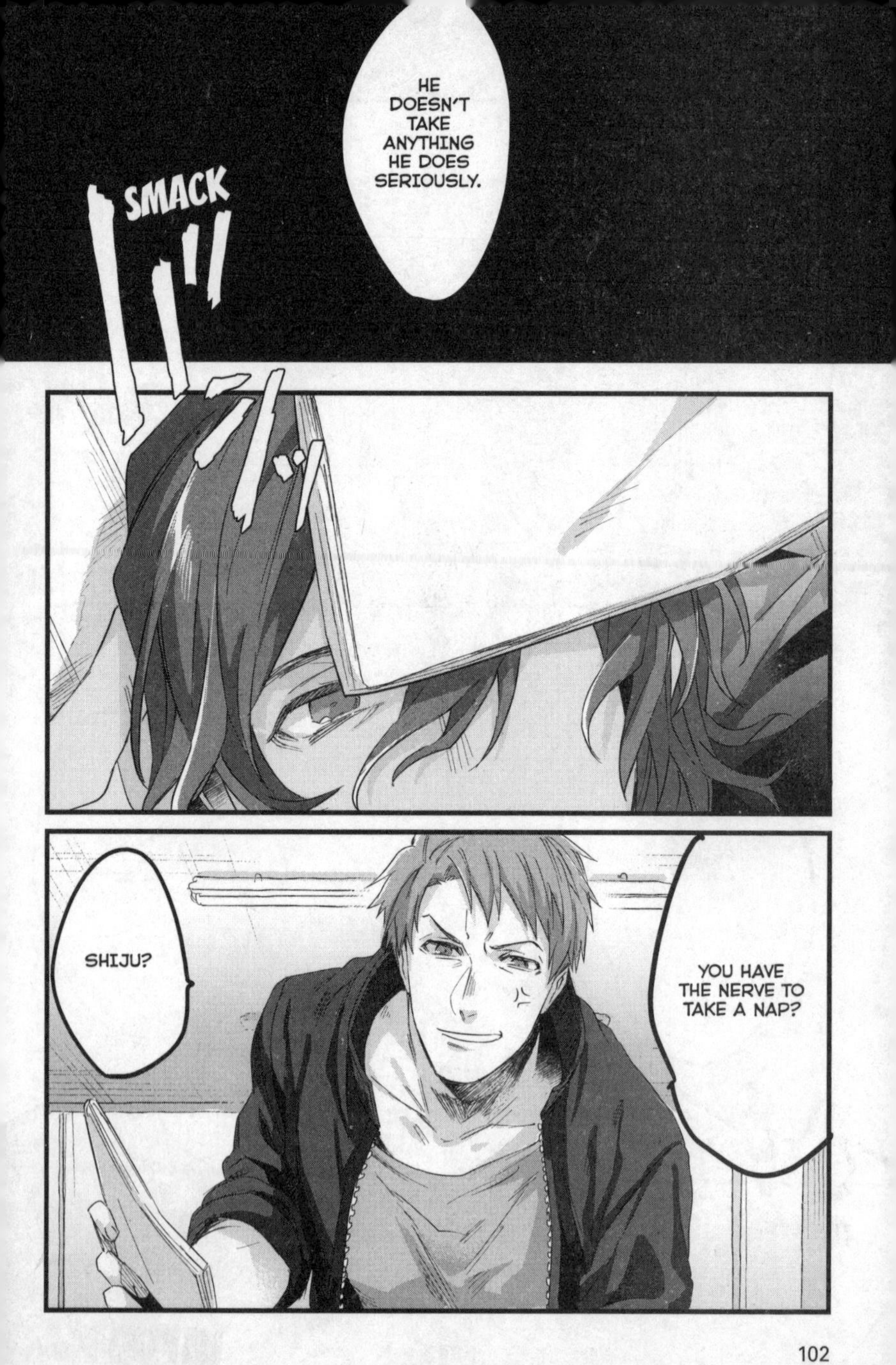
HE DOESN'T TAKE ANYTHING HE DOES SERIOUSLY.
SMACK
YOU HAVE THE NERVE TO TAKE A NAP?
SHIJU?

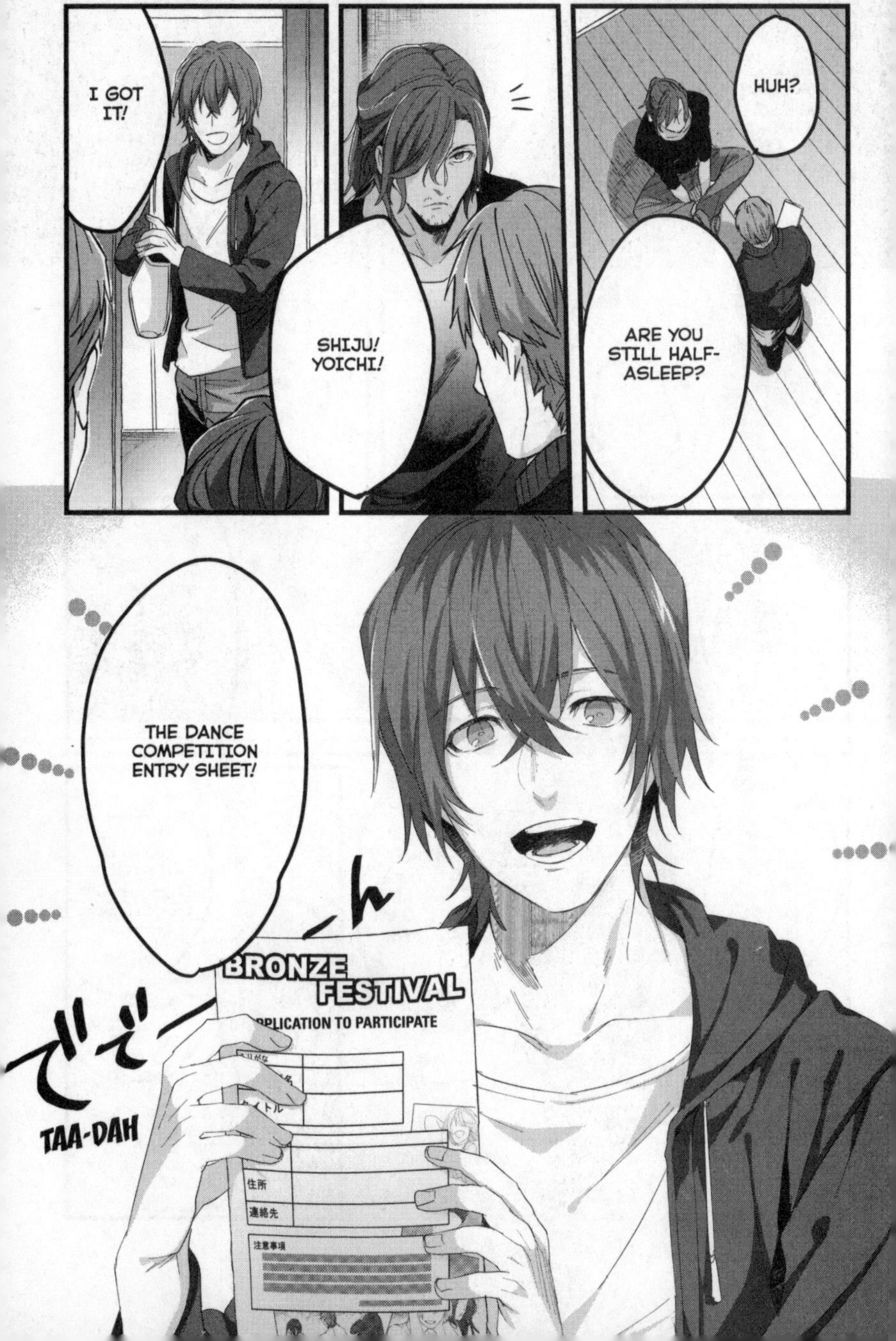
HUH?
ARE YOU STILL HALF-ASLEEP?
SHIJU! YOICHI!
I GOT IT!
THE DANCE COMPETITION ENTRY SHEET!
でで—ん
TAA-DAH
BRONZE FESTIVAL
PPLICATION TO PARTICIPATE
住所
連絡先
注意事項

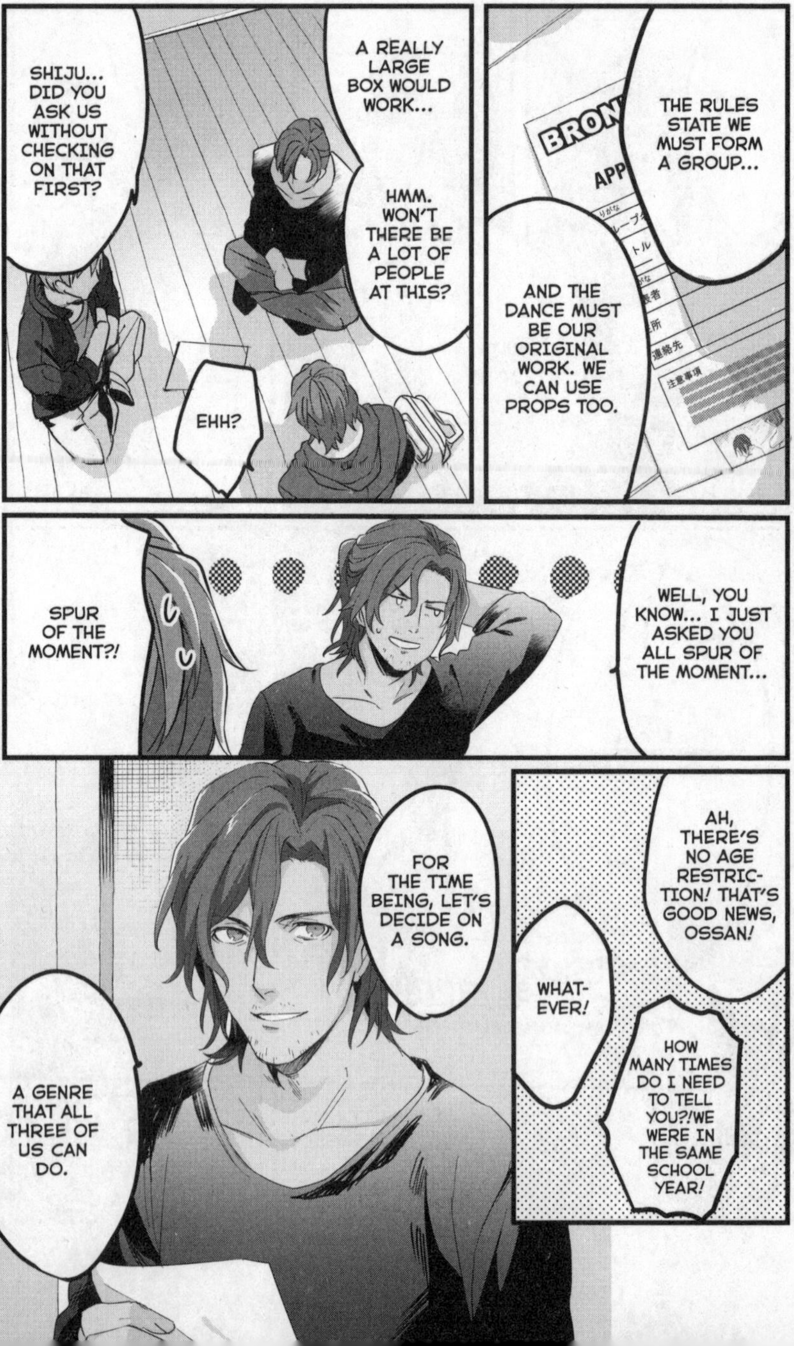
THE RULES STATE WE MUST FORM A GROUP...
AND THE DANCE MUST BE OUR ORIGINAL WORK. WE CAN USE PROPS TOO.
A REALLY LARGE BOX WOULD WORK...
HMM. WON'T THERE BE A LOT OF PEOPLE AT THIS?
EHH?
SHIJU... DID YOU ASK US WITHOUT CHECKING ON THAT FIRST?
WELL, YOU KNOW... I JUST ASKED YOU ALL SPUR OF THE MOMENT...
SPUR OF THE MOMENT?!
AH, THERE'S NO AGE RESTRIC-TION! THAT'S GOOD NEWS, OSSAN!
WHAT-EVER!
HOW MANY TIMES DO I NEED TO TELL YOU?! WE WERE IN THE SAME SCHOOL YEAR!
FOR THE TIME BEING, LET'S DECIDE ON A SONG.
A GENRE THAT ALL THREE OF US CAN DO.

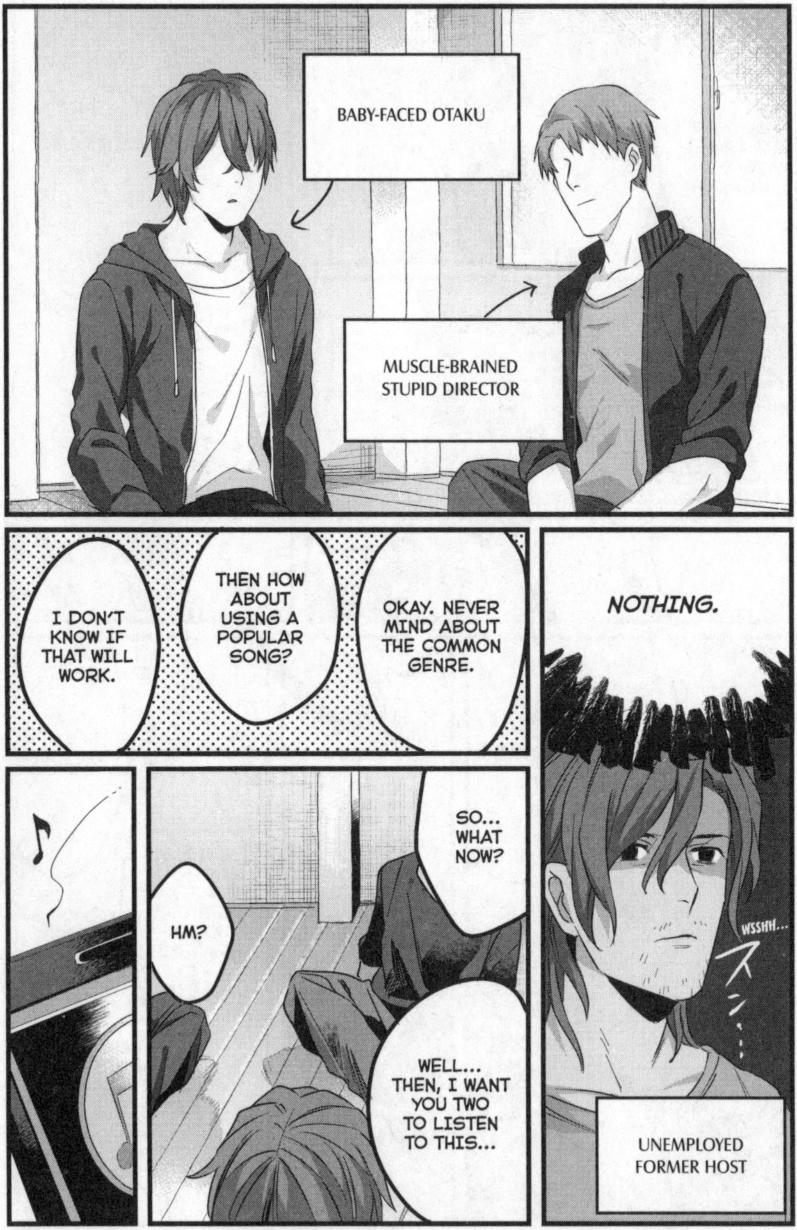
BABY-FACED OTAKU
MUSCLE-BRAINED STUPID DIRECTOR
NOTHING.
WSSHH...
UNEMPLOYED FORMER HOST
OKAY. NEVER MIND ABOUT THE COMMON GENRE.
THEN HOW ABOUT USING A POPULAR SONG?
I DON'T KNOW IF THAT WILL WORK.
SO... WHAT NOW?
HM?
WELL... THEN, I WANT YOU TWO TO LISTEN TO THIS...

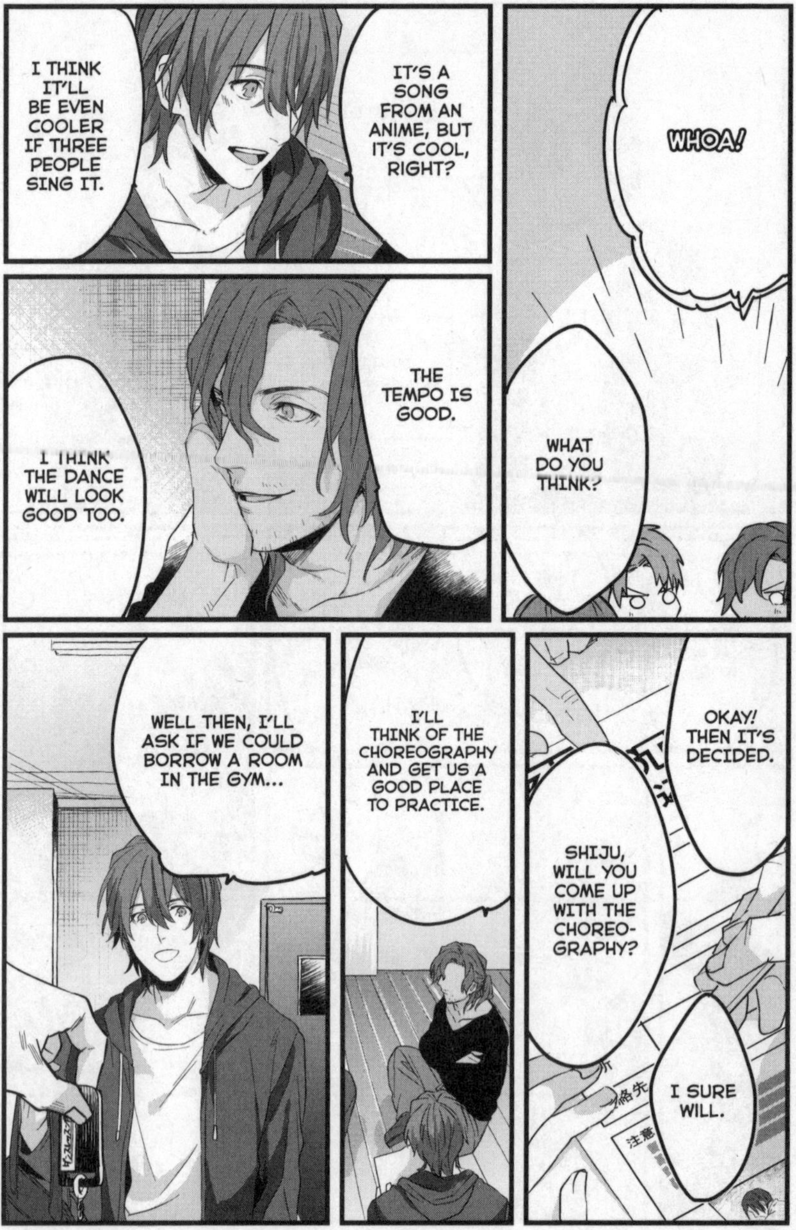
WHOA!
WHAT DO YOU THINK?
IT'S A SONG FROM AN ANIME, BUT IT'S COOL, RIGHT?
I THINK IT'LL BE EVEN COOLER IF THREE PEOPLE SING IT.
THE TEMPO IS GOOD.
I THINK THE DANCE WILL LOOK GOOD TOO.
OKAY! THEN IT'S DECIDED.
SHIJU, WILL YOU COME UP WITH THE CHOREO-GRAPHY?
I SURE WILL.
I'LL THINK OF THE CHOREOGRAPHY AND GET US A GOOD PLACE TO PRACTICE.
WELL THEN, I'LL ASK IF WE COULD BORROW A ROOM IN THE GYM...

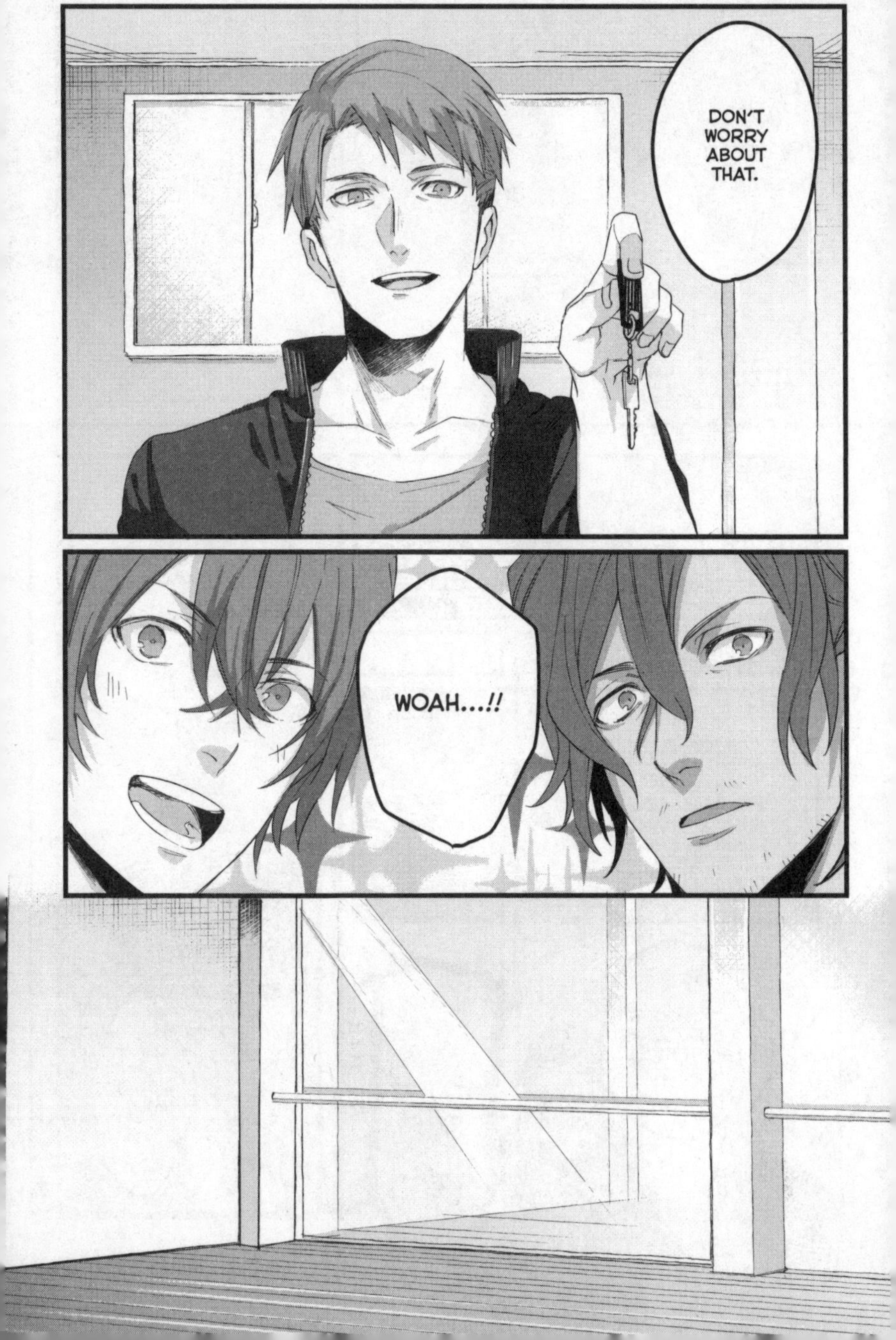
DON'T WORRY ABOUT THAT.
WOAH...!!

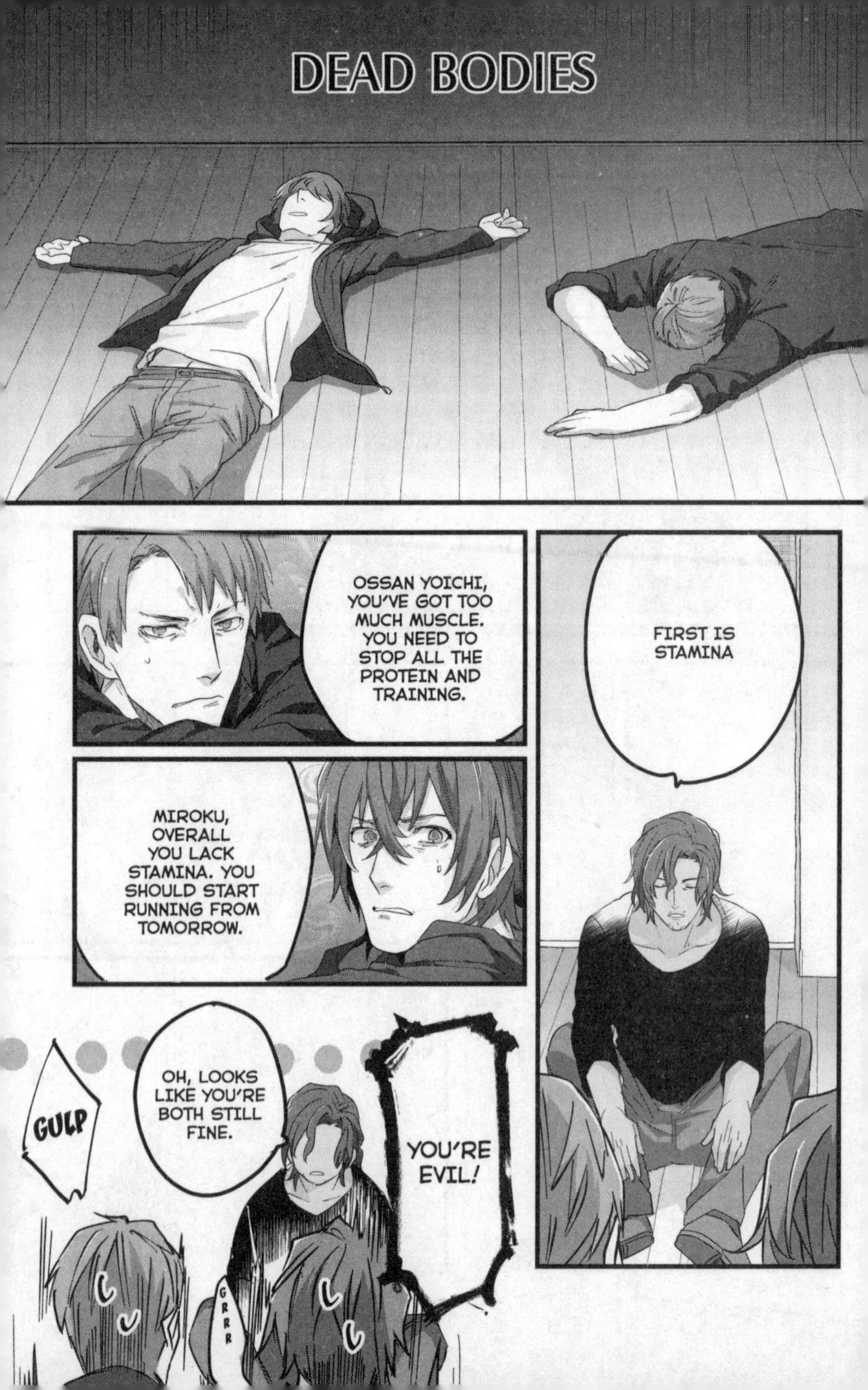
DEAD BODIES
FIRST IS STAMINA
OSSAN YOICHI, YOU'VE GOT TOO MUCH MUSCLE. YOU NEED TO STOP ALL THE PROTEIN AND TRAINING.
MIROKU, OVERALL YOU LACK STAMINA. YOU SHOULD START RUNNING FROM TOMORROW.
YOU'RE EVIL!
OH, LOOKS LIKE YOU'RE BOTH STILL FINE.
GULP
GRRR

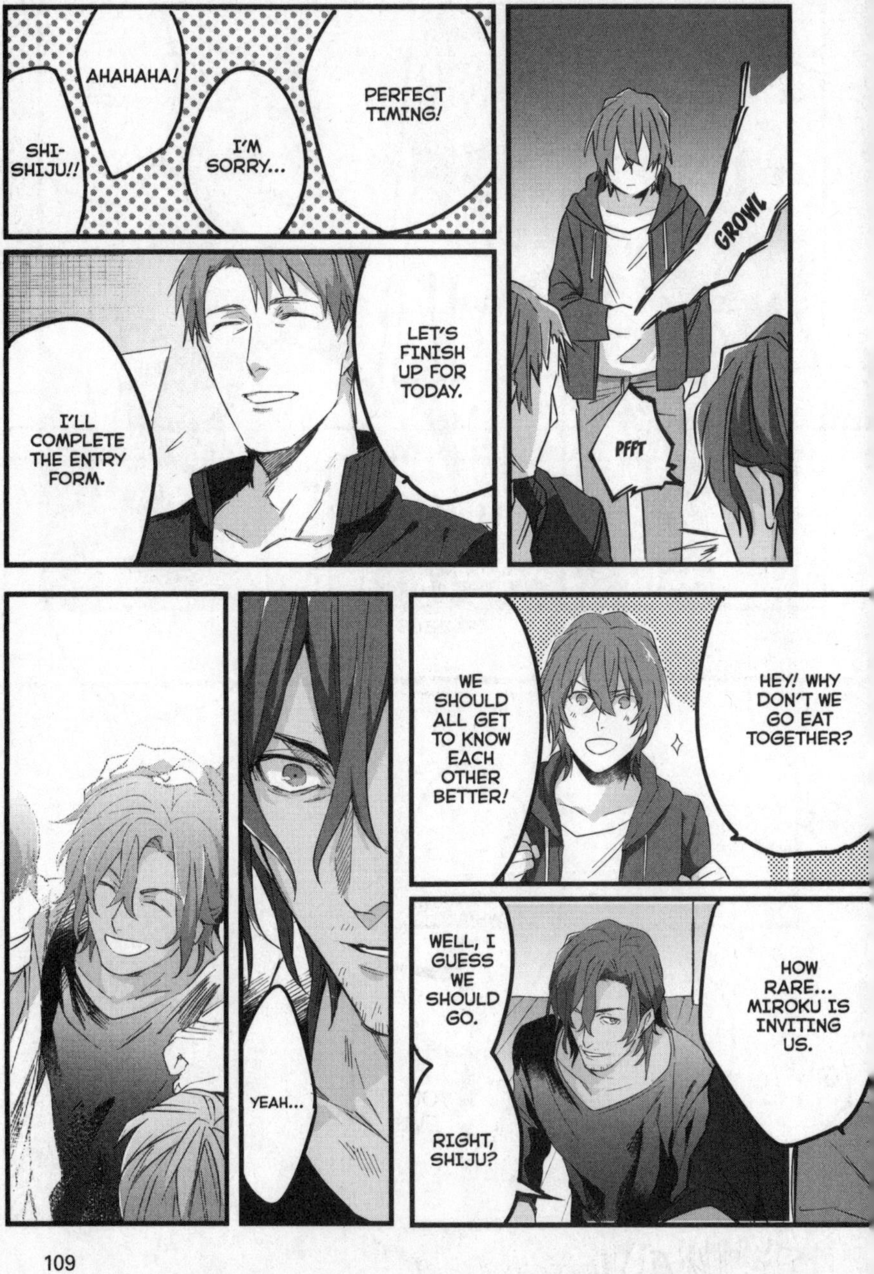
GROWL
PFFT
PERFECT TIMING!
I'M SORRY...
AHAHAHA!
SHI-SHIJU!!
LET'S FINISH UP FOR TODAY.
I'LL COMPLETE THE ENTRY FORM.
HEY! WHY DON'T WE GO EAT TOGETHER?
WE SHOULD ALL GET TO KNOW EACH OTHER BETTER!
HOW RARE... MIROKU IS INVITING US.
WELL, I GUESS WE SHOULD GO.
RIGHT, SHIJU?
YEAH...

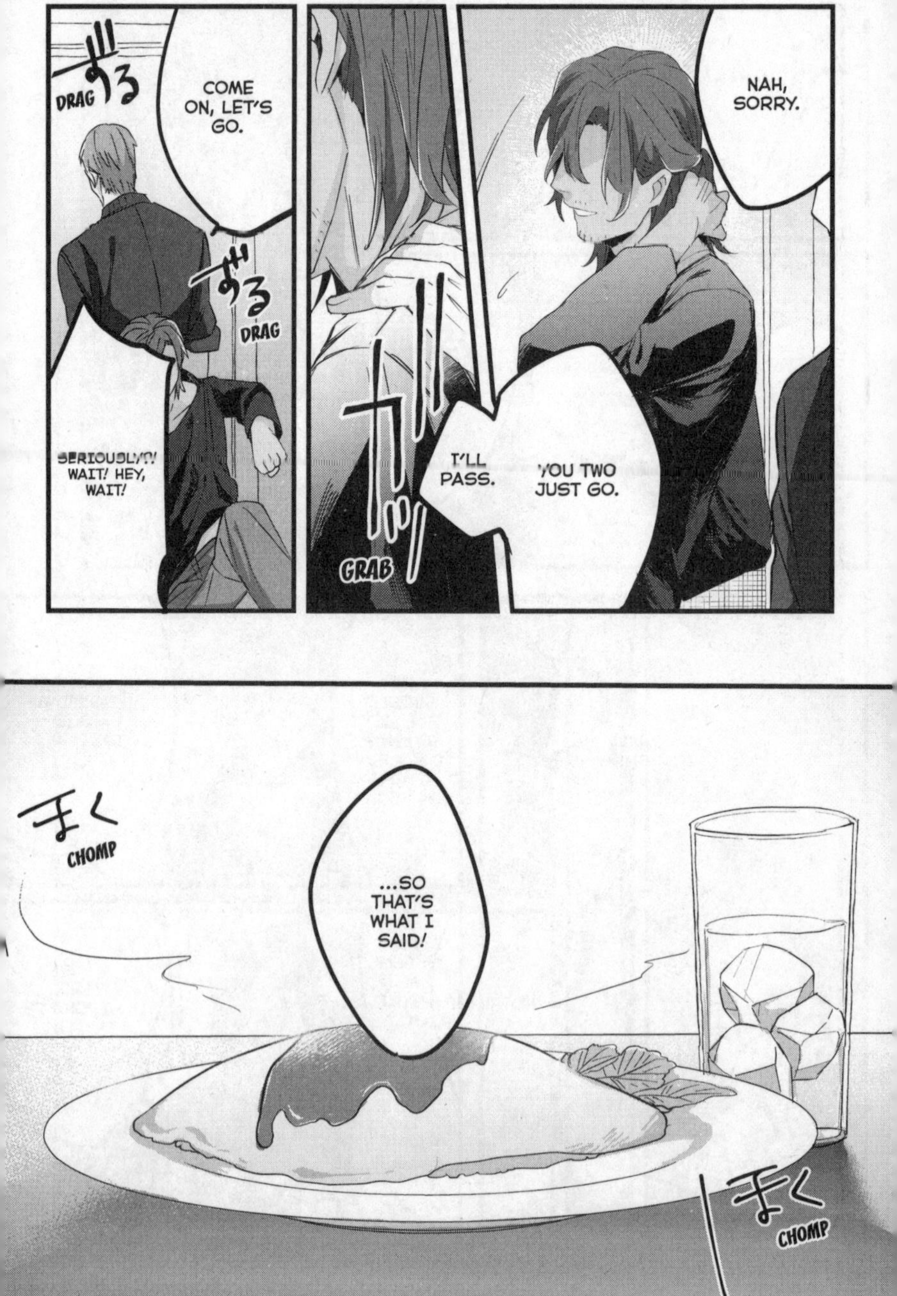
NAH, SORRY.
YOU TWO JUST GO.
I'LL PASS.
GRAB
COME ON, LET'S GO.
ずる
DRAG
ずる
DRAG
SERIOUSLY?! WAIT! HEY, WAIT!
もく
CHOMP
...SO THAT'S WHAT I SAID!
もく
CHOMP

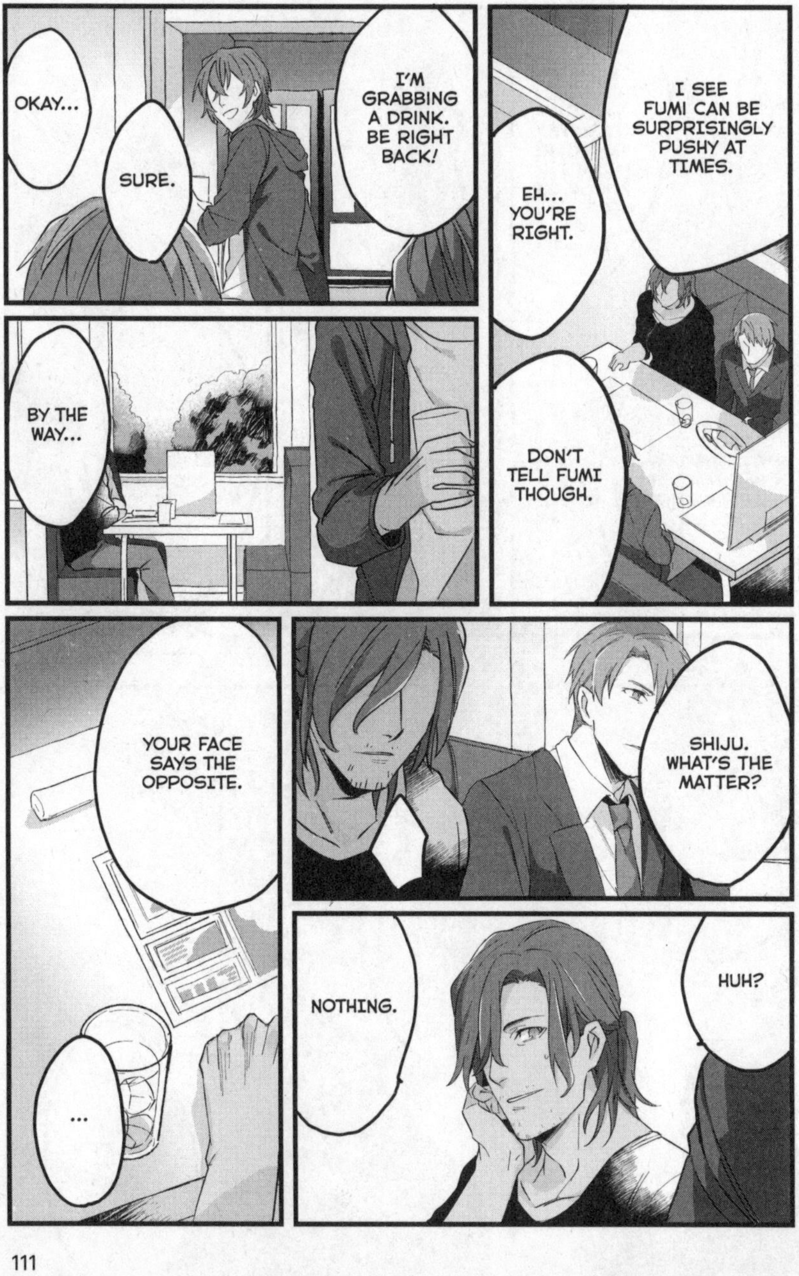
I SEE FUMI CAN BE SURPRISINGLY PUSHY AT TIMES.
EH... YOU'RE RIGHT.
DON'T TELL FUMI THOUGH.
I'M GRABBING A DRINK. BE RIGHT BACK!
SURE.
OKAY...
BY THE WAY...
SHIJU. WHAT'S THE MATTER?
HUH?
NOTHING.
YOUR FACE SAYS THE OPPOSITE.
...

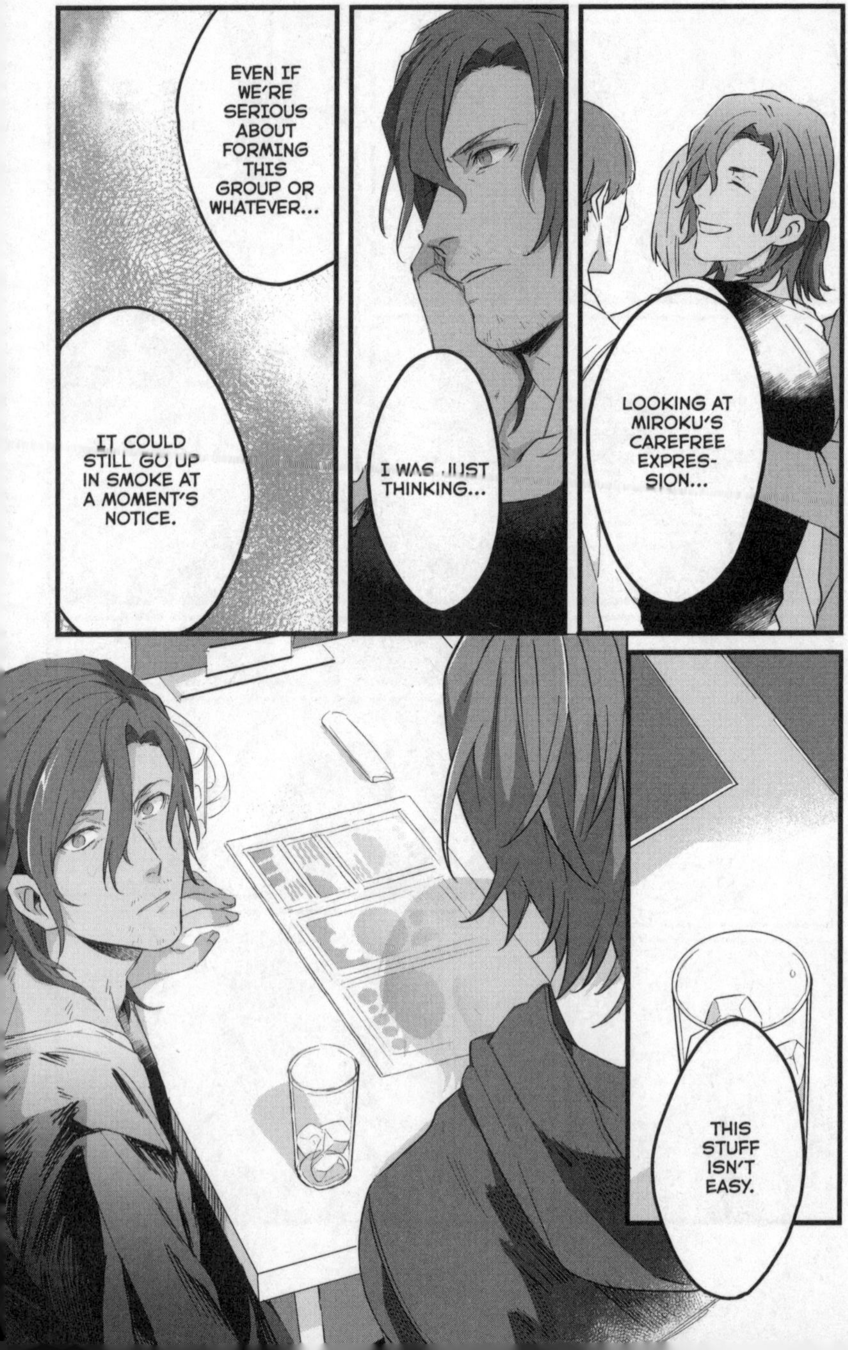
LOOKING AT MIROKU'S CAREFREE EXPRES- SION...
I WAS JUST THINKING...
EVEN IF WE'RE SERIOUS ABOUT FORMING THIS GROUP OR WHATEVER...
IT COULD STILL GO UP IN SMOKE AT A MOMENT'S NOTICE.
THIS STUFF ISN'T EASY.

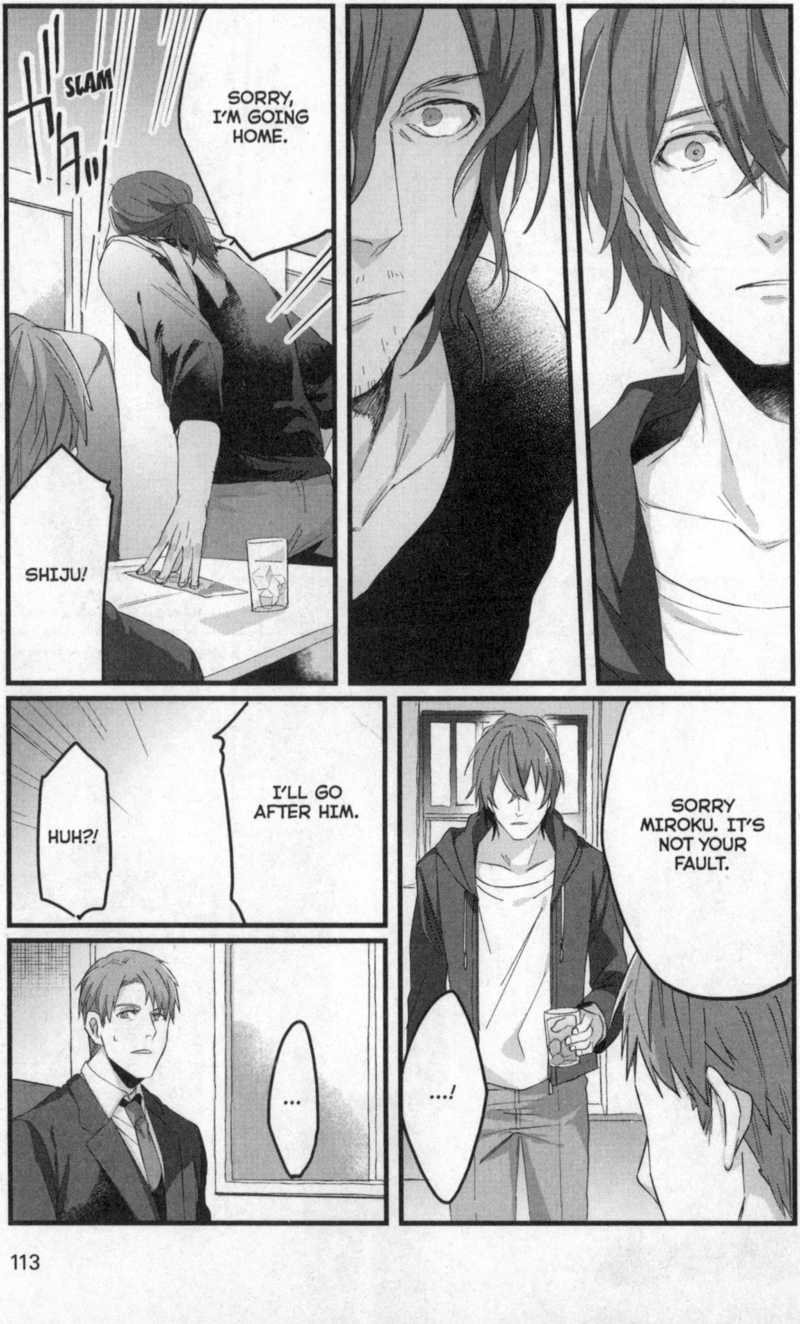
SLAM
SORRY, I'M GOING HOME.
SHIJU!
SORRY MIROKU. IT'S NOT YOUR FAULT.
...!
I'LL GO AFTER HIM.
HUH?!
...

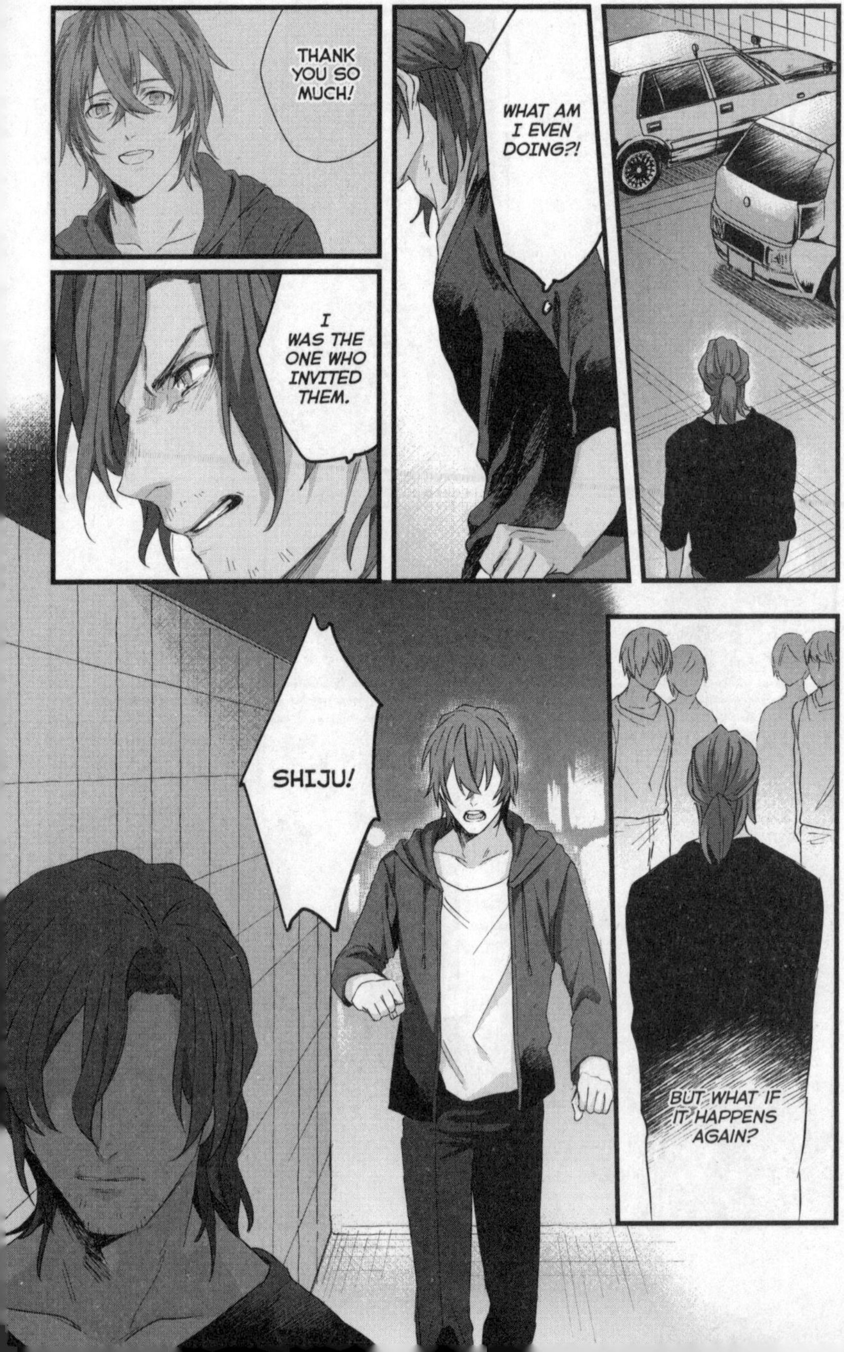
WHAT AM I EVEN DOING?!
THANK YOU SO MUCH!
I WAS THE ONE WHO INVITED THEM.
BUT WHAT IF IT HAPPENS AGAIN?
SHIJU!

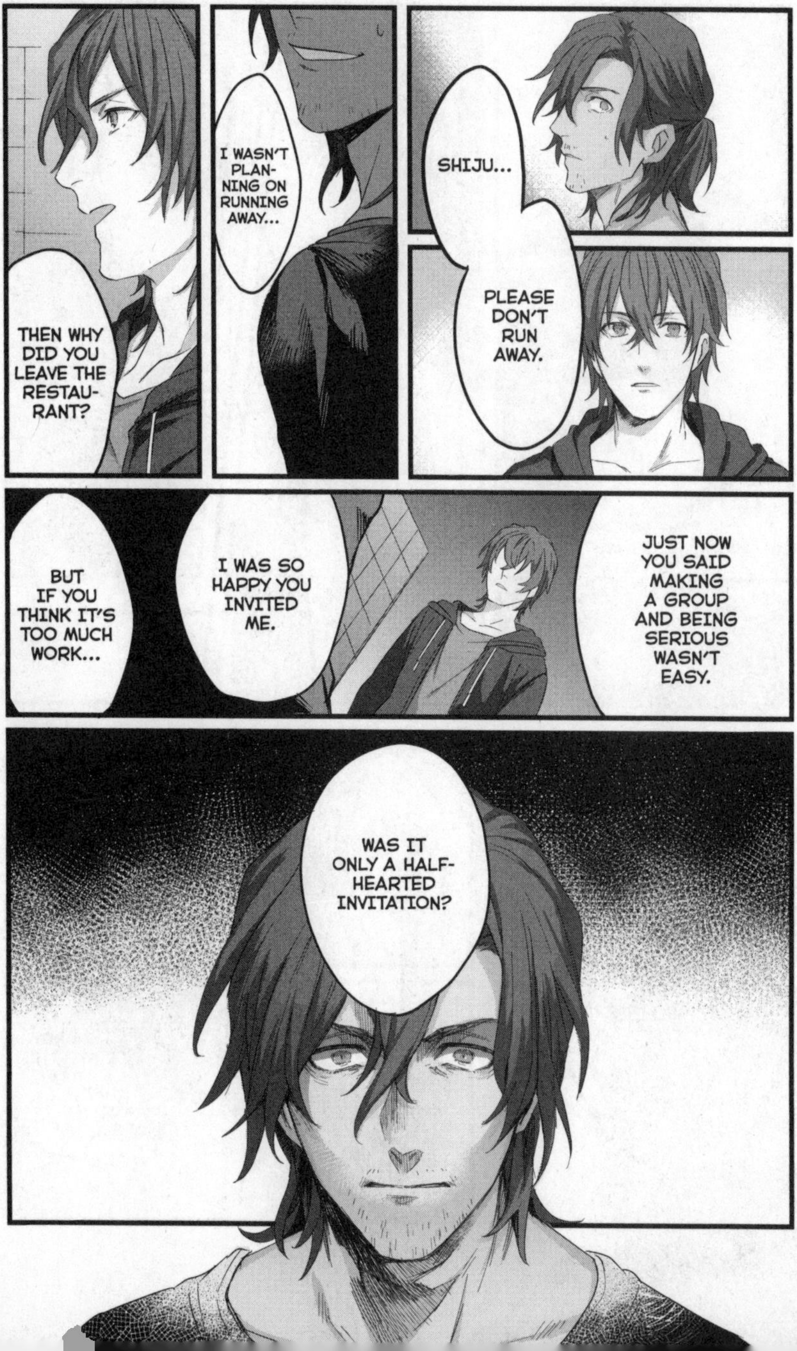
SHIJU...
PLEASE DON'T RUN AWAY.
I WASN'T PLAN-NING ON RUNNING AWAY...
THEN WHY DID YOU LEAVE THE RESTAU-RANT?
JUST NOW YOU SAID MAKING A GROUP AND BEING SERIOUS WASN'T EASY.
I WAS SO HAPPY YOU INVITED ME.
BUT IF YOU THINK IT'S TOO MUCH WORK...
WAS IT ONLY A HALF-HEARTED INVITATION?

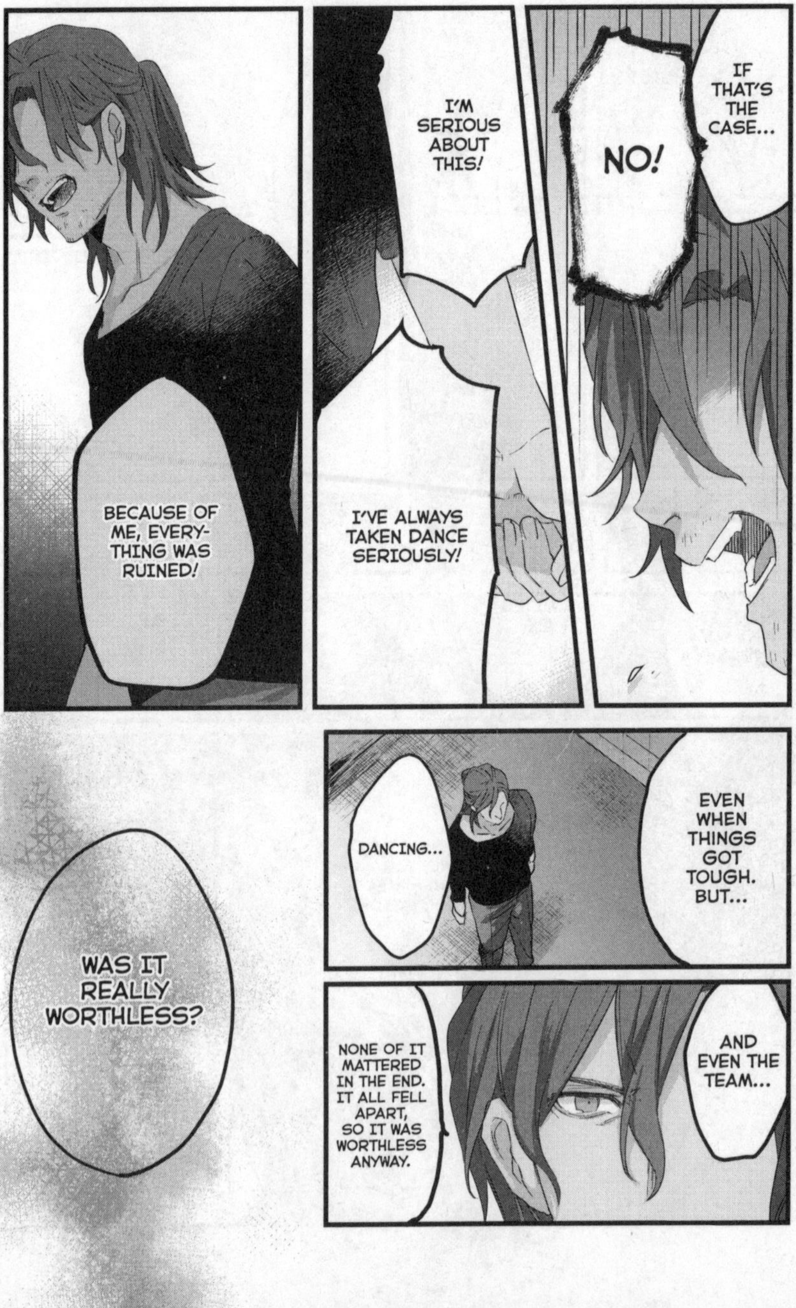
IF THAT'S THE CASE...
NO!
I'M SERIOUS ABOUT THIS!
I'VE ALWAYS TAKEN DANCE SERIOUSLY!
BECAUSE OF ME, EVERYTHING WAS RUINED!
EVEN WHEN THINGS GOT TOUGH. BUT...
DANCING...
AND EVEN THE TEAM...
NONE OF IT MATTERED IN THE END. IT ALL FELL APART, SO IT WAS WORTHLESS ANYWAY.
WAS IT REALLY WORTHLESS?

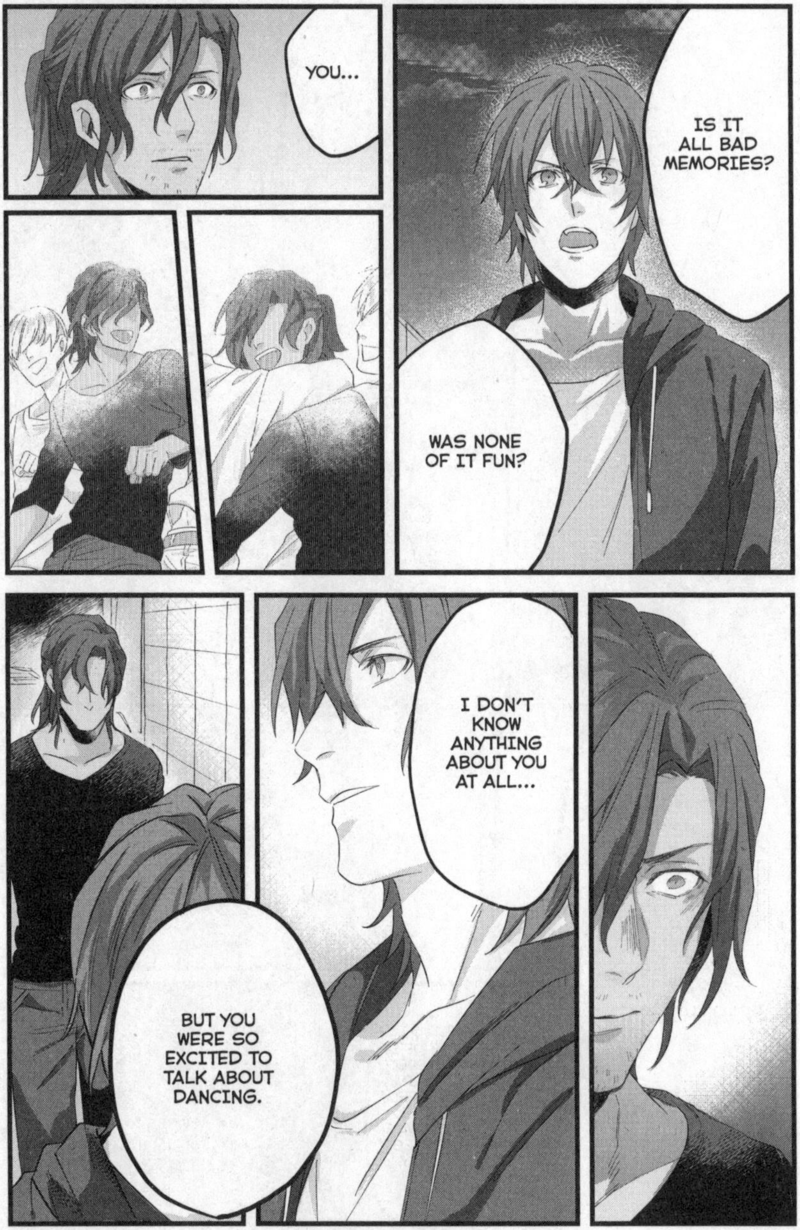
IS IT ALL BAD MEMORIES?
WAS NONE OF IT FUN?
YOU...
I DON'T KNOW ANYTHING ABOUT YOU AT ALL...
BUT YOU WERE SO EXCITED TO TALK ABOUT DANCING.

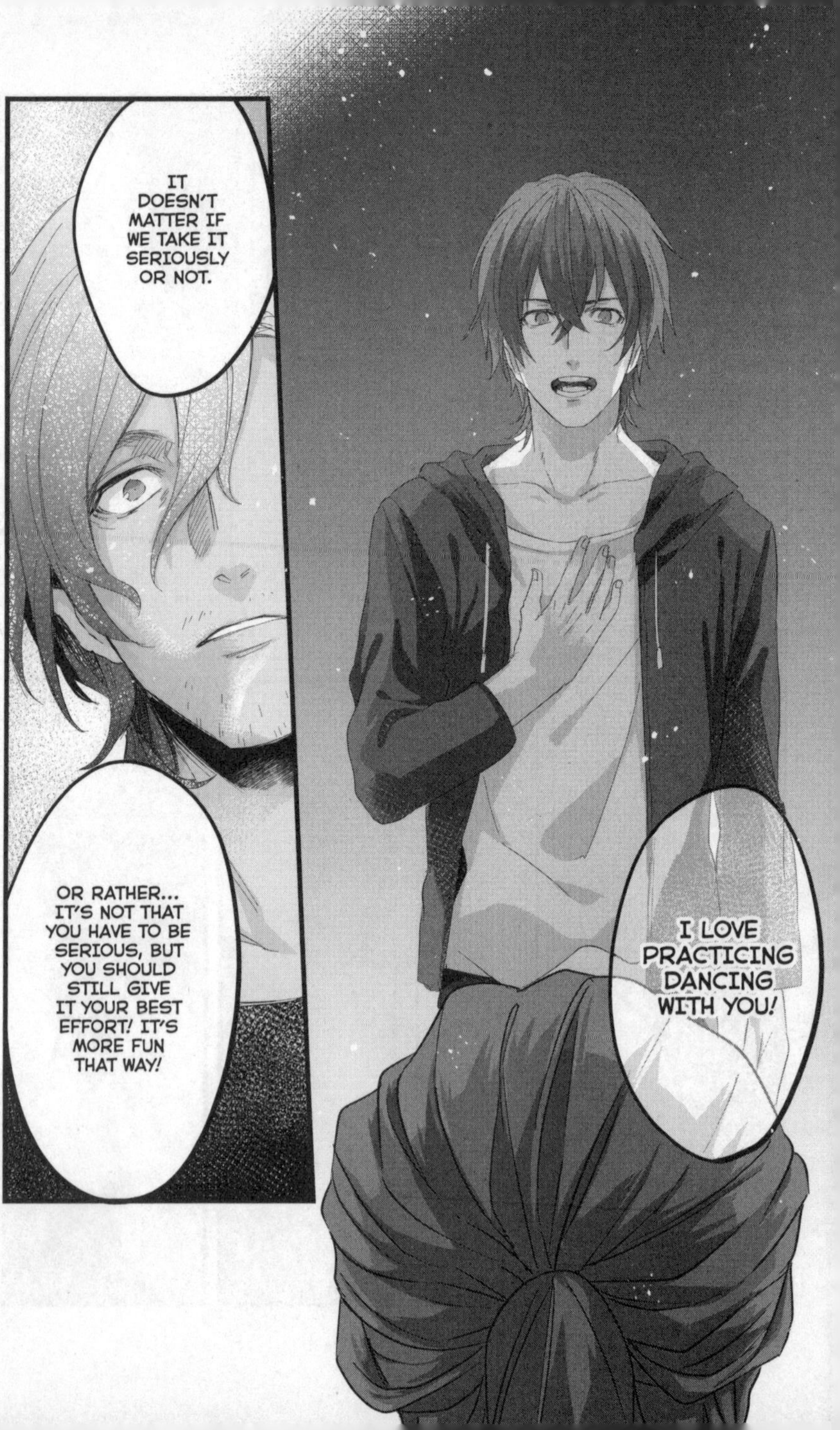
IT DOESN'T MATTER IF WE TAKE IT SERIOUSLY OR NOT.
OR RATHER... IT'S NOT THAT YOU HAVE TO BE SERIOUS, BUT YOU SHOULD STILL GIVE IT YOUR BEST EFFORT! IT'S MORE FUN THAT WAY!
I LOVE PRACTICING DANCING WITH YOU!

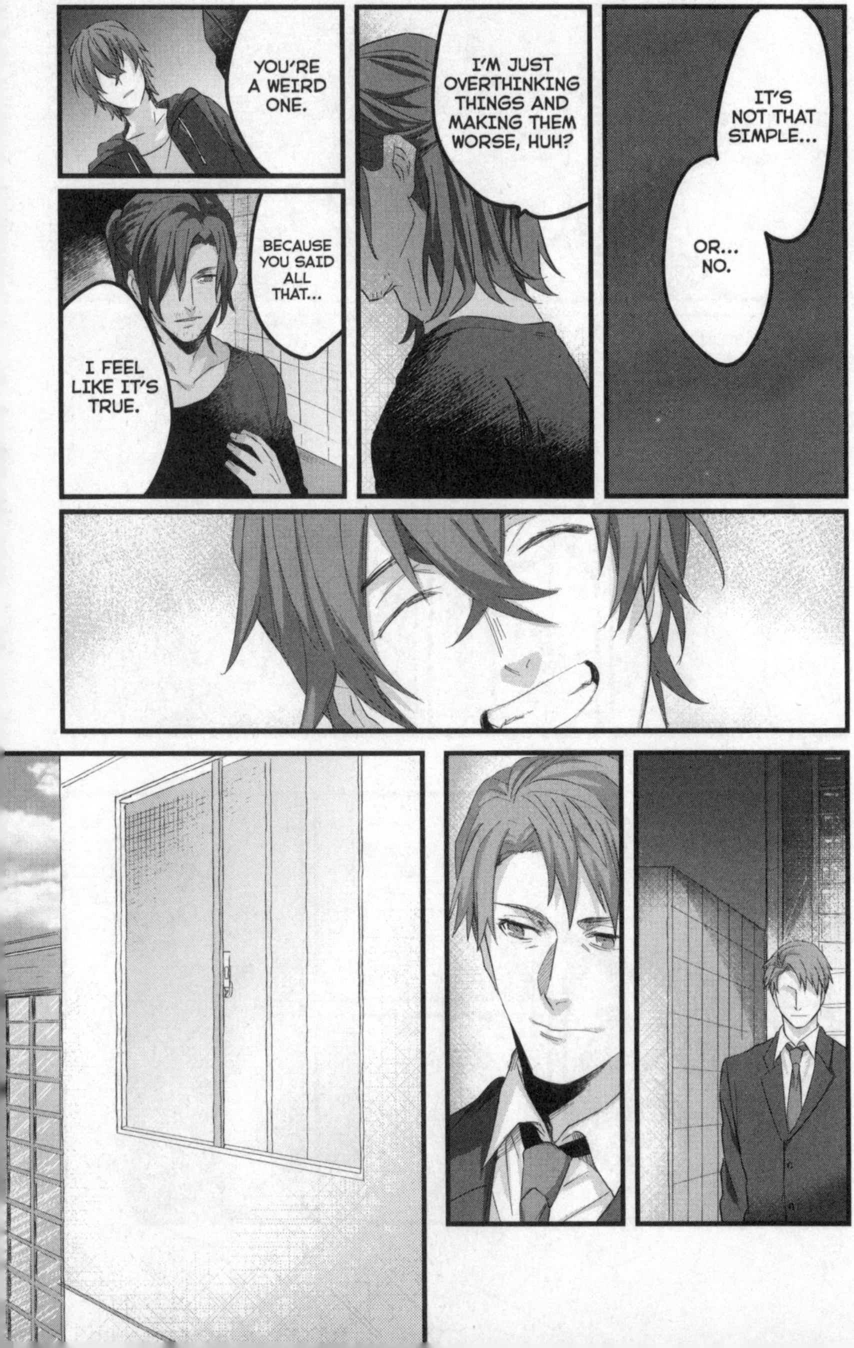
IT'S NOT THAT SIMPLE...
OR... NO.
I'M JUST OVERTHINKING THINGS AND MAKING THEM WORSE, HUH?
YOU'RE A WEIRD ONE.
BECAUSE YOU SAID ALL THAT...
I FEEL LIKE IT'S TRUE.

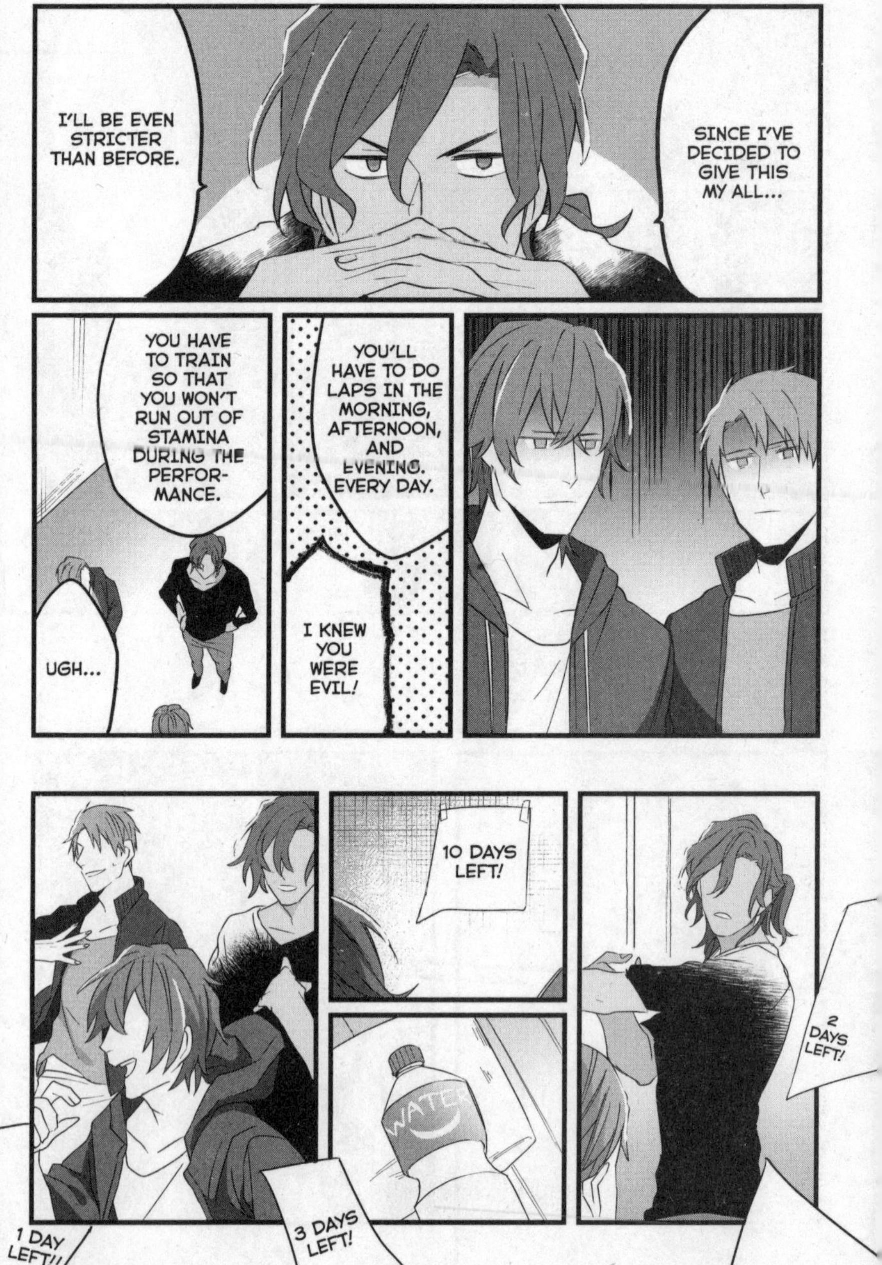
SINCE I'VE DECIDED TO GIVE THIS MY ALL...
I'LL BE EVEN STRICTER THAN BEFORE.
YOU'LL HAVE TO DO LAPS IN THE MORNING, AFTERNOON, AND EVENING. EVERY DAY.
I KNEW YOU WERE EVIL!
YOU HAVE TO TRAIN SO THAT YOU WON'T RUN OUT OF STAMINA DURING THE PERFORMANCE.
UGH...
2 DAYS LEFT!
10 DAYS LEFT!
WATER
3 DAYS LEFT!
1 DAY LEFT!!

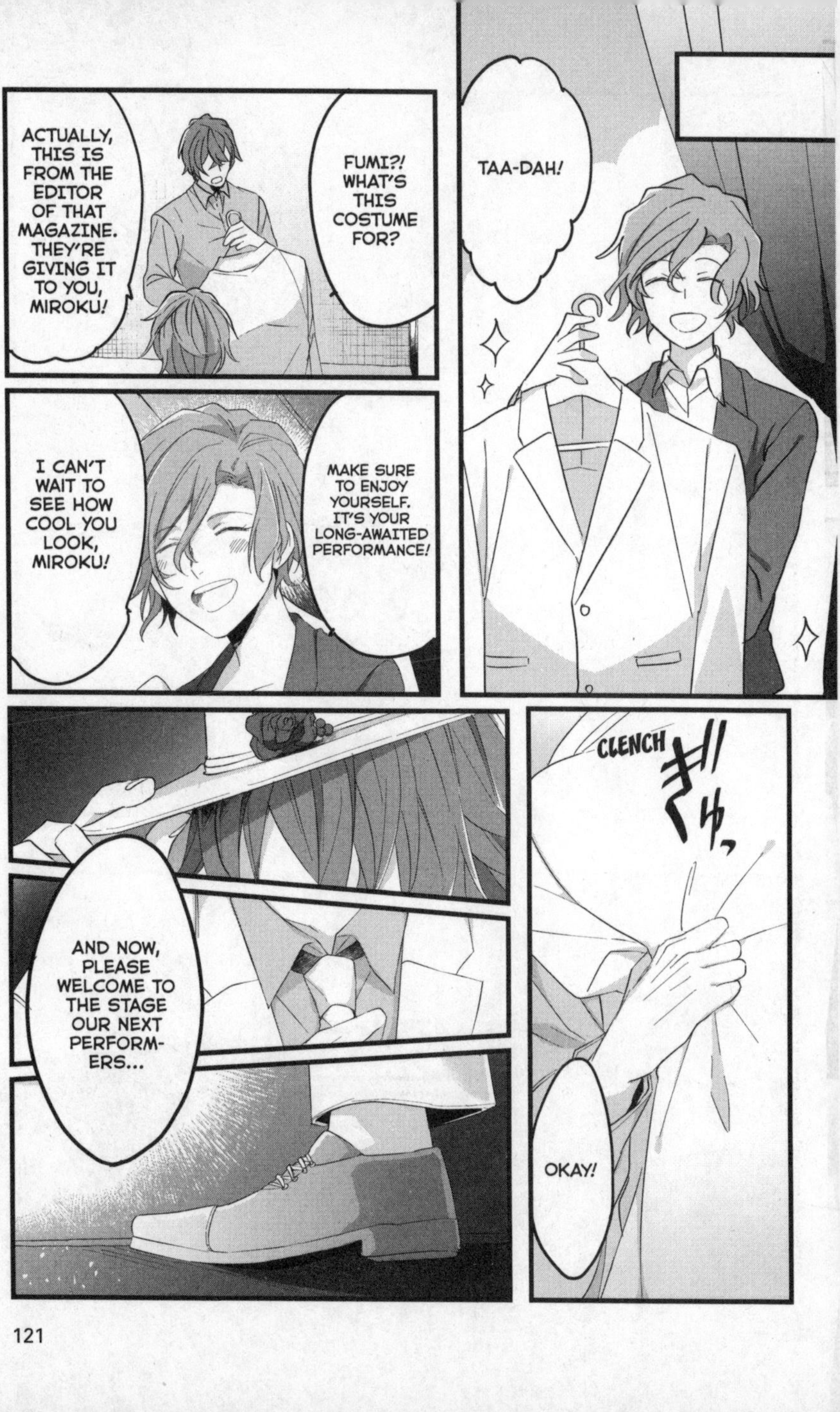
TAA-DAH!
FUMI?! WHAT'S THIS COSTUME FOR?
ACTUALLY, THIS IS FROM THE EDITOR OF THAT MAGAZINE. THEY'RE GIVING IT TO YOU, MIROKU!
MAKE SURE TO ENJOY YOURSELF. IT'S YOUR LONG-AWAITED PERFORMANCE!
I CAN'T WAIT TO SEE HOW COOL YOU LOOK, MIROKU!
CLENCH
ぎゅっ
OKAY!
AND NOW, PLEASE WELCOME TO THE STAGE OUR NEXT PERFORM-ERS...

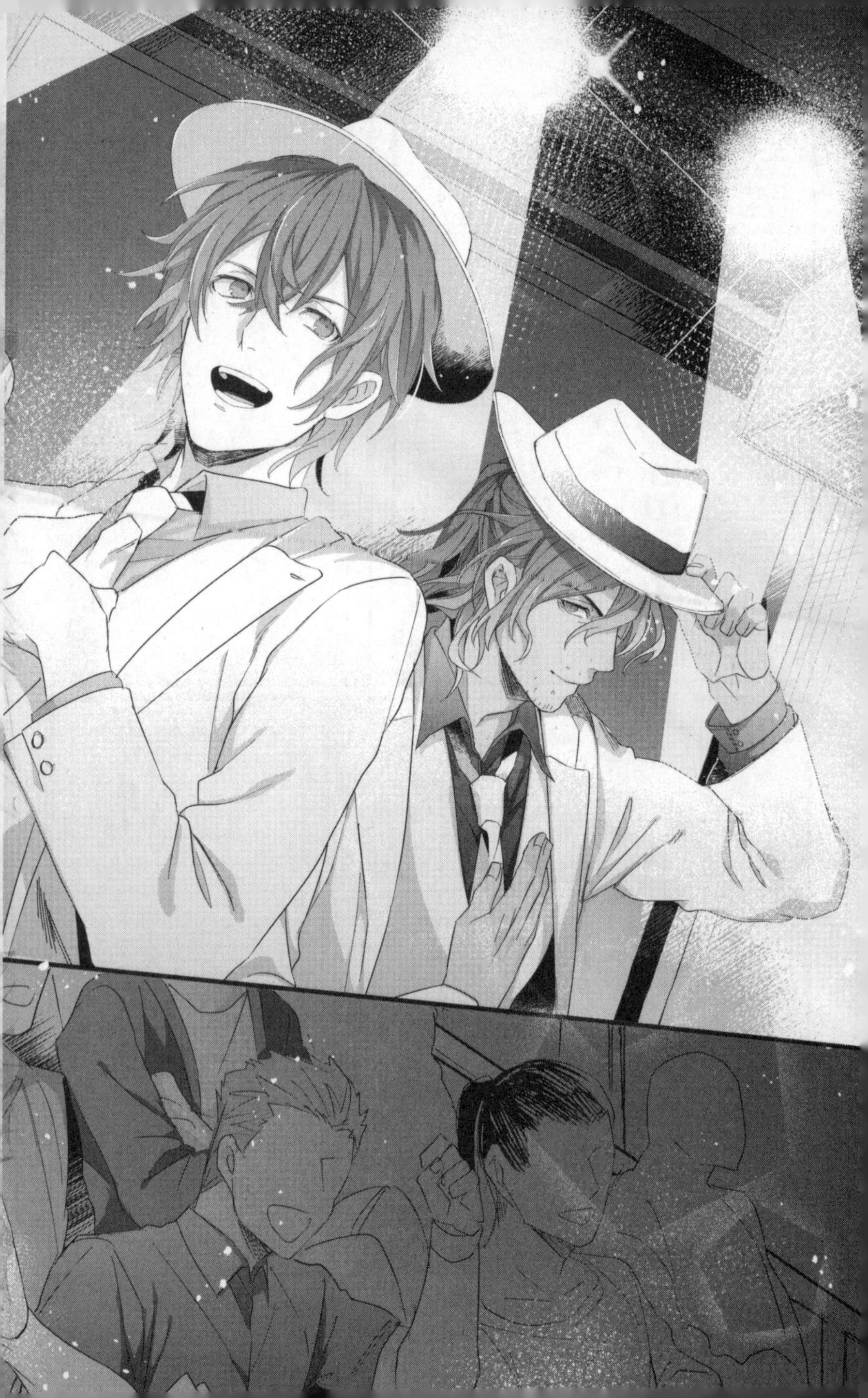

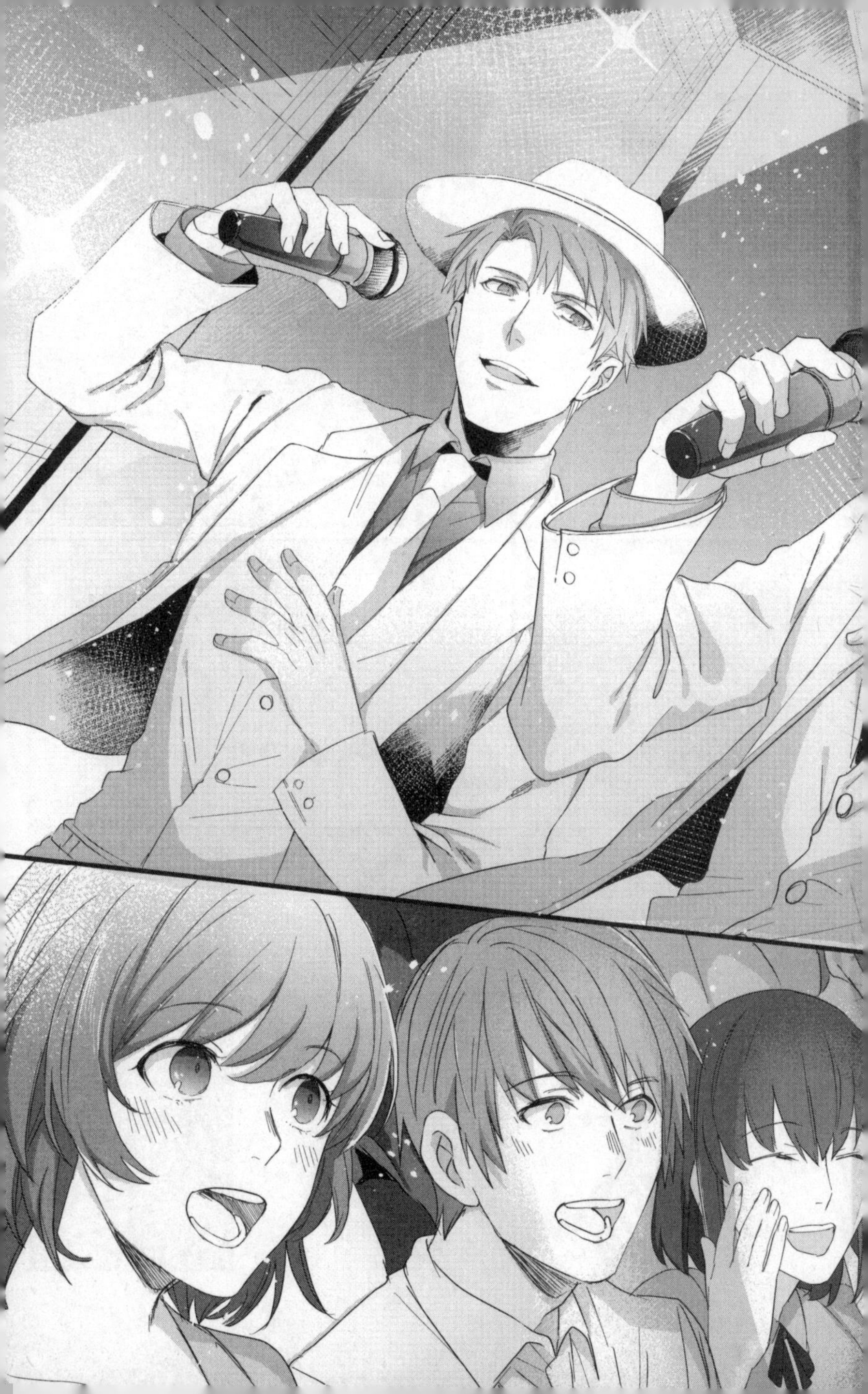

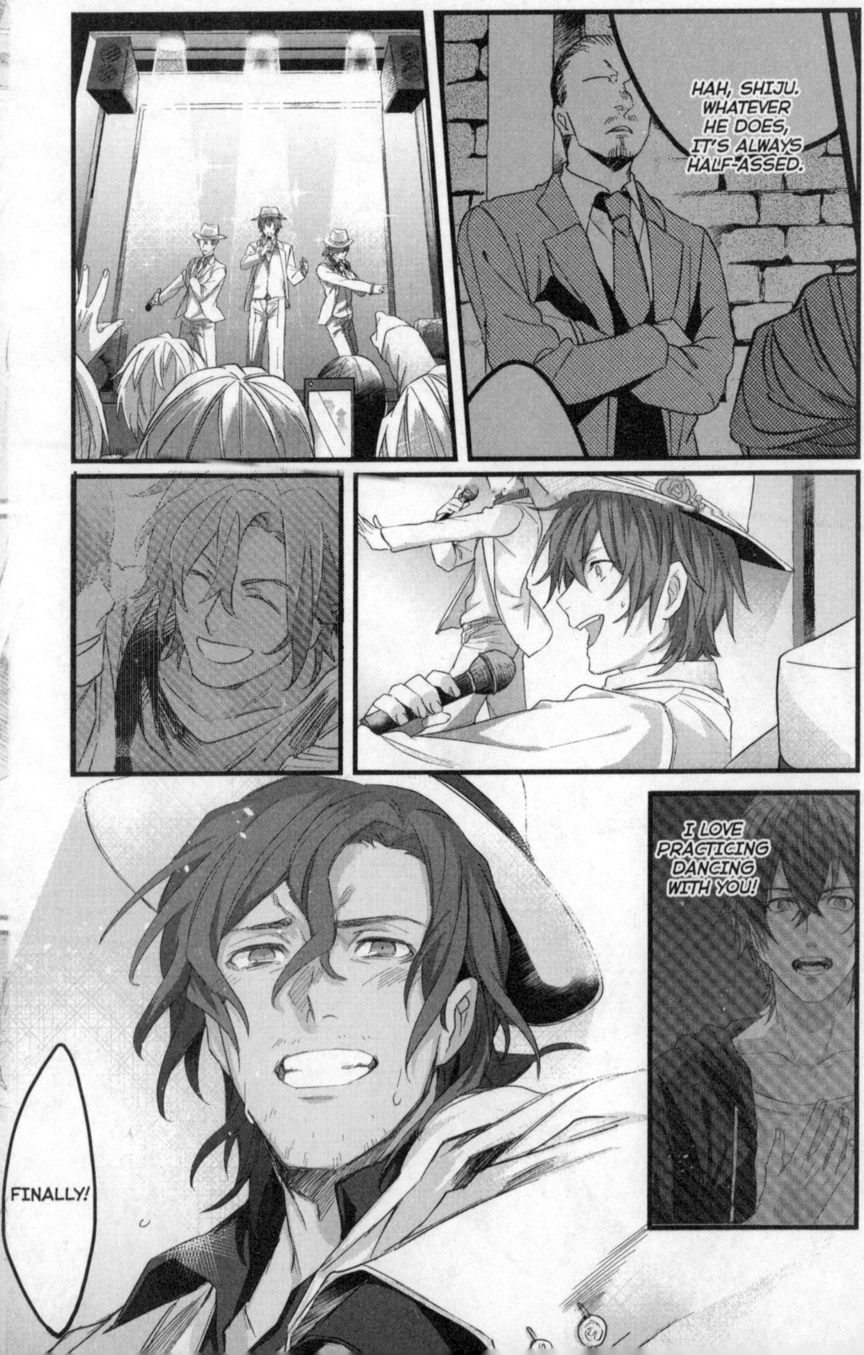
HAH, SHIJU. WHATEVER HE DOES, IT'S ALWAYS HALF-ASSED.
I LOVE PRACTICING DANCING WITH YOU!
FINALLY!

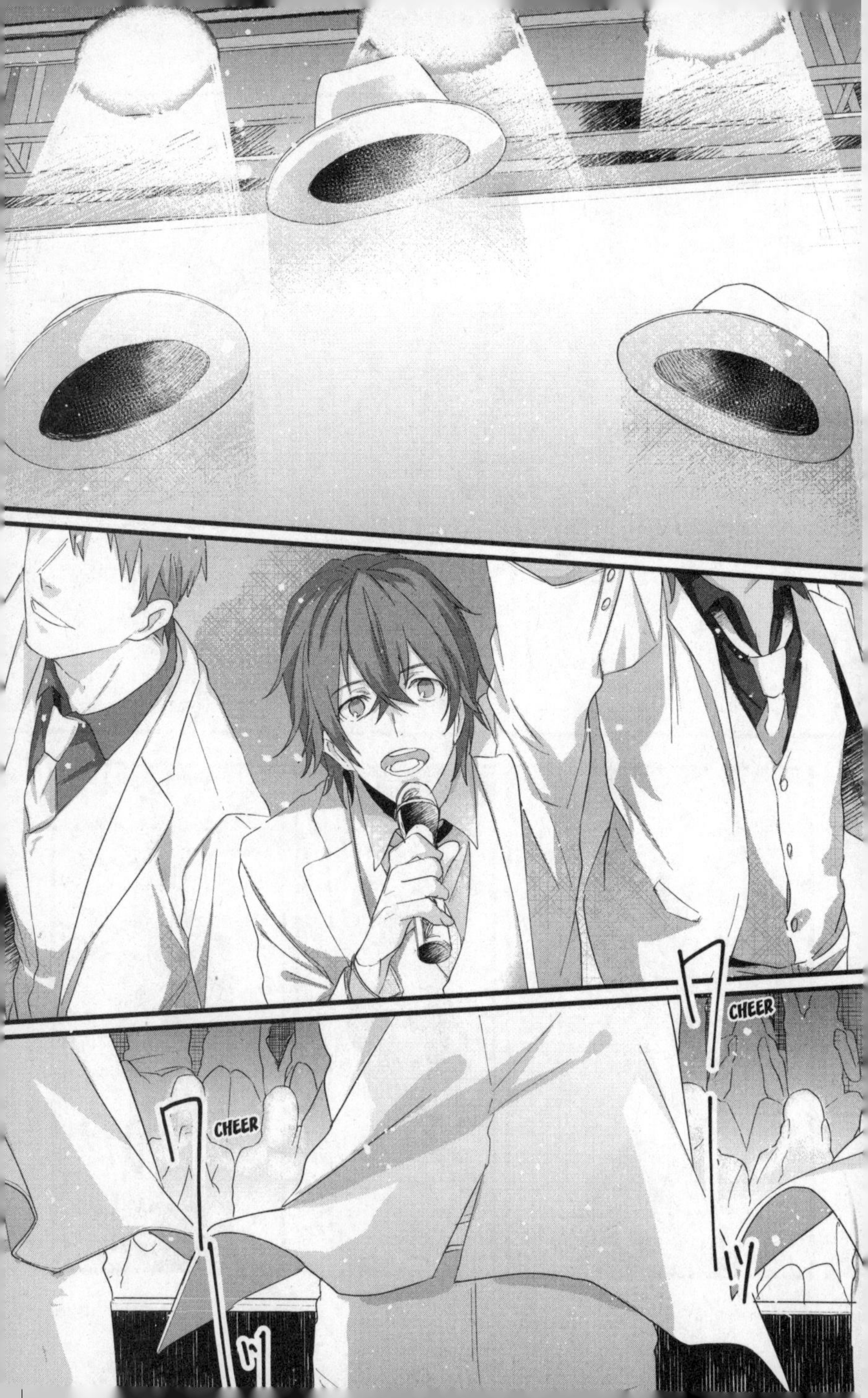
CHEER
CHEER

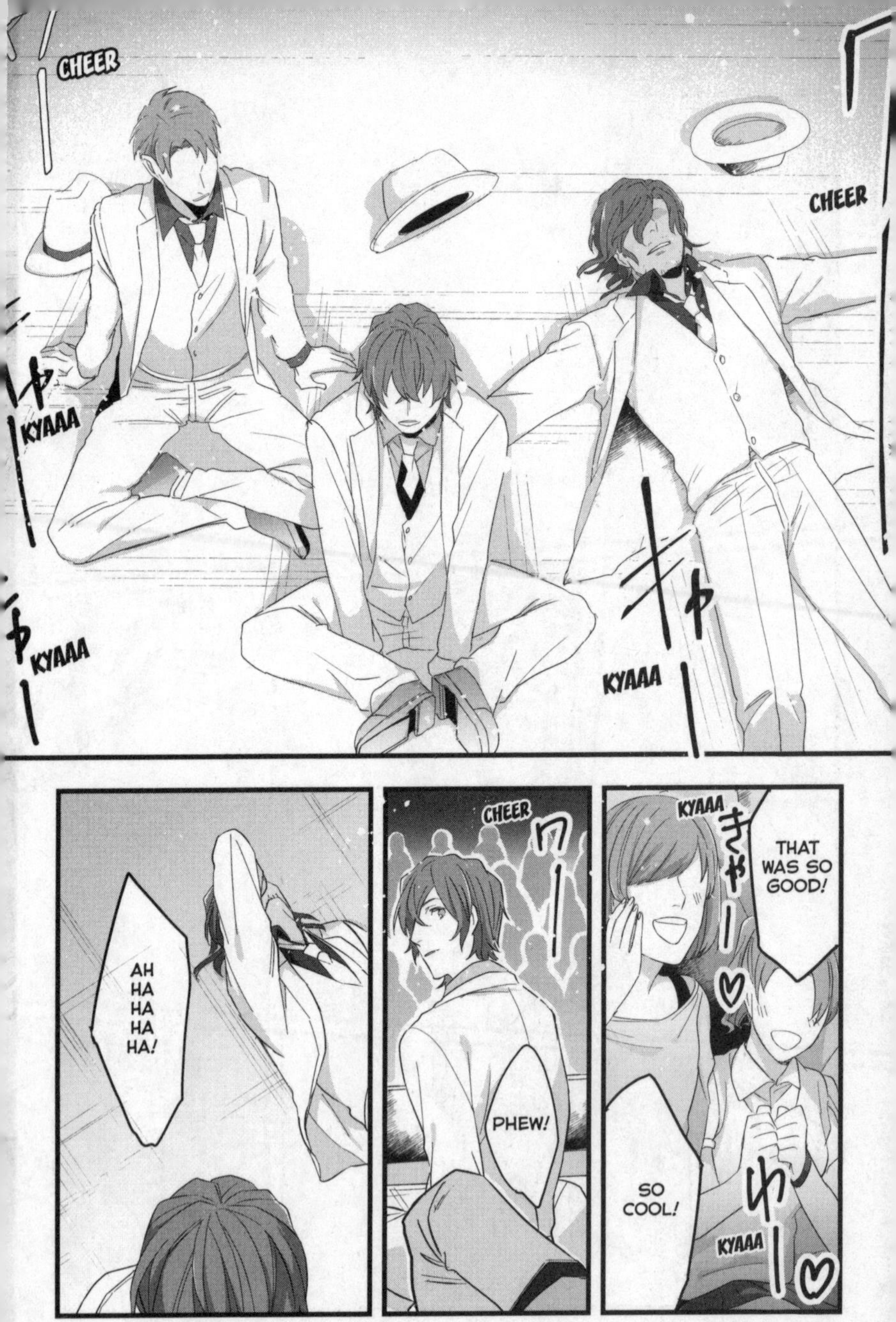
CHEER
KYAAA
CHEER
KYAAA
KYAAA
KYAAA
きゃー
THAT WAS SO GOOD!
SO COOL!
KYAAA
CHEER
ワー
PHEW!
AH HA HA HA HA!

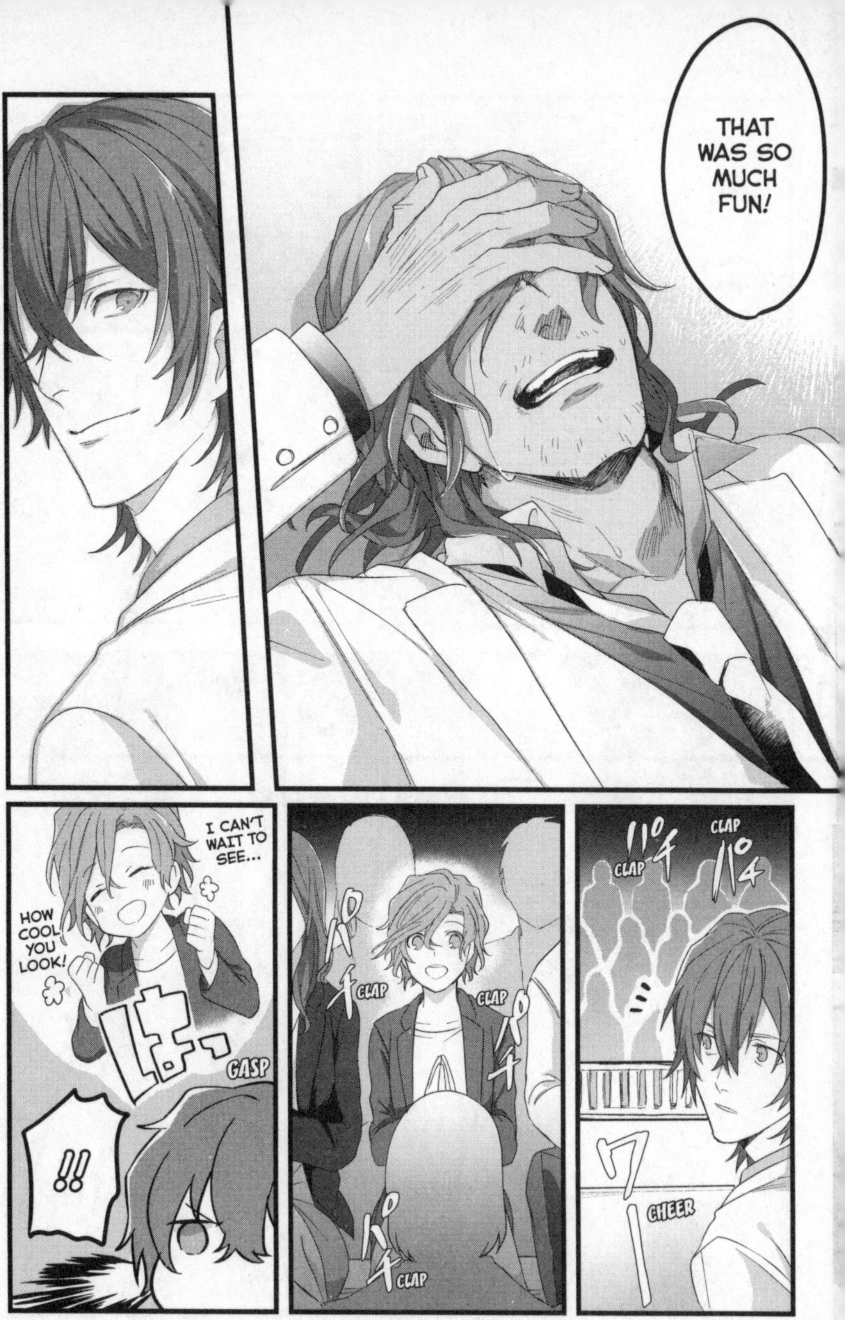
THAT WAS SO MUCH FUN!
CLAP
CLAP
パチ
パチ
...
ワー
CHEER
パチ
CLAP
CLAP
パチ
パチ
CLAP
I CAN'T WAIT TO SEE...
HOW COOL YOU LOOK!
はっ
GASP
!!

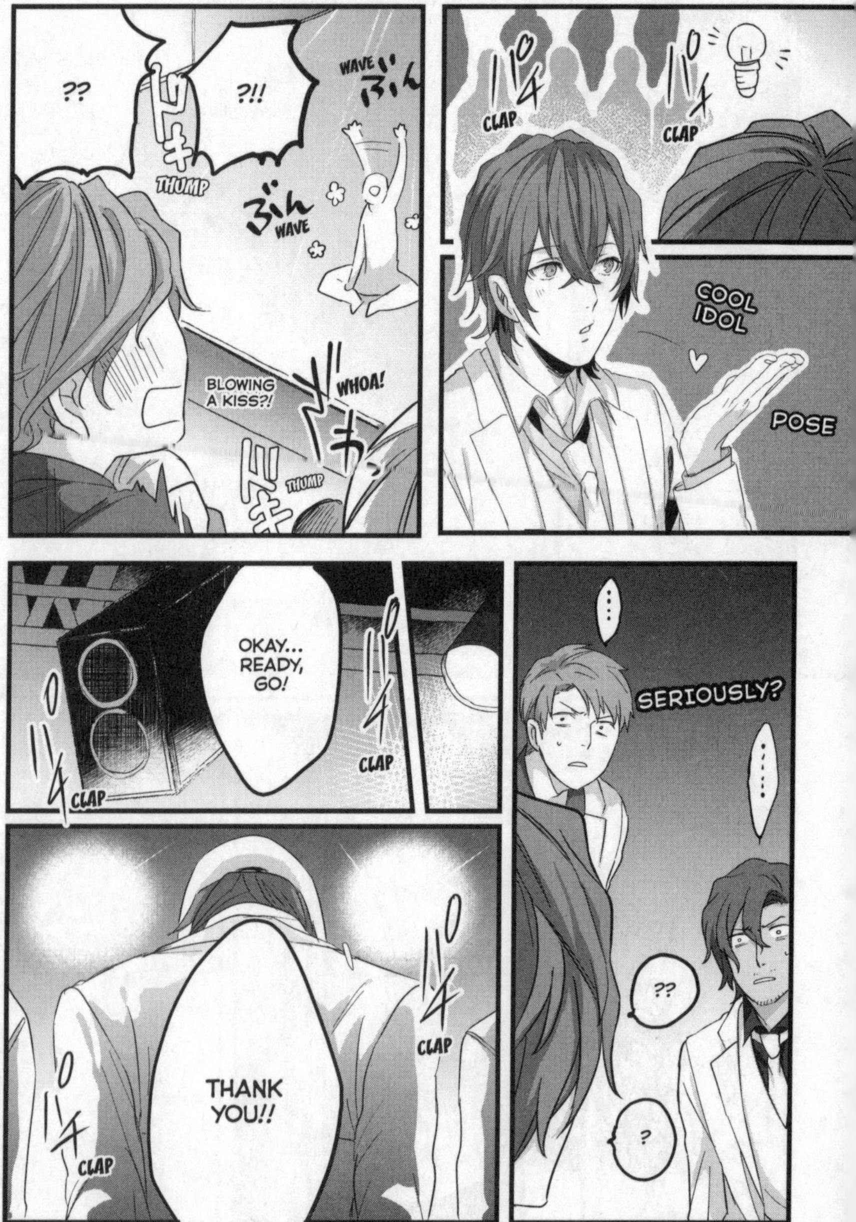
CLAP
CLAP
COOL IDOL
POSE
??
?!!
WAVE
THUMP
WAVE
BLOWING A KISS?!
WHOA!
THUMP
....
SERIOUSLY?
......
??
?
OKAY... READY, GO!
CLAP
CLAP
THANK YOU!!
CLAP
CLAP

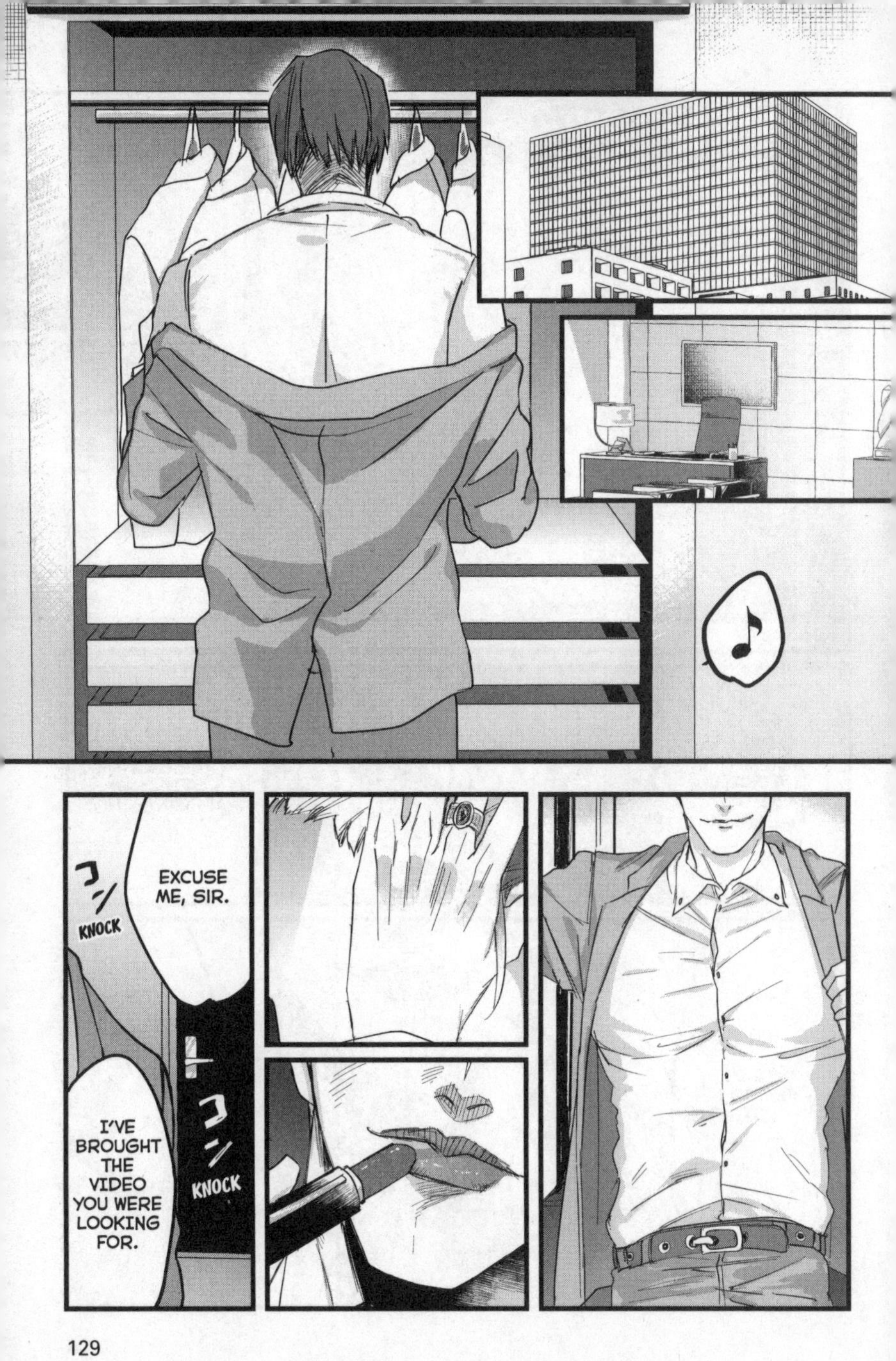
♪
EXCUSE ME, SIR.
コン
KNOCK
コン
KNOCK
I'VE BROUGHT THE VIDEO YOU WERE LOOKING FOR.

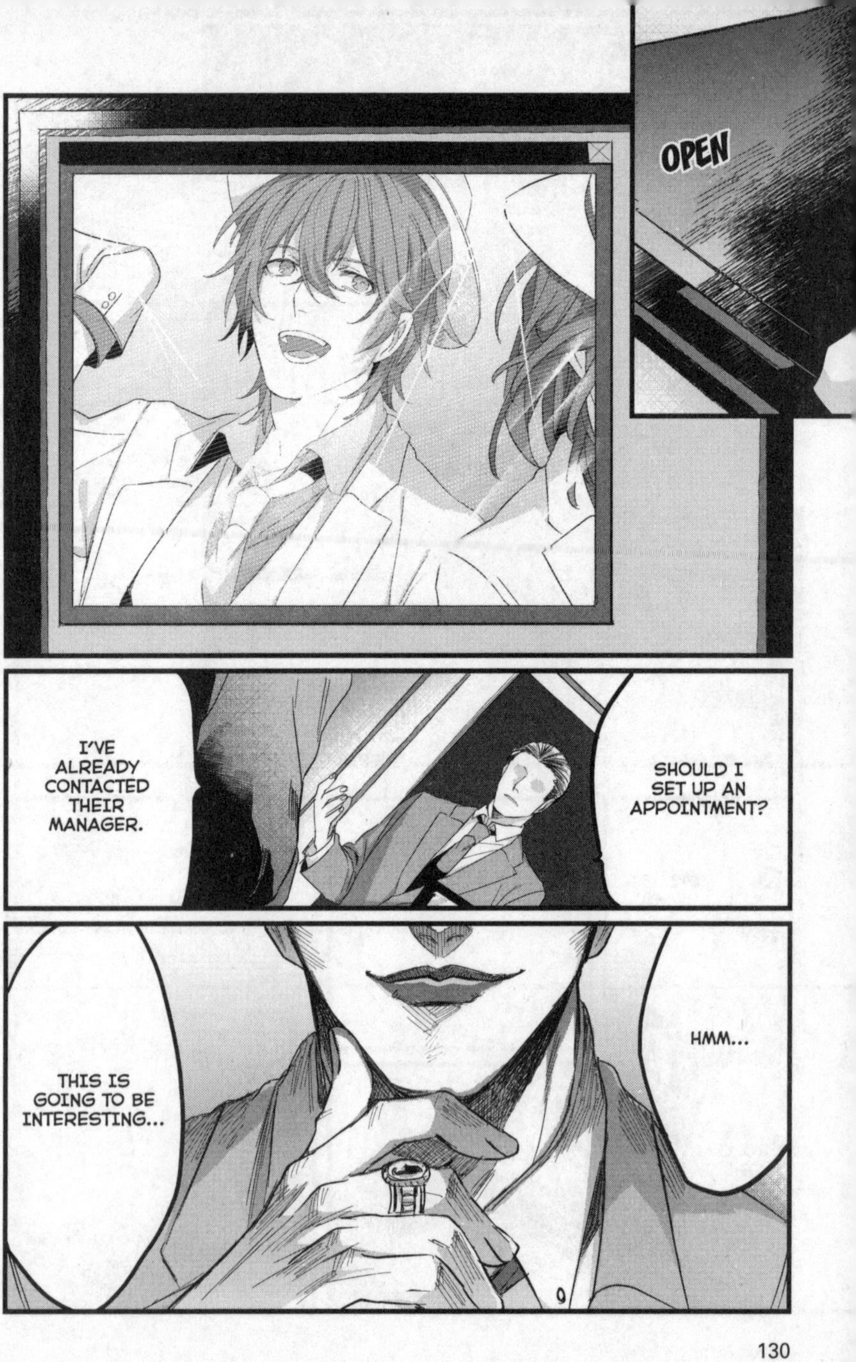
OPEN
I'VE ALREADY CONTACTED THEIR MANAGER.
SHOULD I SET UP AN APPOINTMENT?
HMM...
THIS IS GOING TO BE INTERESTING...

Chapter 5

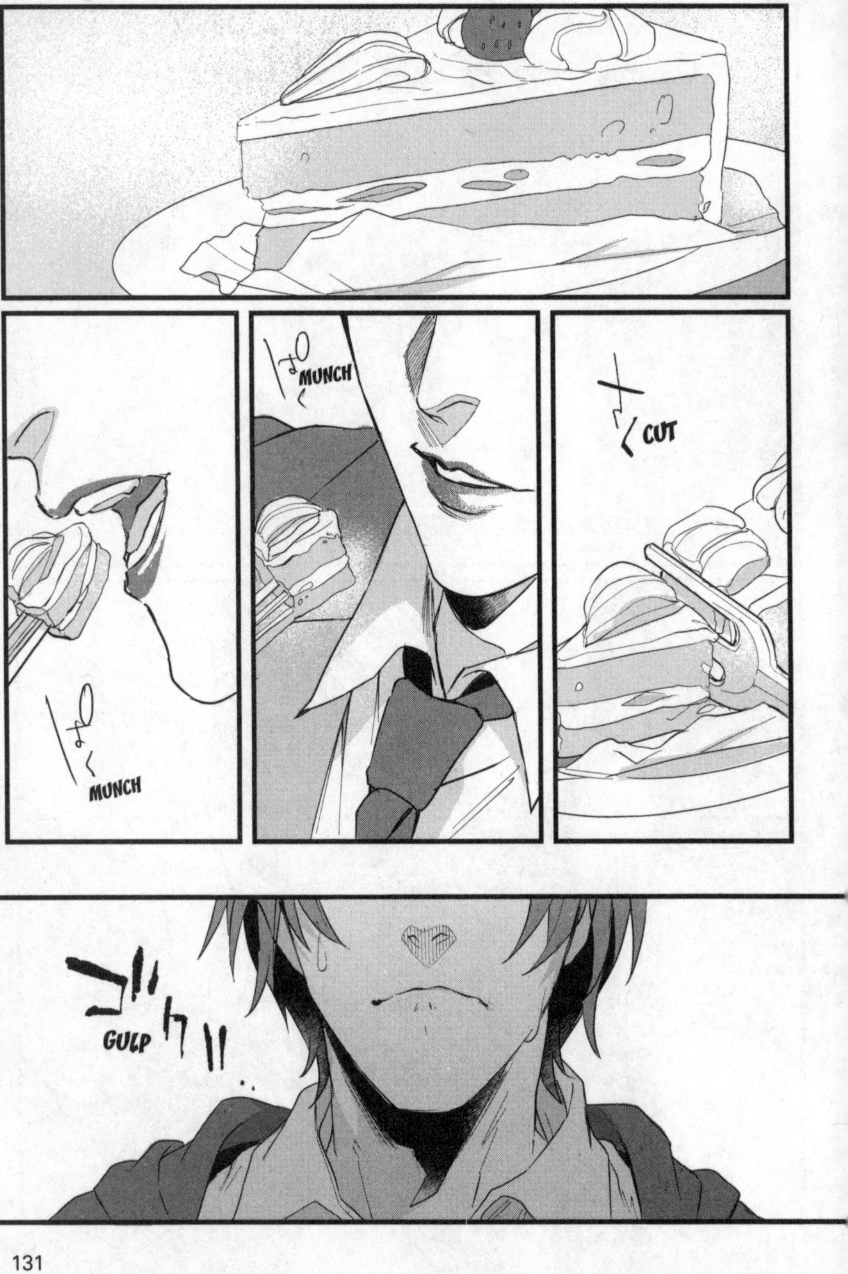
CUT
MUNCH
MUNCH
GULP

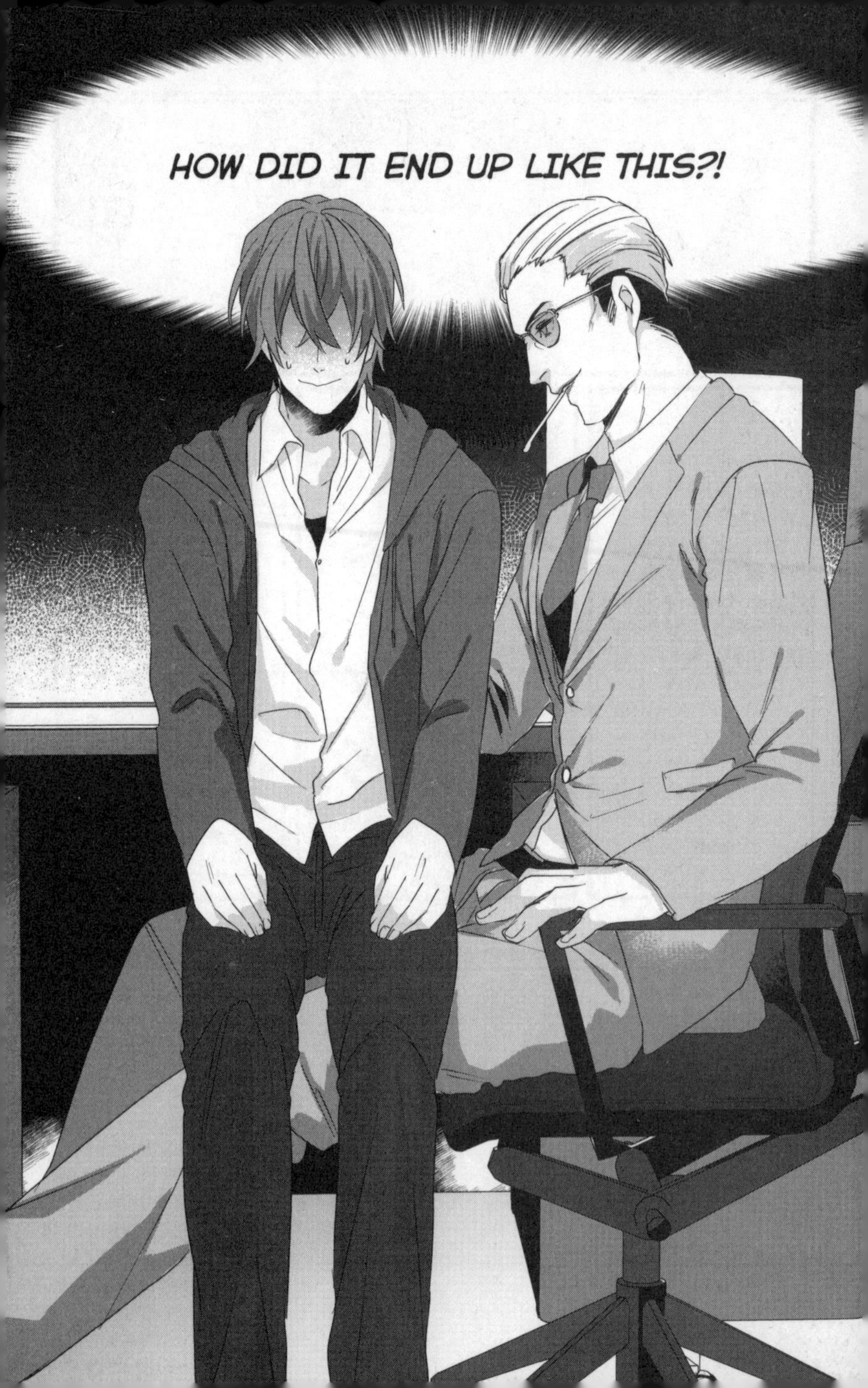
HOW DID IT END UP LIKE THIS?!

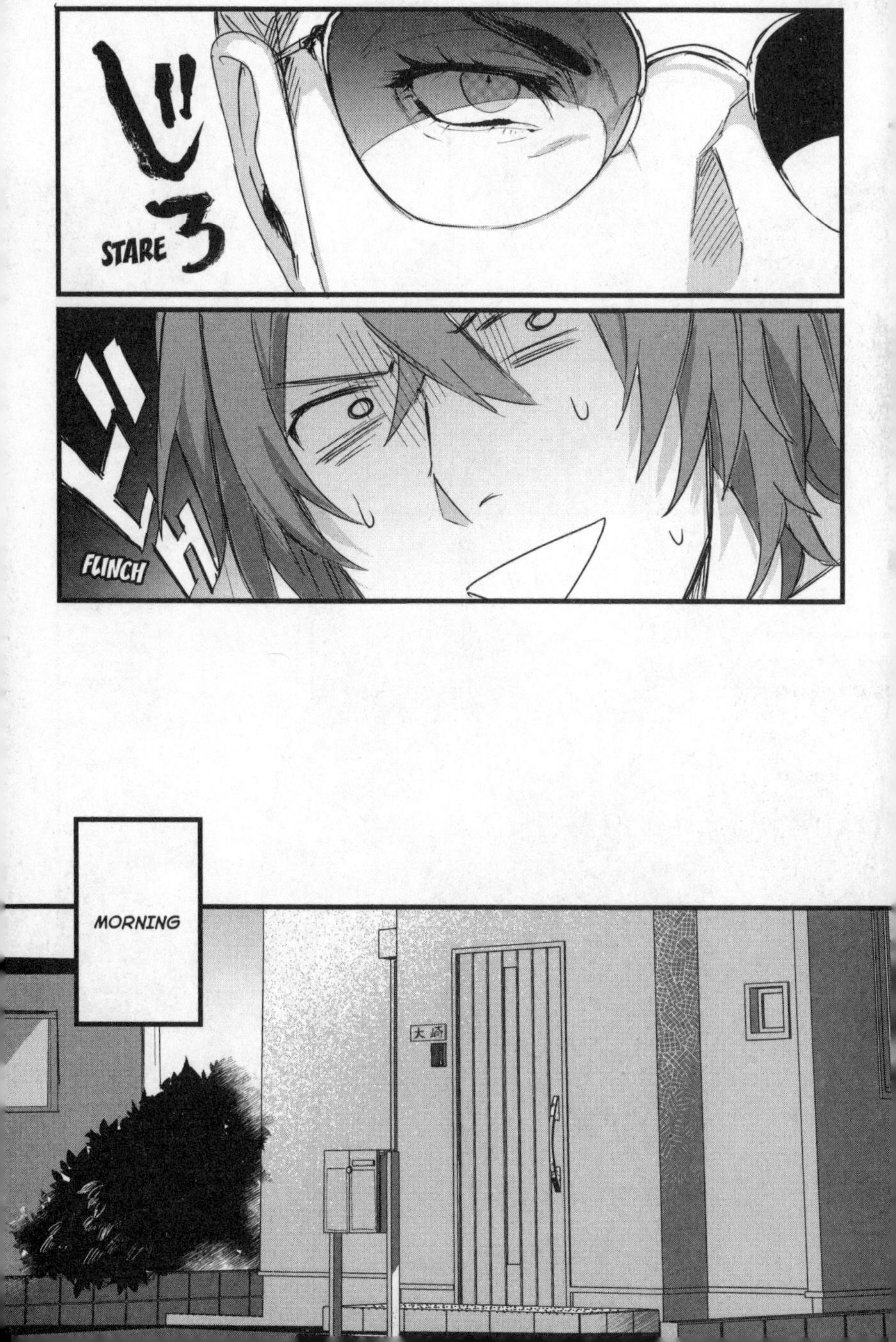
STARE
FLINCH
MORNING
大崎

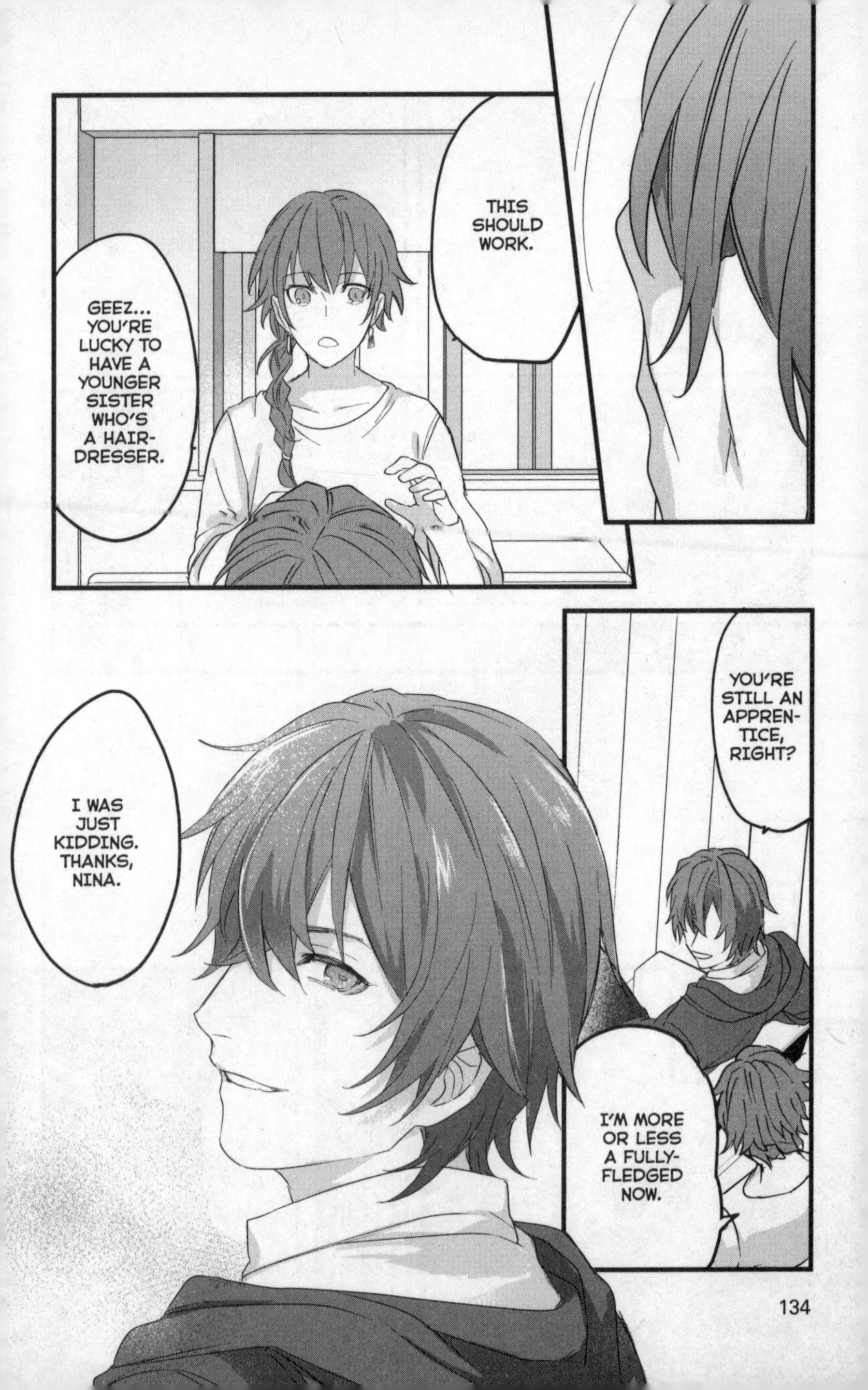
THIS SHOULD WORK.
GEEZ... YOU'RE LUCKY TO HAVE A YOUNGER SISTER WHO'S A HAIR-DRESSER.
YOU'RE STILL AN APPREN-TICE, RIGHT?
I'M MORE OR LESS A FULLY-FLEDGED NOW.
I WAS JUST KIDDING. THANKS, NINA.

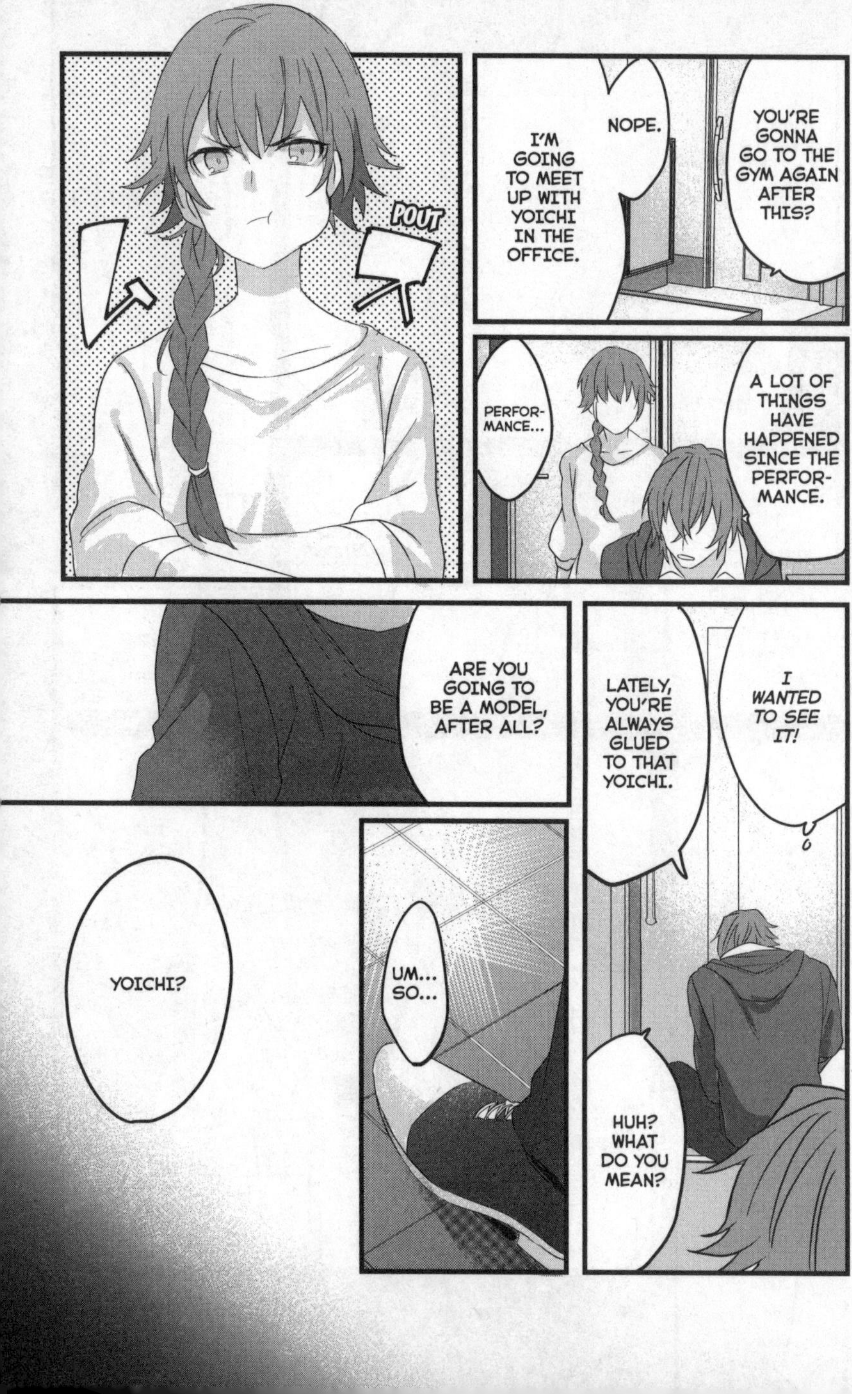
YOU'RE GONNA GO TO THE GYM AGAIN AFTER THIS?
NOPE.
I'M GOING TO MEET UP WITH YOICHI IN THE OFFICE.
A LOT OF THINGS HAVE HAPPENED SINCE THE PERFORMANCE.
PERFORMANCE...
POUT
I WANTED TO SEE IT!
LATELY, YOU'RE ALWAYS GLUED TO THAT YOICHI.
HUH? WHAT DO YOU MEAN?
ARE YOU GOING TO BE A MODEL, AFTER ALL?
UM... SO...
YOICHI?

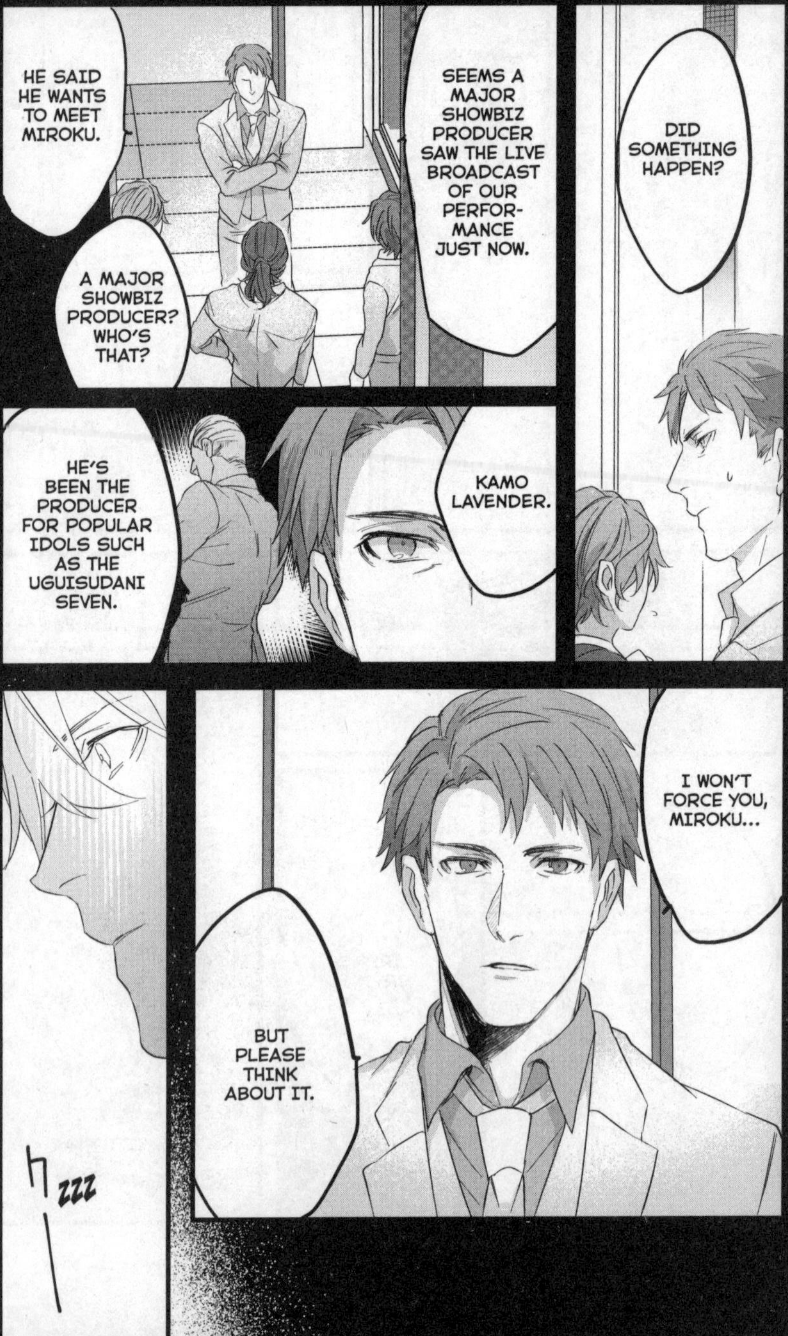
DID SOMETHING HAPPEN?
SEEMS A MAJOR SHOWBIZ PRODUCER SAW THE LIVE BROADCAST OF OUR PERFORMANCE JUST NOW.
HE SAID HE WANTS TO MEET MIROKU.
A MAJOR SHOWBIZ PRODUCER? WHO'S THAT?
KAMO LAVENDER.
HE'S BEEN THE PRODUCER FOR POPULAR IDOLS SUCH AS THE UGUISUDANI SEVEN.
I WON'T FORCE YOU, MIROKU...
BUT PLEASE THINK ABOUT IT.
ZZZ

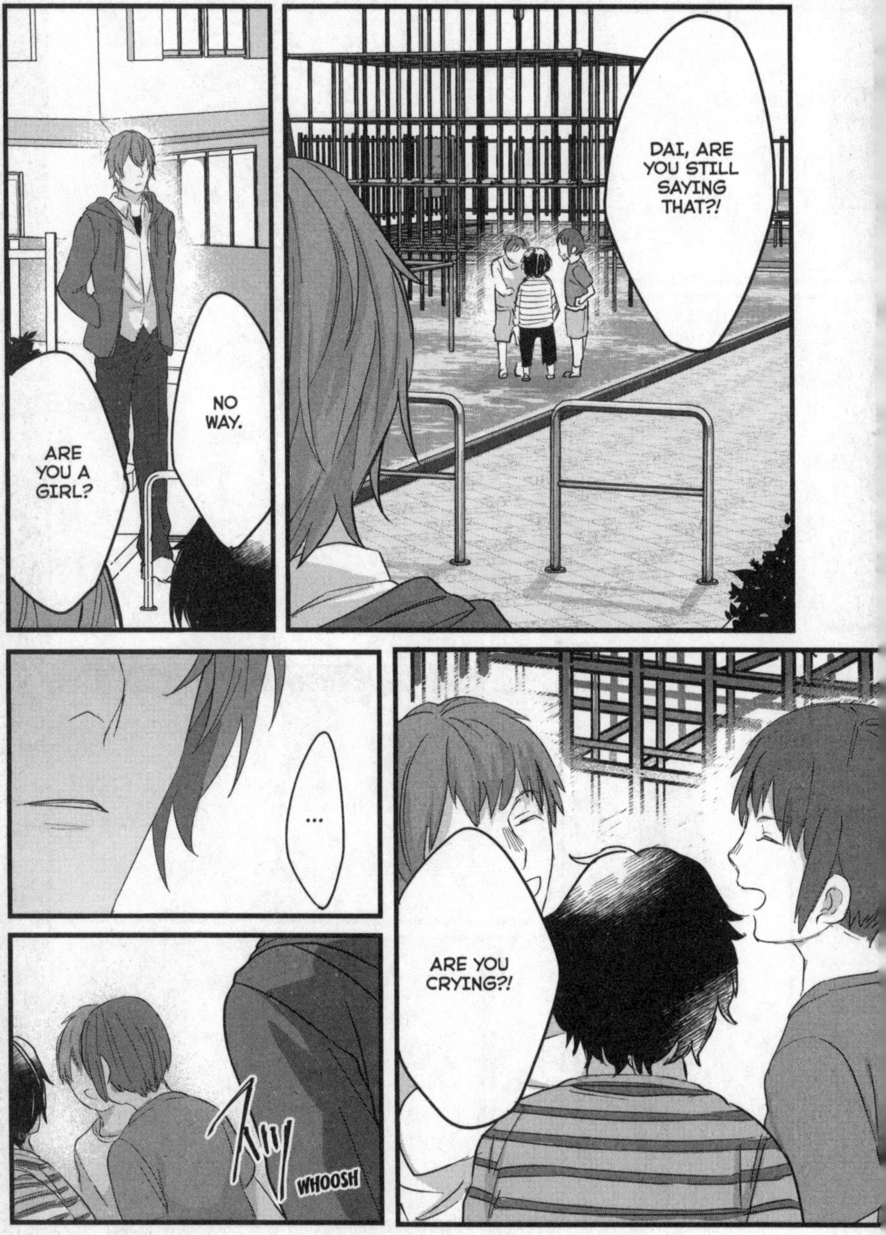
DAI, ARE YOU STILL SAYING THAT?!
NO WAY.
ARE YOU A GIRL?
ARE YOU CRYING?!
...
WHOOSH

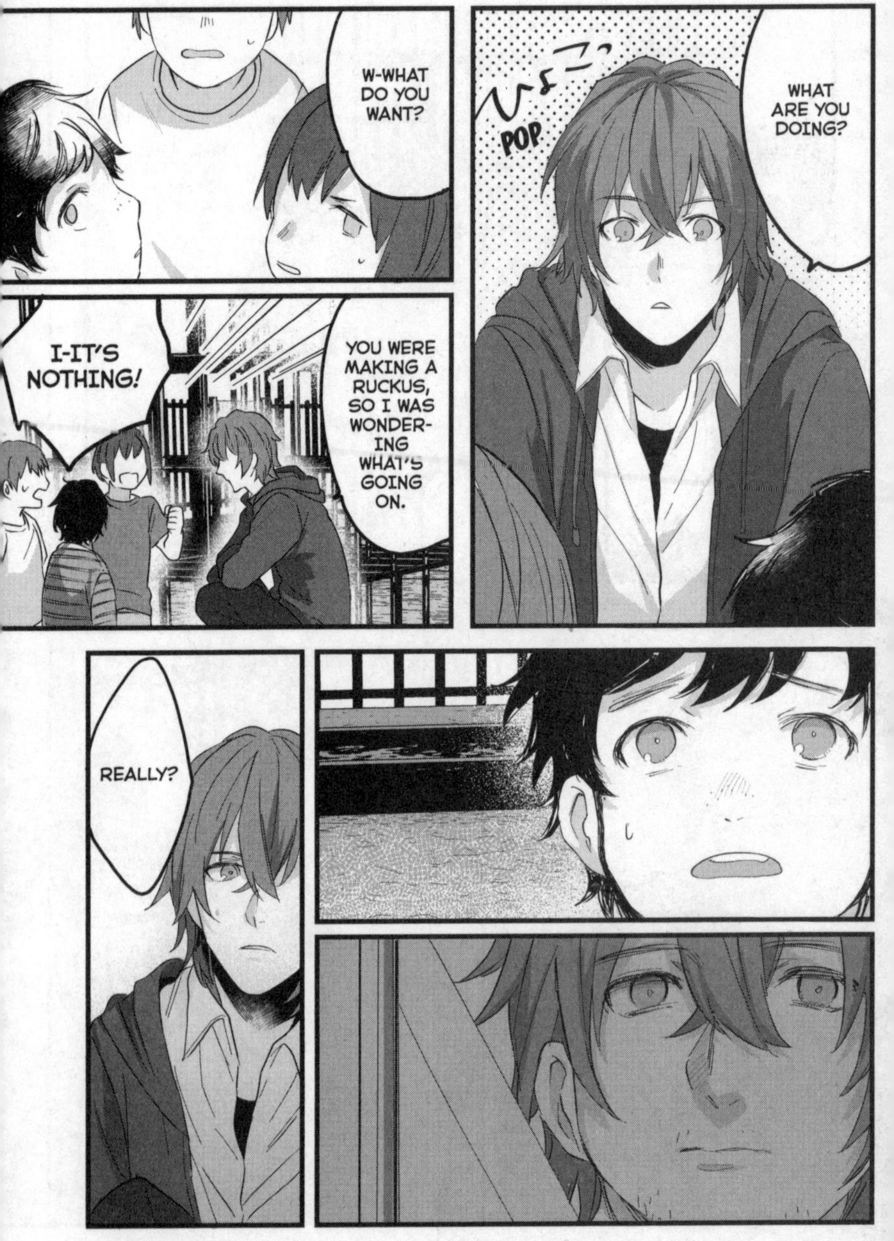
ひょこっ
POP
WHAT ARE YOU DOING?
W-WHAT DO YOU WANT?
YOU WERE MAKING A RUCKUS, SO I WAS WONDERING WHAT'S GOING ON.
I-IT'S NOTHING!
REALLY?

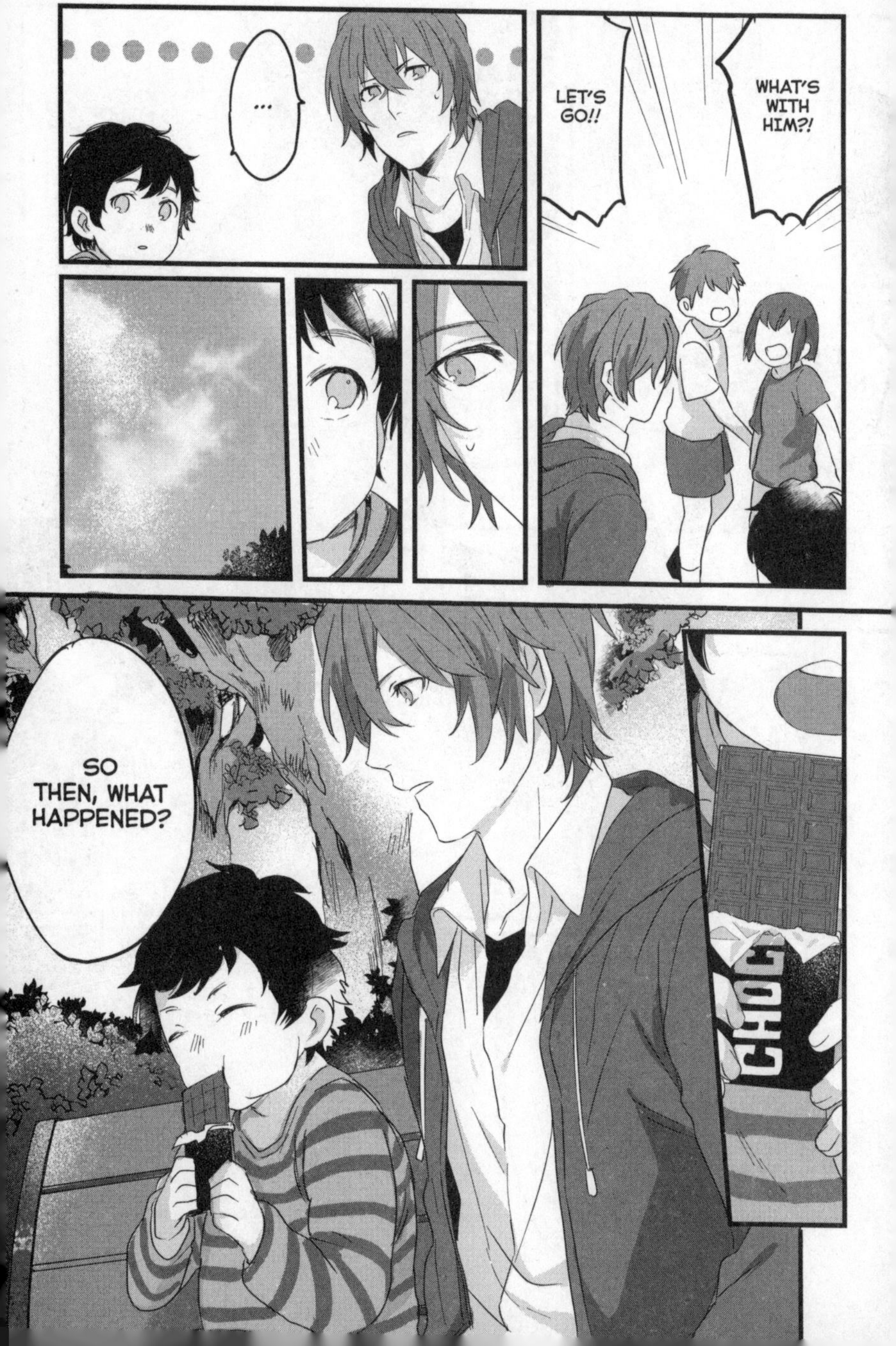
WHAT'S WITH HIM?!
LET'S GO!!
...
CHOC
SO THEN, WHAT HAPPENED?

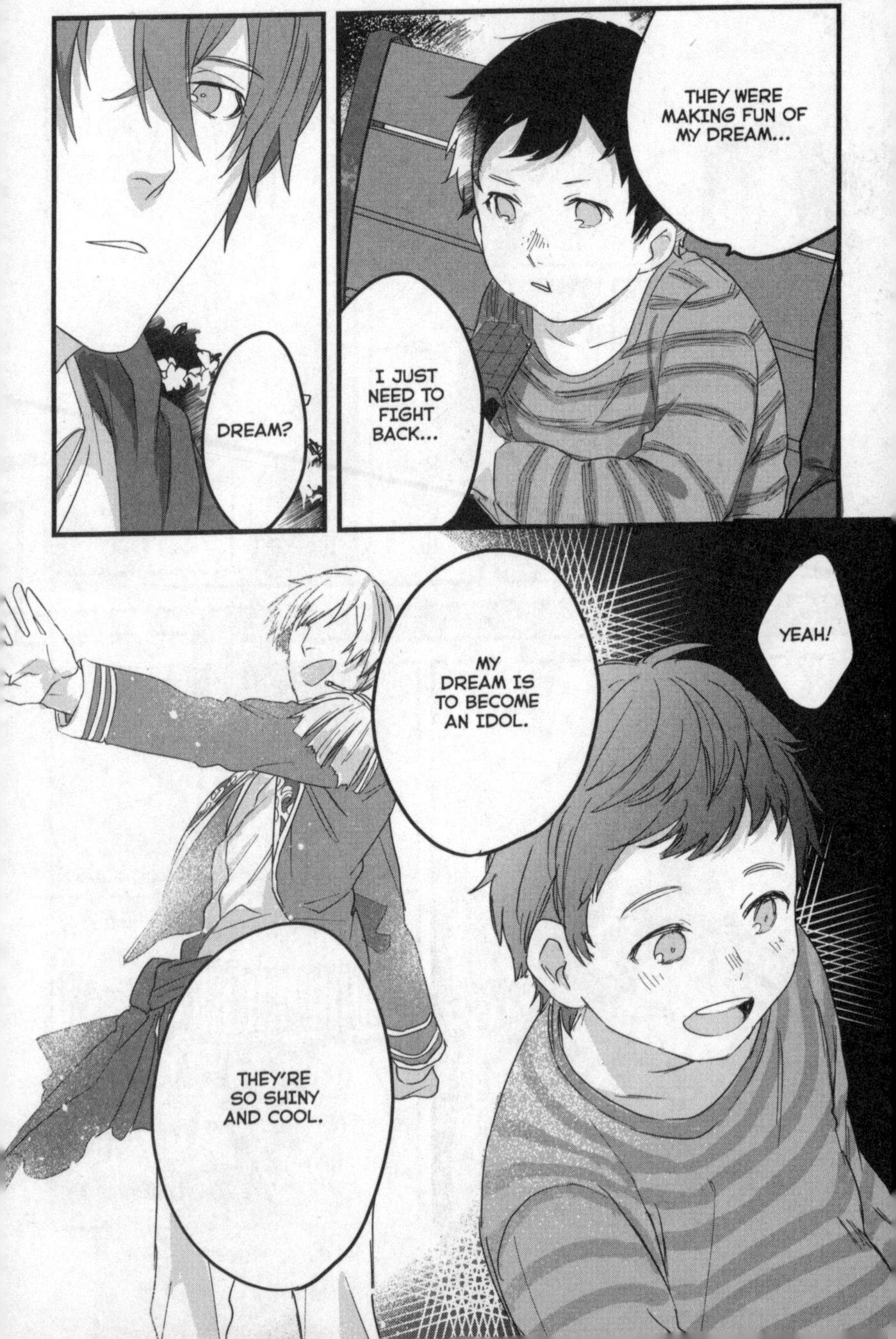
THEY WERE MAKING FUN OF MY DREAM...
I JUST NEED TO FIGHT BACK...
DREAM?
YEAH!
MY DREAM IS TO BECOME AN IDOL.
THEY'RE SO SHINY AND COOL.

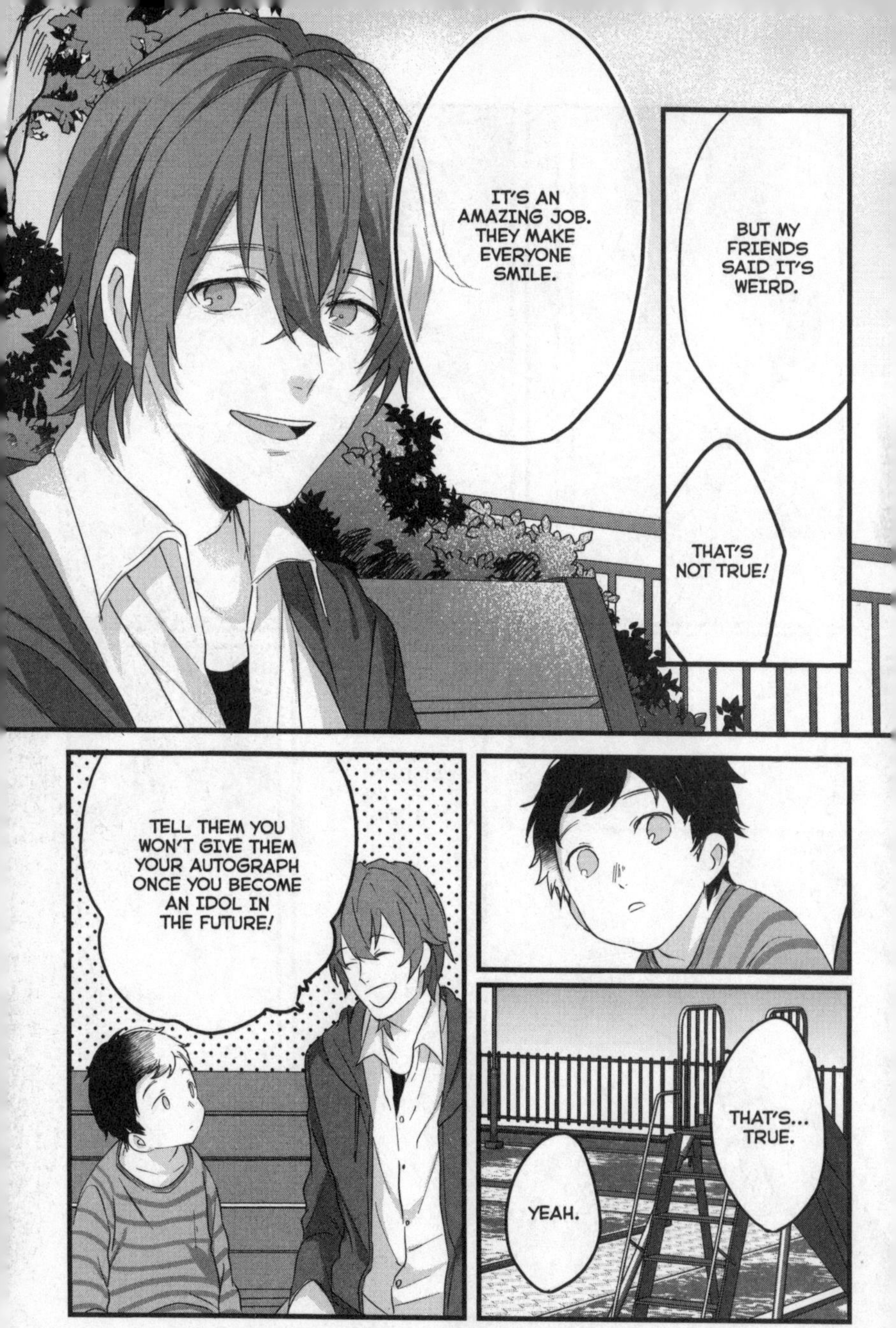
BUT MY FRIENDS SAID IT'S WEIRD.
THAT'S NOT TRUE!
IT'S AN AMAZING JOB. THEY MAKE EVERYONE SMILE.
THAT'S... TRUE.
YEAH.
TELL THEM YOU WON'T GIVE THEM YOUR AUTOGRAPH ONCE YOU BECOME AN IDOL IN THE FUTURE!

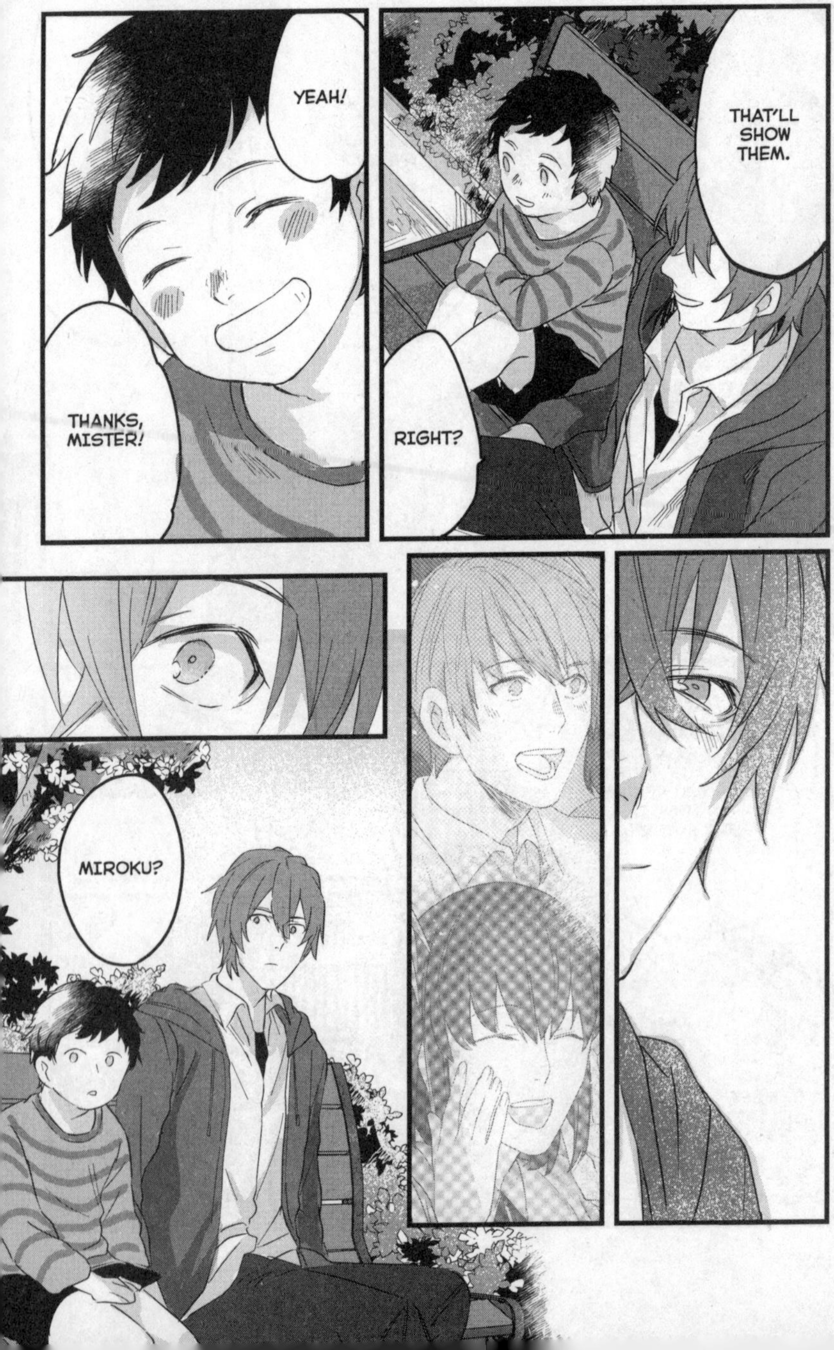
THAT'LL SHOW THEM.
RIGHT?
YEAH!
THANKS, MISTER!
MIROKU?

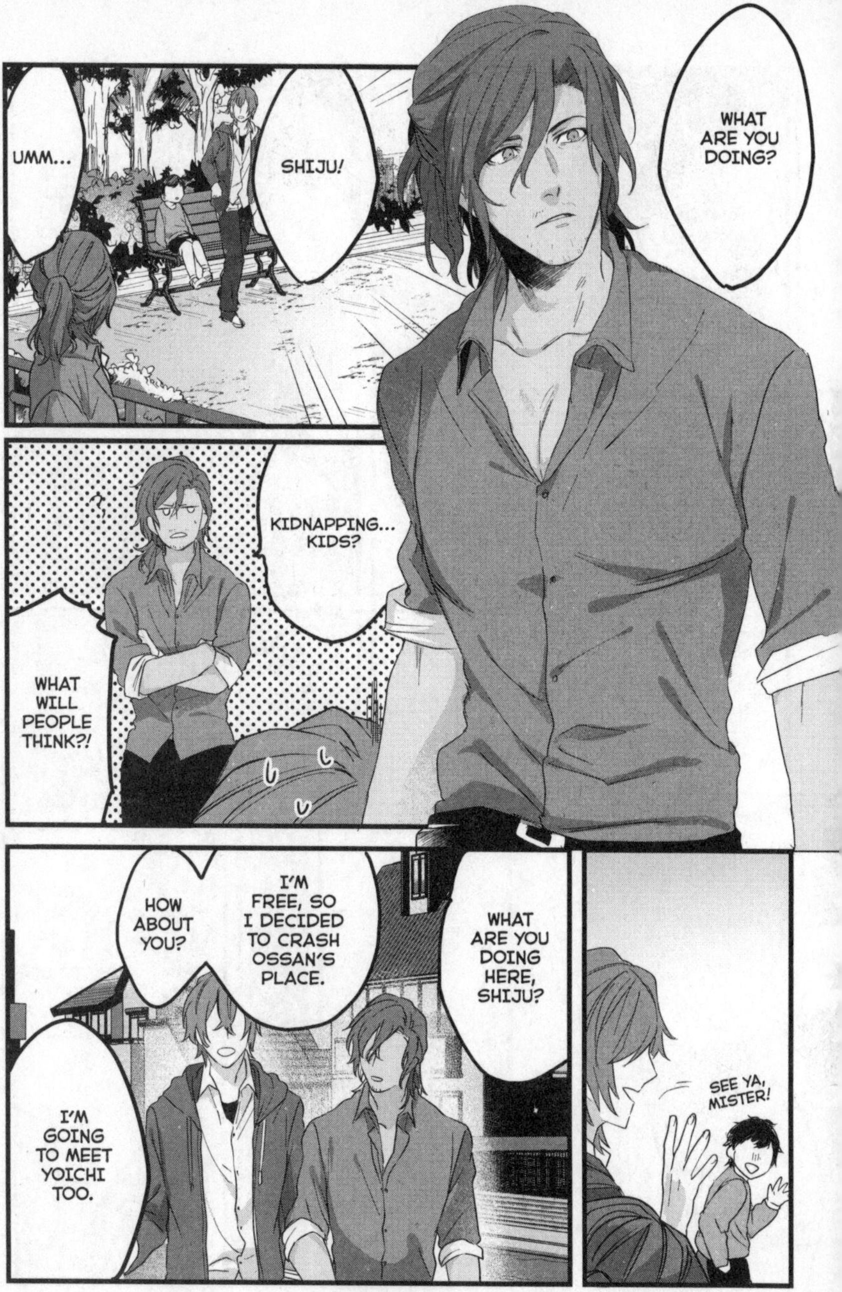
WHAT ARE YOU DOING?
SHIJU!
UMM...
KIDNAPPING... KIDS?
WHAT WILL PEOPLE THINK?!
SEE YA, MISTER!
WHAT ARE YOU DOING HERE, SHIJU?
I'M FREE, SO I DECIDED TO CRASH OSSAN'S PLACE.
HOW ABOUT YOU?
I'M GOING TO MEET YOICHI TOO.

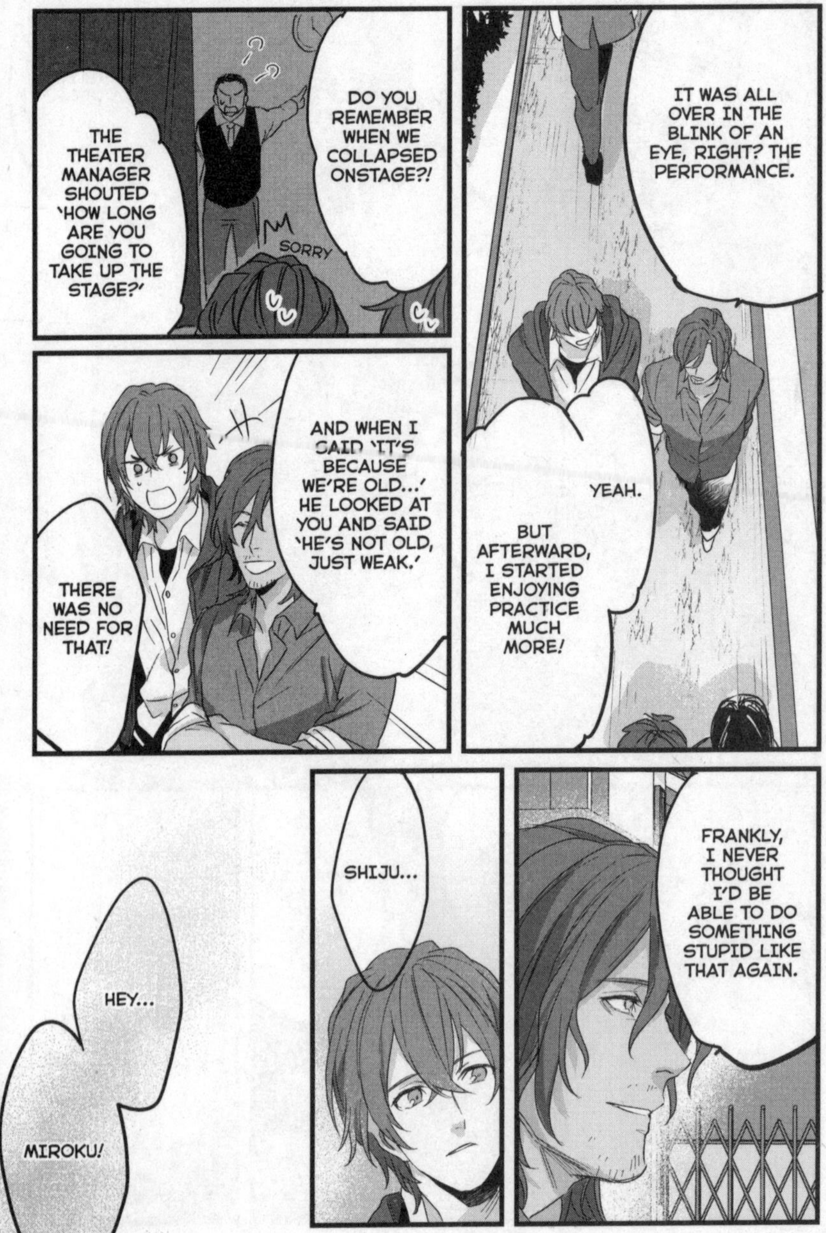
IT WAS ALL OVER IN THE BLINK OF AN EYE, RIGHT? THE PERFORMANCE.
YEAH.
BUT AFTERWARD, I STARTED ENJOYING PRACTICE MUCH MORE!
DO YOU REMEMBER WHEN WE COLLAPSED ONSTAGE?!
THE THEATER MANAGER SHOUTED 'HOW LONG ARE YOU GOING TO TAKE UP THE STAGE?'
SORRY
AND WHEN I SAID 'IT'S BECAUSE WE'RE OLD...' HE LOOKED AT YOU AND SAID 'HE'S NOT OLD, JUST WEAK.'
THERE WAS NO NEED FOR THAT!
FRANKLY, I NEVER THOUGHT I'D BE ABLE TO DO SOMETHING STUPID LIKE THAT AGAIN.
SHIJU...
HEY...
MIROKU!

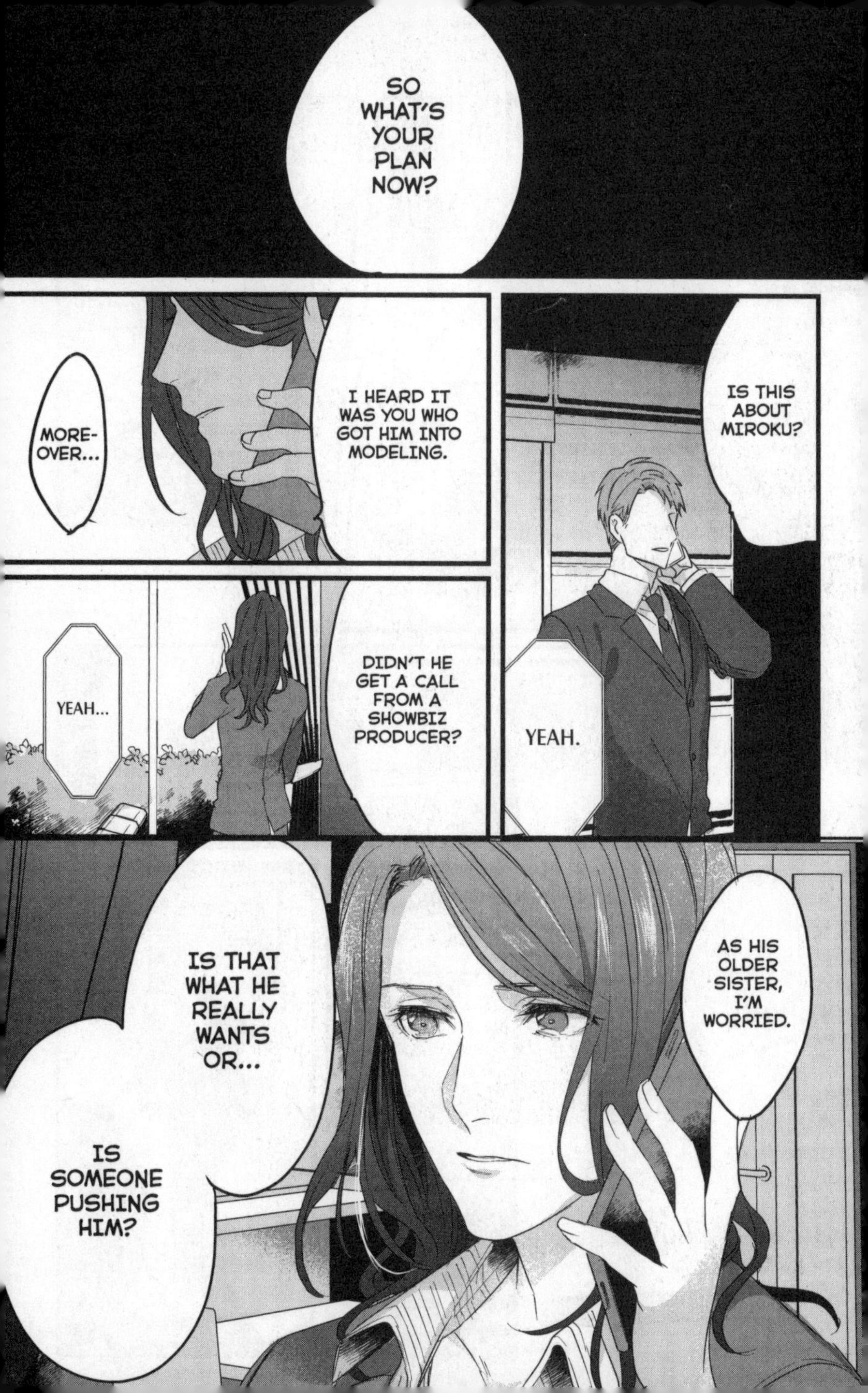
SO WHAT'S YOUR PLAN NOW?
IS THIS ABOUT MIROKU?
YEAH.
I HEARD IT WAS YOU WHO GOT HIM INTO MODELING.
MORE-OVER...
DIDN'T HE GET A CALL FROM A SHOWBIZ PRODUCER?
YEAH...
AS HIS OLDER SISTER, I'M WORRIED.
IS THAT WHAT HE REALLY WANTS OR...
IS SOMEONE PUSHING HIM?

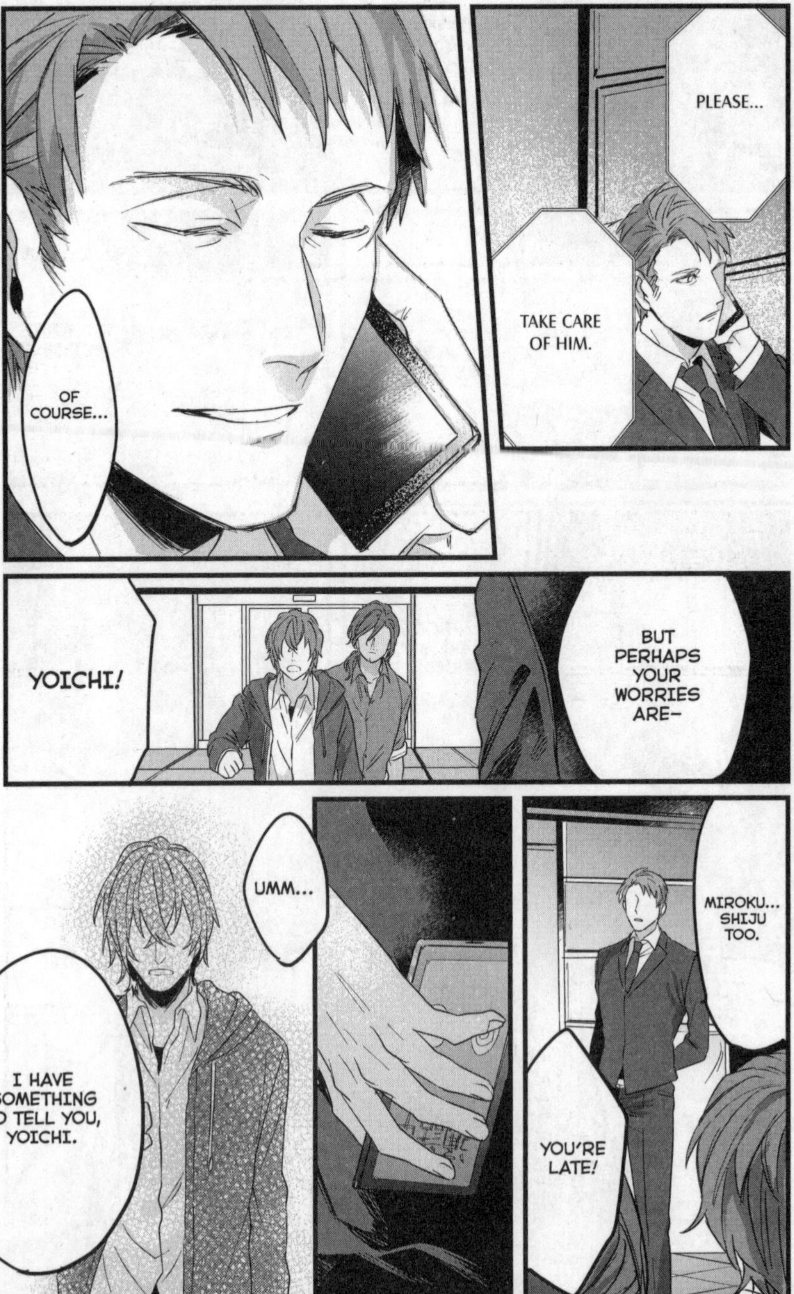
PLEASE...
TAKE CARE OF HIM.
OF COURSE...
BUT PERHAPS YOUR WORRIES ARE–
YOICHI!
MIROKU... SHIJU TOO.
YOU'RE LATE!
UMM...
I HAVE SOMETHING TO TELL YOU, YOICHI.

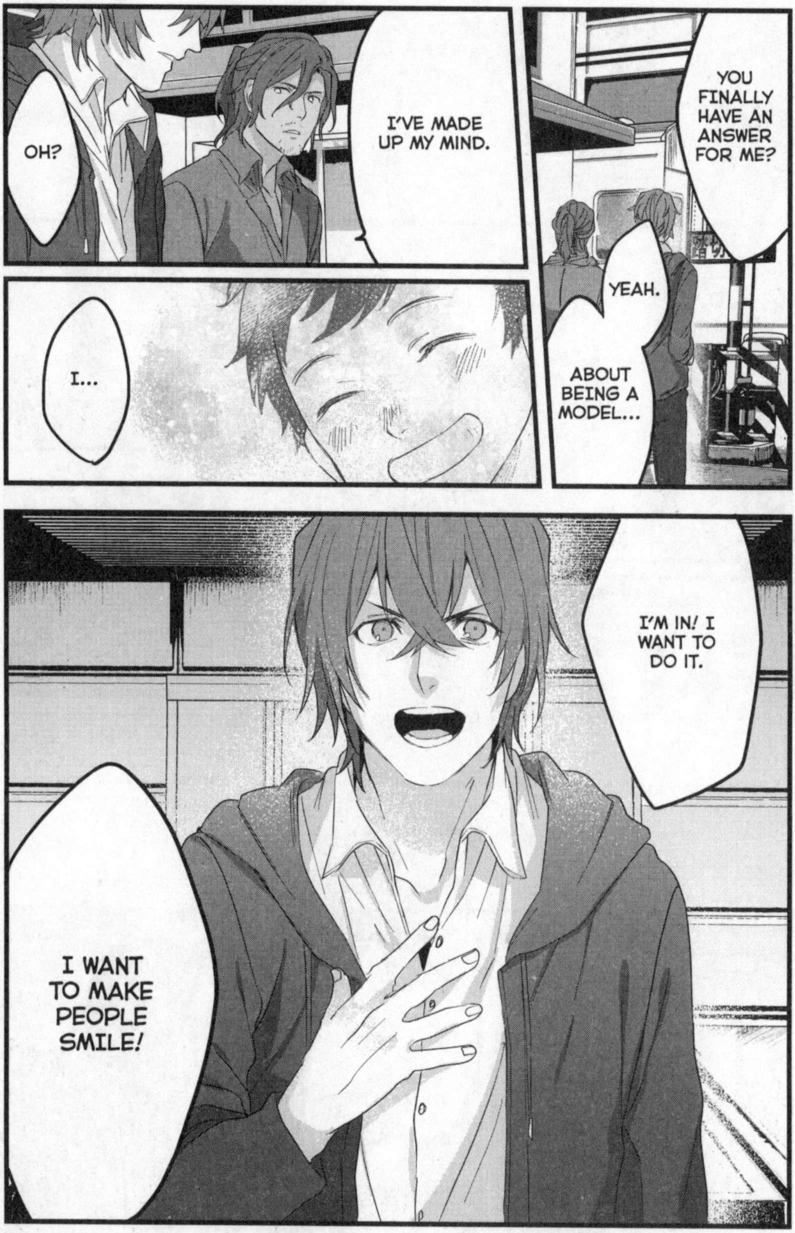
YOU FINALLY HAVE AN ANSWER FOR ME?
YEAH.
ABOUT BEING A MODEL...
I'VE MADE UP MY MIND.
OH?
I...
I'M IN! I WANT TO DO IT.
I WANT TO MAKE PEOPLE SMILE!

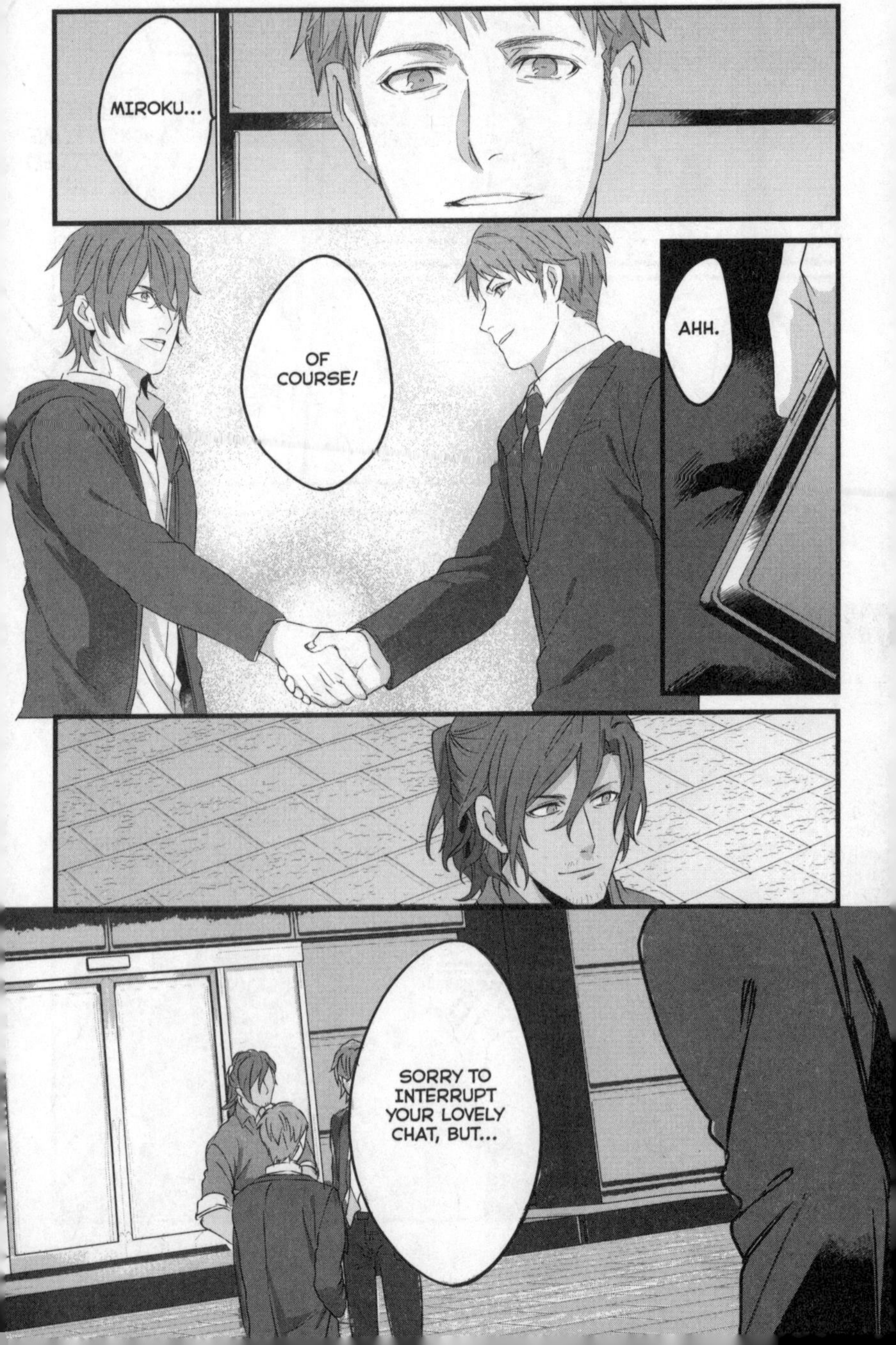
MIROKU...
AHH.
OF COURSE!
SORRY TO INTERRUPT YOUR LOVELY CHAT, BUT...

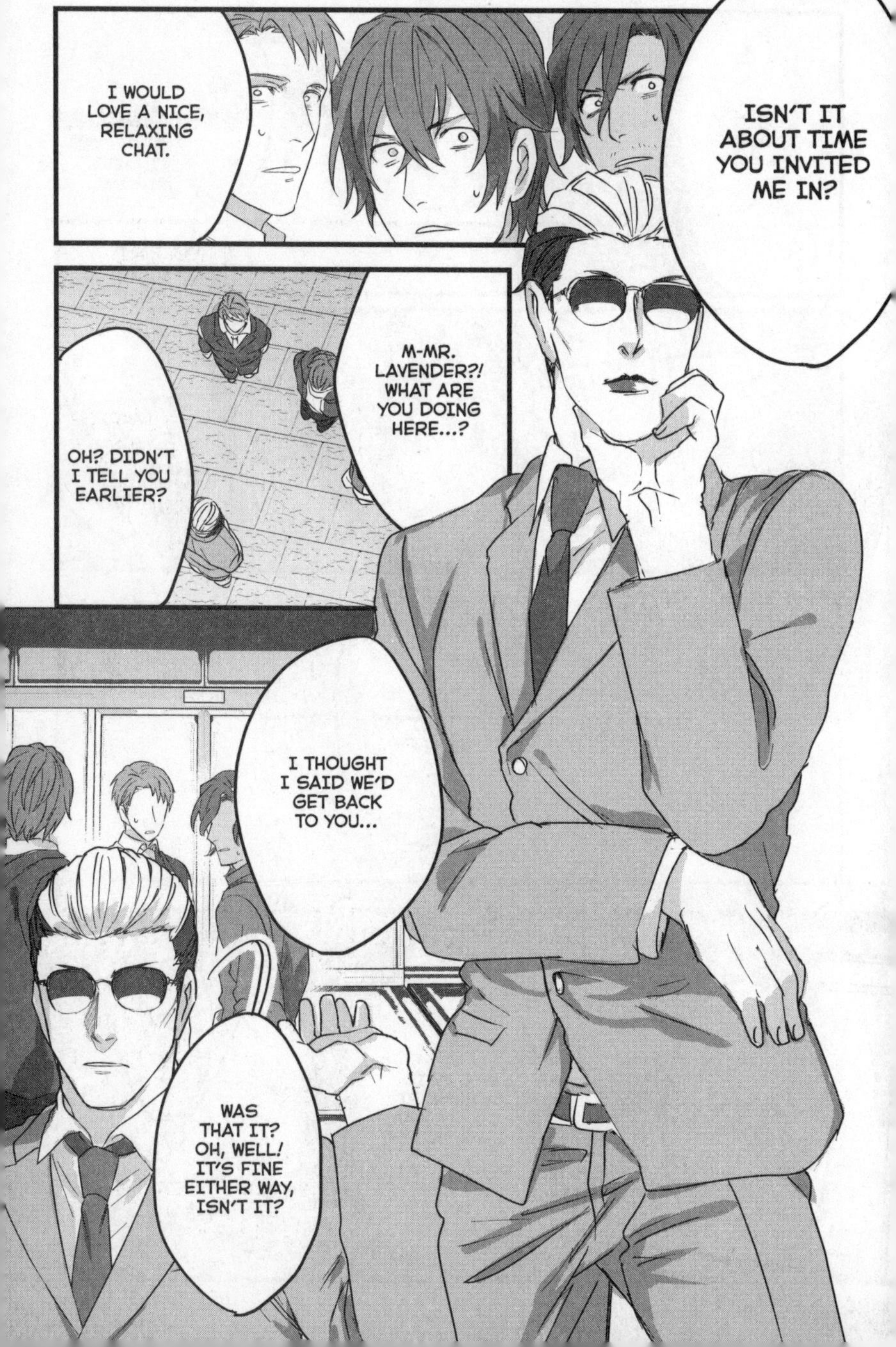
ISN'T IT ABOUT TIME YOU INVITED ME IN?
I WOULD LOVE A NICE, RELAXING CHAT.
M-MR. LAVENDER?! WHAT ARE YOU DOING HERE...?
OH? DIDN'T I TELL YOU EARLIER?
I THOUGHT I SAID WE'D GET BACK TO YOU...
WAS THAT IT? OH, WELL! IT'S FINE EITHER WAY, ISN'T IT?

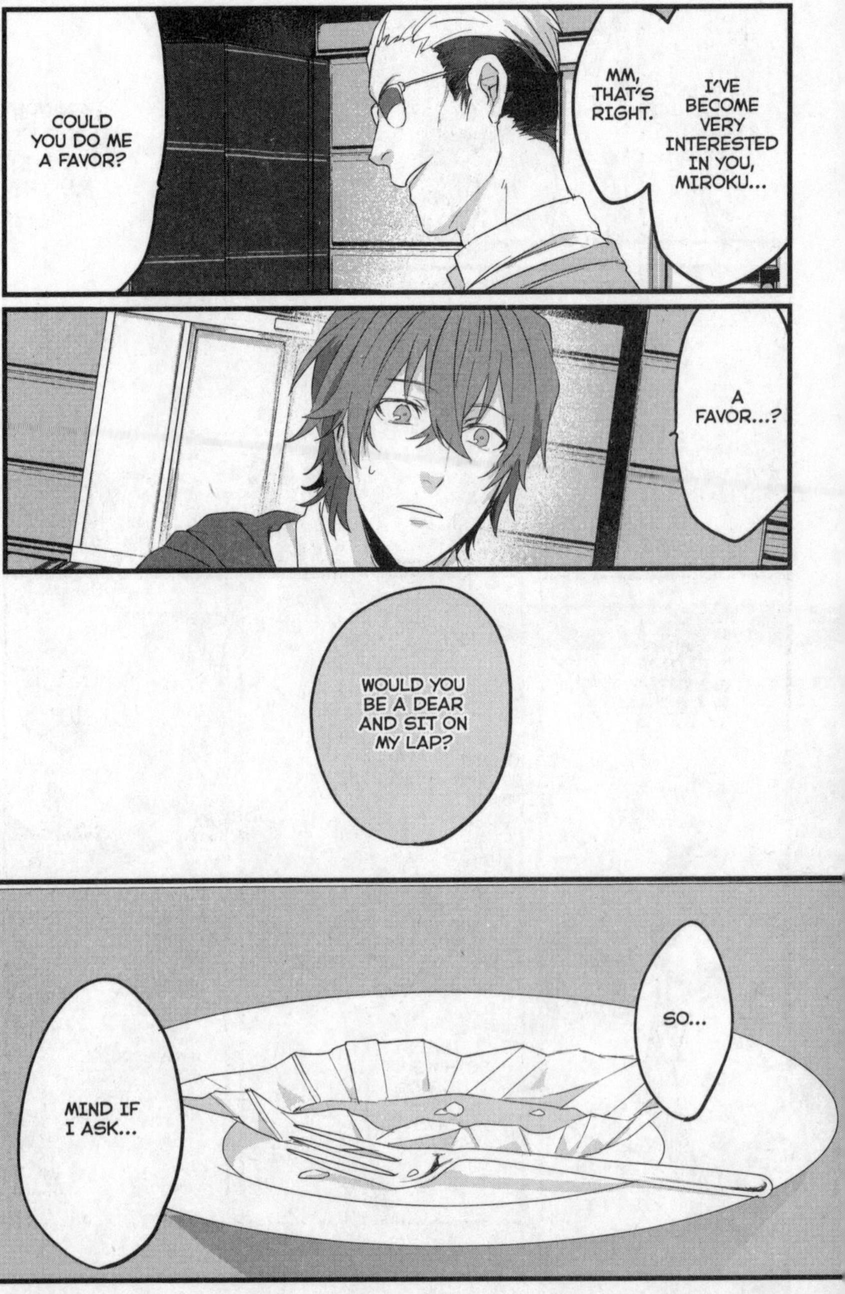
MM, THAT'S RIGHT.
I'VE BECOME VERY INTERESTED IN YOU, MIROKU...
COULD YOU DO ME A FAVOR?
A FAVOR...?
WOULD YOU BE A DEAR AND SIT ON MY LAP?
SO...
MIND IF I ASK...

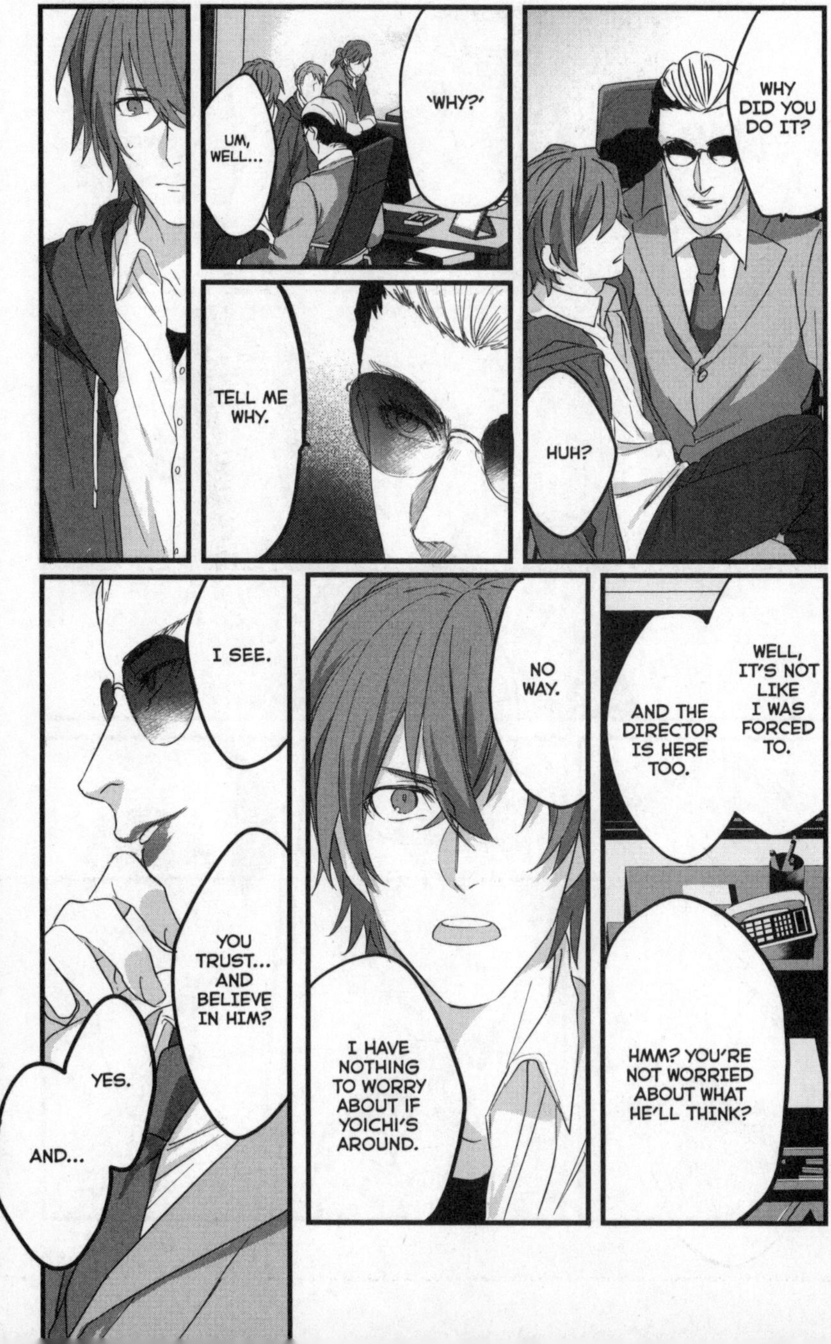
WHY DID YOU DO IT?
HUH?
'WHY?'
UM, WELL...
TELL ME WHY.
WELL, IT'S NOT LIKE I WAS FORCED TO.
AND THE DIRECTOR IS HERE TOO.
HMM? YOU'RE NOT WORRIED ABOUT WHAT HE'LL THINK?
NO WAY.
I HAVE NOTHING TO WORRY ABOUT IF YOICHI'S AROUND.
I SEE.
YOU TRUST... AND BELIEVE IN HIM?
YES.
AND...

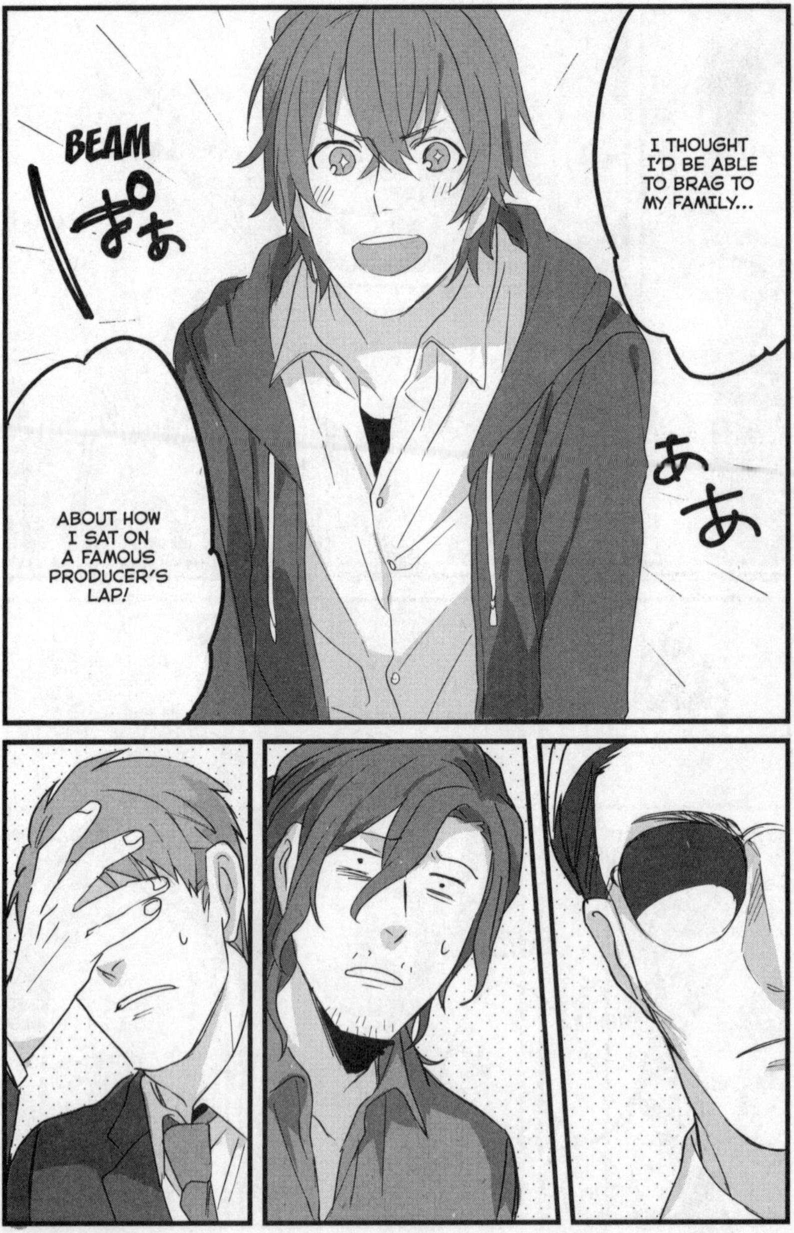
I THOUGHT I'D BE ABLE TO BRAG TO MY FAMILY...
BEAM
ぽぁ
ああ
ABOUT HOW I SAT ON A FAMOUS PRODUCER'S LAP!

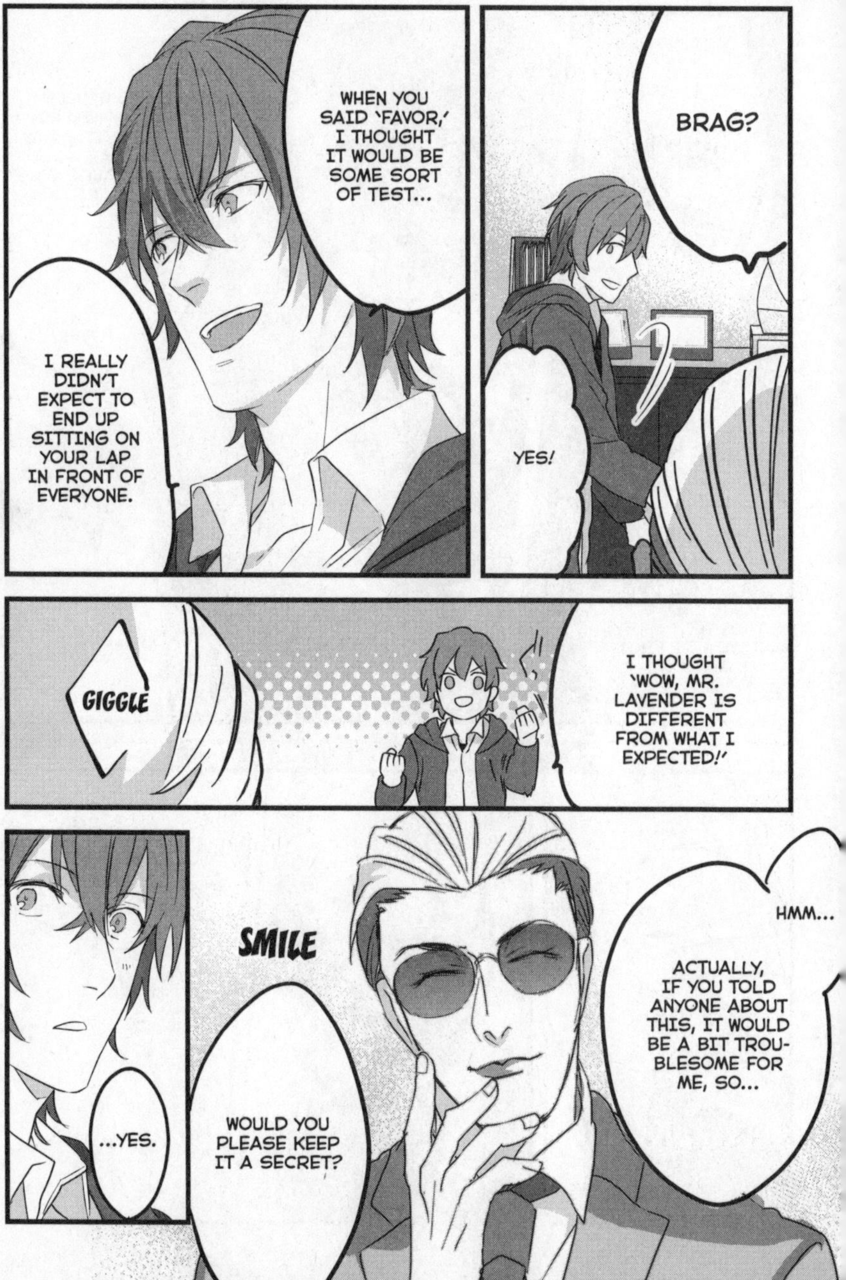
BRAG?
YES!
WHEN YOU SAID 'FAVOR,' I THOUGHT IT WOULD BE SOME SORT OF TEST...
I REALLY DIDN'T EXPECT TO END UP SITTING ON YOUR LAP IN FRONT OF EVERYONE.
I THOUGHT 'WOW, MR. LAVENDER IS DIFFERENT FROM WHAT I EXPECTED!'
GIGGLE
HMM...
ACTUALLY, IF YOU TOLD ANYONE ABOUT THIS, IT WOULD BE A BIT TROU-BLESOME FOR ME, SO...
SMILE
WOULD YOU PLEASE KEEP IT A SECRET?
...YES.

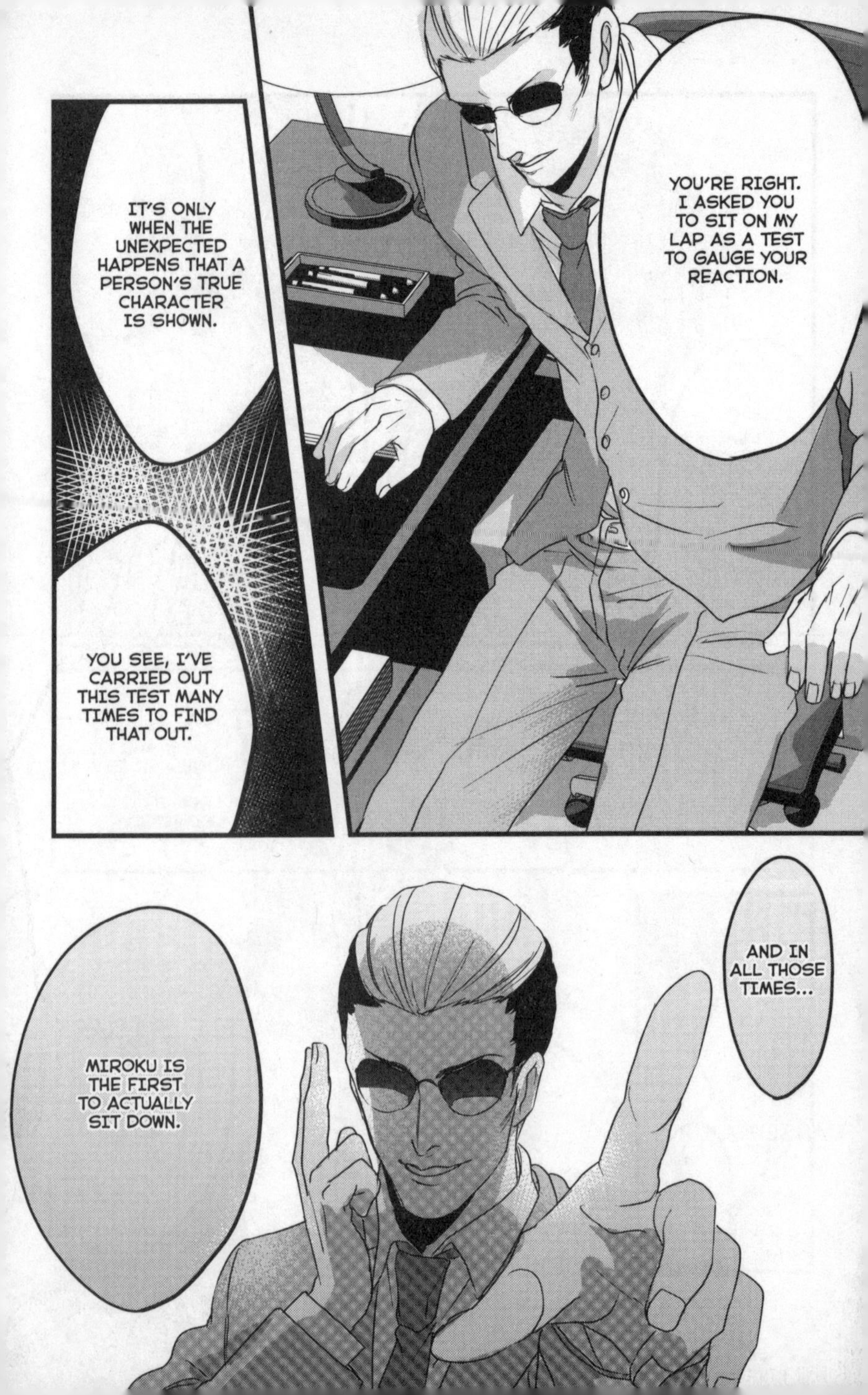
YOU'RE RIGHT. I ASKED YOU TO SIT ON MY LAP AS A TEST TO GAUGE YOUR REACTION.
IT'S ONLY WHEN THE UNEXPECTED HAPPENS THAT A PERSON'S TRUE CHARACTER IS SHOWN.
YOU SEE, I'VE CARRIED OUT THIS TEST MANY TIMES TO FIND THAT OUT.
AND IN ALL THOSE TIMES...
MIROKU IS THE FIRST TO ACTUALLY SIT DOWN.

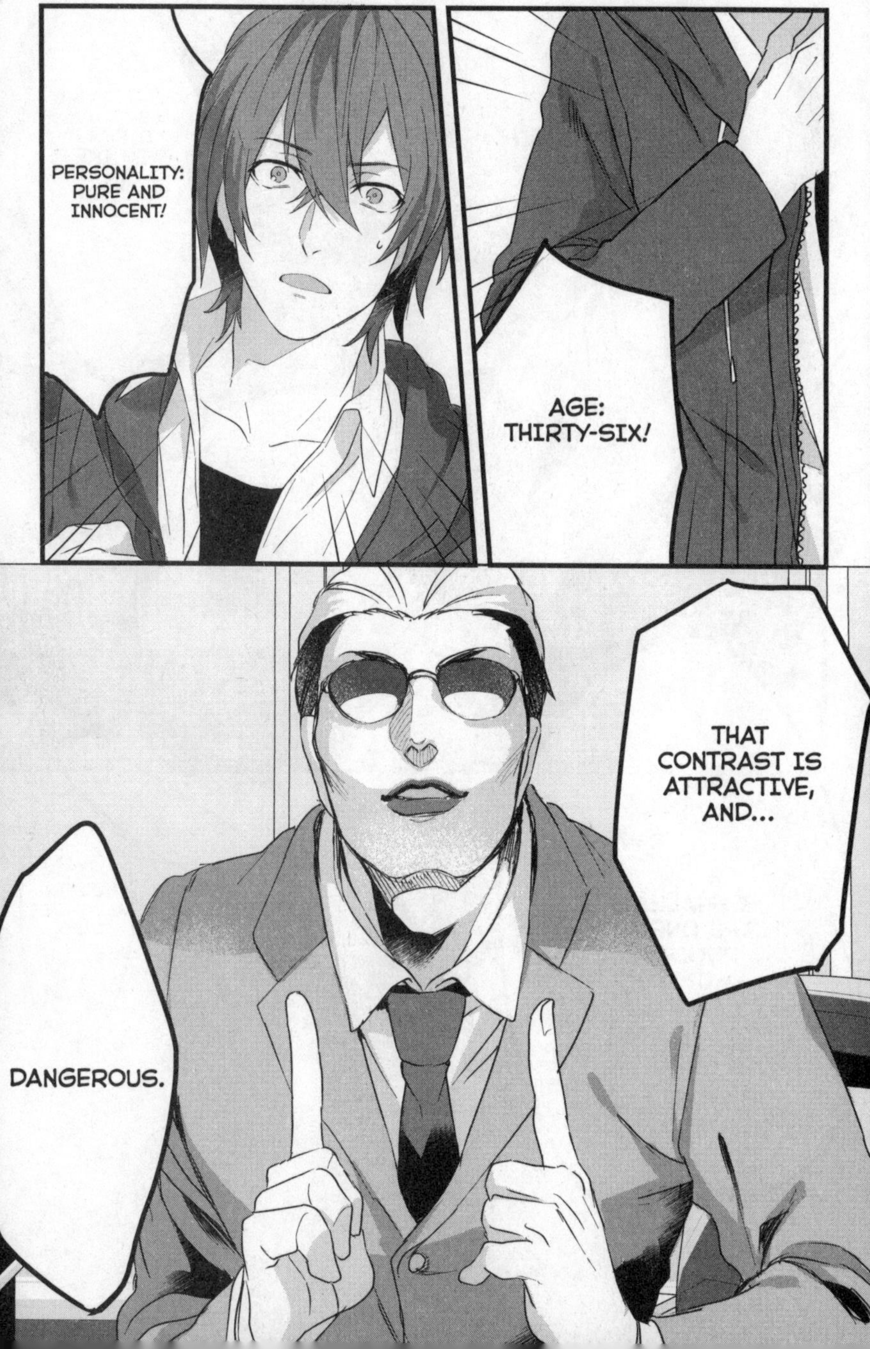
AGE: THIRTY-SIX!
PERSONALITY: PURE AND INNOCENT!
THAT CONTRAST IS ATTRACTIVE, AND...
DANGEROUS.

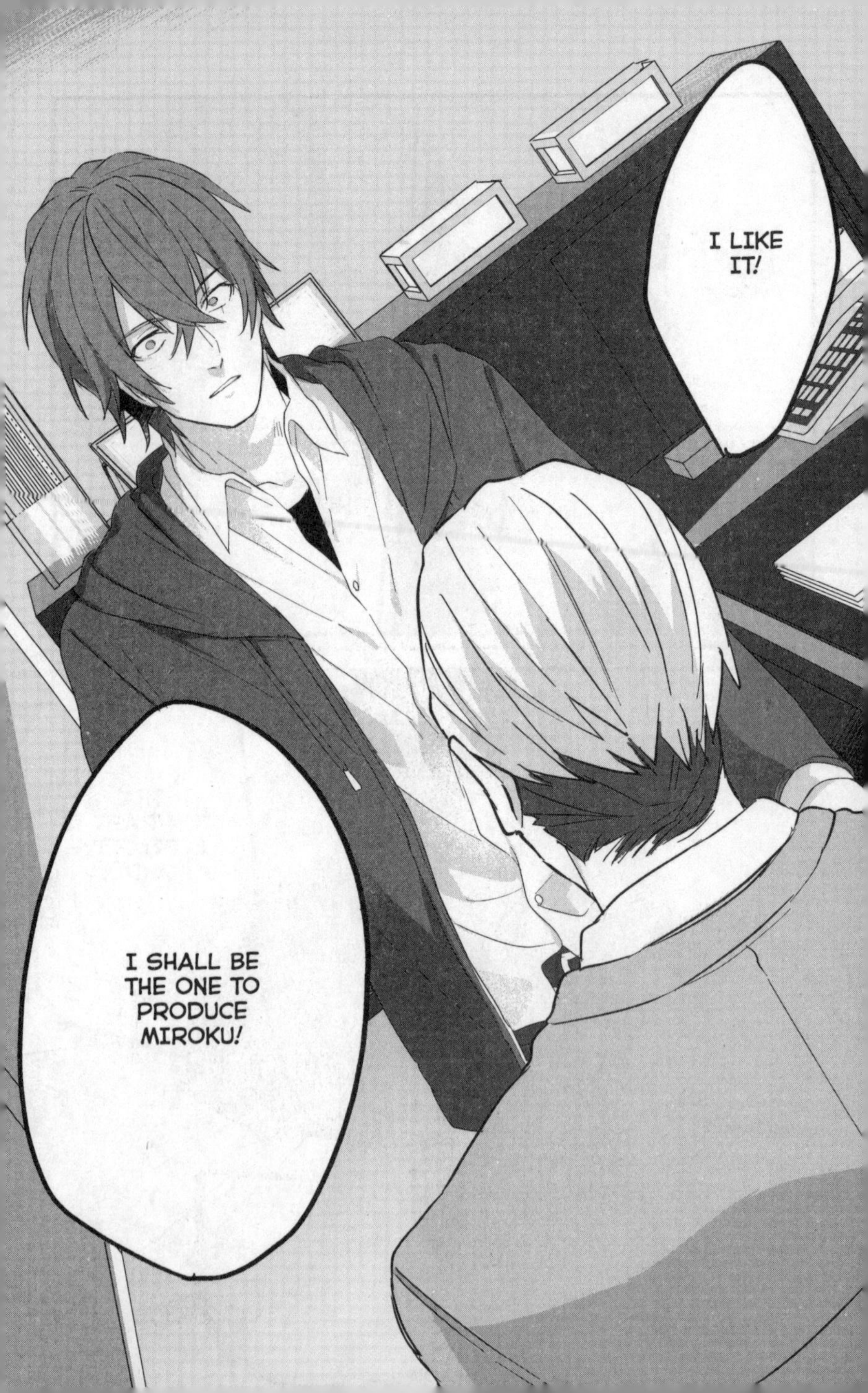
I LIKE IT!
I SHALL BE THE ONE TO PRODUCE MIROKU!

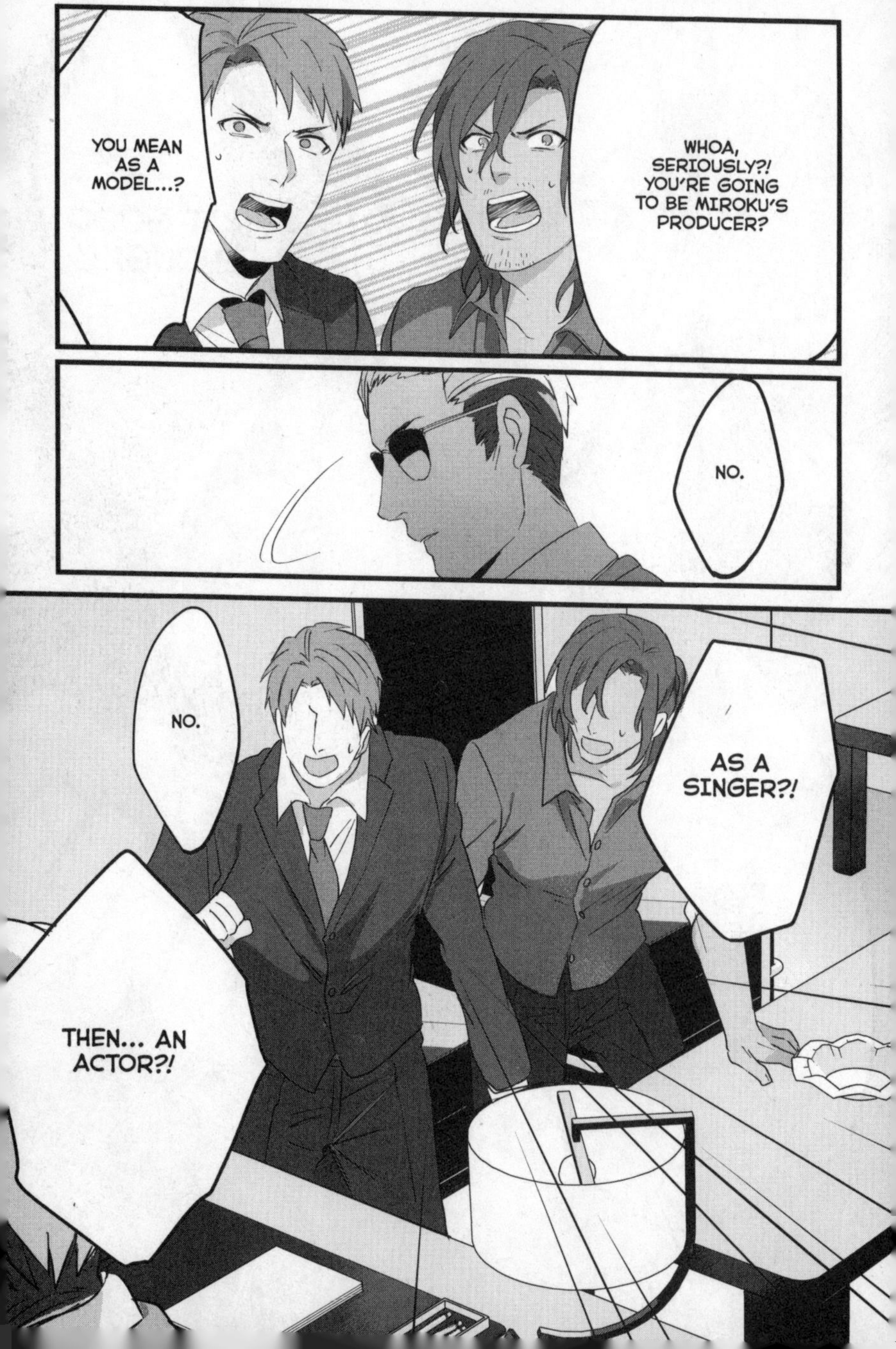
WHOA, SERIOUSLY?! YOU'RE GOING TO BE MIROKU'S PRODUCER?
YOU MEAN AS A MODEL...?
NO.
AS A SINGER?!
NO.
THEN... AN ACTOR?!

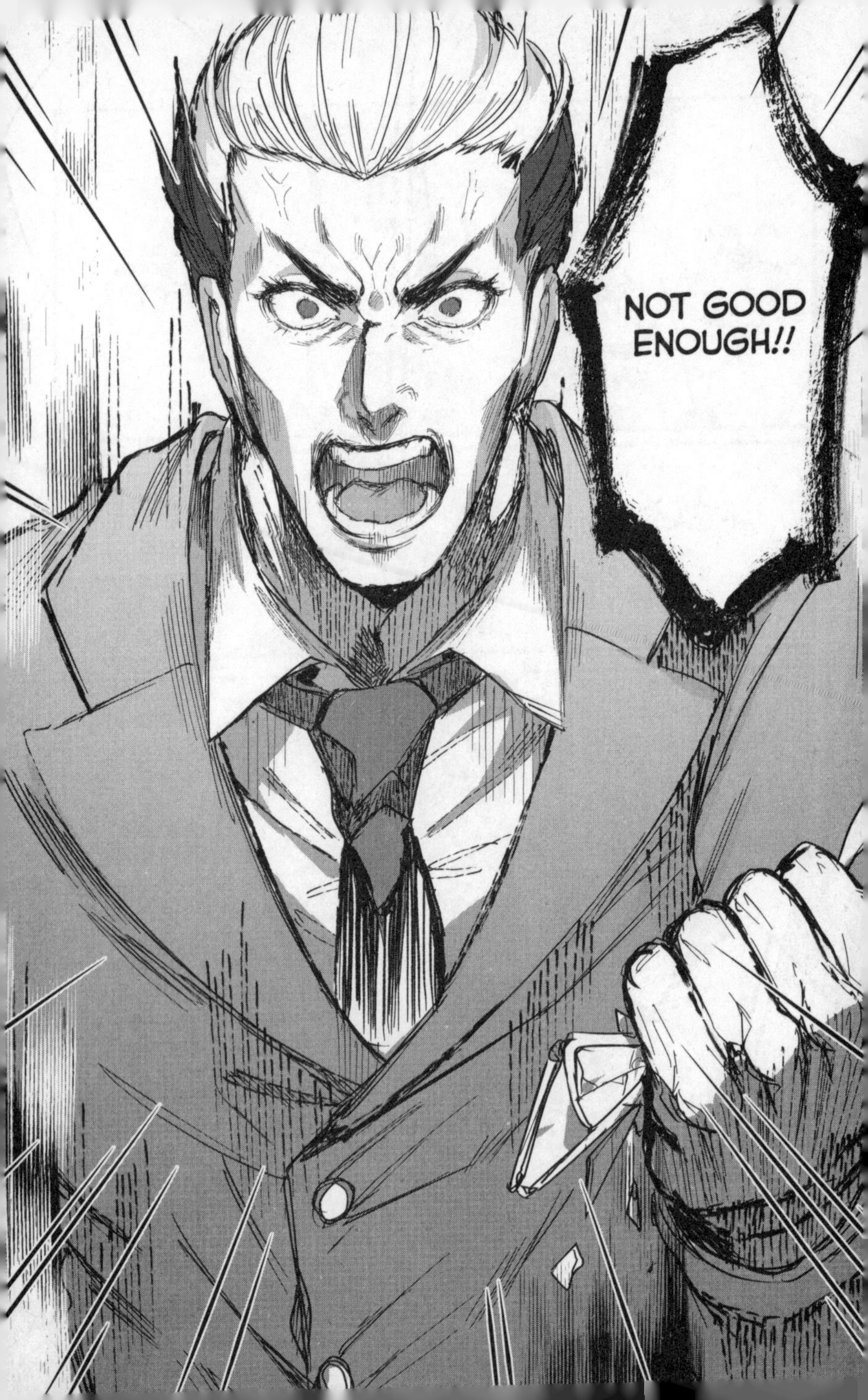
NOT GOOD ENOUGH!!

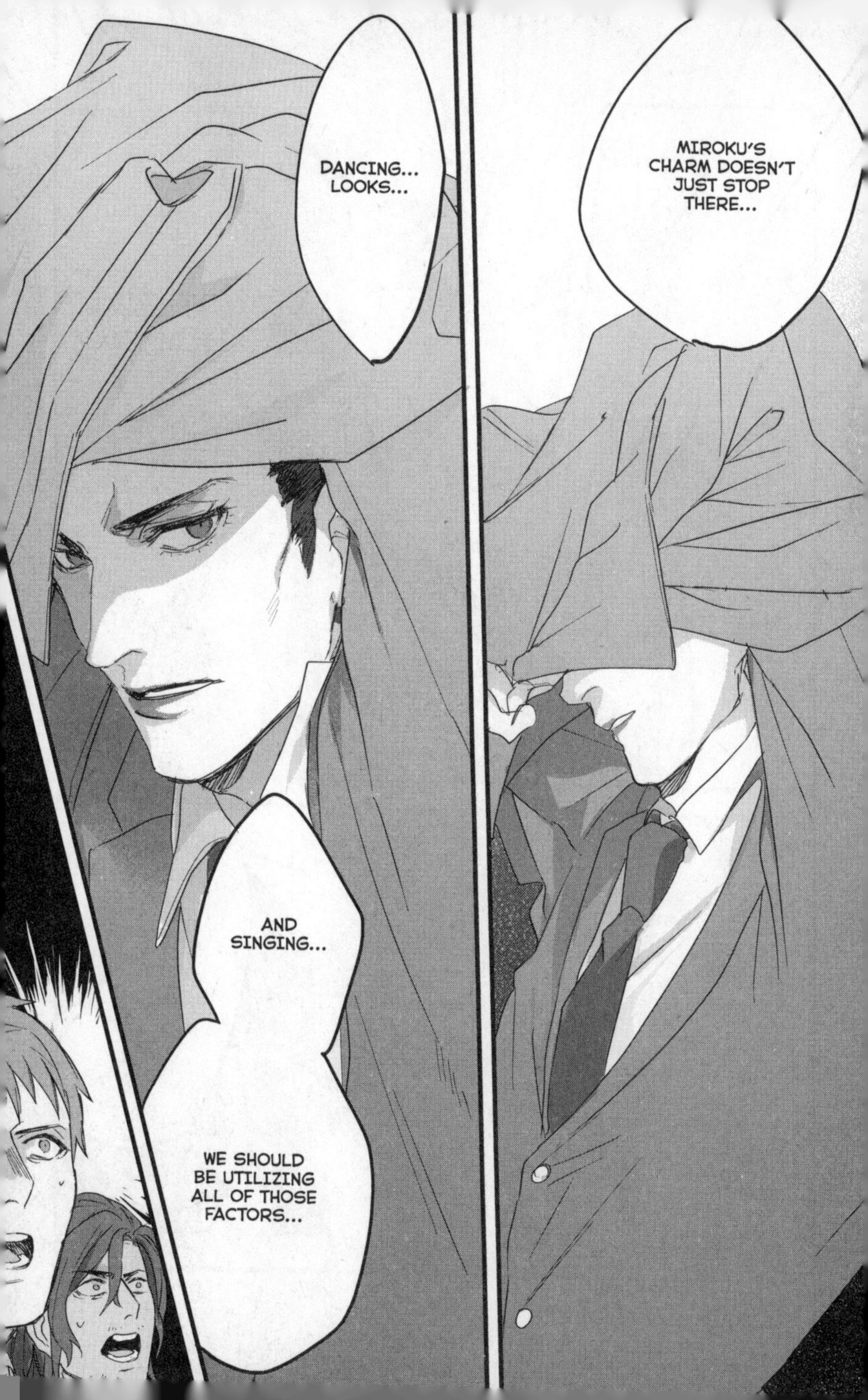
MIROKU'S CHARM DOESN'T JUST STOP THERE...
DANCING... LOOKS...
AND SINGING...
WE SHOULD BE UTILIZING ALL OF THOSE FACTORS...

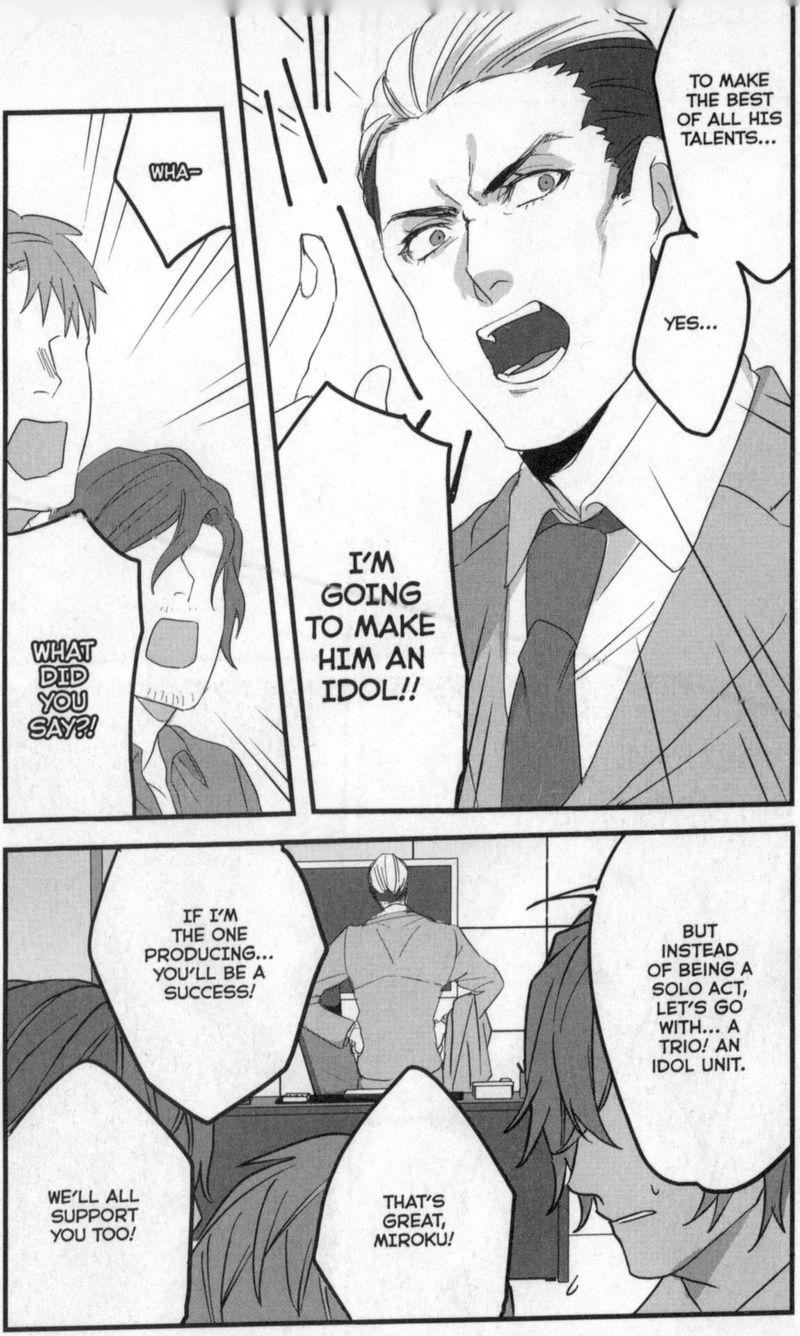
TO MAKE THE BEST OF ALL HIS TALENTS...
YES...
I'M GOING TO MAKE HIM AN IDOL!!
WHA-
WHAT DID YOU SAY?!
BUT INSTEAD OF BEING A SOLO ACT, LET'S GO WITH... A TRIO! AN IDOL UNIT.
IF I'M THE ONE PRODUCING... YOU'LL BE A SUCCESS!
THAT'S GREAT, MIROKU!
WE'LL ALL SUPPORT YOU TOO!

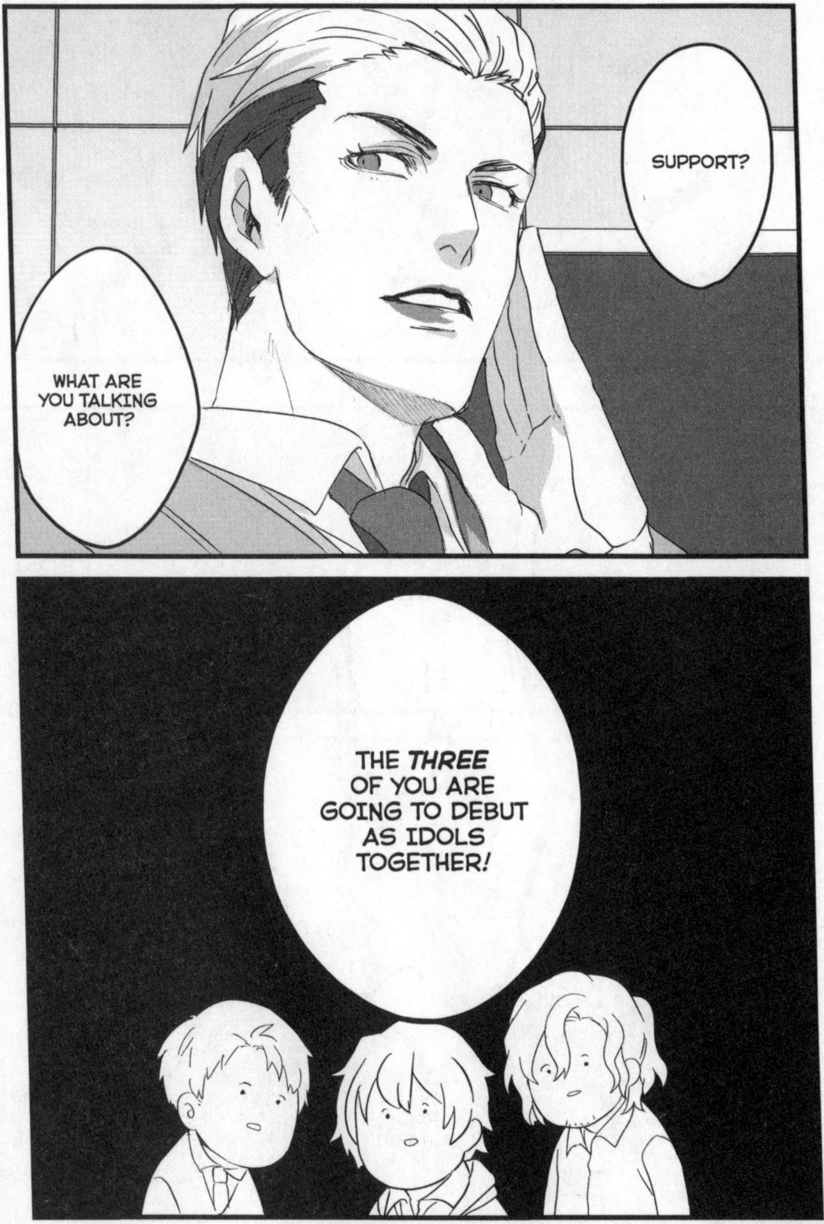
SUPPORT?
WHAT ARE YOU TALKING ABOUT?
THE *THREE* OF YOU ARE GOING TO DEBUT AS IDOLS TOGETHER!

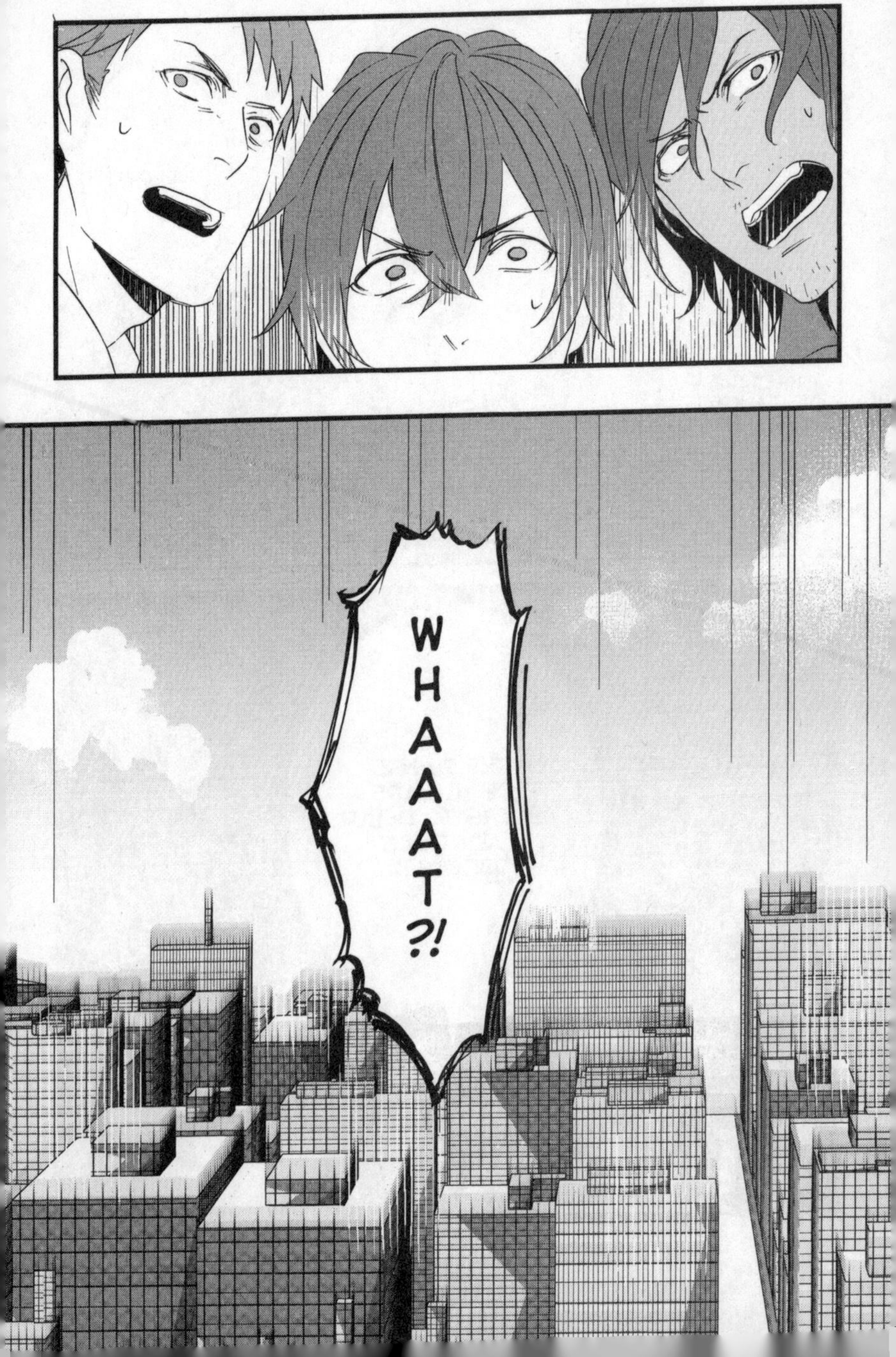
WHAAAT?!

OSSAN IDOL!

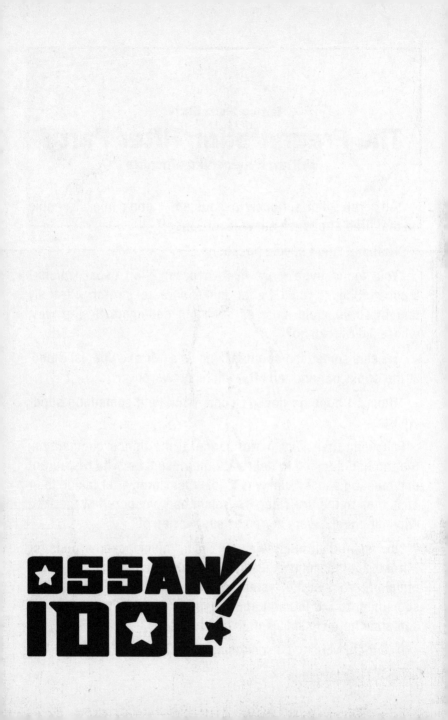

The Presentation After-Party
Written by Mochiko Mochida

"Ah, crap... I'm seriously exhausted! I don't think I should be that tired after such a low-level dance!"

"Hahaha! And I have a backache..."

"You sound even more like an ossan than usual, Yoichi," laughed Shiju. "You'd better make sure to stretch carefully tonight so your old muscles don't get damaged. By the way, where did Miroku go?"

"He said something about making us a 'Miroku Special Blend' at the drinks bar and ran off," Yoichi answered.

"Hmm... I hope he doesn't come back with something super weird."

Following their joint performance at the dance competition, the trio had decided to debrief at their usual favorite restaurant and meeting place. Fumi was to join them later, after taking their costumes to the dry cleaners. Yoichi had wondered at the time why her cheeks were so red as she hurried off.

Now seated at their table with Shiju, Yoichi looked around for Miroku, spotting him in the midst of a conversation with a couple female patrons of the restaurant. He could hear Miroku saying something to the women about adding lemon to tea, while his soft and charming smile left them blushing.

And then, Miroku did something entirely unexpected.

"What on earth did you just do?" demanded Yoichi as Miroku returned to their table.

"Huh? I just made a delicious tea blend for—"

"Not that!"

"You blew a kiss at that woman," Shiju pointed out bluntly with an exasperated sigh.

Miroku sat next to him, cocking his head in confusion.

"Oh, you mean that." Miroku looked a bit sheepish. "Well, Fumi told me she wanted to see me acting cool, so I thought I'd try copying some stuff I've seen idols do at live events..."

"Right. So you were practicing blowing a kiss at Fumi. You sure did get a lot of other people's eyes on you in the meantime."

"Oh... I guess she didn't get to see..."

"That's not what I meant." Shiju shook his head, calmly sipping the drink Miroku had gotten him. Whatever he'd done, it really was delicious. "What idol were you copying, anyway?"

"I can't remember," Miroku admitted. "I just saw an idol on TV a long time ago who blew a kiss out at the audience, and I tried to do the same thing."

"A long time ago? How long ago are we talking?"

"I was in junior high at the time," Miroku said. "I don't remember for sure, but I think that idol group was pretty popular back then. It seemed like they were on TV all the time."

"I see..."

"Hmm." Miroku looked thoughtful. "I think it was an idol duo, actually. What was their name...?"

165

Just as Shiju opened his mouth to ask Miroku something else, Yoichi cut in, redirecting their attention. "Oh, look! Fumi's here."

She was standing near the door with the look of a small animal, wide-eyed as she glanced quickly around the restaurant for them. When she spotted Miroku, she smiled, her fluffy, light brown hair bouncing around her face.

Miroku was just grinning and staring like an idiot at Fumi. Yoichi sighed, turning to shoot Shiju a meaningful, annoyed look.

"It's fine." Shiju waved him off. "Who cares if people talk?"

"No, it's not that. I'm just surprised by the way Miroku's acting. I feel like it's going to come back to bite him in the ass..."

"Like bad karma."

"You don't have to put it that way..." Yoichi muttered, but he couldn't really formulate a proper reply, trailing off as he realized Miroku must have gotten up when he wasn't looking. Now, the idiot was leading Fumi by the hand toward their table, while Fumi blushed bright red.

"Hey, Ossan."

"What is it, Shiju?"

"You really okay with this?"

"You know... I heard from Miroku's sister that in their family, Miroku was taught that he needs to be respectful and kind to women. I think he's trying to honor that with the way he treats Fumi."

Shiju looked skeptical. "You think that's kindness he's showing right now?"

166

"Well, we could debate what counts as kindness forever if you wanted..."

Thankfully, before Miroku's over-the-top hospitality could get any more excessive, the two of them reached the table.

"Miroku," Yoichi grumbled when he was in earshot. "You should learn to keep your hands to yourself."

"Huh? What do you mean?"

"Ugh... You might as well be prince of the airheads."

Fumi, at least, was quick to offer Miroku support while his companions told him off. She shook her head, smiling. "It's all right, really. Miroku was only being nice!"

"Fumi!" Miroku beamed at her, eyes practically sparkling. Happy that Fumi was apparently on his side, Miroku got out of his chair and walked around the table to kneel in front of Fumi, taking her hand and gazing warmly into her eyes.

"I always knew it, Fumi. You're such a lovely and wonderful woman."

Fumi's eyes widened in shock, her cheeks burning bright red at Miroku's ridiculous and yet charming display.

"M-Miroku!"

It seemed she was the only one who appreciated it, though. After that, Miroku was soundly lectured for over an hour by both Shiju and Yoichi.

He still had a long way to go before he could be as cool as the idols on TV.

OSSAN IDOL!

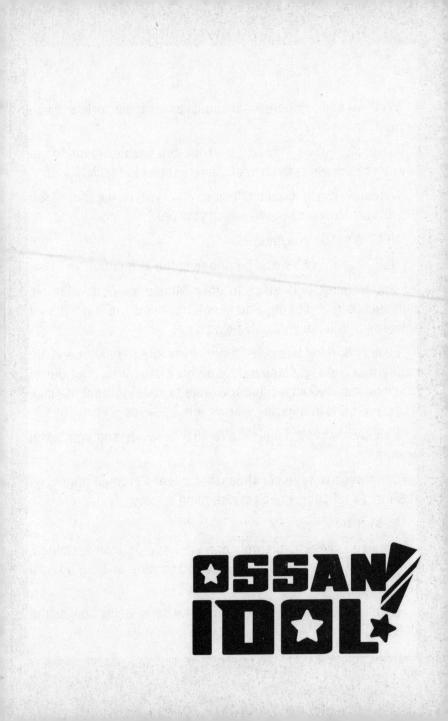

ATOGAKI   AFTERWORD

Nice to meet you! My name is Mochida Mochi, and I'm the author of the original story of Ossan Idol! To the readers of the light novels, I'm doing well. Thank you for choosing this book.

I never expected that Ossan Idol! would get a manga adaptation...I'd always thought it would be amazing if my story could be turned into a manga,, so when I heard about it, I was so happy that my skin became smooth and shiny...!

Please allow me to thank Ichika Kino-sensei for the beautiful manga, and Mizuki Sakakibara-sensei, who designed the characters. And also allow me to yell: "THANK YOU SOOO MUCH! I LOVE OSSANS AND MUSCLES!"

I would also like to thank Y-san, my wonderful editor, H-san, who is completely devoted to pursuing all that is cute, and all the others involved.

Actually, this story was born from a conversation between high school girls that happened to mention something about a 36-year-old being a good age for an ossan. At the beginning of the light novel's release, many people said "men in their thirties aren't ossans," and I kind of think that's true. Men in their thirties are still young, but even so, they're often referred to as ossans. Even though there are a lot of idols in their thirties and forties on TV, they would still be referred to as ossans...

Since that's the case, I thought it'd be great if everyone could fall head over heels for these ossans' charm! "Fall head over heels for them so hard that it makes you squeal in delight!" was the basic thought that went into this work.

I secretly hope that the above-mentioned high school girls might also give it a read!

Mochiko Mochida

January 2019

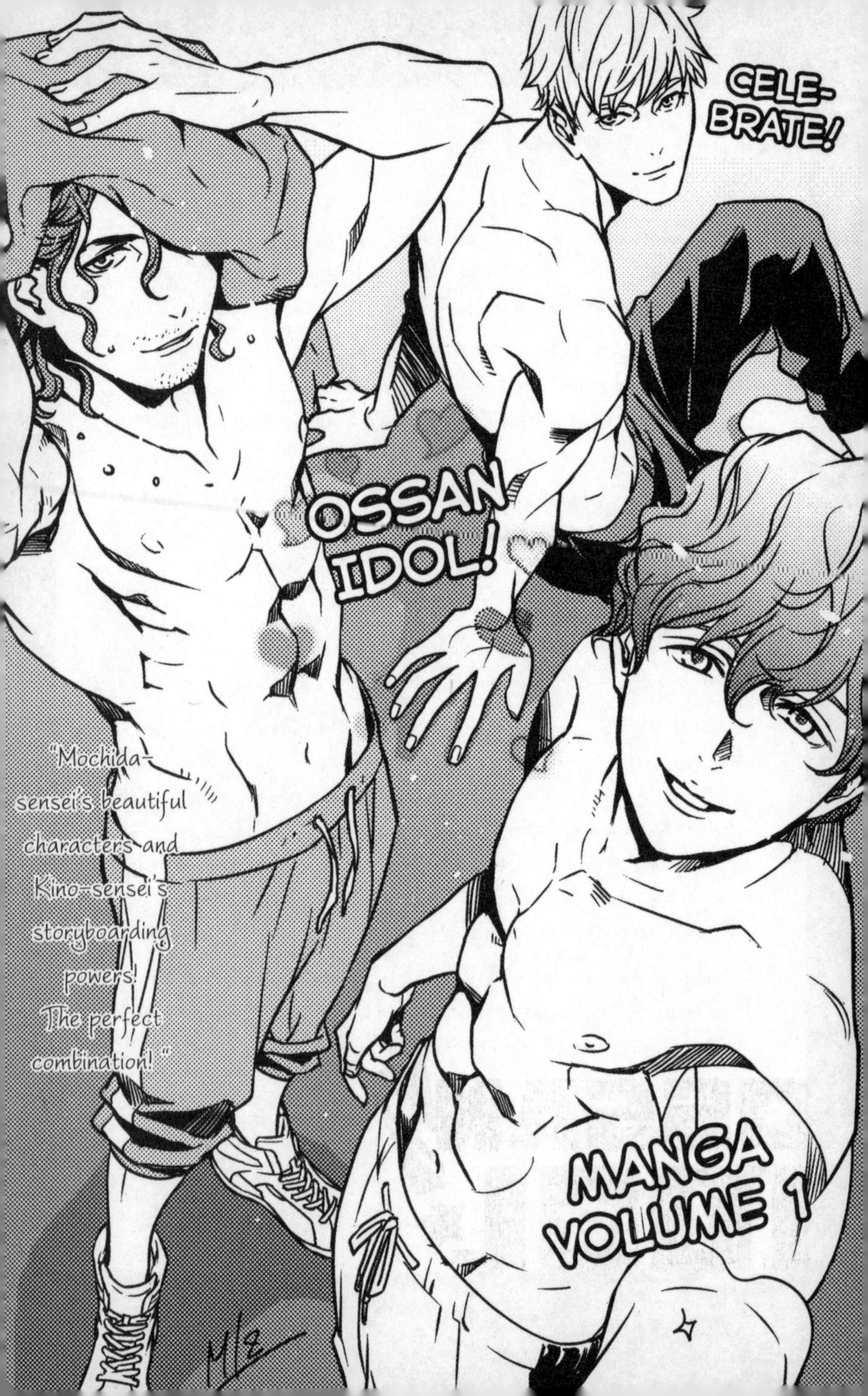
CELE-
BRATE!
OSSAN
IDOL!
"Mochida-sensei's beautiful characters and Kino-sensei's storyboarding powers! The perfect combination!"
MANGA
VOLUME 1

OSSAN IDOL!

BONUS COMIC! LET'S DECIDE ON THE COVER

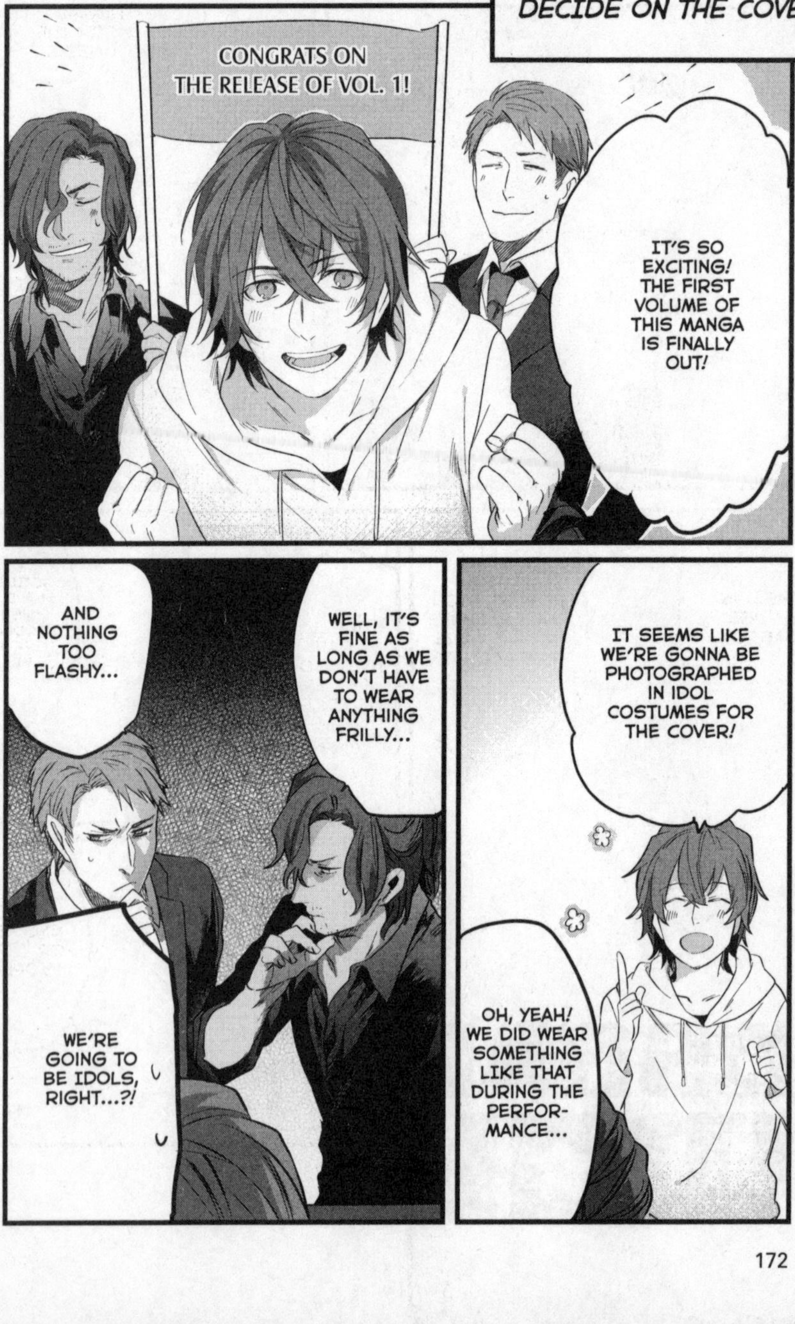

CONGRATS ON THE RELEASE OF VOL. 1!
IT'S SO EXCITING! THE FIRST VOLUME OF THIS MANGA IS FINALLY OUT!
IT SEEMS LIKE WE'RE GONNA BE PHOTOGRAPHED IN IDOL COSTUMES FOR THE COVER!
OH, YEAH! WE DID WEAR SOMETHING LIKE THAT DURING THE PERFOR-MANCE...
WELL, IT'S FINE AS LONG AS WE DON'T HAVE TO WEAR ANYTHING FRILLY...
AND NOTHING TOO FLASHY...
WE'RE GOING TO BE IDOLS, RIGHT...?!

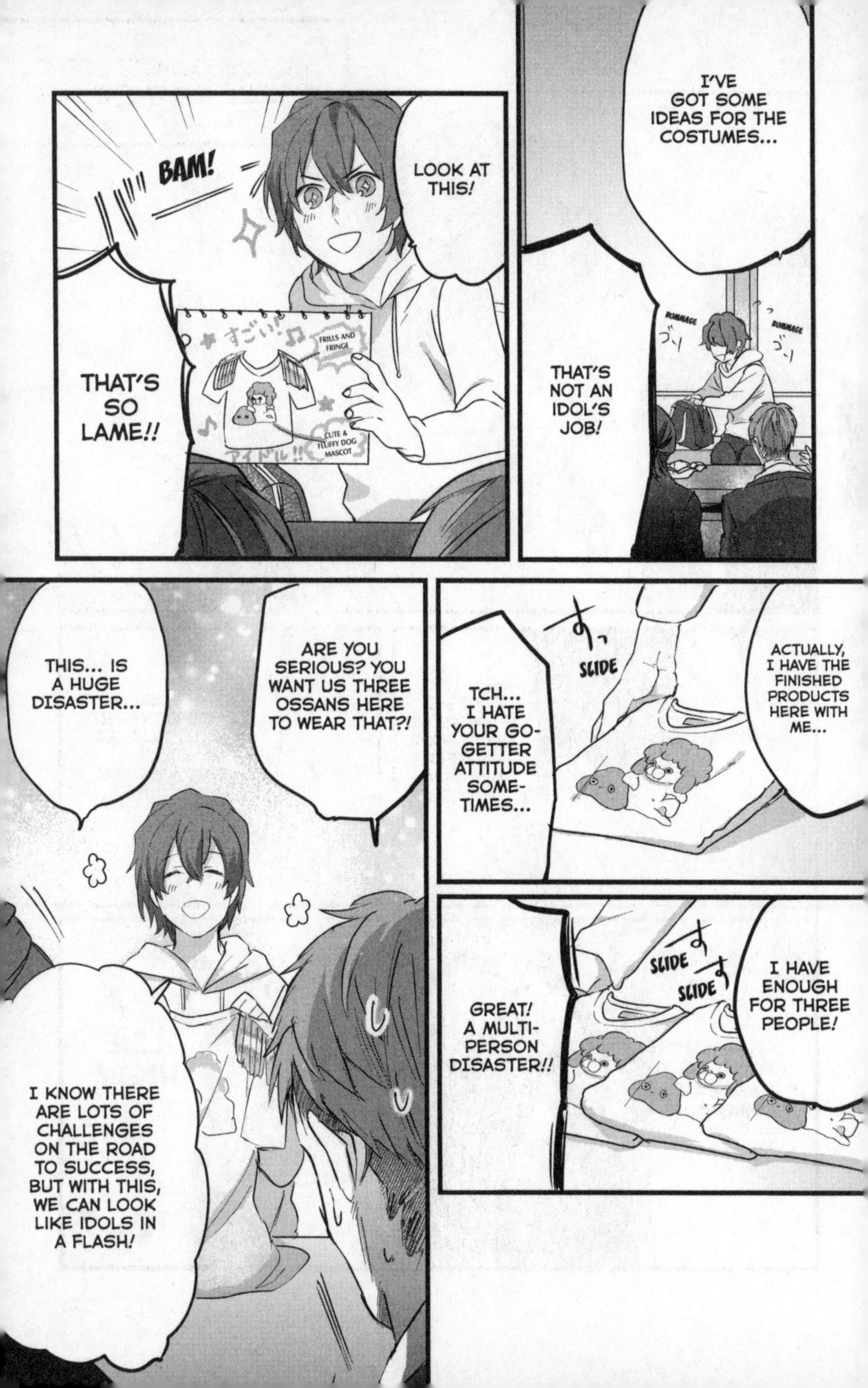
I'VE GOT SOME IDEAS FOR THE COSTUMES...
RUMMAGE
RUMMAGE
THAT'S NOT AN IDOL'S JOB!
LOOK AT THIS!
BAM!
すごい!
FRILLS AND FRINGE
CUTE & FLUFFY DOG MASCOT
アイドル!!
THAT'S SO LAME!!
ACTUALLY, I HAVE THE FINISHED PRODUCTS HERE WITH ME...
SLIDE
TCH... I HATE YOUR GO-GETTER ATTITUDE SOMETIMES...
I HAVE ENOUGH FOR THREE PEOPLE!
SLIDE
SLIDE
GREAT! A MULTI-PERSON DISASTER!!
ARE YOU SERIOUS? YOU WANT US THREE OSSANS HERE TO WEAR THAT?!
THIS... IS A HUGE DISASTER...
I KNOW THERE ARE LOTS OF CHALLENGES ON THE ROAD TO SUCCESS, BUT WITH THIS, WE CAN LOOK LIKE IDOLS IN A FLASH!

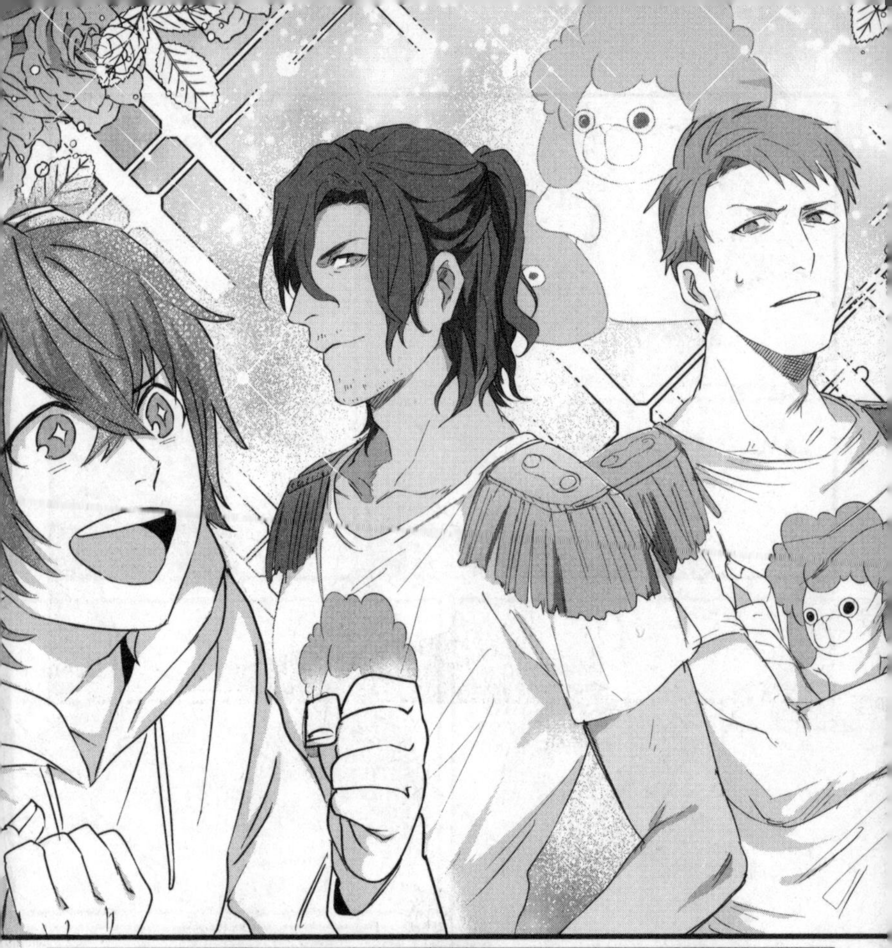

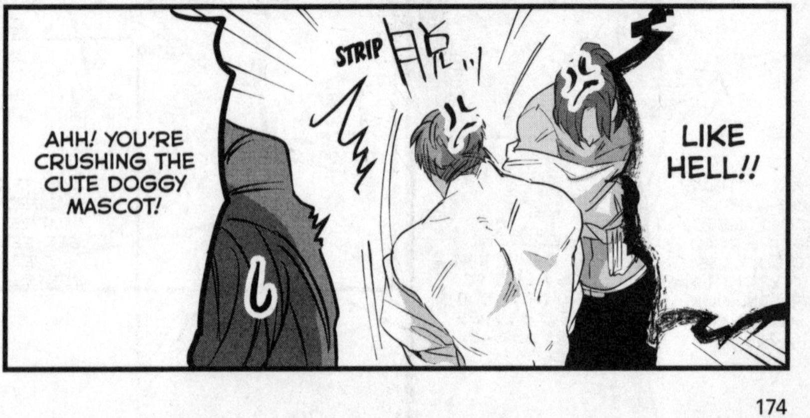
LIKE HELL!!
STRIP
AHH! YOU'RE CRUSHING THE CUTE DOGGY MASCOT!

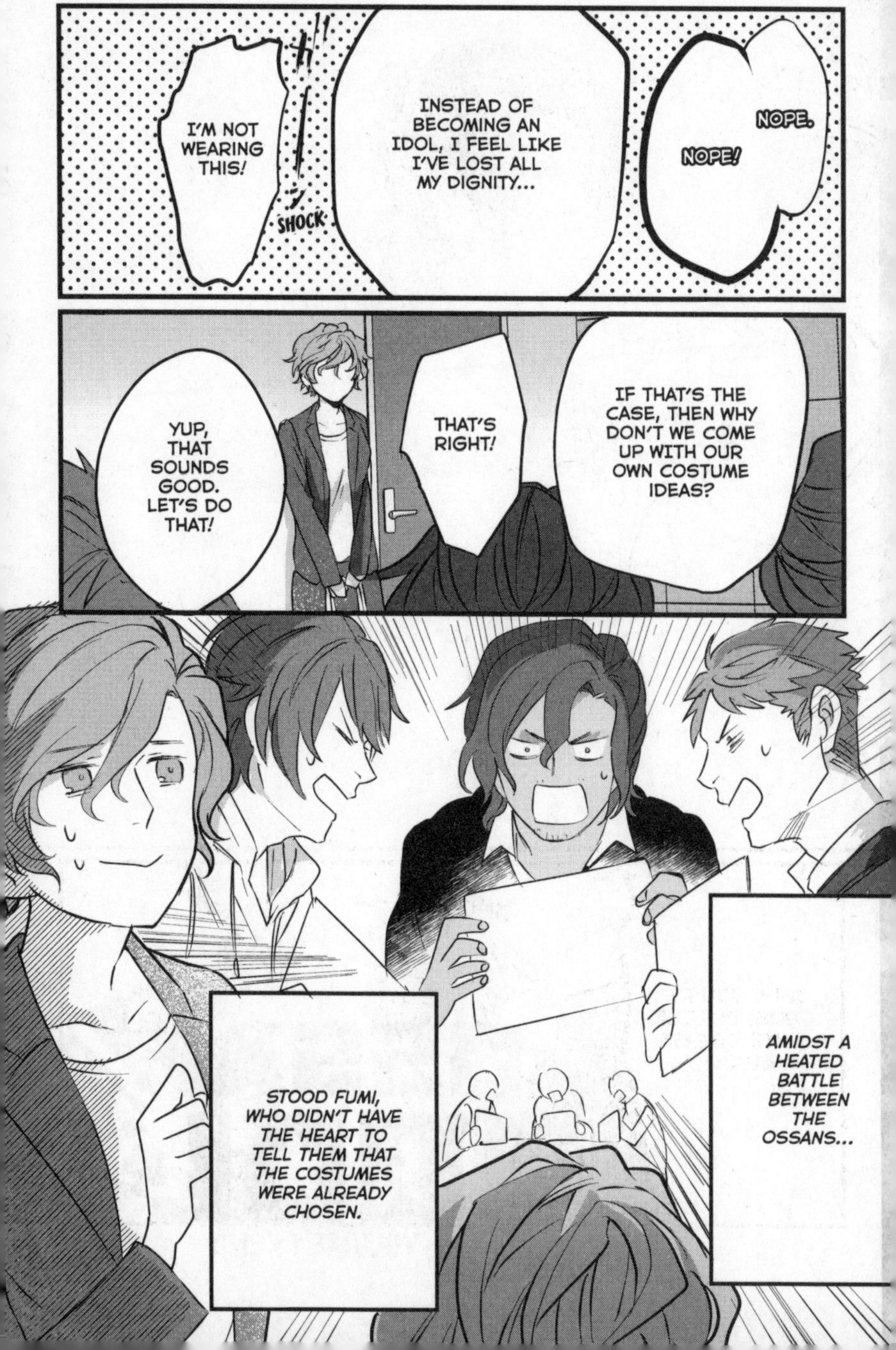
NOPE.
NOPE!
INSTEAD OF BECOMING AN IDOL, I FEEL LIKE I'VE LOST ALL MY DIGNITY...
SHOCK
I'M NOT WEARING THIS!
IF THAT'S THE CASE, THEN WHY DON'T WE COME UP WITH OUR OWN COSTUME IDEAS?
THAT'S RIGHT!
YUP, THAT SOUNDS GOOD. LET'S DO THAT!
AMIDST A HEATED BATTLE BETWEEN THE OSSANS...
STOOD FUMI, WHO DIDN'T HAVE THE HEART TO TELL THEM THAT THE COSTUMES WERE ALREADY CHOSEN.

OSSAN IDOL!

VOLUME 1 • END

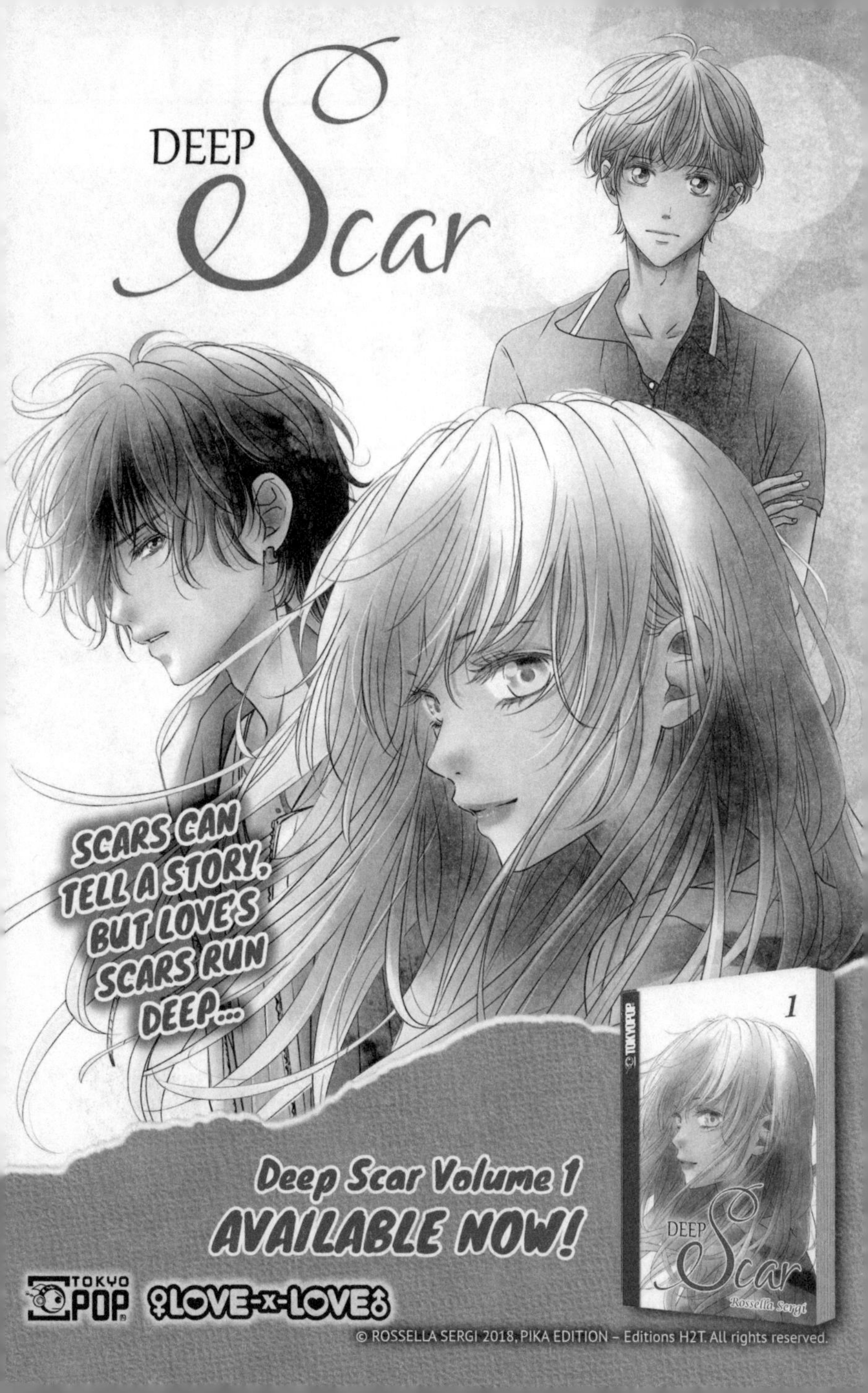
DEEP Scar
SCARS CAN TELL A STORY, BUT LOVE'S SCARS RUN DEEP...
Deep Scar Volume 1
AVAILABLE NOW!
TOKYOPOP
LOVE-x-LOVE
1
TOKYOPOP
DEEP Scar
Rossella Sergi
© ROSSELLA SERGI 2018, PIKA EDITION – Editions H2T. All rights reserved.

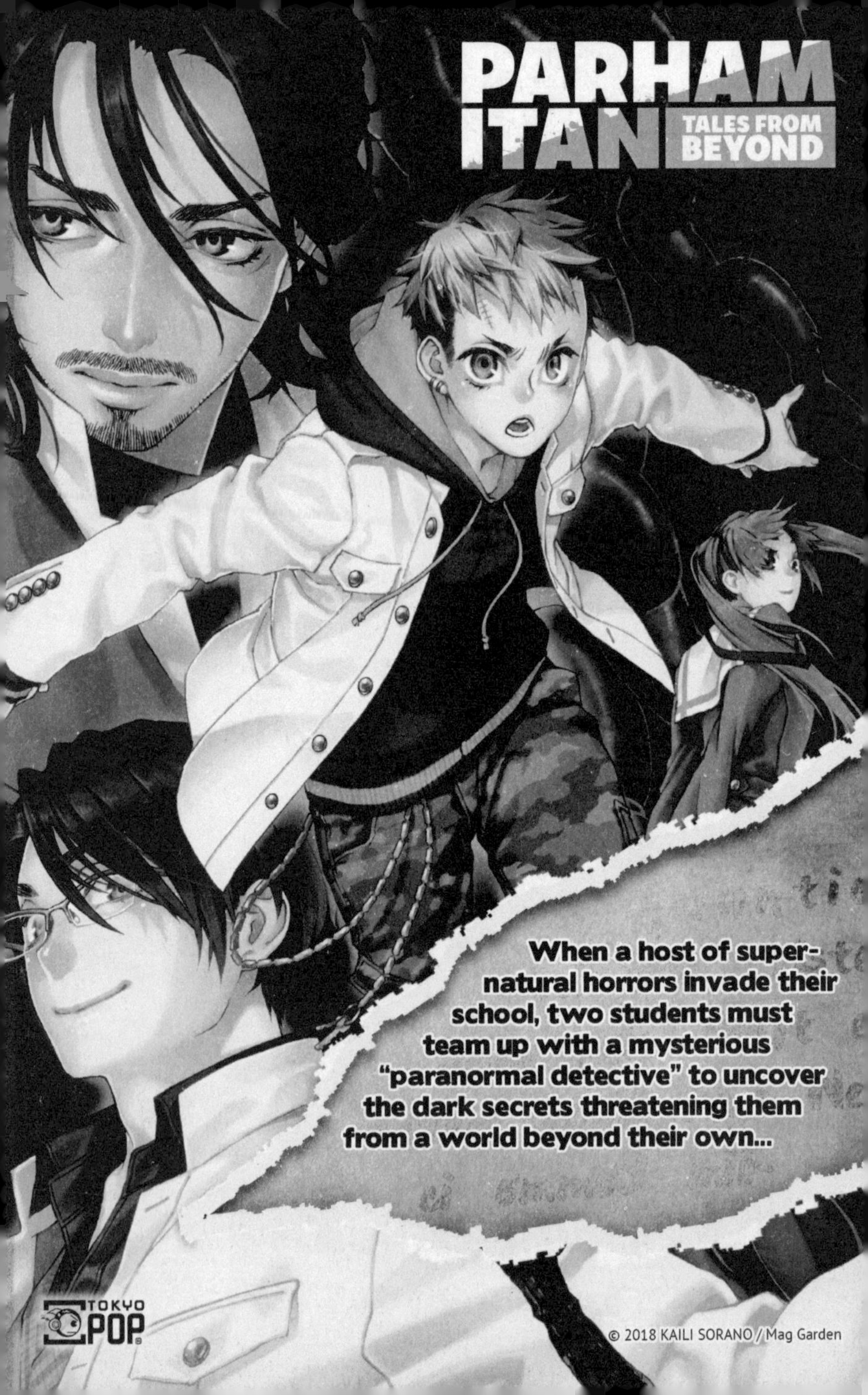
PARHAM ITAN
TALES FROM BEYOND
When a host of super-natural horrors invade their school, two students must team up with a mysterious "paranormal detective" to uncover the dark secrets threatening them from a world beyond their own...
TOKYO POP
© 2018 KAILI SORANO / Mag Garden

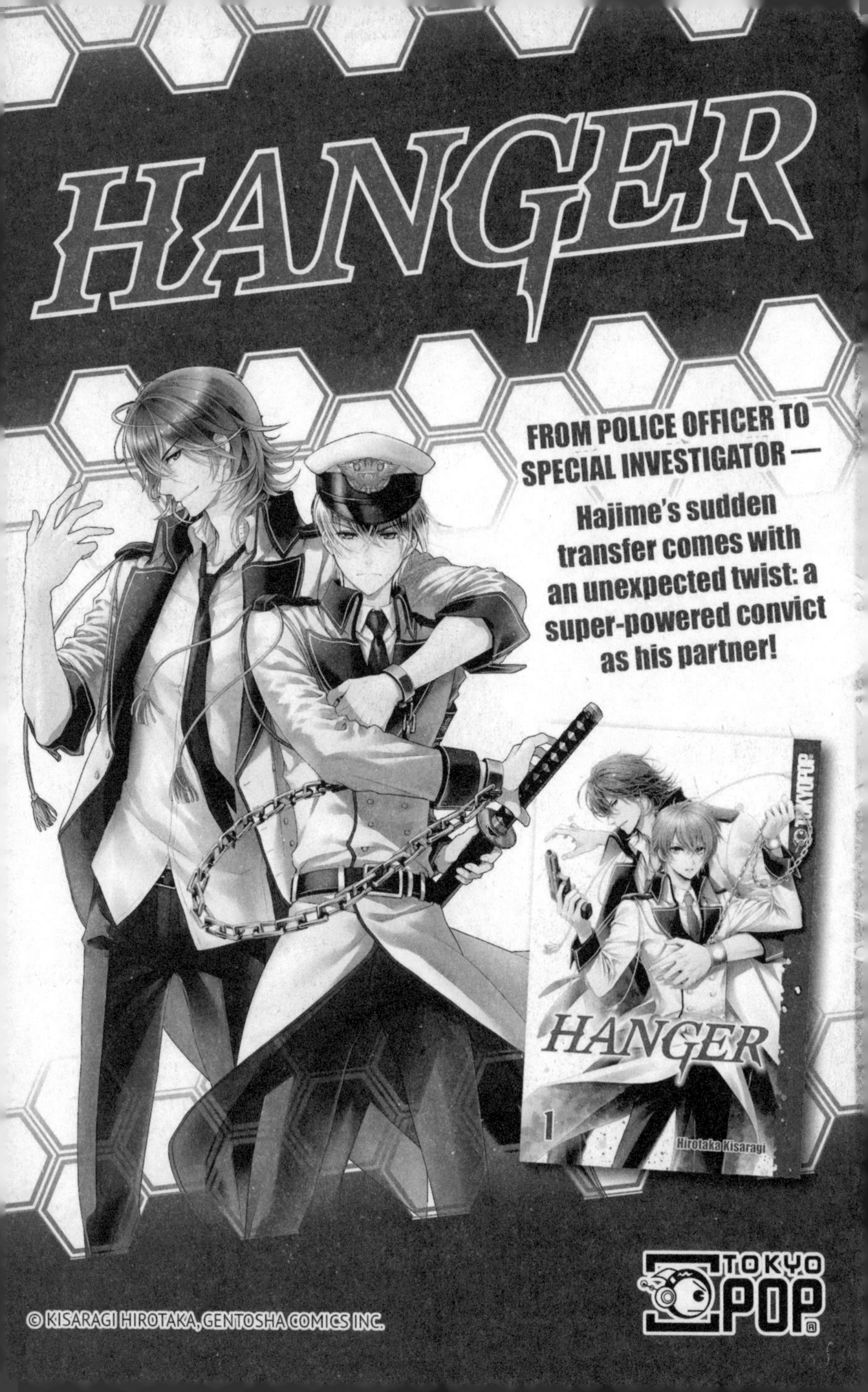
HANGER
FROM POLICE OFFICER TO SPECIAL INVESTIGATOR —
Hajime's sudden transfer comes with an unexpected twist: a super-powered convict as his partner!
HANGER
1
Hirotaka Kisaragi
© KISARAGI HIROTAKA, GENTOSHA COMICS INC.

DEKO-BOKO SUGAR DAYS

SUGAR & SPICE & EVERYTHING NICE!

Yuujirou might be a bit salty about his short stature, but he's been sweet on six-foot-tall Rui since they were both small. The only problem is... Rui is so cute, Yuujirou's too flustered to confess! It's a tall order, but he'll just have to step up!

TOKYOPOP® ⑧LOVE×LOVE⑧

© YUSEN ATSUKO, GENTOSHA COMICS 2018

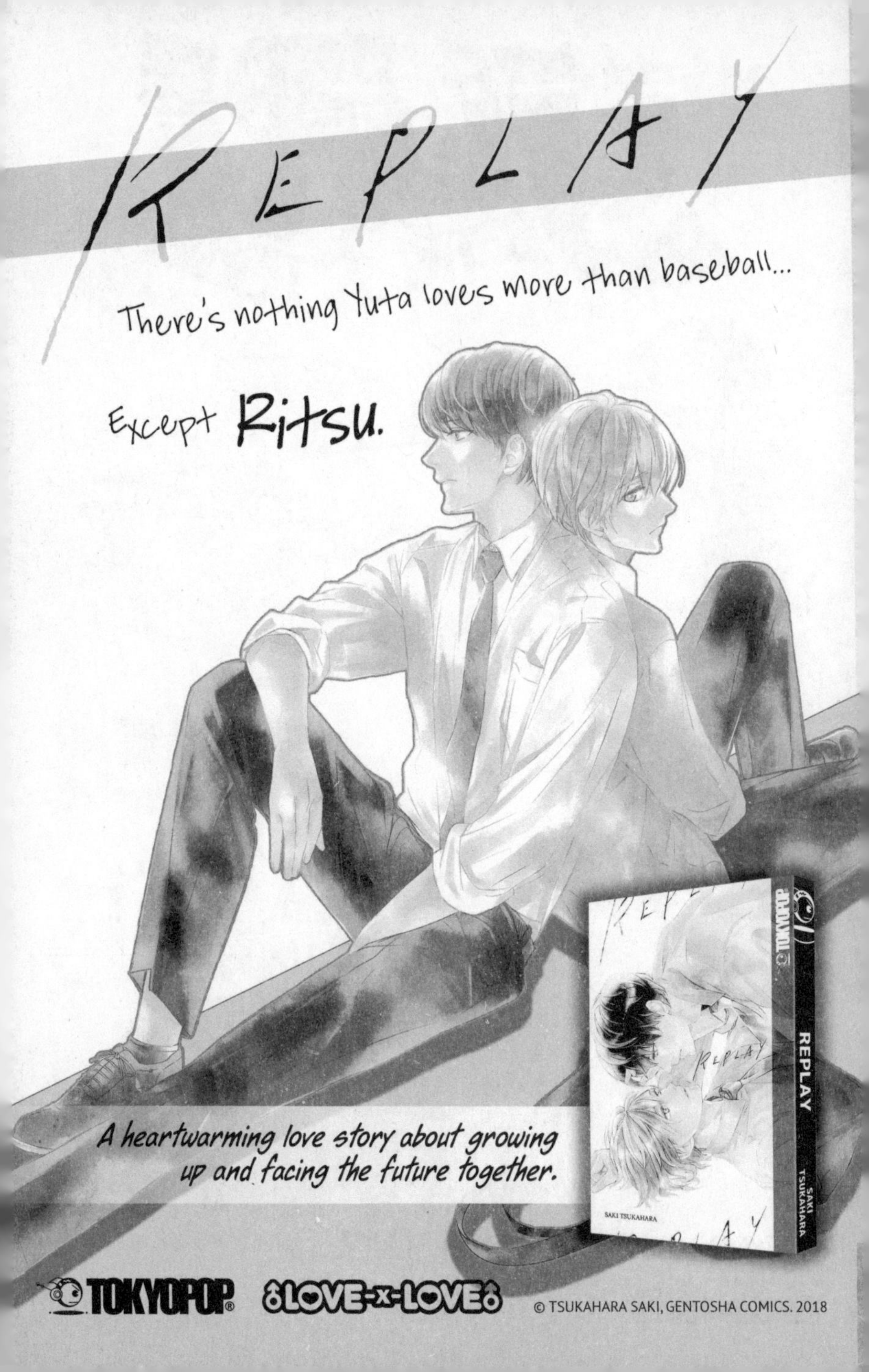
REPLAY
There's nothing Yuta loves more than baseball...
Except Ritsu.
REPLAY
SAKI TSUKAHARA
A heartwarming love story about growing up and facing the future together.
TOKYOPOP
LOVE x LOVE
© TSUKAHARA SAKI, GENTOSHA COMICS. 2018

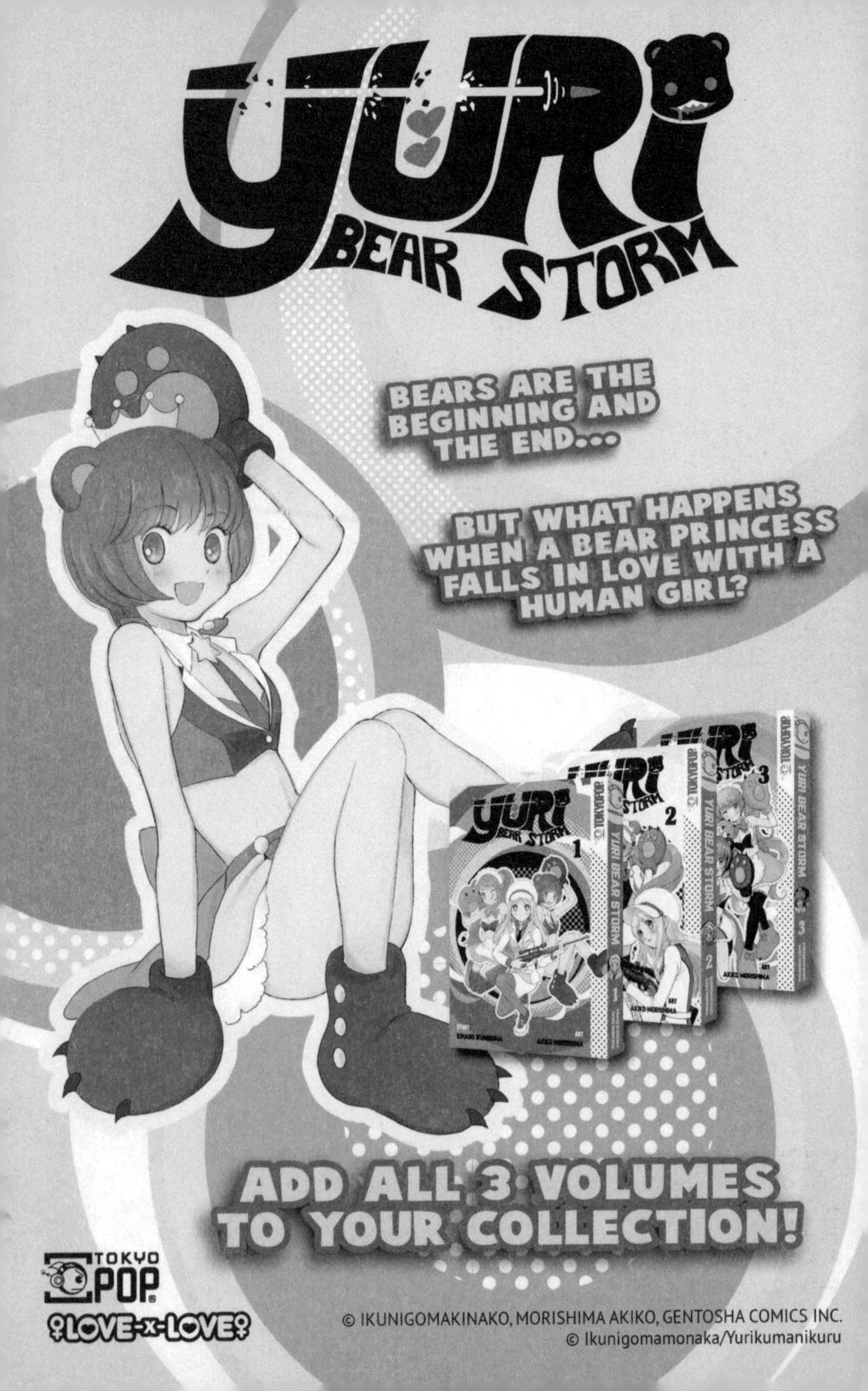
YURI BEAR STORM
BEARS ARE THE BEGINNING AND THE END...
BUT WHAT HAPPENS WHEN A BEAR PRINCESS FALLS IN LOVE WITH A HUMAN GIRL?
ADD ALL 3 VOLUMES TO YOUR COLLECTION!
TOKYO POP
LOVE x LOVE
© IKUNIGOMAKINAKO, MORISHIMA AKIKO, GENTOSHA COMICS INC.
© Ikunigomamonaka/Yurikumanikuru

KONOHANA KITAN

Welcome, valued guest...
to Konohanatei!

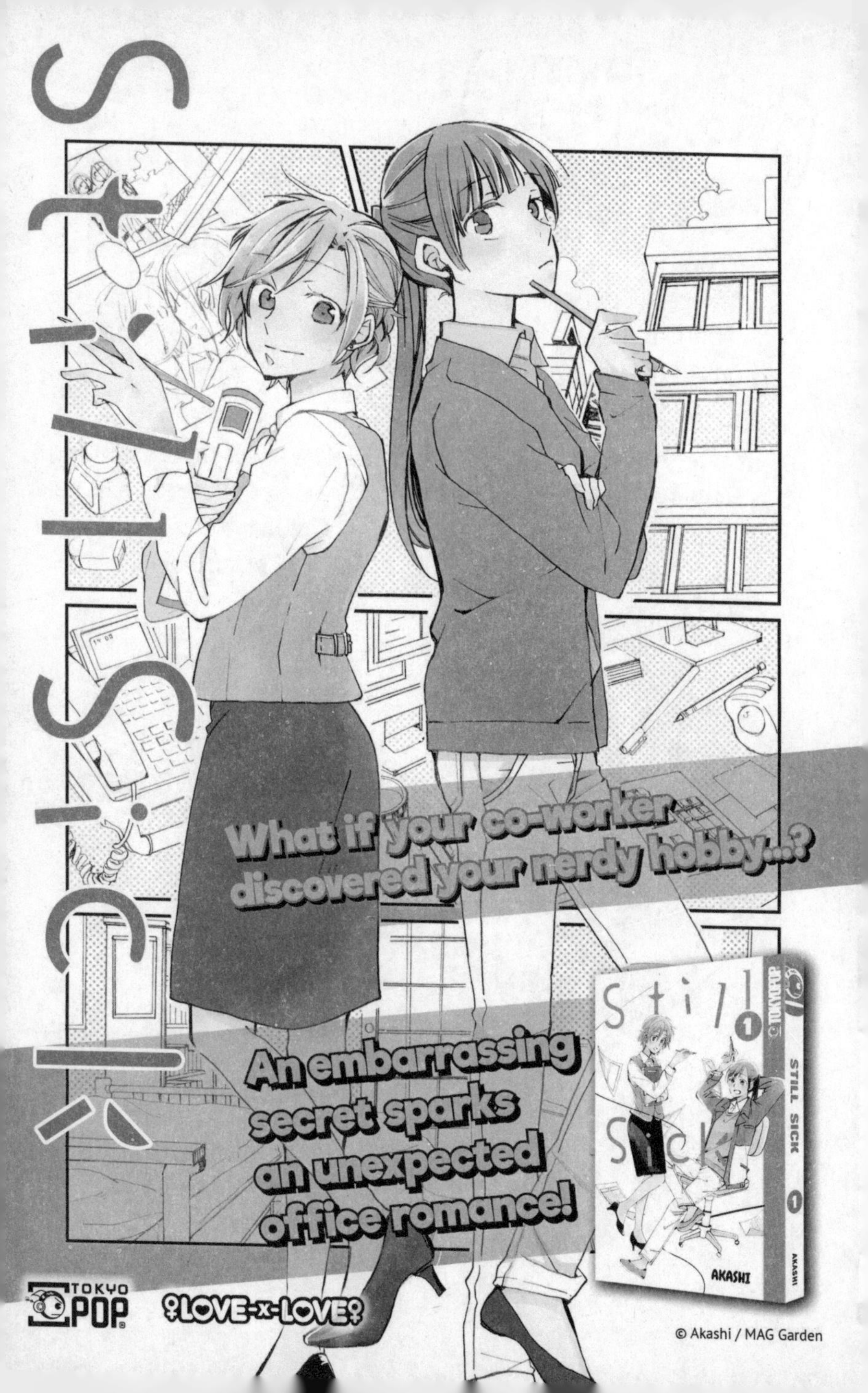
Still Sick
What if your co-worker discovered your nerdy hobby...?
An embarrassing secret sparks an unexpected office romance!
Still Sick 1
STILL SICK 1
AKASHI
TOKYOPOP
LOVE-x-LOVE
© Akashi / MAG Garden

TOKYOPOP PRESENTS

GOLDFISCH

Join Morrey and his swimmingly cute pet Otta on his adventure to reverse his Midas-like powers and save his frozen brother. Mega-hit shonen manga from hot new European creator Nana Yaa!

SCARLET SOUL

Long ago, an ancient hero sealed away the underworld. Now, with that sacred barrier broken, it's up to Rin and the mysterious demon Aghyr to restore balance to the Kingdom of Nohmur!

Ossani Idol! Volume 1
Manga by Ichika Kino
Original story by Mochiko Mochida

Editor - Lena Atanassova
Marketing Associate - Kae Winters
Translator - Milagres Fernandes
Proofreader - Ethan O'Brien
Licensing Specialist - Arika Yanaka
Cover Design - Sol DeLeo
Retouching and Lettering - Vibrraant Publishing Studio
Editor-in-Chief & Publisher - Stu Levy

A **TOKYOPOP®** Manga

TOKYOPOP and are trademarks or registered trademarks of TOKYOPOP Inc.

TOKYOPOP inc.
5200 W Century Blvd
Suite 705
Los Angeles, CA 90045 USA

E-mail: info@TOKYOPOP.com
Come visit us online at www.TOKYOPOP.com

f www.facebook.com/TOKYOPOP
www.twitter.com/TOKYOPOP
www.pinterest.com/TOKYOPOP
www.instagram.com/TOKYOPOP

OSSAN 36 GA IDOL NI NARUHANASHI 1   First published in Japan in 2019 by Shufu To Seikatsu
© 2019 Kino Ichika © 2019 Mochico Mochida   Sha Co., Ltd.
Character designs by Mizuki Sakakibara.   English translation rights reserved by TOKYOPOP. under the license from Shufu To Seikatsu Sha Co., Ltd.

ISBN: 978-1-4278-6408-6
First TOKYOPOP Printing: June 2020
10 9 8 7 6 5 4 3 2 1
Printed in CANADA

STOP

THIS IS THE BACK OF THE BOOK!

How do you read manga-style? It's simple! Let's practice -- just start in the top right panel and follow the numbers below!

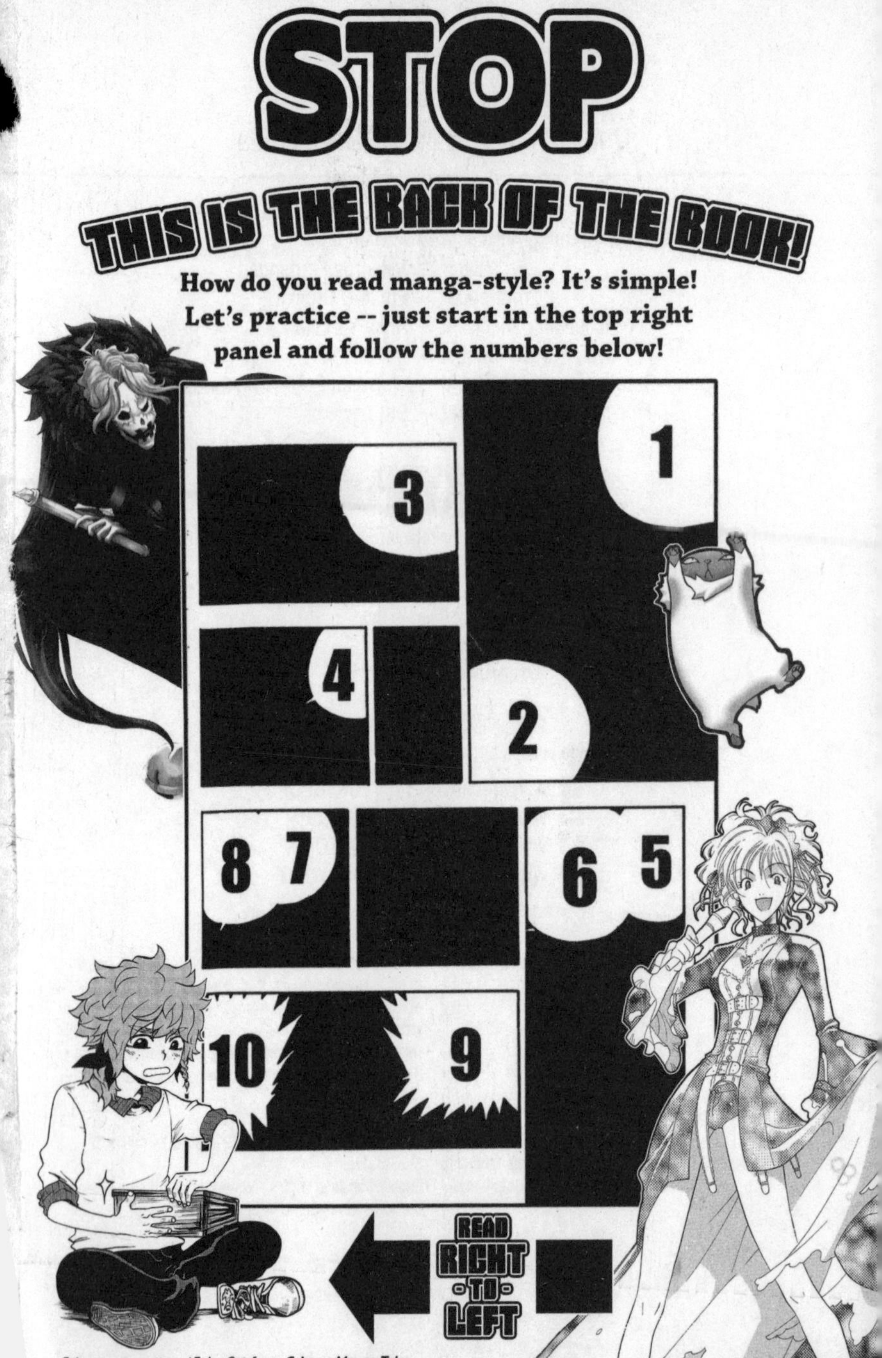
1
2
3
4
5
6
7
8
9
10
READ
RIGHT
-TO-
LEFT

Crimson from *Kamo* / Fairy Cat from *Grimms Manga Tales*
Morrey from *Goldfisch* / Princess Ai from *Princess Ai*